PROJECT MANAGERS AND BUSINESS ANALYST

Delivering Business Value through Projects and Programs Successfully

J ROSS PUBLISHING

BPB PUBLICATIONS

FIRST INDIAN EDITION 2017
REPRINT 2023

ISBN : 978-93-86551-47-4

REPRINTED UNDER A LICENCE FROM AGREEMENT PUBLISHER: J ROSS PUBLISHING, 300 ROAD, #305, S PINE ISLAND PLANTATION, FL 33324 (USA)

FOR SALE IN INDIA, NEPAL, BANGLADESH, SRI LANKA, PAKISTAN, BHUTAN & MALDIVES ONLY.

Distributors:

BPB PUBLICATIONS
20, Ansari Road, Darya Ganj
New Delhi-110002
Ph: 23254990/23254991

BPB BOOK CENTRE
376 Old Lajpat Rai Market,
Delhi-110006
Ph: 23861747

COMPUTER BOOK CENTRE
12, Shrungar Shopping Centre,
M.G.Road, BENGALURU–560001
Ph: 25587923/25584641

DECCAN AGENCIES
4-3-329, Bank Street,
Hyderabad-500195
Ph: 24756967/24756400

MICRO MEDIA
Shop No. 5, Mahendra Chambers, 150
DN Rd. Next to Capital Cinema, V.T.
(C.S.T.) Station, MUMBAI-400 001 Ph:
22078296/22078297

Published by Manish Jain for BPB Publications, 20, Ansari Road, Darya Ganj, New Delhi-110002 and Printed him at Repro India Pvt. Ltd, Mumbai

CONTENTS

PREFACE

Since the first few years of the 21st century, the role of the business analyst (BA) has seen rapid growth, yet project failure rates continue to be quite high. When the BA role is properly executed in collaboration or partnership with the project or program manager (PM) role, higher quality product and project requirements are produced and managed, resulting in higher project or program success rates. With that said, the growth of the BA role has not been fully aligned with the role of the PM and with project needs—resulting in misunderstandings, duplication of efforts, mishandling stakeholder expectations, confusion, and even project failure.

The misalignment was partly driven by the development of certifications that were, and still are, administered by different organizations—the International Institute for Business Analysis (IIBA) and the Project Management Institute (PMI). As the professions started to grow apart, the need for alignment grew, and with it came the PMI-PBA (Professional in Business Analysis) certification that now puts the role of the BA in the project's context; leading to improvement in the alignment between the roles, using the same set of terminology and with it, paving the way to improve the collaboration between the PM and the BA.

With many books and publications dealing separately with project management and business analysis, the need for a consolidated guide that addresses the touch points, the gaps, and the intersections between the two roles has increased. The coauthors of this book have each demonstrated expertise in their respective areas (Cheryl with focus on the business analysis side and Ori with focus on the project management side) and both have worked and excelled in the other field as well. Cheryl, a seasoned BA who was actively involved with the IIBA has also managed multiple projects, and holds the project management professional (PMP) credential in addition to her business analysis designations.

Ori spent his career rotating between both roles, then turned more toward the project management side. Close to a decade ago, Ori was the designer, curriculum developer, and Program Coordinator of one of the first business analysis programs in the world for a Continuing Education department in a Toronto area college.

In fact, the process of writing this book demonstrated the role collaboration between the PM and the BA—successfully testing the same advice that the writers were explaining in the book on forming a streamlined and working partnership between the PM and the BA. It was interesting to see how the characteristics of each of the writers surfaced, especially close to the deadlines, and how the writers leveraged each other's skills to overcome any challenges.

THE FINAL STEPS LEADING TO WRITING THE BOOK

Early in 2014, Cheryl and Ori cofounded the PMI-SOC (Southern Ontario Chapter) Project Business Analysis Community—which at the time, was the first of its kind in the world. Since then they have cochaired the community. The intent behind founding the community was to promote the need for collaboration between the roles of the PM and the BA. The introduction of the PMI-PBA certification was the *push* that helped articulate that need for PM-BA role collaboration that both Cheryl and Ori noticed throughout their careers. After receiving positive feedback from members of the newly formed community and the increased chatter around the need for improving the collaboration between the PM and the BA, the coauthors decided to directly address this growing need in the form of a book.

THE OBJECTIVES OF THIS BOOK

The main objective of this book is to incorporate best practices and concepts into the day-to-day realities of PMs and BAs by addressing the touch points in their roles, areas of overlap, shared responsibilities, gaps, and friction points. Constantly attempting to practice PM-BA collaboration in their careers, Cheryl and Ori strongly believe that it is beneficial to instill the values of such collaboration in more environments and from a cost-benefit perspective, it will provide significant value for those organizations that do it successfully.

The book takes the reader through a journey that incorporates a practical approach to common PM-BA-related challenges, simplified examples, and a touch of humor. It provides the PM and the BA with the ability to think how to work smarter (not harder) and together, by incorporating the value provided by their colleagues to achieve better results while working more efficiently. More specifically, the book helps PMs and BAs think about the situations they face and identify which member of the partnership should step up to lead the related effort—based on a mixture of skills, experience, role definition, interests, access to information, relationships, and practicality.

The book incorporates the coauthors' combined experience and education, including a total of four different project management and business analysis designations that the two earned. This book does not regurgitate these concepts and it does not propose a replacement; it puts the PM and the BA in a state of mind that leverages these concepts and methodologies in the context of the organizational challenges and the realities of the important, intertwined, and often challenging relations between the PM and the BA.

WHAT MAKES THIS BOOK DIFFERENT?

This book offers a new way for both the PM and the BA to work with each other and with the challenges they face. It focuses more on communications, understanding stakeholders' needs, and understanding each other's roles, responsibilities, experience, tendencies, and styles. The book then focuses on a set of value-added activities that address specific areas that are notorious for causing friction to achieve project and organizational success.

The book views the relationship between the PM and the BA as a partnership, and calls for a seamless integration of the roles with each other. The authors of the book strongly disagree with the notion that *PMs are from Mars and BAs are from Venus*. In fact, the book calls the PM and the BA *a duo* that, for the organization's and the project's best interests, must attempt to operate as if they were one entity. Instead of Mars and Venus, PMs and BAs should operate more in the context of a love story. The book's journey toward achieving a close-knit partnership is done through allowing the PM and the BA to each see where their partner is coming from and by that, understand each other and complement one another on an ongoing basis. Achieving such a level of coordination is not an easy task, and the book's structure helps the reader address all the intersecting areas between the roles of the PM and the BA.

THE STRUCTURE OF THIS BOOK

This book takes you through a journey of ideas and thoughts that may be viewed by some as *common sense* or as things that *should go without saying* and by others as *fantasy*, because they are difficult to achieve. However, as the stakes are high, we are aiming high here by attempting to touch on any possible interaction areas between the PM and the BA and by proposing practical ways to achieve better role collaboration. While it may not be possible in most environments to achieve many of the concepts and objectives this book proposes, the modular nature of the book allows for readers to pick and choose any set of benefits to pursue as part of any area that they see fit. Achieving project success through a more effective role collaboration between the PM and the BA comes in many forms, and this book has the recipe for any combination of needs.

This book is not a best practice in the sense that it is not a prescription to follow, but it can be called *an excellent practice,* as each of the areas covered offers multiple opportunities for the PM and the BA to significantly enhance the combined value they provide to the organization with less overall combined effort.

Chapter 1, *Challenges Related to Project Management and Business Analysis*, contains a discussion of common (and some less common) challenges that tend to plague the relationship between the PM and the BA—and with it, the contribution that they provide to the project and the organization. The discussion involves not only the challenges, but also proposed techniques to address them—with the ideas in the chapter serving as a gateway for the rest of the book.

Chapter 2, *Misconceptions of the Roles of the PM and the BA*, discusses misconceptions of the roles of the PM and the BA, as well as misconceptions of the professions of project management and business analysis. These misconceptions include PMs not fully understanding the role of the BA; BAs not fully realizing the extent of the role of the PM; and other stakeholders who fail to realize the value that both PMs and BAs produce for the project and the organization. In short, for those who still need it—this chapter refutes the notion that BAs are *glorified butlers* who are there mainly to take notes in meetings and that PMs are paper pushers and process police.

Chapter 3, *Growing and Integrating the Professions*, provides a clear overview of the differences between the PMI (and specifically regarding the PBA certification) and the IIBA and in a way *picks a side*—recognizing that the PMI-PBA certification provides a meaningful context to the need for collaboration between the PM and the BA. While the IIBA's certification programs develop the role of the BA, they do so with blinders on, alas veering it further away from an effective alignment with the PM role. The chapter then turns the discussion toward growing the PM and the BA skills sets and proposes ideas and techniques on how to better measure the skills of the PM and the BA respectively for hiring, assignment, and professional development purposes. The chapter ties the context of this book (the need for collaboration between the roles) and the chapter's theme for skills development to the reasoning behind project failures—and shows that PM-BA role collaboration and development serve as key components in the recipe for project success.

Chapter 4, *Enterprise Analysis, Portfolio Management, and the PMO*, draws on the similarities between the areas of portfolio management and enterprise analysis (EA) and proposes ways for the PM and the BA to integrate these areas for the benefit of their project. Like two cousins, portfolio management and business analysis share many concepts and activities; and the PM and the BA can integrate them, with focus on achieving efficiencies on the parts that overlap. More specifically, the chapter looks into activities such as project justification, business case, and the process of hand-off to senior management for reviewing, selecting, and chartering the projects. The chapter also looks at the distinctions between the two areas discussed, with the EA process being about identifying opportunities, building business architecture framework, and determining the most suitable investment path for the organization; and the portfolio management process focusing on investments related to projects, operations, and programs and ensuring that the initiatives that are selected align with the organization's strategy.

This chapter also covers the role of the project management office (PMO) as an arm of the portfolio management function—along with how the PM and the BA interact with these processes and organizational functions.

Chapter 5, *Communication and Stakeholder Expectations Management*, looks at the specific contribution of each of the duo's members, as well as the combined value they (can) create in effectively managing stakeholders' expectation. This chapter leverages the authors' vast experience in relationship management and stakeholder expectations management and on practical communication and stakeholder engagement management techniques from Ori's previous book, *Managing Stakeholder Expectations for Project Success* (J. Ross Publishing, 2013).

The chapter also shows the importance of involving the BA in the vital and ongoing tasks of managing communication and stakeholder expectations; not only directly in engaging the BA with stakeholders, but also in relation to the requirements and the due diligence that the BA can provide. The chapter discusses the notion that managing stakeholder expectations has multiple aspects, of which only one directly deals with communication. While the two knowledge areas in the *Project Management Body of Knowledge* (*PMBOK® Guide*)—Manage Communication and Manage Stakeholders—are closely related to each other and at their cores (the area of managing expectations is driven by effective communication, relationship, and engagement planning) there are multiple areas of responsibility that are related or that feed into expectation management.

Chapter 6, *Requirements Definition*, opens with referencing studies (and experiences) that consistently point at requirements as a significant reason for project failures. It then proceeds by elaborating on how to perform the requirements management processes effectively and in such ways that have been proven to directly contribute to reducing project failures. Further, the chapter cites the necessary role and involvement of the PM in the requirements management process, for it to become more effective and in order to ensure the streamlining of the product requirements transition into the project scope.

Referencing concepts from the IIBA's *Business Analysis Body of Knowledge* (*BABOK*®), the *PMBOK*® *Guide* and the *PMI-PBA Handbook*, the chapter takes the reader through a clear review of what it takes to plan for requirements definition and management. It then goes over techniques to align the business analysis and the project management plans—covering specific areas of PM-BA collaboration throughout the various areas of the plans. The next steps involve comparing between product and project scope and going over the requirements elicitation process in detail.

Chapter 7, *Assumptions, Constraints, Dependencies, and Risks*, opens by proposing a new acronym—C-RAID to replace RAID (which stands for risks, assumptions, issues, and dependencies)—so that it includes *constraints*. The chapter discusses issues within the context of risks, and then issues are revisited in Chapter 9 of this book when discussing change management.

Chapter 7 calls for more focus on these areas, as many PMs (and BAs) simply copy and paste them from the business case to the charter; to requirements; to design documents; to test plans; and sometimes through to implementation plans—like a hot potato, but never effectively deal with them. The discussion then shifts and covers techniques to identify, document, consider, manage, and resolve these items. The risk section of the chapter discusses the roles of the PM and the BA to ensure effective management of project risks also—in addition to the need to manage requirements risks and, in turn, how they impact project and business risks.

Chapter 8, *Resource Management*, provides a comprehensive coverage of *anything that is a resource-related issue*, including resource availability, allocation, and management. As this is one of the most common sources of conflict in projects, the chapter discusses a series of practical techniques to leverage both the PM and the BA toward this important cause.

Despite knowing that resources pose a major threat to project success, PMs do not provide a sufficient amount of focus on resource management and often neglect to perform basic activities that can reduce the risks and the impact of resource-related challenges—and in most cases, the BA is segregated from the process of resource allocation and management altogether. The chapter addresses challenges that are common in matrix organizations (weak or balanced). It proposes methods for the PM and the BA to contribute to the effort by leveraging their respective knowledge to improve the resource allocation and management throughout the project by introducing a practical approach to estimating, scheduling, and prioritization. The chapter covers several practical techniques for the PM and the BA to manage their time and help team members and stakeholders to gain more control over their own schedules.

Chapter 9, *Two Types of Change: Project and Organizational Change Management*, is effectively broken into two distinct sections that share the word *change*. The first part covers project change management (i.e., change control) and reviews considerations for improving the effectiveness of the change control process in the organization and to ensure alignment between requirements changes and project changes. The chapter then proceeds to discussing agile considerations for project change.

The second part deals with organizational change. With the growing attention to the connection between project management and organizational change management, the chapter adds another layer to the mix: leveraging the PM-BA collaboration. This collaboration turns out to be a critical-to-success factor in ensuring that the project delivers meaningful value that is aligned with the organizational objectives and the intended change initiative.

Chapter 10, *Project Quality, Recovery, and Lessons Learned*, may appear to some as if it deals with three distinct areas but these areas are actually directly related to each other. The chapter provides context and techniques on how to identify the need for project recovery—and then goes through a detailed process of how to perform project recovery. This chapter is centered on project recovery activities and the interaction between the PM and the BA leading up to and during project recovery. For additional context and relevance, and to instill a culture that values prevention over recovery, the chapter also covers quality considerations that shed light on the importance of measuring the cost of quality (COQ) and additional measures that can be used as project performance indicators. Both the COQ and the indicators are proactive in the sense that they give the PM and the BA indications of performance, and both require information gathering and analysis to be performed jointly by the PM and the BA.

Chapter 11, *Building a Partnership: Shared Responsibility Throughout—Putting It All Together*, draws all the different parts of this book to a meaningful close. Throughout the chapter, concepts previously presented in the book are reinforced and reintroduced within the context of the product and project life cycles to demonstrate the timing and linkages between the PM-BA collaboration concepts. The chapter speaks to a constantly evolving means to conduct project management leading to Project Management 8.4 (Looking similar to Project Management BA)—which plays tribute to the new style of project management that focuses on forming a partnership with the BA. Leveraging the discussions and concepts throughout the book, this section can easily be turned into a checklist for both PMs and BAs on what they need to do at each point in time to effectively work together and to ensure their collaboration produces the desired results.

The chapter explores the area of project integration both from the perspective of integrating all its moving parts, but also by looking at the integration of the project's product into the organization. Related to it is a discussion on product acceptance and benefits realization. To complete the book's picture, the chapter provides a thorough comparison between the skills required for each member of the duo and how to leverage them—especially at and near the touch points.

HOW TO USE THIS BOOK

The great news is that you do not need to read this book from start to finish in order to benefit from it. You can keep it close by and refer to the relevant chapter as you need it, or familiarize yourself with the content of the book and revisit areas that need more focus. This book may turn out to be one of your best friends—whether you are the PM or the BA, as it recognizes simple human behavior characteristics and applies them against the reality of the coexistence of the PM and the BA in project environments. Applying the concepts in this book will make you look good in the eyes of your colleagues and stakeholders—as it gives you means to become more efficient and effective in dealing with your most important partner for success (for a PM it's the BA and for a BA it's the PM).

Reflect on a project that you have worked on where there was seamless collaboration between the PM and BA (rainbows and butterflies come to mind) versus one where it felt like your cohort was from a completely different planet (picturing the devil with the pitchfork). This book will equip you with the means to consistently achieve harmony between the PM and BA roles, like yin and yang, so your project can proceed in a world of rainbows and butterflies to increase the probability of project and program success. We have practiced what we have preached—and are living proof it works!

ABOUT THE AUTHORS

Ori Schibi is the President of PM Konnectors, a Toronto-based, privately held corporation. With a focus on change management, project management, and business analysis, his company provides a variety of services—including facilitation services, workshops and training/professional development, and consulting.

Ori is a thought leader and subject matter expert with over 25 years of experience in driving operational improvements, process streamlining and efficiencies, project recoveries, and complex programs. His expertise also includes the establishment and recovery of PMOs and the creation and improvement of project management and business analysis practices. Finally, in partnership with the coauthor of this book, Cheryl Lee, Ori provides project management and business analysis exam certification preparation courses, as well as a variety of professional development sessions in areas related to project management, business analysis, leadership, and organizational change.

Ori's extensive service offerings help organizations streamline processes, achieve efficiencies, create growth and value, and lead sustainable change. His diverse international and cross-industry experience, combined with high energy and strong leadership skills, have resulted in a track record of delivering outstanding results and achieving customer satisfaction. An underlying theme in his work is a unique and innovative approach to value creation through establishing collaborative relationships between business and IT departments and between businesses and customers—bridging gaps, building partnerships, and getting teams to focus on the main goals of creating value and customer satisfaction.

Large to mid-sized organizations in diverse industries (for example, financial services, telecoms, pharmaceuticals, manufacturing, construction, entertainment, and all levels of governments, including the United Nations High Commissioner for Refugees) have benefited from Ori's innovative services.

Mr. Schibi is a certified PRINCE2® Practitioner and Project Management Professional (PMP®), with an MBA from the Schulich School of Business at York University. He is a highly regarded speaker (and proud member of the Canadian Association of Professional Speakers and National Speakers Association) and a published author (including his first book *Managing Stakeholder Expectations for Project Success*, J. Ross, 2013).

Last, but certainly not least, Ori is a devoted husband and father, who lives with his family in the Greater Toronto Area, Ontario, Canada.

Cheryl Lee is a Certified Business Analysis Professional (CBAP®), certified Professional in Business Analysis (PMI-PBA®) and Project Management Professional (PMP®), with an Honours Bachelor of Science Degree from the University of Toronto.

As a highly experienced business analysis and project management practitioner and trainer, Cheryl has mastered the ability to harmonize the PM and BA roles in order to deliver seamless and successful implementations. This author, speaker, and passionate business analysis nerd never misses an opportunity to help mentor and inspire other PMs and BAs. She has conducted multiple public webinars and presentations at conferences, chapter meetings, and local colleges and universities.

Cheryl's devotion to the profession of business analysis is further demonstrated by her not-for-profit contributions. She served as a Director with the IIBA Toronto Chapter where she initiated and facilitated the CBAP study group and cofounded the PMI Southern Ontario Chapter—Business Analysis Community, the first Business Analysis Community within a PMI chapter, with her coauthor Ori Schibi.

She is also the President of BA Konnectors, a Toronto-based consulting firm that offers consulting and training services within the realm of business analysis, project management, and change management. Clients in both public and private sectors across all industries, including all levels of government, financial services, high tech, telecommunication, transportation, construction, and entertainment have benefited from her company's services. Reliable, efficient, passionate, personable, energetic, and cheerful are a few of the characteristics clients use to describe Cheryl.

Besides being a business analyst enthusiast, Cheryl also loves to cook, travel, and spend time with her family. She lives with her husband in the Greater Toronto Area, Ontario, Canada.

DEDICATION

I dedicate this book to:

Eva, my wife, whom I love more and more every day for being a perfect wife and a loving mom to our two daughters. I simply can't live without you.

Our amazing daughters, Kayla and Maya, who bring light, love, and happiness to our lives.

And to my loving mother, Hava, and my brothers, Naaman and Eitan, who are always there for me.

—Ori Schibi

I dedicate this book to:

My husband, Denny, for his love, patience, and encouragement.

My biggest cheerleaders, in addition to Denny, my parents David and Suzette, Walter, Carolyn, Jenny, Jmee and Julie. Their continued support provides me the courage to tackle anything and everything.

—Cheryl Lee

This book has free material available for download from the Web Added Value™ resource center at *www.jrosspub.com*

At J. Ross Publishing we are committed to providing today's professional with practical, hands-on tools that enhance the learning experience and give readers an opportunity to apply what they have learned. That is why we offer free ancillary materials available for download on this book and all participating Web Added Value™ publications. These online resources may include interactive versions of material that appears in the book or supplemental templates, worksheets, models, plans, case studies, proposals, spreadsheets and assessment tools, among other things. Whenever you see the WAV™ symbol in any of our publications, it means bonus materials accompany the book and are available from the Web Added Value Download Resource Center at www.jrosspub.com.

Downloads for *Effective PM and BA Role Collaboration: Delivering Business Value through Projects and Programs Successfully* consist of:

- A plan requirements activities template
- Sample requirements using requirements attributes
- A requirements risk log template
- An agile suitability scorecard
- A PM-BA contract
- PM and BA role definition and collaboration areas
- A *PMBOK® Guide-BABOK®* comparison
- Tasks and activities by project life cycle stage
- Touchpoints on managing stakeholder expectations
- Requirements management plan guidelines
- A product requirements elicitation checklist
- A traceability matrix
- Use case diagram and scenario examples
- User stories

CHALLENGES RELATED TO PROJECT MANAGEMENT AND BUSINESS ANALYSIS

"We don't grow when things are easy; we grow when we face challenges."—Joyce Meyer

There seems to be a lot of confusion among practitioners and experts alike regarding the division of work and the touch points between the project manager (PM) and the business analyst (BA). While the cause for the confusion ranges from unclear role definition (especially that of the BA) to unclear expectations and lack of understanding on how to effectively utilize the BA in project environments, the bottom line is the same—a mismatch of activities, expectations, ideas, and initiatives—some work well together, others do not, and the rest are in outright conflict with one another.

This chapters sheds light on the challenges in the important, interesting, and at times tense relationship between the PM and the BA—and between the PM-BA duo and the rest of the project team and the organization. The challenges will be addressed in this chapter, and more elaborate resolutions will be presented throughout the book.

DEFINE EFFECTIVE

The word *effective* often comes to mind when describing a PM or a BA; however, there is a wide range of ways to describe effective. Does effective mean impactful? Or rather fast? How about collaborative? Focused? Assertive? Problem solver? We live in an era where projects needs are not only about the individual skills of the people who lead the projects, or those of the team members, but rather the needs shift toward needs that are more integrative, collaborative in nature, and above all—people's ability to communicate with each other and work together toward success.

An effective PM is an individual with leadership skills and style that are appropriate for the circumstances of the project and the organization—one who can work effectively with a BA; who can share responsibility, delegate (once again, effectively), and integrate all points of view, ideas, and actions together toward one cohesive picture. In turn, an effective BA is not only one who understands the project's product, but can work alongside a PM—sharing relevant information, providing clear impact for actions (or inactions), and making recommendations that factor in the full range of considerations to benefit the project and the organization.

As this book is going to illustrate, there is only one way to bring together a PM and a BA and make them into a strong, effective team—a combination of collaboration, integration, and communication that focuses on the strengths that each individual brings to the table, while overcoming the weaknesses and ultimately, turn these two different people into one entity that is designed to take on the challenges at hand.

ONE ENTITY?

Many practitioners may claim that an attempt to turn the PM-BA team into one entity is not going to be as successful as simply utilizing one person for both roles. While in theory it may be true, and it may be applicable for smaller, less complex projects—larger or medium-sized projects require more from this unified role than the capacity of any one individual can produce. Furthermore, despite the many similarities between project management and business analysis, few individuals possess the skills and traits required for both roles. Experience shows that attempts to consolidate the PM and BA roles into one individual on larger, more complex projects ends up backfiring and costing the organization significantly more than the attempted related benefits. Having the PM-BA duo work seamlessly together as one entity on the larger, more complex initiatives generated very favorable results. For smaller, less complex projects, the PM-BA hybrid role has increased in popularity as more organizations shift towards a more change-driven or agile environment. This introduces the need for resources to be cross trained in both disciplines. However, the need still exists for the hybrid PM-BA to understand the integration points between project management and business analysis in order to deliver a successful project.

CHALLENGES

In any scenario where two people need to work together and perform activities that depend on each other, there will be challenges, differences in opinions, and often friction and conflict. Adding to that the existence of many moving parts, uncertainty, differing philosophies on how to perform the work, political pressures, third-party involvement, changes, and shifting priorities may lead to results that are common in most project environments. The PM and the BA have separate backgrounds and areas of focus, and they often report to different parts of the organization—representing different values and priorities. When attempting to combine their knowledge and experience, the PM and the BA often do not get along—they may perform activities that are not aligned and sometimes override each other.

Before diving into the myriad of challenges that impact the relationship between the PM and the BA and in turn, the combined value these two roles produce for the organization, we need to keep in mind that the role of the BA must not be limited to only Information Technology environments. Utilizing a BA to support both the project and the PM can substantially benefit most projects in a variety of disciplines and industries.

It is easy to find challenging areas when reviewing the roles of the PM and the BA; mainly due to the heavy involvement of both roles in the project work. The following pages covers the most common challenges and sets the groundwork for finding ways to address them and ultimately resolve these challenges.

Splitting the Work

Most PMs and BAs do not take the time to discuss how they can work effectively together or how to divide their workload. With multiple areas of responsibility that overlap, it is important to define who does what and where one role ends and the other begins. Different aspects of areas such as risk management, communication, relationship management, and change management need to be addressed by both roles. With no coordination or clear role definition, confusion is likely to ensue—leading to overlaps, redundancies, confusion, and conflict. Clear definition of both the PM's and the BA's roles and responsibilities will clarify *who does what*, both for those who hold the roles and for others (the team and other stakeholders). Further, the role definition will help address the touch points between the roles and the handoffs between the PM and the BA and from the PM-BA *duo* to the rest of the team.

Understanding Each Other's Capacity

As an extension of splitting the work and defining the roles, early discussions of the roles and responsibilities will also allow the PM and the BA to learn about each other's availability, skills, areas of expertise, and capacity. It is common to see PMs and BAs *dump* work on each other, or escalate issues without first understanding whether the other person is capable of handling these issues. As part of becoming one entity, the PM and the BA need to act in full synchronization and become fully aware of each other's experience, skills, availability, and capacity. Bouncing issues and activities from one to the other turns the PM and the BA into a bottleneck and beyond delaying work and resolution of issues, it creates a perception among team members and stakeholders that the PM-BA *duo's* handling of the project work is insufficient. In turn, it contributes to doubts in their skills, slowdowns, and calls to replace either one, or both the PM and the BA. As part of the PM-BA collaboration, they also need to learn of each other's strengths and weaknesses so they can complement each other and divide the work so they can *instinctively* hand over issues, problems, and activities to the most suitable individual to deal with the problem.

Aligning Areas of Focus

The BA's focus is typically on the product and the requirements; that is, what we are trying to produce. In simple terms, they are driven by the business objectives—their role is to create a bridge between the business needs and the technical aspects of the work, and they are ultimately associated with advocating for product quality. This is not to imply that the PM does not strive for product quality, but the PM's areas of focus are mainly project related; deliverables and activities that need to take place to produce the product or service for which the project is undertaken.

Since the project performance will be evaluated based on the scope, time, and cost (a.k.a. *triple constraints*) of the project, the PM and the BA must align their focus areas and activities to ensure that they both work toward achieving the same objectives. A common occurrence on projects is having PMs performing activities to promote their area of focus, often at the expense of the BA's focus, and vice versa. While it is not done intentionally, the unfavorable result is inevitable. For example, when the PMs try to meet the schedule, they may propose removing certain scope items (and hence, requirements), without understanding the full impact on the business objectives, or on other requirements. The same goes for the BAs who often propose a requirements prioritization scheme that does not take resource availability into account, thus leading to a schedule bottleneck.

The aforementioned examples may once again bring up the need to have one person performing both activities; however, the different skills and especially the capacity required for each of the roles usually makes this an unrealistic option. Aligning the areas of focus means a joined process for planning and estimating, ensuring that both the PM and the BA are familiar with their counterpart's considerations, and with the full impact of their actions on their colleague's areas of focus.

Integrating the Requirements

As a significant percentage of defects in projects can be traced back to requirements, there is a strong need to ensure that requirements are not only elicited and managed properly, but also that the entire requirements management process is fully integrated into the project. With requirements being under the *responsibility* of the BA, and with PMs often not being involved in the process, there is a need to ensure that the requirements are fully integrated into the project. This leads to a discussion involving a full division of the roles and responsibilities between the PM and the BA, as well as identifying specific areas to perform the requirements integration. This includes everything from ensuring business value, traceability, incorporation of requirements into the project scope, managing requirements related risks, and ensuring their handling is transferred from the BA to the PM—to requirements prioritization and one integrated change control process. There is no point in getting the BA to cross-train the PM to better understand the product and the requirements, but there is a need to ensure that the BA informs the PM of relevant information that pertains to the impact of the requirements on the project as a whole. At the same time, it is necessary to ensure that the PM consults with the BA to fully understand the dependencies and the impact of scope, as well as other changes in the project on requirements and on the product.

Estimating Techniques

Despite an improvement in the area of estimating a few years ago, there are still multiple standards and resources that project managers can use to estimate work efforts, durations, costs, and the need for resources. Having more organizations moving toward agile project management gets us closer to achieving more consistency and transparency in estimating, but it is still not enough. The PM is not always sufficiently involved in either the estimating process or in the technical work performed and it may reduce the PM's ability to effectively facilitate the estimating process or to provide valid estimates and controls. Moreover, it is common to see team members mixing hope and other subjective considerations into their estimates—and many of those providing the estimates are not the ones actually performing the work. The BA is typically more intimately involved in the technical work that needs to be performed in the project and as such can serve as a liaison between the PM and the team. This will ensure consistent estimating standards are being followed, that terminology is used in a unified manner (i.e., effort vs. duration, specific completion times), and that controls are applied on work performed to allow real time reporting that is as close to representing the actual status as possible.

Reporting

Meaningful project reporting is a common problem in projects. From the timeliness of the reporting to accuracy, completeness, and relevance—reports often not only fail to represent actual progress and status, but they also lead to flaws in decision-making processes and ultimately to an increase in the number of change requests. When senior management does not feel it has the full information or when the information reported does not properly represent progress, it is more likely that senior management will introduce changes to the projects—changes that should not take place whatsoever. The result is waste—extra work, assessments, plans, and work performed to execute the approved changes, which in turn, introduces new risks to the project. Having the PM and the BA design the reports and the reporting standards upfront and bringing the reporting mechanism for approval will save a lot of the potential subsequent misunderstandings and need for changes.

Divide Areas of Responsibility

An important ingredient of the collaboration between the PM and the BA is to identify the areas of shared responsibility, recognize the full scale of both roles, and divide the responsibility of leading each area. This book covers the areas of responsibility for each of the roles extensively. But, it is not sufficient to only identify these areas—it is also important to coordinate and determine for each area whether it is the PM or the BA who is most suitable, appropriate, and qualified to lead. The decision has to be based on capacity, interests, subject matter expertise, the type of project, and stakeholder needs.

Terminology

Project management and business analysis have been governed, for the most part, by different organizations, and as such, both disciplines have grown separate from each other and further—in different directions. PMs and BAs often do not speak the same language or use terminology in the same context. The recent development of the Professional in Business Analysis certification by the Project Management Institute is instrumental in helping PMs and BAs become better partners—starting with using the same terminology and improving collaboration, rather than misunderstanding each other. The bad news is that it takes more than just a methodology to bring two disciplines together. It is now up to the PM and the BA, along with their managers and the organization, to define boundaries, draw interaction maps, set up rules of engagement, develop common vocabulary, and fertilize the new way of doing things through continuous improvement.

COMMON CONFLICT AREAS

It is a known fact that conflict is not a bad thing—that is, when it is managed properly and when it is the *right* type of conflict—about the merits, the work, the domain, and the substance rather than about personalities and styles. Unfortunately, a large portion of the friction between PMs and BAs is due to misunderstandings and *alignment* issues between the two roles, which leads to a lot of waste but fortunately can be easily fixed.

Scope Management

The *project scope* has the potential to become a significant source of conflict in many project environments. This conflict may be caused by a combination of factors including time pressure, lack of understanding of the difference between project scope and product scope, and issues around change control.

- **Time pressure:** This is the reality of virtually all projects and it leads to shortcuts in planning, lack of attention to detail, misunderstandings, and prioritization issues. While it is impossible to stop time, add time, or create new time, this book helps deal effectively with time consuming obstacles—and overcoming them will allow PMs and BAs to focus more on value-added activities such as collaboration, planning, and effective communication.
- **Project scope and product scope:** Project scope defines the activities, time, and resources needed for the project—in order to produce the product, service, or result. It is about the work to get done and the activities that need to be performed in the project. The project scope is articulated through the work breakdown structure and the project activities. Product Scope defines what must be delivered in order to meet the

business need, that is, the major features of the solution. It is articulated in the requirements documentation. One of the major challenges any project faces is to integrate the two seamlessly; take the requirements and integrate them into the project scope by understanding what we have to do and then ask the other *W*s: when, where, who, how, and how much.

While the project may not end up producing the intended product to its entire extent, everything that gets done in the project must be of value for the product at stake. It is not that one is more important than the other, but it is impossible to create project scope with no product scope—and having *product* scope with no *project* scope will likely lead us to a failure.

The boundaries of responsibilities are clear—the BA is primarily responsible for the product scope, but the PM takes the lead with the project scope. However, they are not fully linear processes and both the PM and the BA must provide input and take place in creating both scopes. When defining the requirements, the BA must lead the effort according to the project needs, direction, and constraints that are represented by the PM. In turn, when building the project scope, the PM must ensure that prioritization that are critical to success functionality and technical considerations are taken into account and are transitioned seamlessly from the requirements documentation into the project scope.

- **Change control:** Change control is a contentious issue for many reasons. The PM typically resists adding features or scope in an effort to reduce impact on cost and schedule to protect the plan and reduce shocks to the system in an effort to maintain stability for the team. The BA, on the contrary, is often the driver behind the need to add features, to meet stakeholders' needs and expectations, and to maximize the value produced by the product. The problem with this is that both the PM and the BA are right, but their conflicting interests need to be evaluated by the overall value that can be produced for the customer—taking into consideration all critical to success factors: functionality, time, costs, resource availability, quality, value, and benefits.

  Since most projects do not have properly defined success criteria to highlight the value and benefits the project is slated to produce, it is difficult to determine whether product changes with added features should be included in the project or not—as it is impossible to decide if they will add value to something that was never defined. The decision is then left to the PM and the BA, who arbitrarily debate whether the benefits from added changes warrant the additional costs. Furthermore, the change control process and the decision-making criteria are often tailored toward project needs and not toward product needs, and as such, the process may fail to review certain aspects of the potential benefits or the costs associated with adding features. An unclear, ineffective, or convoluted change control process adds to the chance for a misinformed decision about the change.

Another challenge related to requirements is the unrealistic expectations that project stakeholders develop for quick finalization of product requirements. Any type of issue around product requirements, including the duration that is required to work on developing quality product requirements, is likely to take longer to address and resolve than initially thought. This challenge connects us back to the need to manage expectations, since providing unrealistic promises for quick resolutions will lead to delays, possibly strain the relationship, and ultimately may result in more risks and quality issues due to the need to rush decision making or actions that take longer than anticipated. The majority of PMs and BAs work in silos when it comes to requirements, which is likely the root cause of unrealistic expectations that ultimately lead to project failure.

Attitude

The PM leads the project and is typically more senior than the BA, who is viewed as a team member that reports to the PM. Many PMs tend to develop a bossy attitude toward the BA that sometimes involves demeaning the contribution of the BA, discounting the importance of the BA role, engaging in power struggles, and mistakenly viewing the BA as a type of assistant, instead of treating the BA as a partner and enrolling the BA into collaboration and partnership. The PM and the BA should view each other as equals, where each represents different points of view and interests associated with project stakeholders. Decision making should be done based on information from both the PM and the BA and the PM should not be able to override a need or a recommendation by the BA only by the virtue of seniority. It is ultimately up to the PM—and the PM will be held accountable for the project success—but a truly joint effort is key for achieving project success.

Understanding

The word *understand* is vague and does not represent a set of tangible values. No presenter or individual can guarantee that their partners, in any given conversation, will understand them—even if the presenter explains something in the most articulate way. However, in any project there is a need to understand multiple project-related layers that make up the project context and environment.

The need for understanding spans from the technical aspects of the product or service the project is set to produce—to the industry, market, competition, benefits, organization, and culture—and ends with project management, business analysis, and human resources. It is expected that no one person will have all this knowledge, and therefore, there is a need to identify the areas of expertise the PM and the BA bring to the table, define who serves as a subject matter expert of which area, and with this knowledge identify which additional resources need to be engaged in order to get the missing pieces. Failing to define what the PM and the BA know and what they do not know will guarantee gaps in knowledge that will be counterproductive to achieving project success.

The BA Welcome Package and Early Project Deliverables

Early in the project there are several things that need to be done in order to build a solid foundation for the project. The value of early project deliverables are known to most PMs and BAs, yet this work is rarely completed due to lack of time. Beyond the time and effort involved, which serve as a valid excuse for not performing the early project work, there is a perception that most corporate cultures reward and glorify the *busy* over the *effective* and do not properly differentiate between *tangible* and *valuable*. Therefore, since early project work does not produce tangible progress from a product perspective, it is easy to see why some stakeholders may not see the value it produces.

The early project work involves a list of items that, if performed properly, can serve as a path for success, and with their absence the project will face more risks, challenges, and greater odds of failing to deliver on its promise. Furthermore, even if we manage to achieve success, it will be done with less efficiency and probably through spending more time, energy, frustration, and cost.

The following list represents the bulk of the early project activities; failing to perform them will have a significant and lasting negative impact on the prospect of project success.

- **The BA *welcome package*:** The BA is often involved in pre-project activities related to the business case, feasibility analysis, and other initiation activities. The BA who has worked on the pre-project activities, regardless of whether or not they will continue to work on the project, should be putting together a briefing package for the PM—highlighting the results or findings from the pre-project activities.
- **Project charter:** The charter is the first official document produced by the project; it provides the mandate, expresses the objectives and business case from the pre-project decision-making process, names the

PM, and serves as a marketing document and an important opportunity to set the tone—all in less than three pages, or as Mark Twain said: "I would write you a shorter letter, if I had more time." No matter what the size of the project is, it is critical to keep this document short, since being short serves as one of the major features that will get stakeholders to read it. As the executive summary of the project, it summarizes our current knowledge of what is at stake. It is not the BA's job to write the charter; it is also not the PM's job to do it. However, both the PM and the BA have an important role in putting the charter together.

The BA needs to provide the context, knowledge of the organization, information from the BA *welcome package*, feasibility, risks, product information, and alternative considerations. The PM, who often ends up writing the document, needs to work closely with the sponsor (who is actually supposed to write it) for understanding the mandate and setting the tone. It is the sponsor's project, and the PM must understand the success criteria, objectives, and any unknowns—so they can be documented as assumptions. This type of collaboration between the PM, BA, and the sponsor produces a charter that is likely to reflect conditions as they are and serve as the foundation for future plans and performance. The three parties also collaborate in articulating conditions and considerations, then present them to each other as assumptions that, in turn, get validated and refined. The BA brings in findings from the pre-work activities. The PM arranges the data into meaningful information within the structure of the charter, which makes it easy for the sponsor to view the information and provide feedback. Then the PM can adjust the information, in order for it to reflect the actual project state and needs. We now utilize the value that each of the three aforementioned parties brings to the table and leverage the information into a meaningful and robust project charter.

- **Project readiness assessment:**[1] The readiness assessment measures how prepared you, your team, and the organization are for the upcoming project. There are many ways to measure readiness—and the level of intensity and thoroughness should depend on multiple factors, such as organizational risk attitude, project complexity, and the specific situation you are facing. A *proper* readiness assessment may include evaluations of the organizational culture, processes and procedures, leadership styles, resource management, overall complexity, and historical performance. The readiness assessment can help you identify project and organizational needs and serve as a foundation to planning. The readiness assessment evaluates how prepared the organization and the team are for the project.

Readiness deals with a variety of matters, where the leading issues are related to resources (i.e., availability, capacity, skills, timing, and fit)—other related matters include project dependencies, domain experience, approvals, budgets, and schedule. It can be viewed as a type of gap analysis between where the organization currently is and the capability required for the project. Failing to effectively address these gaps before proceeding with the project will result in elevated levels of complexity and risk. In some cases, the team identifies areas of the project that indicate a lack of readiness, and in others, there is simply a lack of information about some aspects of the project. Either way, these are both warning signs to the organization that this project requires special attention.

The PM and the BA must work in collaboration to measure the true readiness for the project and provide the sponsor with their findings. Having *only the PM* or *only the BA* performing this exercise may produce results that are not based on the full information available.

- **Project complexity assessments:** The project complexity assessment is another important measure for your project that also serves as one of the subsets to readiness. In a world where virtually all organizations engage in running multiple projects simultaneously—resource sharing (and at times dispersed resources), project dependencies, and outsourcing—every project is essentially complex. PMs need to define complexity and how it should be measured, then determine how complex each project is (relative to others), in order to treat every project with the appropriate level of focus and integrity. Obtaining a realistic reading of project complexity will help assess our readiness level and in turn, allow us to plan appropriately.

  There are a few common types of complexity that need to be measured: technical, organizational, environmental, people, and overall complexity. The PM's ability to detect complexity within these generic categories and subsequently prepare for it will have a significant impact downstream on the degree of project success they can deliver. The breakdown of complexity into categories assists in channeling our focus toward the source of the complexity, and the categories can also serve as a checklist to remind us which areas may produce complexity. Generally, not every category identified will end up producing complexity in any given project.

  PMs and BAs need to evaluate all areas of complexity to check if there is an impact on the project readiness then update the project risks accordingly. Details on how to complete this assessment will be discussed in greater depth later in the chapter. Project complexity tends to grow in direct proportion to the size of the project. The complexity assessment may result in a high level of complexity in a specific category or multiple complexities scattered across multiple categories, which also implies the project is complex. The project complexity assessment measures the combination of the project's complexity categories, their magnitude, and the number of interactions between them. All of this should then be factored into the readiness assessment to gauge the organization's and the team's capability to keep the project within the control parameters. PMs should not be deterred from taking on high complexity projects, but having a realistic view of what we are facing in advance will help in the planning process.

- **Stakeholder analysis:** The task of identifying stakeholders starts with the BA collecting information already available from the pre-project activities, then shifts to become a collaborative effort between the BA and the PM once the PM is assigned to the project. Stakeholder analysis is the foundation for designing project communication and setting and managing expectations. It also provides insight regarding potential issues, areas of conflict, the amount of rigor to expect in the project, the magnitude of the change that is expected, as well as risks and quality.

The only way we can understand stakeholders' needs early enough in the game is to perform a stakeholder analysis. There is growing recognition of its importance, yet most PMs do not conduct a stakeholder analysis. Even the PMs who currently conduct some type of stakeholder analysis do not do it sufficiently and fall short of getting the intended results. A hasty and superficial analysis leads to a lack of understanding of stakeholders' needs and their ability to influence the project; it results in overlooking stakeholders' involvement in the project; and ultimately leads to waste—since the half-baked approach still requires effort, time, resources, and money while producing little to no benefit to the project. Failing to perform stakeholder analysis has a negative impact on the project success due to an increased risk of wasting time on items potentially unimportant to the key stakeholders. Project failures can often be traced to missing or poor stakeholder analysis, and although there is never sufficient time to conduct one, there really is no way around it.

The main reasons for not conducting stakeholder analysis is lack of time and the fact that it is usually not a required or tangible deliverable in the organization's project methodology—it is therefore easy to see why many PMs do not perform it. Further, failing to get the BA involved in the process may reduce the analysis' exposure to valuable information about some stakeholders and limits the project team's ability to address stakeholders' needs. In addition, dividing the role of managing stakeholder expectations between the PM and the BA utilizes another set of eyes, and with both the PM and the BA engaged in the process, it becomes easy to approach certain stakeholders; both from a capacity, as well as personality perspective. Since the PM cannot always develop a good rapport with all stakeholders, the BA may deal directly with some of the stakeholders; especially those who are closer to the areas that the BA already leads within the project.

- **Communication planning and ground rules:** While the PM is ultimately accountable for the project success, managing communication is a joint effort and must be done in collaboration between the PM and BA. Due to the nature of the PM and the BA roles, it is common to see gaps—where parts of the communication falls between the cracks, alongside unnecessary duplication of effort that leads to inefficiencies, waste, misunderstandings, and unnecessary conflict. Building a plan for formal flow of communication and a set of ground rules as part of a team contract for general communication and for informal interaction significantly helps streamline communication and address stakeholders' needs.

  Closely related to communication, but not exactly the same is *expectations management*, which is the project's focus on delivering the product, service, or result to the extent that the customer needs. While planning is critical for success, even the best plan might not survive its encounter with reality and will have to be adjusted. The plan's flexibility determines what types of changes and adjustments need to take place and these changes are directly related to definition of project success and to the stakeholders' expectations. Project success may not be determined solely by the product delivered; but also by the management of the stakeholders' expectations and how happy they are with the outcomes that are produced. The PM needs to make sure that the customers' and other stakeholders' expectations are managed with the direct and active involvement of the BA to address any angles and areas that require the BA's subject matter expertise, communication skills, relationship, and business or technical knowledge.

- **Roles and responsibilities:** Most of the fault for failing to set up clear roles and responsibilities lies with the PM. The use of a RASCI chart (responsible, accountable, supports, consulted, and informed), as illustrated in Figure 1.1, is not as common as it should be, and without one, many project resources do not know what is expected of them on the project. Furthermore, resource planning is often not aligned with the requirements or project needs and the process of assigning resources is

Responsibility Assignment Matrix–RAM (RASCI Chart)

Team Member / Task	PM	Sponsor							Remarks
1.1									
1.2									
2.1									
2.2									
2.3									

R=Responsible A=Accountable S=Support C=Consulted I=Informed

This sample Responsibility Assignment Matrix (or RACI/RASCI Chart) can help the PM and the BA identify which resources are going to perform each activity and which resources will be involved with an activity at various capacities. The matching between the resources and activities is an important step on the way to building a realistic schedule.

Figure 1.1 RASCI Chart

not iterative enough to reflect project progress, performance, and overall project needs.

MORE CHALLENGES

It is difficult to predict how the business analysis profession will evolve in the near and the long term, but there has been tremendous growth in business analysis and increased focus on the role of the BA within the last few years.

The following list of challenges complements the challenges already discussed, with the difference that the upcoming list is more about organizational and environmental challenges and the proposed ways for dealing with them—and less about the direct roles of the PM and the BA. Some of these challenges are for the PM and the BA to figure out together (e.g., time management); while others (e.g., strategy) are for the PM and the BA to check and inquire about in the event that they feel there are challenges, misalignments, or lack of clarity with these items.

Strategy and the Organization

A variety of terms can be used to address the need for alignment with organizational needs and strategy, including, but not limited to, enterprise analysis and portfolio management. Regardless of the name we call it, the PM and the BA need to establish a mechanism that involves reporting, checks and balances, and controls—so they can continuously ensure that their recommendations, team members' actions, and stakeholder decisions are all aligned with organizational strategy and business objectives. Performing the alignment task together will lead to more effective results than if the PM and the BA each perform it separately.

- **What is an organization?** There are many ways to interpret the word *organization*—from the company, through its department, to projects and even teams. To clarify, an organization is two or more people working interdependently toward a common goal. Within it there is a need to divide the labor, identify the functions to be performed, assign tasks, and perform the work. The work performed takes the organization closer to accomplishing its goals and objectives and in order to do that, there is a need for a strong alignment throughout the components of the organization. The relevance of the definition of the word *organization* for the PM and the BA is that they belong to many organizations (by reporting lines, the project, the teams) and one of the organizations is the one created by the PM-BA relationship. Treating the relationship between the PM and the BA as an organization may help divide the work and identify the common goals. It can also establish success criteria for this partnership and help measure the performance of the duo. The PM-BA organization is instrumental for project success and without managing it effectively any project success will be in doubt and even if achieved, it will be riddled with challenges and overruns.

Trust Building

Trust is not something that is built on its own or something that can be taken for granted. When a PM and a BA meet for the first time on a project, they cannot simply start working together; they need to establish context for their work, take trust-building measures, learn about each other, define their success criteria, and establish an organization that will help them achieve their objectives. It is not simple to achieve these things, but identifying what needs to get done and putting together a plan will make it easier. Furthermore, it is not only up to the PM and the BA to establish their working relations; as it takes time and effort that may be beyond their capacities and not on their list of priorities. Therefore, the PM and the BA need to enroll their managers into the effort and make sure to request the set-up, permission, and capacity to build trust—and then learn to work together.

Similar to the other early project activities, this set of actions is not about tangible deliverables, nor is it about product related progress. It is likely that some stakeholders approach the PM and the BA with the famous "stop with the planning and show me some progress," and therefore it is the responsibility of the PM and the BA to build a business case and demonstrate the value of these activities to the relevant stakeholders. Without requesting time, permission, and the capacity to perform the early project activities and the trust building measures, they will not take place—and trust issues, lack of coordination and collaboration, and lack of cohesiveness are likely to plague the project performance moving forward. The effort to build trust will also shed valuable light on the PM's and the BA's personalities, tendencies, preferences, and values—which in turn, will help identify each other's strengths and improve the joint ability to enroll other stakeholders and achieve greater buy-in.

Lastly, in order to build trust, both sides must be open—and it involves calculated risks, as both the PM and the BA expose themselves to some level of vulnerability. This exercise, combined with the stakeholder analysis, will help minimize the risk taken and make the trust-building measures meaningful for the other side.

Time Management and Prioritization

The context of time management here is about individuals managing their own time and priorities—not about project schedule management. Time management and prioritization go hand in hand and are critical to the success of every team member, and particularly of the PM and the BA. Deadlines, milestones, multiple unclear (and often conflicting) priorities, and overall *more work than time* are the reality of essentially every PM and BA. Yet, in order to perform their work effectively, the PM and the BA must manage their own time, as well as help others to manage their time and their priorities.

Helping others with priorities and effective usage of time is part of a broader role the PM and the BA need to assume as mentors. As the ones who manage project schedules, identify deliverables, and define activities, the PM and the BA need to serve as an authority figure in their ability to manage their workload, organize their time, and facilitate the prioritization of tasks, activities, issues, and escalations based on the project success, objectives, and mandate provided. Without leading by example, the PM and the BA will have a hard time serving as an authority in time management and will not be able to enroll team members in improving their own processes and effectively managing their days.

It is too often that PMs, BAs and other team members respond with "I don't have time" to requests and needs that are addressed to them. Such responses may be an indication that people in the organization are overworked, but it is often a symptom of one or more of the following problems, which are more foundational and typically involve other stakeholders:

- **Team members do not manage their time effectively:** This may include attending too many meetings or meetings that are too long or unproductive; working on non-value-added activities; multitasking; spending too much time on activities; or poor risk and assumption management.
- **Priorities are not set or clearly articulated:** Priority setting is the role of the project sponsor or other senior stakeholders. However, when priorities are not clearly communicated to the project team, it is the responsibility of the PM and the BA to ask for clarification so the mandate for the team becomes clear. This is a form of managing upward and ensuring that the information from senior management flows effectively to the project team. While we should expect the team members to step forward and ask questions when their priorities are not clear, once again it is the role of the PM and the BA to engage the team and check that the mandate is clearly understood. Often team members do not realize that the priorities are not clear, or they do not suspect that the list of priorities provided to them is flawed. Having the PM and the BA working with the team will help ensure that the team members will work on what the project and the organization need them to work on.

  The reference to both the PM and the BA being responsible for the communication (both upward and with the team) does not imply that the PM and the BA must attend all conversations together; rather it requires the PM-BA duo to divide their tasks and utilize both individuals' skills, relationships, styles, and availability to engage different stakeholders as required.
- **Objectives and success criteria are poorly defined:** The old saying that "when you don't know where you're going, any road will do" is applicable here. When a PM or a BA gives a team member a set of tasks to perform in no particular order, the team member is unlikely to perform the tasks in the sequence the PM or the BA had in mind. Since team members are not mind readers, it is the responsibility of the PM and the BA to provide any context regarding priority, urgency, deadlines, impact areas, or any other information that will pave the way for the team member to do the right thing right—the first time—while maximizing value for the project.
- **Misalignment between the resources and their roles in the project:** This is an integration problem, since it can be originated out of a multitude of factors, including time pressure, unclear communication, flawed sense of urgency, lack of clear prioritization, poor definition of quality, insufficient risk management, unrealistic schedule and resource requirements, mismanaged expectations, and even weak leadership.

Any of these factors can lead to the placement of the *wrong* resource to perform any given activity—where *wrong* refers to availability, seniority, skills, experience, political acumen, communication skills, or technical knowledge.

Matching team members to roles and effectively assigning roles and responsibility requires input from both the PM and the BA and their collaboration in understanding the mandate given to the project, articulating it, and communicating back the true needs for resources to the appropriate part of the organization.

Engaging Others, Elicitation, and Communication

PMs and BAs are the heart of project communication and they are in charge of establishing communication guidelines, facilitating the communication process, providing feedback, and engaging others for information. Unfortunately PMs and BAs are often not trained in communication and they may not be effective communicators. Furthermore, it is typically the BA that is in charge of managing communication, gathering information and eliciting requirements as part of their broader roles in championing the entire requirements process. While it is wrong to blame the BA (or the PM) for other stakeholders' reluctance or inability to be contributing members of the requirements process, it is the responsibility of the PM and the BA to build a process that is not only effective and efficient, but one that is also highly engaging and appealing to other stakeholders.

Many PMs and BAs lead the information gathering, idea generation, and requirements processes with lists and simple brainstorming techniques, which used to be popular and considered effective in the 1990s. However, as illustrated in Chapter 6 of this book, these activities need to be based on the new ways in which people engage each other—which is more interactive, dynamic, and efficient—through gamestorming; storyboarding; and shorter, dynamic and engaging sessions.

Quality and Cost of Quality: The Value Perceptions

The title of this mini-section has potentially enough *meat* in it to fill a couple of books. However, quality, cost of quality (CoQ), and agility are all related—and they appear here in the context of the value proposition that the PM-BA duo bring to the table and the importance of addressing these items together.

Although organizations show emphasis on quality—and there is a lot of talk about quality—not enough is getting done in an effort to achieve the desired level of quality. Furthermore, in many situations quality is either not defined enough or insufficient effort is made toward achieving quality. One of the main factors that may compromise any given project's ability to deliver to the required quality standards is *money*. Cost is often the reason that certain measures do not take place and that certain activities do not get performed to the extent required—or not at all. With that said, the topic of CoQ is severely overlooked; organizations do not have an indication of how much money they spend on quality and on which cost of quality categories. As a result, problems may not be fixed in a timely manner and often there is an attempt to fix or change the wrong item—mistaking it as the root cause.

Cost of quality is a term that is widely used, but often misunderstood. Like any good thing in life, quality comes with a cost, and as articulated by Phillip Crosby[2] in his book *Quality is Free*, it is not a gift, but conceptually, it is free. The actual CoQ[3] was first articulated by Joseph Juran as the cost of poor quality—any cost that would not have been expended if quality were perfect contributes to the CoQ. Quality costs are the sum total of the costs incurred by investing in the prevention of non-conformance to requirements, appraising a product or service for conformance to requirements, and failing to meet requirements.

The goal of quality processes is not to do them simply because it is the right thing to do, but because the return on the investment in quality has a dramatic impact on organizations. A 2002 study reported that software bugs cost the U.S. economy $59.6 billion each year and that one third of the bugs could be eliminated by an improved testing infrastructure.[4] This is in line with other research findings, which indicate that not only can the cost of poor quality reach 20 to 30% of sales or more, but also that most businesses are not even aware of their actual spending on quality, as they do not keep track of it properly. Many people believe that their organizations spend no more than 5% of their total sales on quality.

There is a notion that the cost that an organization incurs in an effort to obtain a new customer is by far higher than the cost to retain an existing one. Similarly, the cost to eliminate a failure once the customer gets the product (a.k.a. external failures) is significantly higher than it is at the development phase. Effective quality management is about early detection of errors in an effort to reduce costs.

CoQ consists of four elements (see Table 1.1): prevention, appraisal, internal failure, and external failure. The total CoQ comprises the cost of conformance (including prevention and appraisal) and the cost of non-conformance (including both types of failure costs). The measure of the CoQ is not the actual price that the organization pays for building a quality product, but rather the cost of failing to create one.[5]

Table 1.1 Quality Cost Components

Cost of Conformance	1. Prevention 2. Appraisal
Cost of Non-conformance	1. Internal Failure 2. External Failure
There are two main types of quality costs: Costs of Conformance and Costs of Non-conformance. The total cost of quality is the result of adding up these two types of costs, as it should account for both prevention and appraisal activities that are performed as part of the effort to achieve quality, as well as for the two types of failure costs that are incurred as a result of failing to achieve quality.	

By nature, prevention costs are the lowest quality cost per item, while appraisal costs get relatively more expensive (albeit the total spending on prevention should be higher than the total spending on appraisal). Failure costs get much higher per item, with external failures potentially becoming dramatically more expensive than internal failure. Unfortunately, the most common way of measuring failure includes only the common costs such as warranty, scrap, and rework. However, true failure costs also include hidden costs such as management time, downtimes, increased inventory, decreased capacity, delivery problems, and lost orders.[6]

In essence, the ways to address the challenges mentioned in this chapter and the approach this book offers to the need for PM-BA collaboration are all about investing in quality. Not knowing what quality cost category money is spent on, or not even realizing that money is spent on quality may negatively impact the decision-making process in the project and the organization and in turn, make the project outcome more expensive to deliver, or possibly lead to failure.

The value proposition introduced by the investment in building a collaborative relationship between the PM and the BA, along with the enhanced focus on planning is proven in delivering meaningful value for the organization by streamlining communication; improving stakeholder buy-in; effectively managing stakeholder expectations; employing a proactive approach to planning, risks and changes; applying lessons effectively and on a timely manner; and overall, increasing the chance of delivering project success.

Project Needs, Business Needs, and Product and Technical Needs

It is not a difficult task to spot projects where there is insufficient collaboration between the PM and the BA. One of the signature symptoms for such lack of collaboration is the presence of conflicting and unclear priorities within the project; such issues translate to a series of misinformed decisions by PMs in relation to delivering value for the organization. These issues typically arise in the areas noted in the following list—and most of them can be avoided by having the PM and the BA work together and share information with each other.

- **Risk management:** Often, PMs and BAs do not see the relationship between *project* risks and *product* risks and consequently, their actions to address the risks may contradict each other.
- **Success criteria:** Project success criteria may be defined and acted upon with limited consideration for organizational success and business value.
- **Assumptions:** PMs often make assumptions that lack factual foundation and thus, are not communicated properly to team members and other stakeholders. These assumptions may not hold under the changing conditions of most projects and result in defects, conflicts, and performance issues.
- **Dependencies:** Cross-project dependencies, as well as dependencies within projects are often overlooked by the PM—mainly due to a lack of time and capacity to attend to all these considerations. The BA's product knowledge and familiarity with organizational constraints can shed light on some of these dependencies that, for the most part, are unknowns for the PM or the project team. Dependencies can be typically categorized under deliverables, resources, and risks.
- **Resource management:** The PM has limited ability to match team members with technical needs—for example, ensuring that a software developer has sufficient relevant experience in the programming language, the type of development life cycle, the type of product, and the level of rigor required and stress involved. The BA can provide valuable context about the matching of team members—thanks to the BA's familiarity with the team members and with the nature of the tasks on hand.
- **Change control:** A healthy change control process should have the BA's contribution incorporated into it; however, including the BA in the recommendations and decision-making processes can ensure that considerations that go beyond the direct project success criteria (i.e., time and budget considerations) get the appropriate level of attention.

Testing and Other Constraints

PMs must consider the voice of the BA in relation to testing needs, time, and resources. Many PMs make decisions throughout the project that lead to shortening or thinning down product testing—inevitably resulting in quality issues. Structuring the PM-BA collaboration in such a way so that considerations typically represented by BAs are heard and incorporated into the decision-making process may prevent late project rushes, emergencies, testing-related problems, and other such issues.

Attention to Detail

Although there are different *types* of PMs and BAs and it is impossible to cast specific characteristics to individuals within these roles, traditionally PMs tend to focus more on the big project picture, while BAs tend to demonstrate more attention to detail. These details include technical, resource, business, and organizational considerations. It is therefore logical to ensure that both points of view are integrated and that the PM's and BA's personalities complement any gaps and address potential duplication of effort and areas of focus.

In this context, it is also important to address the roles' boundaries—in other words, where the PM role ends and the BA role begins. Then for each area (once again considering the personalities of those involved), determine who assumes the leading role and who takes on the supporting role—to complement and leverage relevant skills, experience, personalities, and relationships.

Cross-Functional Conflicts

BAs often finds themselves stuck in the middle of cross-functional conflicts between PMs and functional managers. These situations are often the result of resource allocation related conflicts, and they may lead to escalations and decisions that may address some of the needs of those directly involved—however, with little to no consideration for the needs that are typically represented by the BA.

Having the BA involved in these conversations when the PM already knows the needs that the BA represents, may lead to a solution that is more comprehensive—one that does not compromise the availability and utilization of resources, and also ensures that the right resources are still allocated for the tasks at the required time. The BA can also help reprioritize items, functionalities, or features and provide an impact assessment that can support any decision made.

Bringing the BAs into the conversation at a later stage may force them to *back-pedal* and *reverse engineer* a solution that may put out fires, but not provide the most beneficial solution for the project, the organization, and the business as a whole. It can lead to rushed, misinformed decisions that are based on partial information and are subject to pressures and other considerations that are foreign to the true needs that arise from the situations. From here, it is a short road to outright blaming the BA for failing to facilitate an informed and constructive solution.

Estimates

Estimating is an issue that, despite all the tools and techniques out there, keeps plaguing projects—leading to misinformed, rushed decisions, delays, cost overruns, and ultimately, failures. While we cannot expect technical resources to be estimating *subject matter experts*, the PM can utilize the BA to improve communication, introduce ground rules, and establish a consistent and streamlined approach to estimating. Since estimates are done at various levels of the project and by different resources, if there is no specific guidance regarding terminology, units of measure, constraints, or overhead, PMs may get a result of mixed quality that may indicate the wrong outcome.

Working together, the PM and the BA need to establish a guide that helps engage team members and other stakeholders so they produce estimates that are realistic, unpadded, aligned with project and environmental constraints, communicated, and supported by a process. The guide should: include basic information such as units of measure to use (e.g., days, hours), indicate the type of estimate to employ based on the circumstances, and clarify the need to use effort-based estimates and not duration-driven ones. With effort-based estimates, team members can focus on the task at hand with no regard at the time of estimate to conflicting priorities, utilization and productivity rates, deadlines, time off, or any other constraints. Resources need to provide the rationale behind their estimate, along with context, concerns, availability, or any other issue that they believe can add value to the quality of the estimate. Once the estimates are handed off to the project management team (i.e., the PM and the BA), any constraints are taken into account and the estimates are incorporated into a realistic schedule.

PMs do not have capacity, familiarity, or the necessary relationship with project resources (especially not early on in the project, at the time of producing early estimates) and therefore need to utilize the BA for the estimating task. BAs can also provide additional context about the utilization of appropriate resources, product constraints, and insights about the type of estimate provided, along with the estimator's track record. Accepting estimates as resources provide them; having resources estimating tasks that other people will perform; failing to address the common challenges around effort- and duration-driven estimates; and accepting estimates without the *smoke test* and insights from the BA will reduce the chance that the estimates can be used effectively and will decrease the chance for project success.

To illustrate the value a BA can bring to the table in the estimating effort, we should consider the BA's familiarity with the type of tasks on hand and his or her ability to distinguish between tasks that are effort-driven and those that are duration-driven. For example, if a flight is late to depart, it is not going to shorten its duration if we add another copilot. The BA can provide the value that may prevent misinformed stakeholders from recommending or making the wrong decision—in our case, proposing to add another copilot for a delayed flight to shorten its duration.

Turning a Group of People into a Team

The success of the collaboration between the PM and the BA is not only going to improve project performance, it will also have a direct, positive impact on the project team. Beyond the benefits of the collaboration, the PM-BA duo can also serve as a role model and define a new standard for collaboration in the organization that will set an example for the extended project team and for other stakeholders. Such benefits would be realized in the form of transferring the knowledge and techniques of the collaboration and having the PM and the BA serving as mentors, which helps build more effective and collaborative teams across the organization. Needless to say that since it is a time-consuming task and not all PM-BA duos will engage in such activities—only a select few who excel at both collaboration and in the area of transferring knowledge.

Building an effective team is a difficult, yet important task that can yield significant benefits for the organization and therefore, this activity should be seriously considered by senior management. It also involves a redistribution of work allocation to allow the selected PM and BA to perform the important task of team building successfully.

Although the term *project team* is commonly used, most project teams hardly qualify for the definition of a team—and most fall under what can be called a *working group*. A working group has a leader, but consists of individual work products—accountability is more on the individual level where each person works on their own work product and the group's focus is not unique, but similar to that of the organization.

In contrast, a team may have shared leadership roles and the accountability is not only individual, but also joint and mutual. The team has a unique set of objectives and purposes, and the work is done collectively and interdependently toward a common goal. Discussions in the team are more productive, and the approach to problem solving tends to be more proactive. Success is measured by achieving the joint, collective purpose. Team members also show more rigor and determination to achieve success than working groups.

With the PM and the BA leading the project effort, their focus should be both inward toward improving their own collaboration, as well as outward. This will ensure that in the process, they contribute to turning the group of individuals assigned to work on the project into a an effective, cohesive, and high performing team that has what it takes to deliver project success.

FINAL THOUGHTS ON CHALLENGES RELATED TO PROJECT MANAGEMENT AND BUSINESS ANALYSIS

There is one big *however* to say about the ideas presented in this book—everything has to be done in moderation. Project sponsors and, in turn, PMs and BAs need to perform a cost benefit analysis exercise before each project to ensure that the right investment is made with the appropriate rigor for each project. Similar to risk management or any other project-related decisions, it is possible to overdo things as well as to miss the mark and fail to deliver net value for the project and the organization. Project size, complexity, and the amount of work and rigor required must all be factored in, so the benefits outweigh the costs.

It takes both the PM and the BA to work on reducing friction between the areas they represent and between their personalities. While it is all too common to find conflict and distrust between the PM and the BA, it is first and foremost their responsibility to establish a harmonious and streamlined relationship between them and in turn, to build a team that is based on the same values.

Gone are the days where projects can afford seeing the PM getting annoyed at the BA for taking too long to define requirements, going into too much detail, and putting excellence above project delivery dates and dollars. The BA, on the other hand, should work with the PM on ensuring that technical and project considerations are balanced and no longer view the PM as a racehorse who aims for the end, with no regard to customer satisfaction or business success. In short, the PM and the BA should act as role models for collaboration and not as a source of controversy and constant friction—conditions that with time, turn toxic to project success.

The challenges and concepts presented in this chapter are not about attempting to achieve a perfect world, but rather a recognition that establishing healthy and collaborative working relations between the PM and the BA are key toward healing many of the ailments that so often plague project performances and negatively impact productivity, efficiency, effectiveness, team morale, project success, and organizational objectives.

The next chapters in the book will present benefits for PM-BA collaboration, both from the project perspective—with the BA serving as a supporting role for the PM, as well as from a business analysis perspective—where the benefits of the PM-BA collaboration will help the business analysis function in the organization and contribute to achieving business objectives.

REFERENCES

1. Adapted from Ori Schibi (2013). *Managing Stakeholder Expectations for Project Success*, Chapter 2, J. Ross Publishing, Plantation, FL.
2. Crosby, Philip (1979). *Quality is Free*. New York: McGraw-Hill.
3. *Quality Control Handbook* (1999), New York, New York: McGraw-Hill, 5th edition.
4. RTI International (2002). "*Software Bugs Cost U.S. Economy $59.6 Billion Annually, RTI Study Finds.*"
5. Based on the *ASQ Quality Costs Committee* (1999). *Principles of Quality Costs: Principles, Implementation and Use,* 3rd edition, ed. Jack Campanella, ASQ Quality Press, pages 3-5.
6. Based on Campanella, J. (1999). *Principles of Quality Costs: Principles, Implementation and Use,* 3rd edition. Milwaukee: ASQ Quality Press.

2

MISCONCEPTIONS OF THE ROLES OF THE PM AND THE BA

"Your reality is as you perceive it to be. So, it is true, that by altering this perception we can alter our reality."—William Constantine

This chapter explores the many misconceptions of the roles and responsibilities of project managers (PMs) and business analysts (BAs). Misconceptions of project management and business analysis professions will also be discussed. What the role of the PM and BA should and should not be is fleshed out as each of the misconceptions are listed and explained.

MISCONCEPTIONS OF THE ROLE OF THE PROJECT MANAGER

Many stakeholders view the PM as someone who can be compared to an unfriendly teacher who picks on students for not submitting an assignment on time: A PM may also be described as someone who is constantly angry. Statistics regarding project success criteria—such as those found in the Chaos Report[1]—show that close to 50% of information technology (IT) projects manage to be implemented at close to double their original estimates; and information from the Conference Board of Canada indicates that 40% of IT projects failed to achieve their business case within one year of going live and were on average 25% over budget. It therefore should be no surprise that PMs are seemingly perpetually stressed, under pressure, and act like hard-nosed drill sergeants; projecting their stress upon those around them.

The PM's primary job is to be the process and deliverable police: Related to the previous item, the constant need for the PM to *police* deliverables and *press* stakeholders to deliver on their commitments drives PMs to constantly *ride on people's backs* in the project environment.

PMs do not actually do anything, they just delegate everything: A common view among team members with technical expertise is that PMs do not actually do any work. To their point, the job description of the PM does not involve performing the technical work, but rather facilitating the delivery of the work performed by the team members and ensure the project delivers on its objectives. There should be no need to defend the importance of the role of the PM for project success. Technical resources provide technical expertise in order to design and build the product, where the PM provides scheduling, leadership, communication, risk management, and quality management expertise to ensure all the parts of the product are integrated. Not having a PM to manage the project (or not having a BA) is equivalent to claiming that as long as there is a worker to build a bridge, there is no need for an engineer to design it. The PM and the BA design the project's implementation plan and ensure that the project delivers what it is supposed to deliver, when it is supposed to be delivered, and to the extent that is expected.

On the other hand, many believe (astonishingly, including PMs), that the PM is accountable for each and every activity in the project: This is perhaps one of the most absurd misconceptions, as not only does the PM not have the capacity to be accountable for each activity within the project; but the PM also does not have the technical knowledge to do so. We should view the PM as a chef in a restaurant or the Maestro of an orchestra—the PM is ultimately accountable (to the sponsor) for the entire project; but cannot be accountable for each individual item produced in the project, similar to the chef, who is ultimately accountable for all the dishes that come out of the kitchen, but cannot be there for each and every onion being chopped, or to personally check each plate leaving the kitchen. Delegation, trust, competence, technical knowledge, and teamwork allow the PM to assign work to the team members, who in turn need to perform the work according to the requirements, when they are asked to. Any feedback will then be delivered by the PM to the functional manager (or team lead) for further action, as the functional manager (or team lead) is the one who assigns the resources to the job.

PMs are paper pushers: Dealing with reporting, issues, risks, assumptions, changes, communication, and ensuring that work is getting done makes many people think that PMs are paper pushers and that their job can be replaced by anyone else, or that the PM's job is obsolete. It is understandable that those who are not familiar with project management might think this way but anyone who has worked on a project knows that the task of ensuring the project is managed properly (integration, coordination, collaboration) is not any less, and perhaps even more important than any of the technical roles in the project.

PMs are responsible for the project charter: Many people do not see the value in putting together a project charter or in ensuring that the charter is clear, short, and concise. A project charter is not only the initial document produced by the project, but it also produces the mandate for the project, sets the tone for the project, reiterates the business case, and also names the PM—its main feature being that it is short and that it is high level but clear enough so that it does not need to be changed. Related to this misconception is the misconception that writing the charter is the PM's role. Since the charter actually names the PM, it is not logically sound that the PM would write it. Furthermore, the PM, who has just been named officially to lead the project, does not have enough information about the project and its objectives to write the charter. It is the job of the project sponsor to write the charter, since the sponsor owns the project and will ultimately be accountable for the project's results. In reality many sponsors do not have the knowledge of how to put the charter together—or the time to do it—and therefore they delegate the work to the PM. The PM in return, must ensure access to the sponsor and closely engage the sponsor in the process. A charter that is written without the involvement of the sponsor will most likely lack in focus and misrepresent the original intent for the project—leading to frequent changes, deviations from the objectives, scope creep, cost and schedule overruns, and ultimately failure.

PMs should have product expertise: With the shift that is reflected by the Project Management Institute's move to create a 10th knowledge area in the *Project Management Body of Knowledge* (*PMBOK® Guide*) version 5, an increasing number of practitioners now realize the importance of *people skills* (and their associated three knowledge areas—Human Resources Management, Communication Management, and Stakeholder Management) over technical skills. There are several layers of knowledge and experience that PMs need to bring to the table, including (1) project management skills; (2) people, communication, and leadership skills; (3) industry experience; (4) product expertise; and (5) company specific knowledge. Of these items, project management and people skills are more difficult to acquire and the recognition of their importance keeps growing. While *left brain* skills used to be considered as more important in the past; the shift toward the *right brain* items is pronounced and widely recognized today. Technical and domain knowledge, as well as the other types of skills and experience listed above, are important and can help achieve project success, but in the large majority of projects success cannot be achieved without people and leadership skills. The opposite, however, is not the same—PMs who have people and leadership skills but no technical knowledge are more likely to deliver success than those with only technical expertise.

PMs can do it on their own: Many PMs think they can deliver project success on their own, without a skilled team, without a BA, without sponsor support, and without collaboration with the customer. Having a strong PM is similar to having an excellent coach for a team, but without any skilled players and without understanding the other teams, the team is almost doomed to fail.

PMs have all the answers: Similar to the item above, the role of the PM is more about asking questions than providing answers. It is, however, the art of asking the right questions, in the right context, at the right time, directed at the right people that makes a difference. The questions that PMs ask will help resources, team members, the sponsor, and other stakeholders to make informed decisions.

PMs are only concerned with scope, time, and cost: Project success is measured not only by the extent of delivering the scope, time, and cost; it is also determined by the extent of delivering business objectives, providing post-project value to the customer or organization, minimizing negative impact on operations, along with reducing business and operational risks. The circle of impact outside of the immediate project scope and timelines is sometimes more important than the project's product itself. Many PMs are not fully aware of this circle of impact (BAs typically can provide valuable context surrounding this). For example, an effort to complete a project *on budget* and *on time* may lead to more defects that will need to be dealt with through warranty. While it seems that the project is a success, depending on the impact on the organization, the additional post-project incurred costs may deem the entire project as a failure. PMs must consider at all times the impact of their actions, decisions, and recommendations on the circle of impact outside of the project.

PMs do not believe planning is important: *Show me something*—the need for proper and sufficient planning has been spoken and written about numerous times; yet, it is surprising that there are still people and organizations who do not see the value in planning, and prefer to chug forward through trial and error while racking up significantly higher costs, rather than simply planning first. There is however, a fine line between *not enough* planning and *too much* planning. In fact, we can never fully reach the desired level of planning, because there is no such perfect condition, and we will never have all the information. If we think that we have all the information before we go and do something, it is probably a sign that it is too late. With that said, based on our risk tolerance level, we need to determine what constitutes sufficient planning and follow through with this decision. The PM and the BA are typically at the forefront of the two sides of this discussion—where the BA typically would like to push for more planning, while the PM (recognizing the need) considers additional trade-offs that distract us from planning sufficiently.

The PM's bossy attitude toward the BA is a necessity: PMs need to learn to collaborate with BAs and seek ways to reach out and utilize the tremendous knowledge BAs bring to the table. This is not the time or place for the PM to try to exercise authority (that a PM typically does not have, anyway) or try to undermine and boss the BA around. Realizing that PMs and BAs are on the same side of the challenge at hand and that the BA is not there to compete with the PM will establish a relationship that is based on trust and collaboration; as opposed to competition and friction.

PMs need to tell the stakeholders what they like to hear: An experienced PM once said that when he was studying for an exam, his seven-year-old daughter told him that she could help him—she brought him a book with the title, *Honesty*. Both the PM and the BA need to realize that transparency and honesty are keys to building trust, developing a rapport, and forming relationships. From the start, the PM and the BA need to provide information candidly and not be afraid of asking tough questions. The same is also true when interacting with all other stakeholders. All stakeholders need to follow the rule of honesty as well when discussing the mandate, reports, work performance data, information, and updates.

University-like project management will do: The word *procrastination* is associated with the term *the student syndrome* since it is so common for students to procrastinate and start their studying and assignments at the very last possible minute. Although the fields of project management and business analysis are typically not taught or appreciated until well into people's careers, all stakeholders must realize that university-style project management does not work, and is bound to lead the project into failure (delays, rushing, overtime, cost overruns, defects, conflicts, morale issues, and ultimately failure). There is a reason why we need to plan realistically and allow sufficient time for things to take place—activities take time to perform and approvals require turnaround time. It is unwise to wait until the last minute, as it is not a sustainable or effective way to manage projects and affairs. The information that flows two ways between the PM and the BA should also be done in a timely manner (e.g., requirements, change requests, risks) so there is sufficient time to handle issues, challenges, and problems. Waiting, delaying, and holding back information will never pay off in the long run.

It is not a project; we do not need a PM: In many organizations, small initiatives are not recognized or declared as projects. The result is that processes, reporting requirements, and other due-diligence activities do not take place—leading to failures. These failures are smaller than failures on *real*, bigger initiatives that are called projects, but these small failures add up with time, enough to make a dent in the bottom line. A project is a project, and basic project-related activities need to take place—from a proper requirements and scoping process, to realistic planning, risk management considerations, reporting, and controls. Even if on a smaller scale and with less rigor, the activities performed by the PM and the BA are necessary in any type of project—small or large.

PMs should be measured against tangible success criteria: PMs are measured against their ability to deliver project success in line with stakeholder expectations. This means that the main measures of project success are the scope, timelines, costs, and the overall benefits, value, and quality the project produces. However, throughout the project the PM must focus on a series of additional factors that are critical for project success. These factors include many *behind the scenes*, or *back office* activities and areas of focus that can be labeled as such since they do not produce tangible deliverables toward the project success. They are often not directly measured, as if they are the *meta data* of the project. Experienced PMs know that these activities are the *secrets* for project success, as the driving forces behind the project's ability to deliver meaningful value and meet stakeholder expectations. These activities are the things that PMs need to focus on—they include the project charter, the ability to determine project readiness, risk management, communication and expectations management, change (i.e., project and scope) management, and the effective handling of the resources. One additional factor revolves around the PM's ability to capture and improve on lessons learned. One would argue the project charter is a tangible deliverable, but in many organizations the chartering process is quite ad hoc with no specific criteria or clear structure. By focusing on the things that matter, the PM has a better chance to deliver success on the more commonly measurable items such as scope, time, and cost.

We can get rid of the project manager and have the project management office (PMO) deal with the planning: Confusion around the role of the PMO and the definition of where the PMO ends and the PM begins are a common root cause for PMO failures. The lines need to be clearly drawn as to the role of the PMO. Regardless of the type of PMO, it is not the role of the PMO to replace the PM in the planning or in any of the other project management processes. PMOs are there for support, reporting, controlling, and for providing guidelines, templates, and training so that project management is performed consistently across the organization for higher project success rates, for leveraging successes, and for learning from lessons across projects.

MISCONCEPTIONS OF THE ROLE OF THE BUSINESS ANALYST

The BA's primary job is to document and take notes: While it is true that a portion of the BA role is ensuring that there is a consistent, clear, and complete view of requirements—which usually means requirements need to be documented—it is not the BA's entire job function. Because of this misconception that BAs are there to document, BAs have been invited to countless meetings where they were not really a required attendee, but were expected to simply take notes at the meeting. There are unfortunately many PMs with this misconception. The BA is usually a great note-taker and can certainly assist with this task—as a courtesy to help the PM, so the PM can focus on chairing the meeting—but it is not because it is his or her duty to do so. When it comes time for the BA to chair a meeting, it would be a great gesture for the PM to offer a helping hand by taking notes at the meeting, so the BA can focus on chairing.

BAs should be writing down, word for word, what stakeholders say as requirements: This misconception relates to the previous misconception that the primary role of the BA is to document. BAs are not meant to be court reporters or stenographers. These types of BAs provide very limited value to the project and organization. The value the BA brings to the table is the inquisitive nature to challenge the stakeholders to provide their true requirements. Stakeholders usually do not know what they truly need or what is necessary to solve the root cause of a problem (or what the root cause of the problem is) until the BA asks the right questions to draw this information out of them. This is why we now say that BAs *elicit* requirements instead of going by the traditional saying that BAs *gather* requirements, as requirements are not lying around to be picked up. There is typically much back and forth between the BA and stakeholder before requirements are clearly defined.

BAs hijack meetings to ask a ton of silly questions: If the BA does not ask the right questions but rather, takes what the stakeholder says verbatim as requirements, there is a risk of delivering something that may not actually meet the stakeholder's needs and subsequently may not be used. There is a statistic that states that 64% of the functionality in a system is rarely or never used.[2] The following is a real example of a BA eliciting requirements from a stakeholder. There was a perceived need to be able to archive transactions that were older than a year.

> **BA:** *I think I understand but just to be sure, what are your expectations when you say that the transactions should be archived?*
>
> **Stakeholder:** *All transactions older than 1 year should be physically moved over to another database.*

> **BA:** *May I ask for the rationale for this request? Is it for compliance reasons?*
>
> ***Stakeholder:*** *Our agents work on the most recent requests first and there are historical transactions that have never been cleaned up that show up on the top of the list and the new transactions are on the bottom.*

It is quite obvious from the dialogue that the need was not really to archive transactions; the need was to facilitate the work queue by providing easier access to the most recent transactions. Archiving is also a solution, not a need, but the BA could not tell the stakeholder this up front or they would have risked offending the stakeholder. That is another skill of the BA, to be able to convince the stakeholder what they are asking for is not really what they need without implying they do not know what they need.

> **BA:** *Now that I understand that archiving was not for compliance reasons, there may be an approach to solve your need of providing easier access to the most recent transactions while providing more flexibility should you want to report on or ever see these historical transactions in the future. If they were moved to another database, reporting or retrieving these historical transactions would be more difficult and likely much more costly. We will have the technical leads review the need, and we can present the solution options for you to decide.*

This example is very nonoffensive, focuses on the positives of investigating alternate approaches, and demonstrates the value of asking the *silly questions*. (Image 2.1 illustrates the BA's inquisitive nature.) The solution that was implemented was to allow the agents the ability to sort and filter on the transaction listing to zero in on their work queue. Had the project team gone ahead with the need that was originally communicated by the stakeholder, there may have been use cases that could no longer be executed after the transactions were moved elsewhere—not to mention the expenses associated with setting up an archive database for these transactions would have been much more work than the solution the project team chose.

Soft skills are not important for a BA: Some people wrongfully believe that subject expertise trumps soft skills for a BA. Soft skills or right brain skills are required to perform any of the BA hard skills or left brain skills effectively. This topic is expanded on when we discuss business analysis skills in Chapter 3—*Growing and Integrating the Professions*. In order to elicit requirements from stakeholders and present them for review, there are multiple dialogues

Image 2.1 BAs need to be inquisitive

and sessions that need to be conducted by the BA. Communication is one of the most important skills of the BA; and when a BA is asked to describe their role, many reply with, "I am the middleman between business and IT," (or between the business team and the technical team). The BA is, in fact, the middle person between all stakeholders, not just business and IT, and hence the strong need for soft skills to manage these relationships. The feeling of being a translator between business and IT is definitely relatable to many BAs; while both parties are speaking English there is still the need to translate business talk to technical talk and vice versa. The BA also needs to be able to build a good rapport with their stakeholders in order to gain their trust so they feel comfortable enough to share their requirements and honestly discuss needs and trade-offs.

BAs are the project team's personal assistant: Whenever a meeting needs to be scheduled (whether the BA is required or not), ask the BA. Lunch needs to be ordered for the meeting, ask the BA. The BA is *not* your glorified butler. Whoever is chairing the meeting should be setting up their own meetings and sending out their own invitations instead of e-mailing the list of attendees and agenda with meeting room preferences to the BA. The chairperson would then follow up daily as to who has accepted and not accepted the invitation. That would definitely not be an effective use of the BA's time, and in fact, would probably be more time consuming than if the chairperson did it him or herself.

BAs are Jacks and Jills of all trades: BAs are expected to do anything and everything on a project. BAs are expected to wear multiple hats—the PM, tester, developer, and subject matter expert (SME) in addition to the BA hat. This could be because most practitioners of business analysis did not start their career as a BA. Many say they are a BA by accident and sometimes morphed into the role, but depending on their previous role, there are habits and tendencies that need to be curbed when acting as the BA.

If the BA was previously a PM, they may not get into enough detail in order to move the product from abstract to concrete. PMs are typically used to being at a higher level and not into the details, but the BA role requires digging into details in order to ensure there are not any gaps in requirements. With that said, the act of moving from a PM role to a BA role is a rare one, as it is usually a BA who moves into a PM role. In today's ever evolving project world, it is quite common to come across hybrid PM/BAs. Hybrid PM/BAs need to ensure more than anyone that they understand the handoffs between project management and business analysis.

BAs are sometimes also expected to be developers and design the solution as evidenced by a handful of the modeling techniques listed in the business analysis suite of techniques that are more technical in nature, like data modeling. The fine line between requirements and design sometimes can be blurry—the BA is expected to assist in the design process to a certain degree, but there has to be a collaborative effort between the BA and development team. The requirements drive the design, but the design can often drive additional elicitation and ultimately additional requirements, and if the BA comes from a development background, there is a temptation to solve and design before determining the requirements. This obviously is not the best approach and could lead to solving for the wrong problem or building something that does not meet the needs of the stakeholders.

BAs are also very often expected to be testers and while they are not testers, they have a role in the testing phase of the project and they should work closely with testers in order to ensure the product is being tested appropriately and prove compliance to the requirements. The BA may sometimes need to roll up their sleeves and assist testers with testing activities to meet project deadlines, but they are typically not responsible for the actual testing of requirements. If the BA was previously a tester, sometimes they may be too much in the weeds of things to see the bigger picture.

BAs are also expected to be SMEs and while it is helpful for BAs to have domain knowledge in order to ask the right questions, it is not the role of a BA to have all the answers. BAs are also not decision makers; they should be eliciting all the facts and brainstorming all the various scenarios to facilitate discussions toward a solution or decision. There are many SMEs that cross over into the BA role on projects, and although it is a natural progression (as they have the domain knowledge), the challenge with this is that they have so much domain knowledge, that they are tempted to assume they know what stakeholders want without asking them. This can once again lead to solving for the wrong problem or developing something that will never be used. BAs facilitate the process to define requirements, but BAs should not be the source of the requirements.

BAs need to have an IT background: This is a completely false statement. There are many BAs who are on the business side, and it is more important to be able to facilitate discussions to drive the team toward a solution that will meet the needs of the organization, rather than to be an expert in IT. A BA can be described using this analogy: assume that you are shopping for shoes online at a department store website. You are probably thinking, *online* and *website* implies IT—and it does—but it does *not* imply that the BA needs to be an expert in it. You click on shoes, you click on next, you are presented with a page to enter your credit card information for payment, and you are presented with a confirmation page which states that those shoes will be delivered to you within 5 business days. Now picture what those shoes look like. (Please see the shoes in Image 2.2.) Do the shoes you had in mind look like the shoes in the image? We are willing to bet that they do not, so what went wrong in this process? The

Image 2.2 Shoes—Is this what you had in mind?

website did not ask you what type of shoes you were looking for, the size, or the color. The website did not elicit your requirements and it did not present you with a picture of the shoes ahead of time to obtain your confirmation that these were the shoes you wanted. The website did not specify and model those shoes to ensure they were meeting your needs. BAs are very much like an online shopping tool (that works) and they need to ask the stakeholders the right questions and ask for confirmation that they understood the stakeholder's needs correctly, so that when the shoes arrive at the door, the stakeholders will say, "Yes, that's exactly what I had in mind!" The BA does not need to be an expert in IT in order to facilitate this process.

The BA's job is to advocate for a specific solution: The BA is not here to do the dirty work, but unfortunately many organizations still like to do things backward and determine a solution first and then convince everyone it is the right thing to do. Many BAs can relate to a situation where an executive at the organization goes to a trade show and purchases a *cool*, new software package with the expectation that it is going to meet the organization's needs. Then the BA is asked to create a perceived need to use the *cool*, new software package. Attempting to implement a project with a perceived need is rightfully met with a lot of pushback and negativity, and it is unethical to ask the BA, or any person for that matter, to be the spokesperson for something that they believe to be a bad idea. This is a very delicate situation. It is recommended that the facts are presented, and if the executive team still pushes for a solution that contradicts with the facts, agreeing to disagree has to be the approach to go with.

Another example where BAs are sometimes expected to advocate for a specific solution is when requirements are being presented to the technical team—the technical team deems the requirement to be a bad idea, and instead of explaining why it is a bad idea, a shortcut is taken and an arbitrarily high price tag is attached to the requirement to convince stakeholders not to move forward with it. (Our apologies for airing the dirty little secret of some development teams, but it is unfortunately a reality.) The BA should be eliciting the reasons why the development team thinks it is a bad idea, no matter how complex the rationale may be, and in turn, find a way to communicate this to the stakeholders in a means that they will understand and that will allow them to come to a decision as to whether the requirement should be implemented or not.

BAs are not required at the end of the project: Thankfully, there seems to be a decline in the number of people who believe this misconception. The bulk of the business analysis work on waterfall projects is performed in the beginning—during the analysis phase, when product requirements are being defined. However, BAs still play a very valuable role once product requirements have been completed and signed off. As mentioned earlier, BAs need to work closely with developers and testers during design, development; and testing phases. What if there are changes to the product requirements? The BA is required to analyze product requirement changes and often, that means treating those changes like a mini project in itself.

BAs are not required for all projects: With more organizations moving toward agile practices, many BAs have been afraid of the shift, fearful that they are no longer needed. Regardless of the chosen methodology to implement the project, a resource with requirements definition and management skills is still very much a necessity. The composition of the core project team, however, may change; there may not be a dedicated resource to fill the position of a PM, BA, Developer, or Tester. The competencies of each of these roles are all required, but not necessarily in different people. Again, this increases the need for resources to be trained in multiple disciplines to be able to act in a hybrid capacity. Other examples of projects that people do not feel the need for a BA are those pesky *like-for-like* projects—those where the old system is being replaced with the new system. The perceived need is for the new system to do exactly what the old system is doing, so there is not a need to develop requirements, hence a BA is not required. Like-for-like projects are never completely like-for-like. System replacements are perfect opportunities to evaluate whether there are enhancements that should be made to facilitate more lean processes. There may be functionality in the old system that is no longer used (or never has been) and is not worth the investment in the new system—all of the functions need to be evaluated as to their usefulness. While the functionality may actually be the same between old and new, maybe the interface is different and necessitates a BA to assist with hashing out interface requirements. Another type of project that some believe does not require a BA is an infrastructure upgrade that is seamless to the users. They are not so seamless when the upgrade brings the entire system down unexpectedly and floor managers are frantically opening production support tickets. A BA can evaluate any transition requirements to ensure that the implementation is indeed seamless. Seamless implementations also do not imply communication is not necessary.

BAs are responsible for the project charter: This relates to the misconception that PMs are responsible for the charter. If it is not the PM's nor the BA's responsibility, whose responsibility is it? The charter seems like a hot potato that no one wants accountability for, but it is actually the *sponsor* who should be writing the charter. The sponsor however, often enlists either the named PM or the BA to write the project charter.

MISCONCEPTIONS OF THE PROFESSIONS OF PROJECT MANAGEMENT AND BUSINESS ANALYSIS

This section discusses misconceptions regarding the professions of project management and business analysis, as many people, stakeholders, and team members may either not fully know what these professions are about, or have the wrong ideas about the contribution of these professions to organizational success.

Everything is equally important: Some stakeholders, including customers, believe that the PM and BA need to deliver on all project success criteria. When considering what constitutes project success, scope, time, cost, and quality come to mind. The mix of items within these criteria and the trade-offs among them define project success. While we all try to deliver results that meet the success criteria, many projects face conditions and circumstances that prevent the delivery of the full set of success criteria. This leads to the need to prioritize items and make decisions that will maximize the success, while minimizing the damage of those parts that are not delivered. Since most projects struggle to deliver on all success criteria, PMs need to make recommendations or decisions on which project success criteria will not be met. This is part of project expectations management.

No need for communication and quality plans: Many projects are guilty of not having either one or both of these plans in place. Quality planning is about understanding how we can achieve quality, deliver value, realize benefits, and meet the required standards; it also involves defining process improvement plans, specifications, documentation, measurements, and the cost associated with these items. Without such a plan we will be lost on our journey toward success and we will be clueless regarding how much it really costs us. As for communication—considering that PMs spend close to 90% of their time communicating and that BAs typically champion certain aspects of the project communication—it is surprising to know that most projects do not have a communication plan at all, or even a set of guidelines that take the team and the stakeholders through the process of communicating formally and informally—and how to use them.

Being a PM or a BA is easy; just update your status and you can become one: When people add project management or business analysis skills to their profile, it does not turn them into one. Project management is not just a combination of time management, task delivery, and leadership. A real PM has these skills complemented by communication skills, risk management capabilities, a strong ability to make judgment calls in uncertain conditions and around many moving parts, along with the ability to integrate these efforts. A real BA has strong product understanding, organizational context, end-to-end requirements elicitation and management skills, and the ability to translate these into a meaningful context to benefit the project and the organization. Attention to detail, the ability to remain composed under pressure, and excellent communication skills are only the start of what it takes to become a BA.

Project management software can manage projects effectively: MS Project, Primavera, Eclipse, or any other project management software can be effective in helping a PM manage a project and can serve as effective tools for time management, resource management, and management of interdependencies. With that said, understanding the role of the software and its capabilities is key to ensure effective utilization of the tool. If there is an expectation that project management software will replace the need for an experienced PM or will manage the project for the PM, it is an unrealistic expectation that is bound to end with disappointment and failure. It is more important to ensure that the data entered into the tool is correct and that the constraints are defined properly for the tool to fulfill its role and help the PM.

Purchasing a requirements management software package will solve all of our requirements issues: A requirements management software package does not eliminate the need for an experienced BA. It will not do anything to ensure there are not any gaps in requirements. It will not indicate whether the requirements are complete, consistent, unambiguous, or testable. Not having software to help manage requirements should never be used as an excuse for poor requirements management processes. The tool just helps facilitate processes like tracing requirements, versioning, workflow to obtain comments from reviewers, and signoff from approvers, but anything that can be done through the tool, can be done manually. A broken process is still a broken process—whether executed through the requirements management software or not.

Project management and business analysis focus primarily on IT: The approaches for project management and business analysis are designed to provide a framework for any type of project in any type of industry and are not designed only for IT projects. As such, the software development life cycle is not the same as the project management life cycle and the activities that the PM and BA should focus on go well beyond the technical aspects of the project.

Project management and business analysis are unnecessary overhead: Budget-conscious stakeholders often challenge the need for having PMs or BAs at all and view them as unnecessary overhead, especially in some agile environments where agile practitioners claim that the role of the BA, as well as the role of the PM, is not necessary. It is the same type of approach that asks whether we should be spending time on planning instead of just moving forward and doing something. Virtually every project (whether successful or not) is proof that having a PM and a BA and going through sufficient planning is not a luxury and in fact, is something that we simply cannot live without. Luck, stars that align, and one-time performances may help bring some projects to success, but this is not a sustainable way to provide continuous, consistent results for the organization.

The Project Management Institute's 2012 Pulse of the Profession[3] study found that organizations that reported high project management maturity levels outperformed low-maturity organizations by 28 percent for on-time project delivery, 24 percent for on-budget delivery, and 20 percent for meeting the original goals and business objectives of projects.

Process trumps people: No matter what the setting is, the most important asset of an organization is its people. When any change takes place within an organization (technology or process-related), we must take into consideration the impact on the people—their roles and their potential reactions to the change. People are involved in any activity an organization goes through and hence, the strong need to ensure they are the first priority, their expectations are managed, and the appropriate level of leadership is demonstrated.

Once the risk register is complete, it's full speed ahead: SharePoint repositories and other file sharing environments are filled with the output of an effective risk identification and management process that has been performed as part of the planning process. However, many organizations fail to realize that this is only the start of the risk process. To ensure that no surprises take place from this point on, risk control activities must take place on an ongoing basis by performing the following tasks:

1. Preparing for the risks that were previously identified
2. Assuring that the risk process and effort are appropriate for the type of project, its velocity, rigor, and events
3. Assuring that the risk responses that were put together are sufficient
4. Identifying new risks that may appear or materialize
5. *Retiring* risks that have passed
6. Monitoring the risks that are already listed, in case they have changed

After putting together the risk response plan, the most important tasks are to monitor, track, and control the risks—otherwise, it makes the previous effort moot and the project is going to misfire, get off track, be riddled with bad surprises and unplanned events, which ultimately causes failure.

A project should never be killed: While many stakeholders, including PMs, get emotionally attached to projects and at times fail to see that the only realistic option is to terminate the project, BAs are usually more levelheaded with this decision. Their primary goal is to ensure the requirements provide value to the stakeholders and thus, the organization. Killing a project is not a favorable thing to do—it should only be done after careful consideration, and it is never easy; but sometimes a project gets to the point that it is no longer recoverable and nothing can be done to bring it to a successful outcome. When projects turn into bottomless pits and throwing in more money and resources cannot save them, it is advisable to realize it before too many of the organizational resources have been invested into a losing cause.

Let's just put together a schedule: The process of building a schedule is a long process that starts with the requirements and scoping. Once the deliverables needed to produce the product are known, it's time to think about the activities that need to be performed, their sequence, the resources that will perform them, and the efforts and durations required. It is not prudent to just resort to the project schedule and populate activities with lines on the Gantt chart. The most effective way to ensure we are building a realistic schedule is through the use of a responsibility assignment matrix or a responsible, accountable, consulted, and informed chart to identify the resources who will be involved and their level of involvement in each activity and deliverable. It is an important step that can help ensure that the schedule being put together is closer to being realistic.

Business analysis is a stepping stone into project management: Due to this misconception, the BA is unfortunately seen to be much more junior than, and sometimes inferior to, the PM, and when the BA is treated this way, it causes a lot of animosity. Many do not realize that business analysis is a profession with a career path in its own right. There are senior BAs who act as advisors to executives. They are not usually called BAs but rather, have fancier titles, such as business architects. Business architects work on creating business roadmaps and enterprise analysis activities to generate new projects. PMs and BAs should be treated as equals in order to maintain an effective partnership (see Image 2.3).

Image 2.3 PMs and BAs should be treated as equals in order to maintain an effective partnership

A great project is one that follows the PM or BA practice standards to the letter: There are project teams who execute processes and produce all the project deliverables as documented in the practice standards for project management (the *PMBOK® Guide*) or business analysis (*Business Analysis for Practitioners* or the *Business Analysis Body of Knowledge*) and yet the project is still failing. If it were that easy, a program could be written and projects could be executed by robots. The practice standards are there as a framework or guideline and not as the *be-all, end-all.* Think of it as a restaurant menu—one does not typically order every single item off the menu to eat. The practice standards show the tools and techniques that are available, but common sense must still be employed to understand when it makes sense to use them.

Certification means you are a great PM or BA: Having a project management or business analysis certification does not automatically imply that anyone is a great PM or BA. It means that the practitioner understands the framework of project management or business analysis and has shown commitment to their profession. Certification also provides consistency within the workplace among their practitioners and encourages usage of a common language to communicate in business terms.

FINAL THOUGHTS ON THE MISCONCEPTIONS ABOUT THE ROLES OF THE PM AND THE BA

It is safe to say that there are many misconceptions for both the PM and BA roles as well as project management and business analysis in general. Now that the misconceptions are known, the next step is to be aware of our behavior and not fall into those traps. Being a PM or a BA is never easy—and it is more difficult when people do not understand what they do or the value they bring to the table. It is much easier to describe the roles and responsibilities of a developer or that of a tester. The roles and job responsibilities of a PM or a BA are much more abstract. Projects are also never black and white; there are a lot of gray areas that need to be navigated through. Depending on the project and methodologies chosen, the roles and responsibilities change for the PM and BA, and they need to be able to adapt together to conquer any challenges. Overcoming the misconceptions and having a clear understanding of each other's role boundaries while at the same time being willing to step outside of those boundaries to lend a helping hand is essential to building an effective partnership.

REFERENCES

1. Bryce, T. (2006). *Why Does Project Management Fail?* from http://www.projectsmart.co.uk/why-does-projectmanagement-fail.html.
2. *The Agile Executive*. (2010, January 11). Retrieved February 16, 2015, from http://theagileexecutive.com/2010/01/11/standish-group-chaos-reports-revisited/.
3. www.pmi.org/~/media/PDF/.../2012_Pulse_of_the_profession.ashx.

3

GROWING AND INTEGRATING THE PROFESSIONS

"Alone we can do so little; together we can do so much."—Helen Keller

Compared to the project manager's (PM's) role, the business analyst's (BA's) role is not nearly as standardized, which causes role confusion. If you put a group of people in the same room who share the title of *business analyst*, when they reveal what they actually do, it will vary from industry to industry, company to company, department to department, and maybe even peer to peer within the same department. For example, do BAs perform testing activities as part of their role? Some do and some do not. According to both the Project Management Institute (PMI's) *Business Analysis for Practitioners: A Practice Guide* and the *Business Analysis Body of Knowledge* (*BABOK*®) published by the International Institute of Business Analysis (IIBA), one is not considered to be wearing the BA hat if they are performing testing activities, yet this is inconsistent with the real world and how the BA role is commonly defined. It should probably be clarified that both PMI's *Business Analysis for Practitioners* and the *BABOK*® state that BAs still have a role in the testing phase, but that they are not the ones who actually verify that the solution behaves in accordance with solution requirements, as that is the tester's job. Testing is a complementary activity of the BA—ultimately, the BA, PM, and testers should work together to ensure testing completeness, consistency, and coverage. Nonetheless, it is still inconsistent with how the BA role is defined in many organizations. Training agencies have created courses that cater to the BA on verifying that the solution behaves in accordance with solution requirements (testing of the solution). This decision was based on customer feedback that it was a gap in the business analysis curriculum. The problem with the lack of standardization is evident when working on a project and the PM assumes the BA is going to be performing the testing activities because the last BA they worked with performed the testing activities. This is obviously frustrating for all parties. No one would ever debate whether the PM should be performing testing activities or not since the PM role is much more standardized. It is recommended that organizations clearly define and publish the roles and responsibilities of each of their team members. This also needs to clearly distinguish the difference between a person's title versus their role on a project. This should be reviewed at the beginning of every project and tailored to that project. For instance, a person's title may be *consultant* but on a project they may play the role of the PM, BA, hybrid PM-BA, or scrum master—just to name a few of the team players on a project. Depending on which hat this person is wearing on a given project, their roles and responsibilities will be different—and likely different from their everyday job if they work in a matrix environment. Many operational managers may also play the role of a PM or BA on the business side. The point being that a title does not give any indication as to how that resource should be utilized on any given project. Clarity is important to ensure that expectations are being met and to avoid any role confusion.

With that being said, a group of people may be placed together in a room who *play* the BA role and yet they will all have different titles—e.g., product owner, BA-PM, BA-developer, BA-tester, among many more. This is likely because prior to establishing business analysis as a separate profession, the BA role was split between everyone. The product owner would document their own requirements as a bulleted wish list and provide it to the PM and the developer. The PM would ask any necessary questions to narrow in on scope and timelines, and the developer would clarify whatever was needed in order to build. The tester could then work directly with the developer and the product owners to determine testing coverage and clarify any questions. The problem most organizations realized with this model is that there was not enough focus on requirements management, and while a lot of conversations might have been happening, there was not a single resource who maintained and managed a unified view of the requirements or kept up with all the changes that happened throughout the journey of the project. There is a saying that we all have a little bit of the BA in us. The challenge this provides is that when there is a dedicated BA on the project, the team may not understand what they should be doing versus what the BA is supposed to do, since the team has been performing part of that role all along. Sometimes the team does not want to relinquish the control they previously had over the requirements, thus causing tension.

PROJECT MANAGEMENT INSTITUTE AND INTERNATIONAL INSTITUTE OF BUSINESS ANALYSIS

The IIBA, founded in 2003, has done a great job of promoting the profession of business analysis and has made great strides in standardizing the role by publishing the *BABOK*®. Recalling the role of the BA from 10 years ago, it is clearly not the same as it is today, thanks in part to the IIBA and the progression of the business analysis profession. BAs were, and some still are, Jacks and Jills of all trades. It is unfortunate that a great majority of people still do not understand the role, and quite frankly, many BAs are still not familiar with the IIBA or with the fact that there are business analysis certifications in the marketplace. The way it usually has to be explained is, "You have heard of PMI, right?" Everyone nods *yes*. "Well, the IIBA is the equivalent to PMI, but for business analysts." "Ahhh,"—light bulbs flick on. This is why it is very exciting news that PMI is *entering* the business analysis space (although they have always been in the business analysis space which is evidenced by including requirements management tasks in the *Project Management Body of Knowledge* (*PMBOK*® *Guide)*—for example the *collect requirements* task). If one were to search PMI's repository of publications, there are many business analysis and requirements management articles that date back to before the IIBA was even born. Recent studies conducted by PMI proved the importance of requirements management on project success rates, hence the increased focus on requirements management and business analysis. It is strongly believed that PMI can take the business analysis profession to the next level and provide greater awareness to the community as to what business analysis is and what a BA does. This is very positive news for BAs who have been struggling with an identity crisis for decades. PMI officials have gone on record indicating that PMI had approached the IIBA in 2013 to collaborate, but was declined by the IIBA.[1] That was disappointing news, since partnerships between PMs and BAs have proven to be very positive on projects—a partnership with PMI might have been what the IIBA needed to increase the exposure of the BA profession. Some can also argue that it may actually make the identity crisis worse having PMI represent both the PM and the BA professions. The reason why it is thought to be very positive news is because of the opportunity to highlight the integration points between the PM and BA roles to increase chances of project success. PMI's *Business Analysis for Practitioners: A Practice Guide* that was released in late 2014 has valuable collaboration points for the PM and BA highlighted throughout the guide.

Through speaking with BA peers, many strongly believe their counterpart PMs do not understand what they do. Interestingly enough, many business analysis training curriculum includes an introduction to a project management course yet an introduction to a business analysis course is notably absent from the project management curriculum. There is unfortunately more friction than collaboration between the PM and BA in today's world. PMI's emphasis on requirements management is definitely a step in the right direction. PMI's 2014 North American Global Congress marked the debut of the Business Analysis and Requirements (BAR) track which consisted of several sessions on business analysis and requirements management. PMI's 2015 EMEA Global Congress is continuing this trend with *The Practical BA Experience*.

The sheer size of PMI and the amount of publicity they can generate to highlight the role is very exciting. There were more than 30,000 copies of PMI's *Business Analysis for Practitioners* guide downloaded in the first three months. They also have the resources and experience available to develop a cohesive practice standard that applies to all industries. One of the major criticisms of the *BABOK®* is that it focuses mainly on information technology (IT) where the *PMBOK® Guide* can be applied to all industries—IT or non-IT. There are many who perform the BA role in a non-IT environment and unfortunately, the *BABOK®* is difficult to apply for those folks.

PMI has an audience of over 600,000 certificate holders and over 450,000 members[2]—and has already created quite the buzz by announcing their new Professional in Business Analysis (PBA) certification—a new practice guide on business analysis (similar to PMI practice guides developed for risk management or scheduling) and a full practice standard in requirements management. As mentioned earlier, having the PM and BA professions under the same PMI umbrella will also help work through the challenges of collaboration between the PM and BA roles by providing easier access towards understanding what the other person does—allowing PMs and BAs to leverage each other's skills for increased project success. According to PMI's 2014 Pulse of the Profession® in-depth report on requirements management, 52% of organizations expect an increase in the integration of requirements management and business analysis with project management within the next three to five years. The report goes on to share that *only 46% of organizations believe there is good collaboration between their project managers and business analysts. Yet 68% of organizations indicate this collaboration is essential for project success.*[3] This leaves a lot of room for improvement, and it was naturally one of the key drivers for PMI's recent hefty investment into requirements management.

The authors of this book, in 2014, cofounded the very first business analysis community within a PMI chapter in Southern Ontario, Canada (for the PMI-SOC Chapter). The goal of offering both PM and BA related events within the same chapter will also help bridge the gap between the two roles. There has been positive feedback from the community membership—from both PMs and BAs alike—with this additional opportunity to interact. This trend is expected to continue within other PMI chapters worldwide and, in fact, other chapters are already reaching out to us for advice on how to get started.

PBA vs. CBAP Certification

PMI's focus is more on the BA role within the context of projects and programs where the IIBA does not make this distinction, but most BAs however, do work within the context of projects and programs. Another observation that many have falsely made was that PMI does not focus on enterprise analysis, as that is outside the context of the project where IIBA does have a knowledge area dedicated to enterprise analysis. If one were to look closely at the Requirements Management domains that PMI had introduced, the activities performed in enterprise analysis are apparent in the Needs Assessment domain. So yes, PBA exam takers will still be tested on enterprise analysis concepts. PMI also has an entire practice guide and certification dedicated to portfolio management which in essence, is enterprise analysis. The synergies between enterprise analysis and portfolio management are discussed in Chapter 6 of this book. Furthermore, the remainder of PMI's domains do align with the IIBA's knowledge areas. A chart comparing domains to knowledge areas can be seen in Table 3.1. Therefore, those who are already Certified Business Analysis Professional (CBAP®) should be able to re-use the knowledge to pass the PBA exam.

It is uncertain why the CBAP did not get the demand the IIBA anticipated. Could losing the experienced senior BA to project management be the reason, as the senior BAs did not want to invest in a certification if they were going to abandon the role? This seemed to be the case after conducting a few informal interviews with BA managers and BAs in the field as to why they did not want to pursue BA certification. It is probably safe to say that we all have a little bit of the BA in us and this is where PMI once again shines—in marketing their new certification, they have made it clear that the focus is not on who is doing it, but emphasizing the success of the project depends on resources having the competencies to complete it effectively. This implies that PMs need to, at the very least, have an understanding of requirements management in order to even

Table 3.1 PMI domains—IIBA knowledge areas comparison

PMI PBA domains	IIBA knowledge areas
Needs Assessment	Strategy Analysis
Planning	Business Analysis Planning and Monitoring
Analysis	Elicitation and Collaboration
	Requirements Analysis and Design Definition
Traceability and Monitoring	Requirements Lifecycle Management
Evaluation	Solution Evaluation

A comparison of the PMI *Business Analysis for Practitioners: A Practice Guide's* five domains mapped to the IIBA's *BABOK®* six knowledge areas.

have a chance at succeeding, thus triggering interest in the project management community to take the initiative to learn more. Recent studies that PMI has conducted through its Pulse of the Profession® surveys proved there is still an immense gap within our organizations across all industries highlighting the importance of requirements management for project success regardless of title or who is performing it.

As organizations are attempting to implement functionality more quickly by breaking down projects into smaller increments and moving toward a more agile environment, it is becoming the norm for resources to play hybrid roles while the less dedicated resources are confined to wearing a single hat. There is a definite need to be cross-trained in multiple disciplines including requirements management. A resource who can both manage a project as well as manage the requirements is invaluable. The PBA certification should therefore be attractive for those who are project or program managers and especially those who are already Project Management Professional (PMP) or Program Management Professional (PgMP) certified. The PBA application process is also simplified for those who are already PMP or PgMP certified as the 2,000 hours of experience working on projects has already been met, and therefore this section of the application is automatically skipped. There are also a high number of hybrid PM-BAs out there that should be gravitating toward achieving the new PBA certification.

Interestingly, the concepts are the same between PMI and IIBA, but the specifics may differ. Most people will probably not notice the differences in specifics, but here are a couple of examples:

1. Both PMI and IIBA recognize there are relationships between requirements, but PMI lists the following relationships—subsets, implementation dependency, and benefit or value dependency; where IIBA lists the following relationships—necessity, effort, value, cover, and subset.
2. Both PMI and IIBA suggest it is good practice to capture requirements attributes, but the suggested list of attributes are different. The similarities should not be a surprise as some of the authors of the *BABOK*® also wrote PMI's *Business Analysis for Practitioners*.

The CBAP exam is based on the *BABOK*®, and is therefore easier to prepare for. The PBA is not based on a single book, not even the new practice guide, making it more difficult to study. PMI provides a lengthy reference list as a courtesy with the disclaimer: "Exam candidates should be aware that the PMI Professional in Business Analysis (PMI-PBA) examination is not written according to any single text or singularly supported by any particular reference, the PMI-PBA is a competency-based credential which assesses the integrated set of knowledge, skills, and abilities as gained from both practical and learned experiences."[4] This provides more credibility to those who hold the PBA, as exam takers will have to rely on professional experience as a business analysis practitioner over how well they study a book.

IIBA's *BABOK®* and PMI's *Business Analysis for Practitioners*

The *BABOK®* is more of a theoretical book that lists knowledge areas, tasks, inputs and outputs among other things—almost as if it is the science behind business analysis. PMI's *Business Analysis for Practitioners* is more of a how-to-perform business analysis. As mentioned earlier, the concepts between the two are the same likely because both publications also share some of the same authors. Now where does this book fit in? The *BABOK®* and PMI's practice guide both focus on business analysis and the requirements management life cycle with the practice guide listing collaboration points with the PM. This book will focus on all integration points between the PM and the BA throughout the project life cycle, rather than solely the requirements management life cycle, written from the perspective of both the PM and the BA.

MEASURING AND GROWING THE PM AND BA SKILL SETS

There are several early project activities that, although they have been recognized as important, few organizations engage in performing sufficiently—or even engaging in at all. One of the main reasons for this oversight is that most of these activities lack tangible outcomes or specific criteria for their deliverables and as such, are hard to measure or to focus on. These activities include (but are not limited to) the project charter; stakeholder analysis; project readiness and complexity assessments; the BA package to bring the PM up to speed; sufficient risk management planning; as well as communication and quality plans. With no specific deliverables, many PMs and other project stakeholders get the false impression that skipping these activities would not be harmful for the project. Further, many of these activities are not associated with other *typical* project deliverables, and therefore will not be subject to potential audits or to specific requests from the customer as part of other project deliverables.

One other activity that often does not get sufficient (or rather any) focus in an organization is the measurement of the PM's and BA's skills. Measuring the PM's and BA's skills is one of the most cost effective ways to improve the chances for project success, and failing to do so is one of the leading underlying causes for project failure. An attempt to measure resource's skills should not be overly pricey, long, or cumbersome, and it should not pose any challenges to political correctness. PM and BA skills assessments are simply about checking whether a candidate for a position has the relevant skills for the intended role and should focus on the specific combination of skills and experience to measure whether someone would be suitable for a specific role.

Selecting a PM or a BA is not an easy task and requires a much deeper analysis of the candidate than simply looking at their experience and education. There is a specific and growing need to assess the fit of the candidate to the role. Some of these considerations include the ability to work under pressure, communication skills, ability to manage relationships and expectations, and the candidate's ability to assess and integrate all the moving parts within a project—including understanding the conditions in the organization, the project size, and the stakes involved; then translating them into appropriate and sufficient actions.

The task of finding the right candidate for the PM and BA roles on a project is an important and difficult one, yet most organizations assign PMs and BAs solely on availability, with little to no consideration on whether the candidate is suitable for the role. It is beneficial to measure the skill levels, particularly of the PM and the BA, upon hiring them or prior to assigning them to a project. The measurements will not only help with placement of the most suitable candidates for the project, but also with career growth and professional development. When there is knowledge of the PM and the BA, skill levels within the organization, precious time, and the organization's scarce resources are not spent on meaningless training but rather on developing specific areas that are required for their resources.

Overall, from a benefit-cost perspective, having the PMs and BAs go through a skills assessment is a one-time investment that will pay off for an extended period of time. The PMs and BAs will be placed in the most appropriate roles according to their skills which will allow them to perform at levels that are suitable to their skills, personalities, and capabilities. The assessment results will integrate the findings with the candidate's experience and interests and those findings allow management to make informed decisions about which PMs and BAs to place for each initiative.

The Evaluations Process

The evaluation of PMs and BAs should include two sets of assessments—one for PMs and the other for BAs. The assessment consists of the following steps:

1. A preinterview questionnaire (this questionnaire is intended to collect demographics and other information regarding the education and experience of the candidate). The questionnaire is provided both to

the candidate (self evaluation), as well as to the candidate's colleagues, teammates, and manager.
2. An interview (this is not a job interview; it consists of a set of questions to assess the candidate's specific skills).
3. A detailed questionnaire—as a supplement for the interview, to provide additional context and depth to the interview questions.

The skills assessment is broken down into hard skills (specific PM and BA skills; associated with left brain activities), and soft skills (also known as interpersonal and leadership skills; associated with right brain activities). The technique specified here does not require any psychometric evaluations or additional assessments. The results do not attempt to indicate whether a candidate fits the organizational culture, but rather checks skill levels in relation to the organization's project needs. It serves as a cost effective additional layer to traditional interviewing and is most likely to lead to future savings, as it can help ensure that the most suitable PM and BA are in place.

Right Brain and Left Brain

The breakdown of the assessment to soft and hard project management and business analysis skills aligns with the right and left brain characteristics, and these characteristics point at the type of project management or business analysis skills required to become an effective PM or BA (as shown in Table 3.2).

Why Projects Fail

Beyond priorities, schedules, resource problems, and requirements issues, a common underlying cause for project failures may include overemphasizing formal tools and techniques (associated with the left brain) or underemphasizing

Table 3.2 Left versus right brain characteristics

Left Brain	Right Brain
Logical	Feelings based
Detail oriented	Big picture oriented
Past and present	Present and future
Acknowledge	Appreciate
Strategies	Possibilities
Methodology	Innovation
Analytical	Synthesizing
Process, system	Business acumen, people acumen

A comparison between left and right brain hemispheres' attributes and dominant areas communication and people management skills (typically associated with the right brain), including a lack of proactive thinking, failure to understand project complexity, allowing for unrealistic expectations, and failure to align the solution to the business environment, culture, or organizational needs.

These observations regarding project failures do not attempt to undermine the importance of the left brain skills, but rather to put an added emphasis on the importance of the right brain skills. In short, PMs and BAs with strong left brain skills are still likely to fall short of delivering success if they lack strong right brain skills; which in turn will help further leverage and integrate the left brain skills. The presence of strong right brain skills will benefit the full set of project management and business analysis skills and will position the PM or BA on the path to delivering project success and to satisfying stakeholder needs and expectations.

Project Management Skills Assessment

The ongoing shift in the field of project management toward skills associated with the right side of the brain has been proven effective. While having knowledge of the technical domain of the project can always be of help, PMs who demonstrate strong people skills and effective communication and leadership skills are more likely to get the job done. With that said, when discussing a PM's experience, there is also a need to check the candidate's knowledge of the market, technical domain, and organization in addition to the candidate's experience in project management *hard* skills. Learning about someone's experience is an easy task but the measurement of soft and hard skills is more subjective, less quantitative, and more challenging; hence the PM's soft and hard skills are the focus of this assessment.

Right Brain *Soft* Project Management Skills

- **Stakeholder relations:** The ability to engage stakeholders and manage their expectations.
- **Interpersonal skills:** The ability to build relationships that are genuine and productive.
- **Team building and team management:** The PM's approach to building, developing, and managing teams; as well as addressing team issues, motivation, and cohesiveness.
- **Intuitiveness:** The PM's propensity for picking up on ideas, identifying underlying issues, and *reading between the lines*.
- **Effective communication:** Skills related to translating the relationships into effective communication, clear messages, the establishment and

application of ground rules, and the ability to articulate and deliver the intended message to the intended stakeholder.

- **Focus on results:** Along with interpersonal skills and effective communication this item measures the PM's focus on results and aligning performance with meaningful outcomes for stakeholders.
- **Initiative:** This item is about the PM's proactiveness in addressing needs, tendencies, and issues.
- **Self-awareness:** This item simply checks the alignment between the PM who is assessed and the colleagues, teammates, and manager's view of the candidate. Misalignment in the answers is an indication that goes far beyond just the fact that the PM's view is different than the one of the teammates; it points at potential issues with communication skills, interpersonal skills, effectiveness in communication, and leadership.

Left Brain *Hard* Project Management Skills

This category helps measure the PM's ability in the *hard* project management areas. These results are evaluated in conjunction with the PM's interests, education, and experience, and allow for management to place candidates into roles that are most suitable, considering their skills and experience. It ensures that both the candidate and management select a professional development path that is based on actual needs and that is meaningful for both the candidate and the organization.

The *hard* skills are typically associated with seven of PMI's *PMBOK® Guide* ten knowledge areas, excluding the three knowledge areas that are predominantly associated with *soft* skills—Human Resources, Communication, and Stakeholder Management:

- **Requirements and scope:** Although it is the BA who typically leads the requirements-related effort, the PM needs to understand the process around requirements and take charge of the hand-off from the requirements to project scope. The ability to facilitate a seamless hand-off into the scope is critical for project success.
- **Time management:** This measures the candidate's ability to self-prioritize, as well as provide a clear set of priorities to team members and other stakeholders. Prioritization and the ability to determine the appropriate sense of urgency for competing priorities are keys to successful time management. This area is not about the candidate's skills in relation to schedule management, but rather in the key area of managing their own, as well as team members' time.
- **Schedule development and management:** With the process of progressive elaboration PMs need to be able to take the identified activities for

each section of the project and follow the process toward coming up with a realistic schedule that can be controlled and adjusted as required. This area measures candidate's skills in relation to all stages of developing and managing a project schedule.

- **Cost management:** Measure the candidate's skills in relation to financial management.
- **Planning:** The candidate's attitude toward planning and the approach taken.
- **Governance:** This items ties back to leadership and negotiations, but also considers the candidate's understanding of reporting lines, relations with the project management office, programs and portfolio, as well as relations across organizational boundaries and within the team. It also measures the candidate's ability to delegate.
- **Organizational skills:** In conjunction with the governance area, this item measures the candidate's skills in relation to organizational change management, and alignment to strategy.
- **Human resources processes and policies:** This item is about the candidate's awareness and understanding of human resource theories, reporting lines, and related policies and procedures.
- **Monitor and control; issues and change management:** A good plan can only last so long without a strong control mechanism that helps the PM keep the project under control. Closely related to it is the candidate's ability to manage scope changes, as well as other changes that occur throughout the project and to distinguish between a scope change and an issue. Due to the importance of change control in achieving project success, this item has a shared responsibility with the role of the BA.
- **Vendor and procurement:** These items measure both the candidate's awareness of policies and procedures and actual experience in relation to procurement. It ties back to the stakeholder relationship area under the *soft* skills.
- **Quality:** Measuring awareness and attitude toward quality planning, best practices, and approach.
- **Risks, assumptions, and dependencies:** In addition to change control these items produce most of the remaining instability in projects and as such, these items require close attention. The growing need to document assumptions and the assumptions' relation to risks requires a systematic and consistent approach throughout the project. This area also determines the PM's ability to define and manage dependencies effectively.
- **Constraints and success criteria:** PMs need to manage constraints and have the ability to translate them into success criteria. Further, the ability to articulate success criteria and manage them in the context of

the organizational needs is critical to delivering value and benefits to stakeholders.

The assessment should also include the following topics that, although they appear to be focusing on right brain skills, they combine both left and right brain capabilities:

- **Leadership:** Under the umbrella of leadership, the assessment looks for a set of skills related to self-confidence, sensitivity, the ability to inspire, vision, focus, direction, delegation, facilitation, motivation, team building, and coaching. The assessment also measures the PM's ability to gain and handle followers, to set direction, ensure alignment to organizational objectives, and provide support.
- **Influencing and motivating:** Although related to leadership, the PM's ability to influence and motivate is measured separately, due to the PM's ongoing need to manage upward, and deal with multiple stakeholders while having responsibility without authority. The assessment measures the PM's ability to engage stakeholders and motivate them, and the ability to use and leverage formal and informal power.
- **Problem solving:** Changes, issues, risks, assumptions, dependencies, conflicts, and bottlenecks introduce challenging situations to the project on an ongoing basis, and the PM needs to have a systematic approach to handle these situations and to seek a resolution that serves the best interests of the project, while keeping the stakeholder satisfied. The assessment looks for these abilities, along with skills related to problem identification, creativity and flexibility, the ability to clarify problems as opposed to symptoms, and a systematic approach to conflict management. The PM must demonstrate the ability to present resolutions, recommendations, and decisions while factoring in internal and external considerations, as well as technical, political, and interpersonal elements, along with the presentation of options, alternative considerations, and timely selection of the solution while maintaining the appropriate sense of urgency.
- **Negotiation:** This area comes to show the PM's ability; to juggle conflicting priorities, make appropriate concessions, and leverage power; to understand different personalities, competing demands, scope, contracts, and assignments; along with being able to build commitment and identify resource requirements while establishing and maintaining lasting relationships.
- **Organizational considerations:** The PM must also demonstrate skills that are related to the ability to understand strategic implications and ensure that project needs are aligned with business objectives

and considerations, and that risks are viewed not only from a project perspective; but also from a business point of view. Organizational skills also include understanding organizational politics (utilizing it, as well as being aware of negative aspects), managing across organizational boundaries, dealing with functional managers, networking, and building informal relationships. The assessment also detects skills and awareness related to human resources, effectiveness, productivity, and customer relations.

- **Integration:** It is difficult to measure integration—or even to fully define integration. Measuring integration is evaluating the candidate's ability to put things together, to consider all aspects of the project, and to weigh every action, recommendation, and decision against all surrounding factors—from the project success, to organizational needs, business objectives, strategy, and stakeholder expectations and needs.

Business Analysis Skills Assessment

The left and right brain business analysis factors are strikingly similar to the project management left and right brain factors. This should not be a surprise as this is why a PM and BA partnership is natural and necessary. This is possibly why there is a widespread career progression of BAs moving into PM roles. There are, however, different facets of these skills that are emphasized in the PM versus the BA role debate. Similar to the project management skills assessment, there is also more emphasis on right brain factors over left brain aspects and probably more so for BAs. BAs rely heavily on soft skills in order to execute their job successfully. Even when performing the left brain skills, the ability for the BA to perform them effectively is highly dependent on how well they are integrated with the right brain skills.

Right Brain *Soft* Business Analysis Skills

- **Stakeholder relations:** The BA needs to engage stakeholders for requirements and manage their expectations while being objective and neutral. Usually if there is a single BA on a project, he or she is typically assigned from a pool that belongs to the IT department for IT projects. The BA needs to ensure he or she is not always siding with IT.
- **Interpersonal skills:** The BA has to earn the trust of the stakeholders to discuss their requirements openly and honestly.
- **Team building and team management:** The BA is a core team member and should partner with the PM to motivate the rest of the project team, but the BA also needs to manage the requirements management team which includes the core project team as well as subject matter experts.

- **Intuitiveness:** The BA needs to have the ability to see five steps ahead to identify gaps, uncover all nuances in a scenario, identify risks, and be able to play devil's advocate while taking the team through this journey—convincing them it was their idea all along.
- **Effective communication:** The BA needs to select an appropriate elicitation technique to suit the stakeholder, realizing that each elicitation technique requires different communication skills. The BA also needs to ensure when explaining concepts, that everyone has the same understanding.
- **Active listening:** Listening is a vital component of effective communication. It provides the confirmation that the recipient of the communication, in this case the BA, understands the information by paraphrasing it back to the sender.
- **Focus on results:** The BA needs to ensure all requirements provide value to the overall project goals and business requirements.
- **Initiative:** The BA also needs to be proactive in addressing needs, tendencies, and issues.
- **Self-awareness:** Similar to the PM assessment, this item simply checks the alignment between the BA who is assessed and the colleague's, teammate's, and manager's views of the candidate. Misalignment here also points to potential issues with communication skills, interpersonal skills, and effectiveness in communication and leadership.

Left Brain *Hard* Business Analysis Skills

- **Requirements and scope:** Requirements management is a primary function of the BA, thus the BA needs to be well versed in requirements and scope management practices and standards in order to lead this effort. The BA will also need to work with the PM to translate product requirements into project requirements.
- **Requirements elicitation and facilitation:** This ties into communication and selecting the right elicitation technique for the right situations, along with how effectively the BA can execute the elicitation technique. Does the BA need to schedule multiple sessions to discuss the same topic because he or she was not able to think on the fly and ask the right questions the first time around? This skill also requires organizational knowledge in order to discern who holds the most authentic information from which to elicit the requirements. This should also measure how well the candidate is able to manage conflicting stakeholder requirements.

- **Determine underlying needs:** The BA needs to be measured on how effective he or she is in determining the underlying needs. Does the delivered product meet the needs? Are the solutions being built actually being used? How well is the BA able to convince stakeholders that what they are asking for is sometimes not what they really need, without offending them by accusing them of not knowing what they want?
- **Requirements documentation:** Requirements, regardless of which methodology is used, needs to be unambiguous, concise, accurate, and complete. Everyone reading the documentation needs to have the same understanding because all other project work is built on top of the product requirements. The BA needs to be able to break down abstract thoughts into more details and be able to trace high-level requirements down to low-level requirements. The BA will also need to cater their writing style to different audiences and use different mediums such as diagrams and models to convey more complex requirements.
- **Modeling:** The models supplement the text and in some scenarios, the models themselves represent the requirements in more change-driven environments. The BA needs to be able to use the right modeling technique to convey different concepts and cater to different audiences.
- **Time management:** The BA, as with any team member, will need to be effective at prioritizing his or her own efforts. Time management at a larger scale for the entire project team is the responsibility of the PM, but the BA will still need to manage the time of the requirements team members in order to meet the milestones that were communicated to the PM for the overall project.
- **Schedule development and management:** The PM is responsible for the project schedule development and management, whereas the BA will need to develop and manage the schedule for the requirements development phase of the project. This however, should not be looked upon lightly as this is usually the phase of the project where there is the highest probability of schedule overruns.
- **Planning:** The candidate's ability to plan their business analysis activities and collaborate with the PM to develop the requirements management plan and other suite of project management plans should be evaluated. Attention should also be paid to their ability to rework the plan when necessary.
- **Monitor and control issues and changes:** Similar to the PM, the BA also needs to be able to monitor and control issues and changes. In fact, how well the BA partners with the PM on this activity should be measured.

- **Risks, assumptions, constraints, and dependencies:** The BA specifically would be measured on his or her ability to manage the requirement level risks, assumptions, constraints, and dependencies which the PM manages at the project level. Due to the correlation between project level and requirement level risks, assumptions, constraints, and dependencies, the ability of the PM and BA to work together should be evaluated.
- **Organizational change:** The ability of the BA to become a change agent by coaching stakeholders to accept change should also be measured.
- **Leadership, influencing, and motivating:** BAs sometimes are not seen as leaders, but they should be. BAs also need to be able to manage upward and deal with multiple stakeholders without authority. They need to influence and motivate stakeholders in order to elicit their requirements and work through any conflicts and/or issues.
- **Problem solving:** There are always multiple ways a challenge can be tackled. The BA's ability to be creative, to brainstorm, and to objectively present solutions that fall within constraints that need to be dealt with in a timely manner is an important talent.
- **Negotiation:** Balancing the options and doing the right thing for the organization within the constraints of the project is no easy feat. Sometimes there are also conflicting demands between competing departments that the BA needs to be able to effectively sort though.
- **Integration:** BAs sometimes need to be able to get out of the weeds and see the bigger picture. Similar to PMs, the BAs need to be measured on their ability to see all the moving parts and ensure they align with the project goals, other projects within the organization, the organizational needs, and most of all, the stakeholder's expectations and needs.

Findings

The results of the skills assessment can allow project sponsors to *rank* the PMs and BAs and categorize their skills based on their scores of left and right brain skills. This will point out each PM's or BA's ability to manage certain project types and sizes, along with their associated impact on the organization and the stakeholders. In a simplified view, there are four main categories of PMs or BAs based on the assessment results:

- **Low hard and low soft skills:** These candidates can be assigned to managing a single project that has lower stakes and with stakeholders that are easier to engage.
- **Low hard and high soft skills:** These candidates can be assigned to smaller initiatives that involve more challenges to engage stakeholders

with more competing demands. The implementation approach, however, should involve straightforward methodologies and procedures.

- **High hard and low soft skills:** These candidates would be most suitable to initiatives that are more complex from a methodology point of view, but they involve a more straightforward interaction with stakeholders who typically do not have significantly challenging needs or conflicting priorities.
- **High hard and high soft:** These candidates could be assigned to high stakes, complex initiatives that require strong interaction with the stakeholder and significant application of methodology, including larger projects, as well as programs.

At the same time, the pairing of the PM and BA should involve taking into consideration what skills are required to execute the project, then deciding on resources who have that skill. It may also be strategic to pair a PM and BA with complementary skills instead of a pairing with the same competency in each skill. This provides the opportunity for each pairing to leverage each others' strengths and weaknesses to successfully implement the project.

FINAL THOUGHTS ON GROWING AND INTEGRATING THE PROFESSIONS

Project management and business analysis are both rapidly growing fields. Although business analysis is a bit behind in evolving, there is a projected 19 percent growth in business analysis jobs by 2022[5] compared to a projected 15 percent growth in project management jobs by 2022,[6] according to the United States Department of Labor. It will be interesting to see how PMI and IIBA will compete in the business analysis certification field in the next few years. While it is believed that there is room for both organizations to thrive, based on the amount PMI has invested into growing the business analysis area of their organization and the amount of resources they have at their disposal, it would not be a surprise if the PMI-PBA gains much more traction than the IIBA CBAP and CCBA certifications. It is definitely exciting to see this much attention given to the BA role, and it will be thrilling to see both professions grow over the next few years. With more organizations seeing the need for resources with project management and business analysis skills on projects, there will be an increased focus on figuring out how to most effectively integrate the PM and BA roles and have them work nicely together. The PM-BA relationship has many times been compared to a marriage. Both partners need to work together to manage the finances, the children (or stakeholders), long-term goals (or scope), and timelines to meet those goals through effective communication and risk planning, in order to achieve balance (or quality) in the household (or project). Furthermore, just like a marriage, there should be less focus on the stereotypes of who should be doing what—for example, gender stereotypes such as the woman should be doing all the household chores or the BA should be doing all the administrative work. There should be, however, more emphasis on leveraging the skills of each member in the partnership and working through the peaks and valleys to lend each other a helping hand to complete the required tasks.

REFERENCES

1. Project Management Institute. (2014, April 7). *Requirements Management CoP SPECIAL WEBINAR*. Retrieved January 28, 2015, from ProjectManagement.com: http://www.projectmanagement.com/videos/286343/Requirements-Management-CoP-SPECIAL-WEBINAR.
2. According to PMI's 2013 Annual Report, published by the Project Management Institute.
3. Project Management Institute Pulse of the Profession®. (2014). *Requirements Management: A Core Competency for Project and Program Success*. Newton Square, PA: Project Management Institute.
4. Project Management Institute. (2014). *Reference Materials for PMI Professional in Business Analysis (PMI-PBA) Examination*. Project Management Institute.
5. Project Management Institute. (n.d.). Retrieved April 11, 2015, from PMI Professional in Business Analysis (PMI-PBA): http://www.pmi.org/Certification/PMI-Professional-in-Business-Analysis-PMI-PBA.aspx.
6. United States Department of Labor. (n.d.). Retrieved April 11, 2015, from Bureau of Labor Statistics: http://www.bls.gov/ooh/management/computer-and-information-systems-managers.htm.

4

ENTERPRISE ANALYSIS, PORTFOLIO MANAGEMENT, AND THE PMO

"If I had an hour to solve a problem I'd spend 55 minutes thinking about the problem and 5 minutes thinking about solutions."—Albert Einstein[1]

Enterprise analysis (EA) and portfolio management are similar to each other in many ways. The result of the EA process is the identification of a set of projects that integrate into the portfolio of projects—and in certain ways, the EA activities overlap with some of the portfolio management activities. These activities include providing project justification and business case, and a hand-off to senior management for the process of reviewing, selecting, and chartering the projects. While the EA process is about identifying opportunities, building business architecture framework, and determining the most suitable investment path for the organization; the portfolio management process focuses on investments related to projects, operations and programs, and ensuring that the initiatives that are selected align with the organization's strategy. In a sense, the EA process serves as a filter to identify and determine business requirements for future investments in projects and initiatives and portfolio management serves as an additional filter, since not every good idea can turn into a project that is worth investing in. The portfolio management process will evaluate the ideas presented by EA, prioritize them, and come up with a short list of ideas that are most aligned with the organizational needs. Over time, these ideas will turn into projects and programs. Since portfolio management centralizes the efforts toward achieving the strategic objectives of the organization (to invest or not to invest), it contains within it the EA process.

This chapter covers the areas of enterprise analysis and portfolio management, along with a discussion about the role of the project management office (PMO) and how the project manager (PM) and the business analyst (BA) interact with these processes and organizational functions.

ENTERPRISE ANALYSIS

Where do projects come from? There are many PMs and BAs alike who work strictly on projects and do not get involved in any of the pre-project work that happens in enterprise analysis. "Enterprise analysis, or EA, is the portion of business analysis most closely associated with portfolio management. The output of EA is a set of projects that go into the project portfolio, complete with business case support and ready for management to examine, choose, and charter."[2] PMs and project BAs typically get assigned after the business case has been approved and we are ready to begin work on the project. EA is a function of business analysis. It may not necessarily be the person with the BA title who is working on EA, including business casing activities, but they would definitely be using business analysis skills. It may not be the same BA who conducts EA, then continues on to execute the project, either. A PM (again, not necessarily the same PM who will continue to work on the project—although this would be ideal) should be engaged to assist in EA, but the resource with business analysis skills is who should lead these activities. When working on a project, it is the PM who is the pilot and the BA is the navigator. In EA, it is the other way around; collaboration is still imperative even before the project is born to ensure we have a solid foundation.

What is scary is that most of the project resources do not have visibility into the business case prior to starting their work on the project. What might be even worse is that EA is not happening at all and bright ideas by executives with personal agendas convert into projects where organizations invest millions of dollars without providing any justification as to whether it was a good investment to begin with. Actually, an even worse scenario is where an organization conducts EA, but then manipulates the results to demonstrate that the preferred project is a good investment. Unfortunately these scenarios are reality in many organizations. The end result is a project team that is not invested and therefore not motivated in the product they are building—with the consequence being a project that will run severely over time and cost and a product that is never or rarely used. It is no wonder why only 56% of strategic initiatives (and according to other research, even less) meet their goals and business intent. Admitting there is a problem is half the battle, as the same Program Management Institute (PMI) study also published the statistic that only 9% of organizations rate themselves as excellent on successfully executing initiatives to deliver strategic results.[3]

Defining Business Needs

How do we fix the reality that so many strategic initiatives fail? We start from the beginning and move forward, instead of starting with a solution and working backward. We start with a needs assessment. There is great temptation to provide solutions prior to investigating the root causes of problems, and even though we have the best intentions in mind, without root cause analysis we are simply masking the symptoms instead of addressing the underlying need. We must ensure that we are taking the time necessary to conduct proper EA to develop needs into business requirements—as all other requirements, both project and product, are built on top of these business needs. Without a strong base, the entire project will topple, as illustrated by Image 4.1. Consider this very simplistic example: your car will not start. There could be a million reasons

Image 4.1 Falling toppling blocks

One of the keys for project success is building the project on solid foundations. Without building a sufficient foundation—leading from the definition of the business case to its planning—it will be difficult to deliver success or to realize all the promised project's benefits.

why your car won't start. Wouldn't you want to figure out what is wrong with the car before you start to fix it? We could fix the starter, replace the engine, but the reason why your car does not start could actually be because your kids forgot to fill the tank after they used it. Seems obvious, yet we fail to conduct root cause analysis when embarking on new initiatives within our organization.

The Problem Statement

When defining business needs, we need to first define the problem and we can start with a very rudimentary problem statement:

> ***There has been an increase in employee turnover.***

This problem statement does not provide any additional details other than letting you know people have been leaving the company. So what? Why should I care? This may not actually be a problem yet, if it is only a nominal increase. The statement is still very arbitrary, and there are additional aspects of the problem we need to be able to answer in order to fully understand what we are dealing with:

1. **What is the problem?** When defining the problem, we need to elicit additional information to expand the initial problem statement into further detail, similar to how we elicit scope features into detailed requirements. What is the severity of the problem? The initial statement indicates an increase in employee turnover, so how much of an increase and over what time period?
2. **What are the effects of the problem?** Think about the impact of the problem. Is it costing the company more time and/or money? Is there a customer satisfaction impact? We can break this part down into 2 subquestions:
    a. *Who is affected by the problem?* List all stakeholder groups—they may be internal or external to the organization—that are affected.
    b. *What is the impact of the problem on each group who is affected?* We break down the impacts by stakeholder groups to ensure we have full coverage of the severity of the problem.

We can use the information we collected on the problem to create a revised and much more detailed problem statement:

> *Over the past year, we have seen employee turnover rates increase by approximately 18% resulting in an additional $200,000 in onboarding*

costs for new employees as well as a decrease in customer satisfaction, which translates into a $x loss in revenues due to being understaffed.

We now have something much more tangible to work with in order to elaborate further. The pain points identified will also assist in building a case for the business case. Executives love to see hard figures and if estimates can be provided as to how this is impacting their bottom line, there is a higher probability of getting their attention. PMs typically have access to strong financial and number crunching resources and this is where the BA may want to partner with a PM to help with the estimates. Involving the PM this early on means the PM is invested and has the opportunity to see the value they could provide to the organization if they were to pursue a project to solve the problem at hand.

Conduct Root Cause Analysis

Now that we have a good grasp of the problem, we need to figure out why it is happening. *Why* is the most important question to ask when trying to elicit underlying needs. It therefore should not be a surprise that *why* is also the fundamental question used in root cause analysis. We could very well take the problem of employee turnover for what it is and start a possible solution immediately by offering across-the-board raises and free lunches in the cafeteria, but we want to make sure that these actions will ultimately decrease the turnover rate within the organization. Two common techniques used in root cause analysis are the *Five Whys* and the *Fishbone* or *Ishikawa diagram*. The Five Whys, as suggested by the name of the technique, has the facilitator asking why, five times. We start with the problem and ask why it is happening—and by the fifth why, we should be down to the root cause of the problem. We have to be cautious when conducting root cause analysis not to come off as being overly offensive. Asking *why* multiple times can offend some stakeholders, as they may feel as if we are accusing them of having superficial needs. We have to learn to ask *why* without actually directly asking *why*. Table 4.1 is an excerpt from PMI's *Business Analysis for Practitioners* showing sample dialogue between a BA and the sponsor using the Five Whys technique without directly asking why five times.[4]

The Fishbone or Ishikawa is favorable for more complex problems as there are sometimes multiple reasons why a problem is occurring. Not that the Five Whys technique does not give the same result, but the Fishbone diagram helps to visually depict the sources of the problem. The concept of creating a Fishbone diagram is the same as Five Whys: starting with the problem at the head of the Fishbone and asking why it is happening. Each reason for the problem is a new branch, and we ask why again to expand on each branch. Figure 4.1 is an example of a completed Fishbone diagram for the previous employee turnover

Table 4.1 Five Whys Technique Excerpt: A sample dialogue between a BA and the sponsor

Role	Question/Reply
Sponsor	We would like to add the ability for policyholders to submit claims from their mobile phones. We figure it would speed up claims processing considerably.
Business analyst	I'm new on this team. Can you help me to understand why this is a problem? ***[Why 1]***
Sponsor	Well, the problem is that claims take too long to process. With a mobile application, we can encourage customers to file claims as soon as an accident or storm happens. Plus, there are other features of smart phones we can exploit, like using cameras and video technology.
Business analyst	What do you think is the major delay in processing claims? ***[Why 2]***
Sponsor	Partly it's the lag between the time of an incident and when the policyholder files a claim, which can add several days to a week to the process time. The delay also results from our corporate policy that we need to investigate every claim we think will exceed certain limits. That tends to be 80% of all claims.
Business analyst	Can you tell me the reason behind the need to investigate so many claims personally? ***[Why 3]***
Sponsor	We're a pretty conservative company, and to avoid fraud, we like to personally view the damage.
Business analyst	What other alternatives for speeding up claims have you tried in the past, and why didn't they work? ***[Why 4]***
Sponsor	Well, we tried skipping the investigation for all but the highest claim amounts, and our losses jumped way up. We also tried encouraging customers to call us on a dedicated line from their mobile phones but for some reason they didn't seem to have our number handy or who knows completely why, but we didn't get enough calls to warrant continuing.
Business analyst	What did you attribute the higher losses to? ***[Why 5]***
Sponsor	We found out that many of the damages were not as bad as the claims indicated. I think we overpaid by around 20%. If I remember correctly.

Source: Project Management Institute, *Business Analysis for Practitioners: A Practice Guide*, Project Management Institute, Inc., 2014.

example. The source of information for root cause analysis can be interviewing the affected stakeholder groups, and in our example we could have conducted the root cause analysis exercise with a couple of different sources:

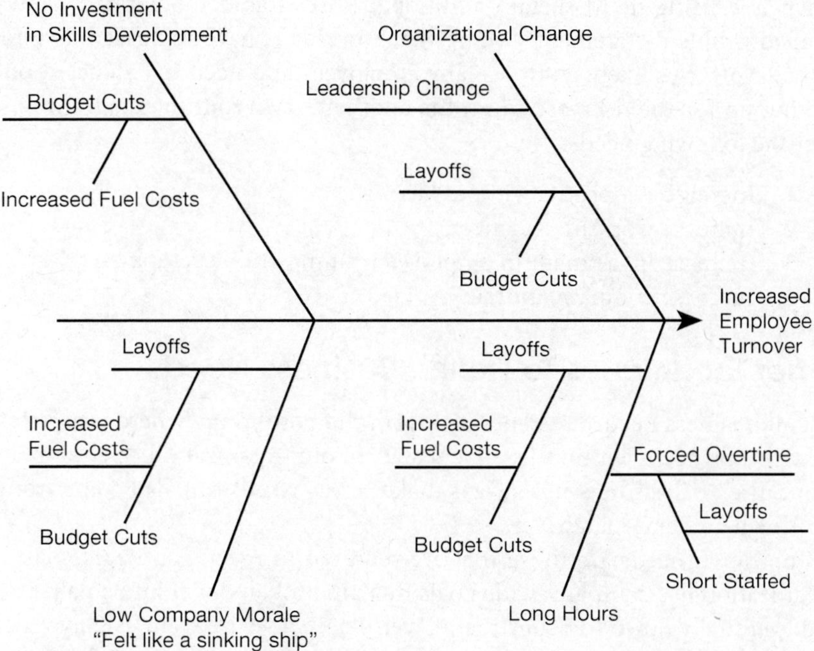

The Ishikawa diagram (also known as a fishbone diagram or cause-and-effect diagram) is created to brainstorm and figure out the potential cause(s) of a specific event.

Figure 4.1 Fishbone or Ishikawa diagram

- Conduct a workshop with management to see why they think the employees are leaving
- Review the exit interviews to determine why people are leaving

Ideally, multiple sources should be used to ensure that we are eliciting underlying needs. It would also be interesting to see if there was a gap between perception and reality.

The Fishbone diagram shows that most of the branches lead to the same reason—budget cuts due to the increased cost of producing our product. This resulted in layoffs which, in turn, caused organizational change, long hours, elimination of employee development programs, and low morale. The initial solution to increase wages would have been a temporary fix, but likely one it would not sustain given the budget cuts. We ultimately need to make up for the increased costs in some way other than additional layoffs. The budget cuts are a real hardship, but it appears that we have been taking it out on the employees, which is causing us to sustain additional losses—as demonstrated from our detailed problem statement. Seeing that workloads have increased as a result of the layoffs, we likely cut too many employees and need to balance it out by making up for the decrease in profits another way. From the diagram we can infer the following needs:

1. Increase net profits without layoffs
2. Increase work/life balance
3. Increase investment in employee training and development
4. Increase company morale

Other Techniques to Define Business Needs

Not all business needs are generated from the bottom up, where we are tasked to solve a problem within the current state of our organization. Therefore using root cause analysis may not always make sense. Needs can also come from the top-down and external drivers.

Top-down needs are those that are required to meet a strategic goal. Each organization has company-wide goals that are broken down into smaller pieces and eventually down to department level. These objectives are usually reflected on the employee performance scorecards, and the department is then tasked with breaking down those goals and objectives into smaller more manageable pieces. In turn, those more manageable pieces become business requirements that projects or programs will solve for. Using functional decomposition to break down the higher-level goals and objectives into project-level goals and objectives will ensure that the project aligns to organizational strategy. Figure 4.2 will assist in visually depicting which organizational goals and objectives the project maps back to.

Needs that are produced from external drivers can be uncovered through benchmarking studies by comparing your organization to the competition, however, it will not give innovative solutions—as benchmarking will only result in catching up. With everything splashed on the internet nowadays, it is a lot easier to conduct benchmarking studies. A bank can compare its products to a competing bank by simply going online and reviewing detailed product listings—right down to terms and conditions.

Defining Business Requirements

Business needs can be elaborated into business requirements—and business requirements "describe the higher-level needs of the organization as a whole, such as business issues or opportunities, and reasons why a project has been

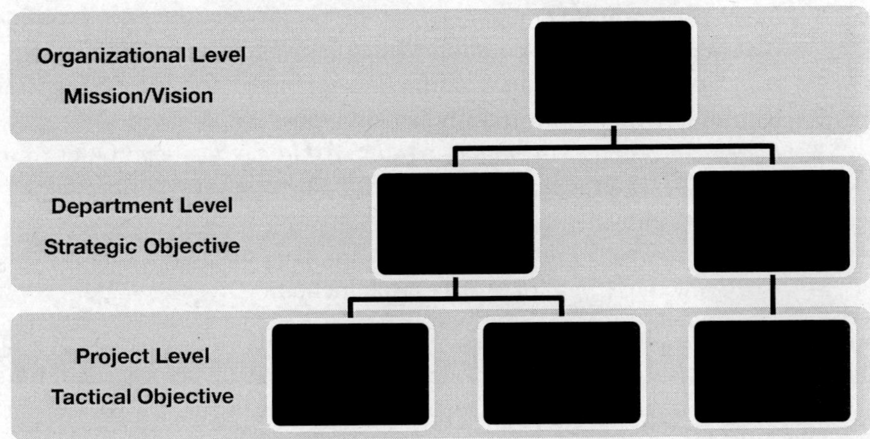

Mapping the hierarchy of goals and objectives is a visual depiction of the organizational goals and objectives; it can help stakeholders realize what the project connects and maps back to.

Figure 4.2 Mapping the hierarchy of goals and objectives

undertaken."[5] Many organizations are still not aware of the different types of requirements or the hierarchy of requirements, so they call all requirements business requirements. Business requirements—per the definition provided—are special in that all other requirements need to trace back to the business requirements to ensure that they provide value. Business requirements, like business objectives should be written in the SMART format as defined below:

- **Specific:** High level does not mean vague. The business requirements still need to be clear and concise.
- **Measurable:** There must be a way to prove that the business requirement has been met.
- **Achievable:** The business requirement still must be realistic in that it is attainable or feasible within our environment. The *A* in SMART can also stand for Attainable.
- **Relevant:** The business requirement must align with organizational goals, mission, vision, and strategy and not violate any core values.
- **Time-bound:** The time period in which the business requirement will be satisfied should be specified so we know when to measure the results.

Using the SMART criteria, we can now convert each of the business needs into SMART business requirements:

1. *Increase net profits without layoffs*: Increase net profits by 10% within a year of project implementation without any additional layoffs.
2. *Increase work/life balance*: Eliminate the need for forced overtime within 3 months of project implementation.
3. *Increase investment in employee training and development*: Offer training and development opportunities for all employees within 9 months of project implementation.
4. *Increase company morale*: Increase employee satisfaction survey scores by 20% within a year of project implementation.

The process is simplified for this case study, but a lot of work has to be put into gathering and analyzing statistics to determine realistic percentages and timeframes in which to achieve these business requirements. Again, the BA can partner with a PM to assist with setting realistic goals, as these are estimates after all. The PM can also help with identifying assumptions associated with these estimates. The SMART business requirements can then be reused as the success criteria for the project if/when it gets approved via the business casing process. By involving the PM in the business requirements definition, again, they have a sense of ownership and control over the success criteria for the project they could potentially be leading, instead of having this handed to them and asked to deliver.

Assessing Capability Gaps

In order to understand how to solve for the business need, there is a need to understand where we stand today and what is preventing us from meeting our needs. The delta will provide us with capabilities we will need to deliver. A capability is, "the ability to add value or achieve objectives in an organization through a function, process, service, or other proficiency."[6] We need to understand the enterprise architecture of the organization, which is defined as, "a collection of the business and technology components needed to operate an enterprise." It includes the people, processes, "applications, information, and supporting technology to form a complete blueprint of an organization."[7] The following questions need to be asked:

- Who are the stakeholder groups impacted?
- What are the current business procedures?
- What are the functions the teams perform today?
- What systems/technologies are being used?
- Are there any projects in flight that may be affecting the area of study that could alter the current state in the near future?

The last question in the list is often overlooked, as the organization is always changing and the potential project is probably not the only thing going on. Meeting with portfolio and program managers and with PMs can help gather a lot of information about the changing landscape and provide opportunities to collaborate on potential shared components. In addition, it will be beneficial to ensure that current projects that are in flight are not counterproductive to the business requirements and project objectives. It would be a shame to invest time and effort implementing, only to spend more time and effort to reverse it. Trying to find the interdependencies between projects is tough, and it usually takes place through word of mouth and hallway conversations. Team meetings are effective ways to provide brief overviews of projects that are coming down the pipeline, and they help keep the lines of communication open.

Much of the current-state analysis can be done using existing documentation that is available and supplemented with interviews. Remember that we are still in EA and much of the detailed analysis is still to come, should we decide to pursue these business requirements. The goal of the analysis done here is to help identify gaps or areas that we could improve on to meet our business requirements. For the employee turnover example, some of the pain points were long hours and high costs. We may want to look at operational procedures to see if there are opportunities for streamlining and identifying process steps that are wasteful or do not provide value. We may also want to evaluate employee development programs that were available in the past and which ones were taken away.

Brainstorming Potential Projects

Organizations usually do not have the flexibility of pie-in-the-sky solutions, but at the same time they need to make an effort to avoid stifling the brainstorming efforts—so it is recommended that they brainstorm first and filter things out, based on constraints, later. There may be some solutions that seem far-fetched, but with a different set of eyes looking at it there may be creative ways to make it happen. Also, if the idea is absolutely brilliant, it may convince stakeholders to loosen some of those constraints.

Ideas generated for potential projects could come from multiple sources. Each of the business requirements should be tackled separately, then examined for areas of overlap. A single project does not need to address all of our business requirements at once. Looking at our set of business requirements, here are a few ideas to address them:

1. Increase net profits by 10% within a year of project implementation without any additional layoffs: To undertake this business requirement a working session with senior management can help with the effort to elicit ideas.

Many organizations are looking at more creative ways to brainstorm and are turning to gamestorming, which uses interactive techniques that enable the team to visually think and be part of the solution. While some of the games may not be new, it is still a great way to get everyone involved and is much more fun than having a dry roundtable session. A carousel can be used for the gamestorming session—where the team prepares a handful of flip charts asking targeted questions about the problem:

- What are some factors that are driving costs up?
- How can we lower our costs?
- How can we increase profits?
- What do customers love about our product? (We don't want to change something that will alter these items.)
- Are there processes that can be streamlined?

During the session, the facilitator forms groups of two or more people (depending on the number of participants). Each group takes two to three minutes to rotate through each flip chart. This will allow everyone the opportunity to provide their input and be engaged in the process. The end result should be a good list of ideas that can be investigated further.

2. Eliminate the need for forced overtime within three months of project implementation: This one can probably be tackled from a couple of angles. One of them involves an in-depth study of the existing processes to identify any areas that can be streamlined. This may involve physically job shadowing and measuring how long each process step is taking, to identify bottlenecks in the process. Gamestorming and affinity mapping can also be used to elicit additional ideas; starting with the question—"how can we eliminate the need for forced overtime?" Participants are asked to silently document ideas using sticky notes for about 10 minutes; utilizing one sticky note per idea. A facilitator will take the sticky notes and arrange them on a board, and once the time is up, the team can work together to categorize the thoughts by moving the sticky notes around. Duplicate sticky notes can be placed on top of each other to show how many participants had the same idea. Figure 4.3 demonstrates what the process could look like. The findings can then be balanced against any constraints and used as topics for further discussions.

3. Offer training and development opportunities for all employees within nine months of project implementation: One of the best ways to identify solutions is to simply ask the affected stakeholder groups. In many environments the input of our end users is left out and the EA process ends up leading the team toward devising solutions that they think will work. There is a reliance on middle management to represent the end users, but members of middle management are not the ones performing the work on a daily basis. It is better to get

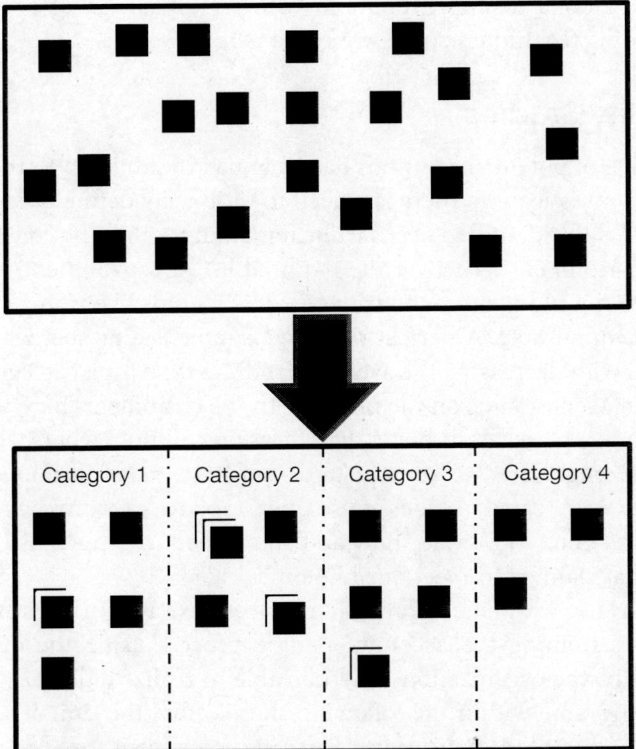

The affinity diagram is used to organize ideas and data. It is one of the seven management and planning tools.

Figure 4.3 Affinity diagram

relevant input directly from the source. It will be helpful to survey the employees and ask—if more training and development opportunities were available, would they take advantage of it? This is a means to confirm the need for training and development opportunities. The survey should also elicit what types of training and development opportunities the employees would be interested in. Categories of training can be included so that the results are not as open ended, but still leave space for participants to share open-ended feedback. Follow-up interviews could also be conducted if more information is required, and once the information elicited has been analyzed and organized, it is time to schedule a follow-up session with managers to determine the most effective way to make it happen within the project constraints.

4. Increase employee satisfaction survey scores by 20% within a year of project implementation: There should be input from the employees regarding what can be done to improve employee morale—surveying or the previous gamestorming techniques could work well here as well.

Feasibility Studies

Once the list of potential solutions has been narrowed down to those warranting further investigation, there is a need to ultimately define potential projects that will meet the identified needs while remaining within the constraints of our current environment to deliver the required list of capabilities. Creating projects that do not fit in with our current environment is like trying to fit a square peg into a round hole. A perfect real-life example is a project where the team was tasked with decreasing the average handling time for a call center, which is the time an agent spends on the phone with the customer. There were multiple issues with this project, one being that it was one of those where a business case was reverse engineered to attempt to demonstrate value in implementing the project that was created in order to use a new tool. An executive within the organization had gone to a trade show and was duped into purchasing a software package that claimed to meet our undefined needs. It was an account opening application, and without conducting any root cause analysis, it was determined that by streamlining the account opening process using the out-of-the-box functionality, the organization would be able to realize a decrease in the average handling time within the following six months (the time it would take to configure and test the application). The call center agents used a custom-coded solution to service customers, and the purchased software package needed to integrate seamlessly with the existing custom-coded system. Forcing the software package to play nicely within the existing system, with minimal custom coding, was a real challenge. With the multiple (and not so seamless) integration points of passing information back and forth between the two systems, the average handling times actually increased as the system spent a lot of time clocking. The six month timeline turned into a year and a half and was 250% over budget, with the additional custom coding and troubleshooting, along with expensive consultants from the software vendor.

Feasibility studies need to be conducted as a checkpoint to determine if the organization is on the right track before any further time and effort is spent. With the call center example, we could have had technical resources study the software package with the help of the vendor, then make a decision on how well it integrated with our existing systems prior to purchasing it. In the employee turnover example we could conduct follow-up sessions to ensure the training programs that we decided on would actually be used. Some low-cost suggestions could be scheduling lunch-and-learns where employees can learn from each other. Would employees be willing to give up their lunch hour for these sessions? Do we have experts in house that can conduct these sessions?

Defining Scope

For each of the potential projects that need investigating, there is a need to define the scope boundaries; specifically, what is in and out of scope. In practice, each time an in-scope item is identified, a corresponding out-of-scope item should also be documented to show the boundary—even if it seems obvious. For example, if training that is to be provided in English is considered in scope, out of scope should be training provided in any language other than English. If this is not explicitly stated, it may be questioned as to whether Spanish or French or any other language would be in scope. This clearly indicates that the team considered it but decided that only English will be provided at this time. Scope can also have many dimensions:

- **Functional scope:** processes or features that will be in/out of scope
- **Organizational scope:** organizational units that will be in/out of scope
- **Technical scope:** technologies/systems that will be in/out of scope

Listing scope items is the norm, but diagrams are better for stakeholders to digest. Models such as Process Models, Use Case Diagrams, and Context Diagrams can be used to show scope.

Preparing the Business Case

The business case is the major output out of EA. The business case consists of a costs and benefits analysis to provide justification as to why we should invest in a particular initiative. Each of the potential projects we are investigating needs to have the same level of detail and effort put into the analysis. Sometimes we think the best option is obvious and unintentionally bias the results to favor a certain project. The following list includes the key components of a business case:

- **Executive summary:** Even though it is found at the beginning of the business case, it should be written last. The executive summary reviews all of the components in the business case, including background information, top options, and any major risks along with providing a recommendation to the reader, based on the findings. It should follow the flow of the remainder of the document.
- **Background information:** This information should describe how the problem or situation came to light. The problem statement should be included here.
- **Business requirements:** It is good practice to also include the business goals and objectives hierarchy to show alignment to organizational strategy.

- **Solution options:** This information should consist of a brief description of each of the options that were investigated including the in/out of scope items. Each of the solution options should be elaborated further to include the following:
    1. **Benefits:** Benefits are much harder to express than costs. All benefits, including hard and soft benefits should be included although it is ideal if all benefits are expressed as hard benefits using a common denominator. Hard benefits are those that can be measured, and soft benefits are those that cannot. Using assumptions, all soft benefits can be converted into hard benefits. For example, increased employee satisfaction can be converted into a hard benefit by using the satisfaction survey scores as a measurement. It can also be taken a step further and converted to a financial hard benefit by linking employee satisfaction to cost of employee turnover. Assuming that 30 percent of employees who are not happy will leave and it costs $10,000 to onboard a new resource. Based on satisfaction scores, approximately 100 of the employees are currently not happy. The benefit can therefore be expressed as a savings of $300,000 (30 percent of 100 employees, multiplied by $10,000 to replace each of them) in onboarding costs for new employees. These benefit assumptions need to be clearly articulated in the business case. It would be a good idea to have them validated by someone who is trusted by the sponsor prior to presentation. If the business case is based on exaggerated assumptions, all of the work may be dismissed.
    2. **Costs:** Remember to include the total cost of ownership which includes not only the project related costs, but also any operational or ongoing maintenance costs including service agreements, licensing costs, and additional hires. Any cost assumptions should also be documented and shared with a trusted advisor of the sponsor.
    3. **Outcome:** Private sector companies like financial institutions typically use financial outcomes to measure projects. Some of the common financial outcomes are net present value (NPV), internal rate of return (IRR), return on investment (ROI), cost/benefits ratio, and payback period, just to name a few. This requires all of the benefits and costs to be expressed in financials. If using financials, the projects with the highest NPV, IRR, or ROI but lowest payback period would be selected. When evaluating the costs/benefits ratio, if the ratio is pre-

sented as benefits/costs then *greater than* (>) 1 is favorable. If the ratio is presented as costs/benefits then *less than* (<) 1 is favorable. You obviously want the benefits to be greater than the costs.

Public sector agencies, such as government or not-for-profit organizations do not usually measure their projects using financial outcomes, as their businesses are not about making money. They would have to find a common denominator to measure all of their projects using the same criteria in order to compare apples to apples. For example, a local government agency is looking to improve public view by 10% within a year of project implementation. The common denominator that can be used is public opinion poll results, which aligns to the goal of the project.

4. **Risks:** An initial risk assessment should be completed for each potential project. This can sometimes be a deciding factor for risk-adverse organizations like government agencies that have to be very careful how public tax dollars are spent. PMs can be a valuable asset when creating the business case, as not only can they help with their estimation skills, they can also serve as subject matter experts if the project is similar to one that has been performed in the past. The PMs will be able to provide actual costs that can help in baselining the estimates; with lessons learned collected from the previous projects; and with risk identification.

Business Case Decision

A business case may be approved, sent back for rework, put on hold, or declined:

- **Approved:** The projects in an approved business case are rubber stamped to move on to chartering. A project team will then be assembled, where a PM and BA will be assigned. The PM and BA assigned may not necessarily be the same PM and BA duo who worked on the business case. Business cases should therefore be shared with the project team as a starting point so the team understands the value of the work they are doing. It may also eliminate a lot of rework as many components can be re-used or built on. The PM can reuse and build on the information that was provided in the business case to prepare the project charter. In situations where there may be more than one project required to meet the business requirements, a program manager may also be assigned to manage the multiple projects and teams.

- **Rework:** Rework is often the worst case scenario. This could be because the sponsor determined that there was not enough information provided in order for them to make a sound decision or the sponsor did not agree with the assumptions. This is why it is recommended to review the assumptions and the business case presentation with the sponsor's trusted advisor to vet through these issues prior to presenting it to the sponsor.
- **On Hold:** It might be a great project, but not for now, as other higher priority initiatives require the organization's attention now. The BA may be invited to present the business case again at the next project selection meeting, once the more pressing needs have been addressed.
- **Declined:** Despite what most may think, this is not necessarily a bad thing; in fact, it is probably a great thing. This means that enough information was presented to the sponsor to make a decision not to waste time and money on something that did not provide value. This scenario is much better than an approved business case for a project that delivered functionality that was never or rarely used once implemented. A 2002 study by the Standish Group indicated that 64% of functionality delivered is rarely or never used.[8]

MANAGING PROJECTS FOR VALUE

After the business case is approved and the project is well on its way, the business case should never be shelved. It should be dusted off at the end of every phase of the project to facilitate go/no-go decisions to ensure the project is still going to provide the intended value as promised in the business case. The project team would have significant challenges with a task if they do not have visibility into the business case. Through progressive elaboration—"the iterative process of increasing the level of detail in a project management plan as greater amounts of information and more accurate estimates become available"[9]—many things can change. A lot can happen from the time the project was selected—assumptions can change, risks may be realized, business objectives may change, or you may realize you had unrealistic cost and benefit models. If this is the case, it may make sense to modify the business case accordingly and decide if it still makes sense to proceed. If the answer is no, the idea of sunk cost should not deter the team from recommending the project be canceled. (Sunk cost is the concept of taking into consideration that the money that was already invested in the project would be wasted if we canceled, so we should just finish what we started.)

The concept of sunk cost always brings up memories of a beloved old car that we thought had a few years left in it, so we invested in new winter tires for the car. When summer time came, the air conditioner broke, and because we had just invested money in the new winter tires, we then invested more money into the air conditioning. Shortly thereafter, the brake pads needed to be replaced and the same line of thinking came to mind, and we sank more money into the car. When the next problem emerged, that time with the starter, it was finally time to give up on the darn car. From a project prospective, wasting a fraction of the project budget is much better than blowing the full amount on something you know would not provide the value as anticipated.

Tracking Project Benefits

We invest millions and sometimes billions of dollars on projects, we take the time to document measurable business requirements and success criteria, but many organizations do not take the time to actually measure if these projects actually meet their project objectives. We choose not to learn from our past experiences before we are ready to jump into the next pricey endeavor. The large majority of organizations do not look back six months or a year after the project is implemented to check if the project delivered the intended value. It is quite shocking that organizations, including government agencies, do not bother to check back to see if they realized the value from the project they had undertaken. Looking back is a low-cost and highly effective way to learn from mistakes, learn from successes, and tweak the implemented solution so it addresses the actual needs for which it was undertaken.

One of the reasons the benefits realization check does not take place is that projects are temporary in nature and the resources have all moved on to other projects. Many organizations also rely on contract resources that may no longer be with the company by the time benefits are ready to be tracked. The project team, however, can ensure there are tracking mechanisms in place so the data is available to be collected and analyzed when the time comes. A PMO could assist with this task, by having the PMO diarize when project benefits should be tracked, and have them assign a team to conduct the analysis to measure it against the success criteria. If it turns out that the project benefits were realized, it is both a great feel-good story and company morale booster (including the opportunity to leverage some of the good things that took place in the project) and if not, it is a great learning opportunity for the next time around.

The analysis could also uncover additional opportunities for improvement, thus kicking off the EA again. Sometimes there may be situations where the project failed the success criteria, yet the project can still be seen as a success depending on what factors you were looking at. Consider the example of a call center project: the success criterion was to decrease the average handling time (time spent on the phone with the customer) by 20 percent within six months of project implementation. The project did not decrease the average handling time, in fact the time it took to complete the account opening process remained stagnant, but the call center agents were much more satisfied with the newly streamlined process. The old process had them logging into another application and rekeying data which was also prone to more errors. The project is deemed a failure if measured against the average handling time, but possibly a success if measured against employee satisfaction.

RECAP: ENTERPRISE ANALYSIS

Many project teams are assigned to a new project without understanding the business justification, but a project has a much higher chance of success if people understand the benefits of what they are delivering. Some projects are spread across years. Imagine spending that much time dedicated to this work and not understanding the value of doing it? It may be de-motivating. The same takes place when a project's benefits are not explained to the end users, resulting in pushback and negativity around the change. Working through the steps of EA will ensure that all approved projects align to the organization's strategy and subsequently completed more successfully. PMI's Pulse of the Profession 2015 report indicates one of the factors that help an organization build and sustain its growth capacity and become a high performer is aligning projects to strategy.[10] More often than not, a project is thought up, then we dream up superficial costs and benefits, making the business case simply a formality. This is a source of much of the misalignment. The integration points in the pre-project work will help the project team understand the value of the project and how it fits into organizational strategy.

PORTFOLIO AND THE PMO

Since EA and portfolio management are so closely linked to each other, it serves as an opportunity to leverage the roles of the PM and the BA in their respective areas and benefit both the project and the organization. With the BA already adding value to another portfolio function—the PMO—and having the PMO representing both the needs of the PMs as well as those of the BAs, we can ensure better business alignment between the ideas generated in the EA process and the organization's strategic goals. Other benefits include a more informed decision-making process that considers both product as well as portfolio capabilities and capacities, along with a reduced duplication of effort, and enhanced integration and focus of organizational capacities and resources.

Many organizations fail to fully leverage the value that the BA brings to the table from conducting the EA process, which results in wasted efforts and, in turn, a flawed decision-making process that may prevent the organization from directing its capacity where it is needed the most. Identifying business opportunities, building their business architecture framework, and determining the optimum project investment path for the enterprise are three of the core functions of EA, but they also serve as integral parts of portfolio management.

From EA to Portfolio Management

Another way of looking at the distinction and similarities between the EA and portfolio management is to view EA as a product-driven foundational step of portfolio management, as during EA activities, business requirements for future project investments are identified and documented as higher-level statements of the goals, objectives, and needs of the organization. We then take this product-driven justification process, and move toward translating it into organizational investment decisions, capacity management, project selection criteria, and other considerations that ensure alignment of the tactical initiatives under consideration with the organizational objectives and strategy.

Portfolio management also provides facilitation and oversight for focus management and resource allocation, as it helps projects deliver their success by ensuring that each project and activities within it receive the appropriate level of rigor and resources to perform it in line with the organizational strategy. The PMO arm is there to provide expertise and to ensure consistency and use of tools and terminology in an effort to maximize the benefits each project produces, and to serve as an escalation mechanism to identify and manage performance exceptions.

Better Business Alignment with Strategic Goals

Better business alignment with strategic goals is not only about ensuring that the PM is aware of the organizational strategy, but also to produce additional benefits that help maximize benefits:

- **Improved processes:** It is important to improve the planning processes so the project plan focuses on producing meaningful value without wasting resources on non-value-added activities.
- **Risk mitigation:** Many PMs focus on project risks with little to no consideration of product risks, business risks, and operational risks. While it is important to deliver project success (namely scope, time, and cost targets), PMs must consider the impact of promoting their project goals at the potential expense of business objectives. For example, removing

product features in order to reduce the timeline and meet schedule constraints may be important, but portfolio management comes into play to ensure that such decisions do not compromise the value the project produces for the organization. When there is a conflict between project and business objectives, portfolio management helps facilitate the process of defining and doing the right thing for the organization.

- **Improved integration of resources:** For instance, people, processes, machines, and tools—when there is a clear idea of the benefits to realize, it is easier to perform resource allocation and to make sure capacities are in line with the organizational needs.

What's in a Name

The name of the activities we perform becomes secondary to the need to integrate the EA with portfolio management. Despite coming from two different disciplines, the two sets of activities are very closely tied together and as such, require the collaboration of those who perform them and the integration of both efforts into the organization's decision-making process. Furthermore, the BA plays an important role in this collaboration for several reasons:

1. Taking part in the EA process
2. Being part of the PMO
3. Helping the PM ensure that the project is aligned with strategic goals and objectives
4. Providing additional due diligence to senior management as a result of the EA activities and by being involved in the process—ensuring continuity and focus as well as using the same measurements, considerations, parameters, and project selection criteria

Roles Involved

On the portfolio level we can find the heads of the portfolios such as the Strategic Business Unit (SBU) managers defining the strategic goals and prioritizing proposed and existing projects—both activities factoring in findings from the EA process that provide context and depth.

The functional or technical managers lead the effort to align their own areas with the strategic objectives and they provide context regarding the current state of their area and its ability to take on initiatives and carry the mandate from senior management.

Technical team members provide their expertise in their respective areas to ensure delivery of the mandate. They also provide details regarding the technical considerations related to their work and the value they produce.

The BA plays a key role here by facilitating the communication between the technical teams and the business, providing context to the information that is discussed, as well as performing the following activities:

- Participating in creating a high-level business case for initiatives that are under consideration, and for those selected for further review, leading the feasibility studies
- Helping set up score cards and other criteria to review, prioritize, and rank proposed initiatives
- Identifying gaps between the current state and the identified goals—both from a technical and a business perspective
- Providing the PM with context when an initiative is chartered to become a project
- Identifying areas to address as part of the desired state and propose relevant and related process improvements

The PM typically gets involved only when the initiative is chartered and becomes an approved project. Therefore, the PM is responsible to reach out to the BA and to any portfolio *officers* (including the project sponsor) who have been involved in the process and inquire about the initiative, its priority, the sense of urgency, and any assumptions, constraints, and risks that are worth noting for the chartering process.

Hands-on Portfolio Management Utilizing the PMO

PMOs are established for a variety of reasons in different types of organizations, to oversee multiple projects and attempt to deliver a variety of benefits. Some of the key characteristics that PMOs need to have are related to their ability to evolve and change over time, to ensure the value the PMO adds to the organization is relevant, current, and growing. Similar to evolution in the style of leadership that PMs need to demonstrate throughout the project—from directive, to facilitative, and eventually supportive—the PMOs also need to evolve, to address the changing needs and expectations of their organizations.

In the early days of the project, the PMO must learn the needs of the organization and orient itself toward the value it needs to produce—upward for senior management and downward for PMs. The orientation involves the establishment of tools, templates, guidelines, and ground rules to support PMs in their work and define good and best practices. A common mistake that PMOs make is to attempt to continue enforcing these areas and to keep establishing new practices, with the inevitable consequence that PMs start viewing the PMO as project management police and a producer of taxes and red tape. Before long,

PMs no longer buy in to the PMO processes and cease to see the value the PMO provides.

Furthermore, additional motion in this direction takes place with the reorientation of the PMO upward toward the portfolio side of the organization, neglecting to address the growing gap between the PMO and the PMs. What the PMO should do is reinvent itself, almost to the extent of making its most recent role obsolete, by reestablishing itself as the producer of new value for both the portfolio and the PMs. Instead of simply increasing the capacity and the number of projects under its wing, the PMO should evolve toward helping in project selection, and playing an increasing role in resource allocation, resource sharing, dependency management, cross-project interactions, and building a culture of overall collaboration and open dialogue among PMs. Furthermore, the PMO should continue its continuous improvement process by constantly questioning the current value it produces for the organization and periodically trying to reinvent itself for the benefit of all those involved.

With the constant recreation of value, the PMO also subconsciously engages in self-preservation, without appearing to do it deliberately. A common challenge with PMOs is their attempt to enforce the need for their own existence with the introduction of more red tape and more policing, instead of thinking how to let go of previous sources of power and reinventing itself with new sources, as seen in Table 4.2.

Challenges with PMOs

A PMO is often established with no clear mandate or vision and for no practical reason other than realizing that many other organizations have one. For a PMO to be successful in adding and realizing value for the organization there has to be a clear vision for it, as well as specific reasons to establish it that are rooted in the senior levels of the organization as a function of portfolio management. Within the first couple of years of their existence, many PMOs will not only fail to deliver the expected value for the organization, but will also be labeled as failures and may even shut down. Becoming aware of the common causes for failure can help PMO sponsors, senior management, PMs, and PMO managers extrapolate relevant information for their organizations and circumstances and also combat any challenges or potential deficiencies they encounter.

The causes of PMO failure listed here appear in no particular order, and each one is followed by a short explanation with suggestions as to how to address the problem:

1. **Inexperienced PMs:** Many PMOs provide processes, coaching, and mentoring services that benefit PMs who are less experienced—while the more experienced PMs do not realize any benefit from the PMO.

Table 4.2 Basic and advanced PMO roles

Basic PMO Roles	Advanced "Reinvented" PMO Roles
Capacity management	Proactive resource sharing
Resource management	Cross project dependencies
Risk management processes and practices	Risk management center of excellence; proactive, collaborative, cross project; project vs. business risks
Prioritization of projects and other work	Define urgencies and their criteria
Processes, tools, techniques, and templates	Continuous improvement
Project selection	Alignment to organizational strategy
Training and professional development	PM and BA skills assessment for hiring, resource allocation, and focused training
Establishing best practices	Sharing lessons across projects, in real time
Agile practices	Meaningful dose of agility
Providing guidelines for communication planning	Establishing and supporting ground rules for communication and conduct; escalation procedures
Helping with quality planning	Providing a meaningful quality plan with support in defining standards, specifications, and documentation; measuring and acting upon cost of quality findings
Ensure project mandate is clear	Providing criteria for defining project success
Project management support	Management by exception; management of assumptions, constraints, issues, change, and dependencies
Simple communication and HR policies	Conflict resolution and expectations management
Providing above the surface value	Focus value for PMs and for the organization
Reporting guidelines	Focused reporting; incorporating Earned Value techniques
Limited scope of involvement	Establishing culture of collaboration; a hybrid of consulting, directing, and supporting roles
Project management practices	A broader scope including leadership, negotiations, relationship management, and expectations management

This table lists "traditional" roles that basic PMOs serve in many organizations versus a more advanced set of benefits dynamic and adaptive ("reinvented") PMOs bring to the table.

PMOs should tailor their offerings toward all PMs and attempt to establish a perception that they are a trusted partner to all PMs, while providing a collaborative environment that involves team building, cross-training, and information sharing.

2. **Inexperienced PMO staff:** With the role of the PMO staff often perceived as mostly administrative, supportive, and reporting-based, organizations often place employees in the PMO who have insufficient project management experience. The PMO staff must have strong project management experience, and they need to understand the hurdles and challenges PMs are facing. With relevant experience, PMO staff members can free up time to focus on more valuable activities for both the projects they oversee and the organization.
3. **Mismanaged and unrealistic stakeholder expectations:** Senior stakeholders often have many misconceptions about PMOs, thanks to their lack of understanding of why the PMO is in place, along with a lack of clear objectives for the PMO. This leads to the wrong perception about what the PMO is about and the value it is intended to produce for the organization, and in turn, to negative attitudes, lack of buy-in, and even feelings of resentment. Common misconceptions and unrealistic expectations include:
   a. *Audits*: They are often perceived negatively—predominantly as a means to discipline and even penalize team members for noncompliance and to look for flaws. Audits often lack specific focus and do not produce tangible recommendations, or they do not result in their findings being implemented. The notion that audits are part of continuous improvement and that their recommendations will help stakeholders in these respective areas must be communicated upfront to all relevant stakeholders as part of trust-building. At times, PMOs are perceived only as *audit police*, rather than as a value-added function for projects and the organization.
   b. *The PMO is perceived as offering little or no value*: The PMO reports to senior management and therefore, is structured toward delivering value to them. As such, PMOs tend to forget that they are also intended to deliver value to PMs. When PMs perceive the PMO as representing red tape and are considered to be a liability, it is a breakdown that must be addressed by ensuring that the PMO works closely with the PMs to establish and deliver value to them. Unfortunately, even when PMOs focus on producing value to senior management, it is not always viewed as value, since some members of senior management often lack a basic understanding of project management concepts. It has long been said that project management training should be provided to all levels of the organization, since it is critical that all stakeholders understand basic concepts in project management.

The PMO must not forget that it has multiple customers in the organization and there is a need to manage the expectations of all stakeholders; specifically the PMs', senior management, and resource/functional managers.

c. *Red tape*: Processes and technology are a means of improving people's ability to perform their work, but project success is driven by people and their abilities. Technology and tools cannot replace the need for skilled people, but rather complement it. If the PMO is viewed as leaning heavily toward representing theories, tools, and regulations, there will be no buy-in from stakeholders, since the latter are interested in useful ideas, practicality, improvement, and streamlining opportunities. The PMO must portray itself as a value-adding function and focus first and foremost on the people, their needs and their ability to work in collaboration with the PMO staff and the approaches it represents.
d. *Stakeholder expectations management and gap alignment*: With varying levels of stakeholder involvement in the PMO's operations and in understanding the project management processes altogether, along with a culture of instant gratification that prevails in many organizations, it is important to set the right expectations about what the PMO can deliver from the start. This includes not only a specific, measurable, realistic, and quantifiable set of benefits, but also timelines, areas of impact, and non-tangible benefits to be realized. Stakeholders should not expect benefits to be realized immediately, and when value is delivered, it should be attributed to the appropriate source. The expectations should also be set regarding the type of the PMO; when a PMO is established in the context of Project Management, it will deliver a different set of benefits than one associated with portfolio management. Portfolio management PMOs take part in project selection, specific resource allocation, and strategy formulation, while project PMOs are much more tactical in their focus.[11]
e. *Boundaries and definitions*: It is important to define the PMO's boundaries in relation to other functions of the organization—its overall scope (including areas it does not cover) and the expectations around roles and responsibilities between the projects and the PMO. The touch points should be clear and defined, so there is no duplication of effort and no gaps are discovered. Related to this is also the need to set up boundaries to define where the

PMO ends and projects begin, so there is no false expectation that the PMO is going to serve as a safety net or a fallback plan for PMs—with PMs thinking that when things get derailed to a certain extent, the PMO will step in to save the day. This also leads to the need to define the role the PMO should play in project recovery, in the event that projects reach a point where they need recovery and rescue actions.

f. *Keep it simple*: The most effective and efficient processes, tools, techniques, approaches, and methodologies are often simple and straightforward. The PMO must ensure that following its processes is simple to do and easy to rationalize. To be motivated, people need to know what they need to do, why they need to do it, and what's in it for them. If processes become convoluted and difficult to follow, the stakeholder's attention will be diverted from adding value to trying to figure out how to perform the work. PMO processes should also not restrict workers, but rather focus on helping to make them easier for everyone.

4. **Lack of senior-level support:** PMOs must have a senior sponsor or champion—not having one increases the chance for PMO failure. It is also important for the sponsor to understand what project management is about and the full set of values the PMO is set to deliver. Senior managers often think that the PMOs primary function is consolidated reporting, template creation, and resource coordination. This viewpoint often results in the senior manager providing little support to the PMO to perform its duties, which becomes even more pronounced when there is a conflict between PMs and the PMO that is escalated to the sponsor. This will often lead to the senior manager believing that the PMO is the cause of project difficulties.

   A related cause for PMO failure is its lack of authority. While there is a senior manager who serves as a sponsor, the PMO is not given the appropriate mandate and authority to perform its work and as a result, PMs often view the PMO's requests for information and collaboration as low-priority.

5. **Poor resource management:** Whether or not resources report to the PMO, the PMO needs to develop the ability to quantify resource demand. Depending on the type of organization, the PMO needs to develop projections and forecasts for resource usage, or make recommendations to decision makers regarding the need to mobilize, allocate, and reallocate resources. The PMO can help in the development of a process for time-tracking while remaining cognizant of the fact that

timekeeping is not the goal, but the means to achieving success and for finding opportunities to add value to the organization.

6. **Poorly defined benefits and value definitions, measurements, and realization:** There has to be a built-in mechanism to define, measure, control, and adjust the benefits the PMO is set to produce. It can be helpful to refocus the PMO's efforts to ensure it aligns with the organization's strategy and during times of change and reorganization, it can help reestablish the business case and the justification for the PMO without scrambling for information and measurements.
7. **Self-serving PMOs:** Over time, the PMO naturally evolves from being a supporting function to becoming a self-serving entity. Instead of focusing on adding value to the organization and to projects, the PMO begins focusing on self-preservation, where processes are driven by political considerations to justify the existence of the PMO, and no longer addresses projects' concerns, failing to act as a trusted partner. The organization's senior leadership needs to ensure that a clear and direct line of communication exists between PMs and other stakeholders, and must constantly be on the lookout for informal feedback about the PMO via these channels.
8. **Not providing real support:** Beyond its official scope, the PMO needs to constantly search for new ways to add value to projects and to other stakeholders. These include providing input on establishing communication management guidelines for projects, deploying consistent risk, change, issues and assumption management approaches, and capturing and implementing lessons learned in real time and across all projects within the PMO's area of responsibility. All the while, the PMO must ensure they are collaborating with PMs, while not suppressing the PM's creativity, innovation, or ability to think outside the box. Although the PMO is mandated to introduce (and at times enforce) structure and process, it must leave room for PMs to excel in their respective areas of expertise.
9. **Poor capacity management and organizational alignment:** Most PMOs have no portfolio functions, do not take part in project selection, and do not own project resources. However, the organization tends to continuously trickle more work, coverage areas, responsibilities, and projects into the scope of the PMO, and the PMO finds itself having to manage more with less. With no *voice* at the senior level of the organization, the PMO slowly becomes overwhelmed and in extreme cases, loses the ability to deliver benefits outright, finding itself in an advisory and consulting capacity, with diminished ability to deliver value to projects or the organization. Similarly, PMOs often find themselves

delivering their mandated value, only to realize that the organizational strategy has shifted. This misalignment will ultimately result in the perception that the PMO is failing to add value, even though it has been delivering on its intended mandate. Building-in a mechanism to ensure alignment and perform checks in predefined intervals will help ensure that the value produced by the PMO is both meaningful and on target.

10. **Establishing a PMO for the wrong reasons:** Before setting up a PMO, the stakeholders involved should go back to the question of why they should establish a PMO. It is not a sufficient reason to do so just because everyone else has a PMO, or because some projects are failing. PMOs can be established for any one or more of the following reasons: the desire for an organizational entity that will facilitate continuous improvement in the area of project management; to improve accuracy of project estimates; to help prioritize projects; to coordinate resources; to provide guidance for consistent project management; to improve support from senior management for projects, skills development, or facilitation and application of lessons learned. PMOs should have a clear set of objectives, success criteria, and challenges they are trying to address, which will help define the purpose of the PMO.

PMOs can help with a variety of causes and their functions, scope, span, staffing, and support levels should be determined based on the cause(s) for which they were undertaken. When setting up the PMO, we must keep in mind that no single PMO fits all organizations and even within the same organization, people, context, and expectations are different from one department to the next. This notion specifically applies to organizations that already have a PMO (e.g., for information technology) and are not attempting to duplicate the success to the business side. To address this, the organization can attempt to leverage success areas from an existing PMO, while keeping in mind that it may not be received in the same fashion across organizational boundaries.

Doing More with Less

Partially related to the capacity discussion, organizations are constantly trying to do more with less. The goal of the PMO and that of PMs is to do less with less. This is not about achieving less or completing less work, but rather, it is about focusing more on time management, prioritization, urgency assessment, and productivity. The PMO should become a center of excellence in helping PMs prioritize their work based on the organizational objectives and the projects' success criteria while taking on the function of helping resources manage their time more effectively. By becoming more proactive, productive, and efficient, PMOs will achieve their objectives with less effort. By providing guidance about basic communications, e-mail management, meeting management, and time management, the PMO can further increase the value it produces by helping stakeholders focus on value-added activities, while reducing non-value-added ones.

Lack of Communication, People Skills, Leadership, and Interpersonal Skills Management

With the growing recognition of the importance of interpersonal skills, leadership, and stakeholder expectations management in project management, PMOs should also shift more toward focusing on these areas. Without discounting the importance of resource coordination, reporting, training, consistency, and process management and improvement, these soft skills turn out to have significant impact on the ability of PMOs to deliver their intended value and help the organization grow. Rapport, trust, team building, motivating, influencing, inspiring, and becoming a trusted partner are skills and competencies that each member of the PMO must possess. In many organizations, the success of the PMO will, in fact, hinge on the rapport that is established between PMs and their PMO *representatives* and without these characteristics, little progress will be made in the areas of collaboration, innovation, taking initiative, and helping each other. Focusing on *right-brain* activities also involves fewer numbers and auto-pilot thinking and more consideration for people's needs.

What to Do so That PMOs Do Not Fail

There are two main approaches to reducing the failure rate of PMOs:

1. Properly set up the PMO from the start, with a clear business case, a specific and articulated reasoning for establishing it, understanding of its goals and which challenges it is set to address, a vision, a charter, a clear road map, roles and responsibilities, stakeholder analysis, and expectations management.
2. Review the common causes for PMO failure, focusing on these areas in the setup of the PMO (as a preventive measure), as well as while running it (as a corrective measure). Understanding the reasons why PMOs fail is the first step in developing special measures so that the PMO does not fail.

How to Establish a Successful PMO

Building a successful PMO involves steps that, although not complicated to perform, are often overlooked:

- **Position the PMO for success:** The PMO's level of sophistication, structure, and its funding will vary depending on the area it intends to improve. Before establishing a PMO, ensure that there is a sponsor and that senior management has a clear idea as to why they need a PMO. Merely establishing a PMO is not sufficient to ensure that the PMO delivers expected results, hence organizational leadership should set expectations upfront, define the organizational needs, and identify the desired value of the PMO to achieve this goal.
- **Ensure that accountability for the PMO comes from the top:** Whoever sets up the PMO needs to secure senior management support, establish a culture of collaboration, provide access to standardized tools and templates, set up transparent methods for selecting team members, build a knowledge library, put reporting mechanisms in place, and allow for the implementation of lessons learned programs.

Follow Logical Steps

1. Build a foundation for a successful PMO by identifying senior stakeholders and get their commitment to the PMO, write a PMO charter and a value proposition, specify the PMO funding source, identify resources, define desired results and goals, and select projects to be included.
2. Identify short-term objectives and initiatives, including targets for launching the PMO, acquisition of resources, tracking and reviewing projects, supporting new projects, and establishing criteria for PMO support and support for projects in need.
3. Specify long-term solutions including the development of areas of expertise, identification of process improvement and streamlining opportunities, building a mechanism to help identify, realize, and apply lessons learned, customization of project processes and methodology, and identification of tools and techniques.
4. Provide improvement and support by establishing baselines for project reporting metrics, improving project management processes, creating a process to identify areas of potential added value to be provided by the PMO, building personnel needs assessments and training programs, and establishing governance procedures.

RECAP: PORTFOLIO MANAGEMENT AND THE PMO

With PMOs established for a variety of reasons and with multiple scopes and mandates, it is important to define the reasons, mandate, and scope of each

PMO. Failing to do so is the first step toward mismanaging the PMO or the expectations of it, and both ultimately lead to PMO failure. In many organizations, PMOs face an environment that is similar to a pendulum, over time—shifting from too much focus on them, to too little, then back again—with this alone serving as a contributor to mismanaging expectations and PMO failures.

When establishing a PMO, the person heading it must act like a four-year-old in a way (albeit only one aspect of the behavior of a four-year-old) and ask *why* as many times as it takes, until there is a clear answer from high up in the organization regarding the reason for establishing a PMO. The answer should involve addressing real organizational requirements that are more than a set of *desire*ments, where the PMO is in search of a problem, instead of serving as an answer to a known issue.

With a staggering 25% of PMOs shut down after one year, 50% after two years, and 75% after three years, organizations must take care in establishing a PMO that will deliver on its promise and produce the intended value for the organization. As such, it must put an emphasis on people skills, leadership, trust building and motivation, so it becomes and is perceived to be a trusted partner to all stakeholders and PMs in particular.

PMO success hinges on having a clear vision, strong leadership, emphasis on stakeholder expectations management, a consistent approach to project management, well-defined roles and responsibilities, and strong risk management. These ingredients serve as the foundation for PMOs to deliver on their promises.

BAs TO THE RESCUE

The majority of the factors mentioned previously in relation to doing the right things to establish and effectively manage a PMO, may need to be supported by a BA—and if they are supported, they are more likely to succeed. Further, the typical causes for PMO failure are also related to business analysis and are rooted with the absence of effective BAs in the setup, day-to-day operations, and analysis of a PMO. In addition, excluding business analysis from PMOs diverts them away from fulfilling their value by serving as a direct arm of the portfolio function of the organization.

From the analysis of the organizational needs as part of the process to build a PMO, the articulating criteria for measuring the value produced by the PMO, business analysis skills are an integral part of these activities. Beyond the setup, BAs should also be part of the ongoing operation of the PMO, as well—including the integration of the EA into the portfolio matters that are under consideration. The PMO should also function as a project management office-business analysis office (PMO-BAO) to provide support for the discipline of business analysis in the organization in a similar fashion to the way PMOs support the project management discipline.

In fact, failing to integrate business analysis into the establishment, operations, and orientation of the PMO is not only damaging to the performance of the portfolio, the PMO, and the organization as a whole, but it is also a betrayal in the notion of integrating EA and portfolio management.

FINAL THOUGHTS ON ENTERPRISE ANALYSIS, PORTFOLIO MANAGEMENT, AND THE PMO

Despite the elaboration on the role of the PMO, this discussion clarifies that business analysis and specifically EA are integrated parts of delivering value through portfolio management and PMOs. The breakdown of each of the roles PMOs can assume in an organization shows the need for business analysis skills and therefore the need to support such skills under one umbrella. The activities reviewed in this section for which PMOs provide support for PMs and for organizations, such as communication management, change control, and risk management, all have specific areas related to the business analysis portion of the project, as well as to areas that require skills that BAs typically bring to the table—product expertise, business context, process management and improvement, communication skills, scope and requirements management, root-cause analysis, business case and feasibility analysis, identification of capability gaps, quality orientation, and the ability to articulate success criteria.

REFERENCES

1. Goodreads. (n.d.). Retrieved February 05, 2015, from http://www.goodreads.com/quotes/60780-if-i-had-an-hour-to-solve-a-problem-i-d.
2. Tenerowicz, C. L. (2009, January 22). *Cornell University*. Retrieved February 5, 2015, from https://confluence.cornell.edu/display/BAF/Enterprise+Analysis.
3. Project Management Institute Pulse of the Profession. (2014). *The High Cost of Low Performance.* Newton Square, PA: Project Management Institute.
4. Project Management Institute. (2015). *Business Analysis for Practitioners: A Practice Guide.* Newton Square, PA: Project Management Institute.

5. Project Management Institute. (2015). *Business Analysis for Practitioners: A Practice Guide.* Newton Square, PA: Project Management Institute.
6. Project Management Institute. (2015). *Business Analysis for Practitioners: A Practice Guide.* Newton Square, PA: Project Management Institute.
7. Project Management Institute. (2015). *Business Analysis for Practitioners: A Practice Guide.* Newton Square, PA: Project Management Institute.
8. The Agile Executive. (2010, January 11). *Standish Group Chaos Reports Revisited.* Retrieved February 9, 2015, from http://theagileexecutive.com/2010/01/11/standish-group-chaos-reports-revisited/.
9. Project Management Institute. (2013). *A Guide to the Project Management Body of Knowledge (PMBOK® Guide)—Fifth Edition.* Newton Square, Pennsylvania, USA: Project Management Institute, Inc.
10. Project Management Institute Pulse of the Profession. (2015). *Capturing the Value of Project Management.* Newton Square, PA: Project Management Institute.
11. http://solutions.sukad.com/.

5

COMMUNICATION AND STAKEHOLDER EXPECTATIONS MANAGEMENT

"The single biggest problem in communication is the illusion that it has taken place."—George Bernard Shaw

It is widely believed that the role of managing stakeholder expectations is almost exclusively associated with the project manager (PM). However, it is easy to explain what the role of the business analyst (BA) in managing stakeholder expectations should be—similar to that of the PM. In reality, however, it is more complicated, as there are some misconceptions around the role of the PM in managing expectations (let alone the misconceptions as to the role of the BA in managing expectations); as well as lack of clarity about the work division, the touch points, the integration of the two roles, and efforts to effectively and realistically manage expectations.

It is important to note that managing stakeholder expectations has multiple aspects, of which only one directly deals with communication. While the two knowledge areas in the *Project Management Body of Knowledge* (*PMBOK® Guide*)—Manage Communication and Manage Stakeholders—are closely related to each other, at its core (the area of managing expectations is driven by effective communication, relationship, and engagement planning) there are multiple areas of responsibility that are related or that feed into expectations management.

Managing stakeholder expectations requires an integrated approach—considering every action, the associated reaction to situations, impact areas, dependencies, resources, responses, and downstream effects. Furthermore, the effect has to be measured against both the project objectives and the business objectives. It is imperative that project decisions should not have uncontrolled or unknown negative implications on the organization, the business, or anything that feeds off the project. Even if project decisions end up producing a negative impact, it should be realized as early as possible, with its impacts articulated and approved by the appropriate level of authority.

THE SOURCE OF MOST PROBLEMS ON PROJECTS IS PEOPLE

The importance that stakeholder analysis has on project success is recognized, for the most part, by project stakeholders; however, we still lack in the process of translating this recognition into actions and allowing sufficient resources to conduct a meaningful stakeholder analysis. To clarify—the word *resources* refers to time, money, capacity, and the utilization of the right people at the right time; the word *meaningful* refers to performing the stakeholder analysis in context—that is, with the appropriate level of rigor, utilizing relevant knowledge and attempting to maximize the amount of meaningful information about stakeholders upon which to act.

In many environments the PM's attempts to engage in conducting stakeholder analysis do not produce the desired results and in addition to falling short of being effective, the effort is also inefficient. The PM—with limited knowledge of the project at its infant stages—does not know who to engage, does not ask the right questions, and lacks the ability to extrapolate meaningful information from the answers and the data collected. What makes the situation even worse is the lack of resources within the project that can shed meaningful light on a better understanding of the stakeholders' needs, leading to a reduction in wasted effort at later stages of the project that are due to miscalculated steps and lack of insight about stakeholders' needs, actions, and reactions.

When thinking of knowledgeable resources within the project team, the role that first comes to mind is the BA. Even if the BA assigned to the project is not the same one who took part in conducting the case study and feasibility analysis prior to the initiation of the project, the BA is typically more familiar with the organization than the PM, and the BA can utilize this knowledge to reach out to other people who were involved in the pre-project assessment and selection criteria. The BA is also more likely to gain access to additional information about the nature and needs of those involved, organizational structure, reporting lines, and other anecdotes about what to expect from stakeholders.

Involving the BA in the process of stakeholder analysis does not imply that the BA takes the lead in this role, or that the PM relies solely on the BA's knowledge. However, as part of the ongoing partnership between the PM and the BA, both of their insights will be significantly more valuable than if one of them conducts the stakeholder analysis on his or her own. When the BA conducts the stakeholder analysis, he or she is looking at it from a different angle—identifying stakeholders who will hold the most authentic information as sources for requirements. This additional lens often reveals additional stakeholders that the PM may have never considered.

The goal of stakeholder analysis is to understand what people and organizations around us want and need, and to determine which ones are more significant (due to their interest, ability to influence, status, or position). We do not need to know everything about everyone, and we do not try to build strategies to please everyone. Following the stakeholder analysis, we build a roadmap on how to engage the stakeholders by determining what type of communication style will accommodate their needs and how to set and manage their expectations. Informed stakeholders, who feel that they are included in the process to their level of satisfaction, will always be happier and more content than those who feel misinformed and excluded. Stakeholder analysis also helps us *pick our battles* so we can channel our efforts in directions that produce benefits and that are worth our effort.

MINI PM-BA ANALYSIS

As part of the process of conducting a stakeholder analysis the PM and the BA should also engage in assessing each other. Collaboration cannot be achieved if any one of the parties is unable or unwilling to cooperate and to pull their own weight. Becoming *one entity* and having a streamlined, focused, and aligned relationship with each other requires significant effort, coordination, and establishment of rules of engagement and ground rules—first between the PM and the BA, and subsequently with the other team members and stakeholders.

The keys for success of the PM-BA duo not only lie with the success of establishing positive relationships that are based on trust, partnership, and accountability, along with being of an ego-less nature; but also on the duo's ability to serve as role models and even as mentors for the rest of the team in the areas of stakeholder engagement management, expectations management, and communication.

The mini analysis is not quite the same as the regular analysis, as it involves only the PM-BA duo, and its core is based on conversations between the two—unlike the full-scale stakeholder analysis for the project that includes learning about stakeholders' needs, rather than asking them direct questions. The mini analysis involves five stages:

1. Collect insights about each other
2. Engage in a conversation and ask direct questions related to style, history, tendencies, drivers, and motivators
3. Retreat to assess the information collected and organize it into an action plan
4. Draft a strategy of how to engage each other and work together
5. Get together to discuss the findings and recommendations; put together an engagement and collaboration plan

Although these steps take time and effort, following them is absolutely critical for the success of the PM-BA collaboration, as this is the only way the members of this duo can achieve the desired level of collaboration in such a short period of time. The result of the mini stakeholder analysis is the first step in the PM-BA duo's effort to work together; moving forward, touch points should be established at regular intervals in order to make the necessary adjustments to maintain a sufficient level of collaboration, discuss issues, and work on improvements. Adopting a tactic of avoidance or accommodation (which are both common in conflict resolution) may backfire in the long run, as it will allow issues and challenges to go untreated and accumulate, which will inevitably lead to trust issues and to cracks in the working relations.

The PM-BA Contract

The PM-BA contract assists in setting up a collaborative working environment between the two individuals holding these roles. The intent is to turn the two into one entity that works seamlessly, effectively manages the project, and sets an example for the rest of the project team and the organization on how to work together effectively. This contract is the main enabler of the PM and the BA to build a new reality for these two roles and in turn, for a new path for success that they will create in their projects. In essence, it is about taking the reality of a lack of sufficient communication (that so many projects face) and turning it into effective communication through the establishment of a healthy dialogue between the two roles.

The dialogue is facilitated by aligning the methodologies of both roles and ensuring there is no duplication of effort, mixed messages, redundancies, or gaps in project areas. According to the *PMBOK® Guide* and the *Business Analysis Body of Knowledge* (*BABOK®*), sometimes speaking in different languages and using terminology in different contexts creates two competing realities—one for the PM and the other for the BA. We are now moving toward having a new reality where the Project Management Institute Project Business Analysis (PMI-PBA) methodology for BAs is fully aligned with the project management methodology.

Having the methodologies aligned, however, is not sufficient on its own. It serves only as the first step in enhancing the communication between the PM and the BA toward becoming a fruitful dialogue where both sides express their desires, needs, agendas, interests, and approaches; and in turn, each side listens and provides feedback until the PM-BA duo can achieve the collaboration required for project success.

The PM-BA contract is where the duo's shared values are expressed, documented, and developed, under the following headers:

- **Alignment to organizational strategy, policies, and rules:** The alignment can be achieved with the support of the project management office (PMO) or the project sponsor, who should act as a facilitator for the alignment process.
- **Standards and best practices:** Once again, the PMO (along with the business analysis function within it) should facilitate and regulate any standards, practices, processes, and other organizational process assets to support the project work of the PM and the BA.
- **The PM-BA duo's shared values:** The contract should also address the PM-BA duo's shared values and the culture they are trying to establish for the project—including values related to integrity, accountability, respect, partnership, commitment, and other personal values. Alongside these values, the contract should stipulate what specific actions the PM and the BA should take to ensure these values are fulfilled.

The PM-BA contract includes additional sections that will further streamline their working relations, including the following:

- **Define roles and responsibilities:** Address all the touch points between the PM and the BA—define who does what, and how information will flow between the members of the duo, as well as between the PM-BA and the team and other stakeholders. This section also defines the specific roles of the PM and the BA to ensure all their associated activities and tasks are assigned.
- **Skills review:** The contract discusses the experience and skills the PM and the BA bring to the table and assigns specific tasks to each individual in a way that ensures both the PM and the BA engage in activities they are each good at and that each individual also gets a chance to develop their skills.

- **Rules of engagement:** Similar to the set of ground rules established for the entire project team, the contract specifies rules of engagement for the PM and the BA; including the frequency of update meetings, how information should flow between the two individuals, the reports they will produce for each other, and the style of the communication. The contract should also address escalation procedures for disputes and disagreements, and a mechanism for conflict resolution between the members of the duo. The escalation procedures and conflict resolution mechanism should also address anything related to the PM-BA duo's communication with team members and other stakeholders.
- **Decision making:** As not all decisions in the project are to be made by the PM, the contract also specifies how decisions will be made, and it divides the authority between the PM and the BA according to their areas of responsibility and expertise. The contract also divides the areas of communication between the PM and the BA to ensure there is no duplication of effort or mixed messages in the interaction with team members and stakeholders. Furthermore, the contract should have placeholders for future decisions on who will be in charge of engaging specific stakeholders. Due to the specific stakeholders' needs, the different communication styles that stakeholders have, and the different areas of expertise that the PM and the BA have, it is important to ensure that the most appropriate person addresses each stakeholder to facilitate the flow of information and capitalize on the relationships based on the unique styles and areas of focus the PM and the BA bring to the table.
- **Friction points:** The contract also directly addresses the traditional friction points and areas that may produce conflict between the PM and the BA—for example, what each individual expects from the other, any expectations that each individual has for their role and from the other person, as well as assumptions, constraints, issues, and obstacles.

The BA Package

An important deliverable the BA should produce in the early stage of the project is the BA package. This is an information package that the BA who worked on the pre-project activities produces for the PM and the project BA (if a different BA is assigned to work on the project) in an effort to bring the PM and the project BA up to speed and inform them about basic considerations, objectives, and business needs related to the project. Creating such a package does not require extensive effort, and it would provide significant value for the PM-BA duo toward understanding the context of the project.

Although the information package is not a traditional part of the mini stakeholder analysis, the information in the package will help serve as a foundation that will shape the need to define areas of focus and other touch points between the PM and the BA.

THE REAL DEAL—UNDERSTANDING STAKEHOLDERS

Project failures can often be traced to a missing or poorly conducted stakeholder analysis, and although there is never sufficient time to conduct one, there really is no way around it. Working together, the PM and the BA can achieve a level of understanding of stakeholder needs that is sufficient for project needs and takes less combined effort than if the PM attempts to perform it alone.

Stakeholder analysis is one of several early project activities that does not get sufficient attention by PMs, and as a result creates deficiencies that escalate throughout the project life cycle and end up costing the project dearly in terms of time, money, misunderstandings, conflicts, and wasted effort. Stakeholder analysis is not the goal, but rather the means of the PM to channel the project team's effort effectively and efficiently, and it is a proven approach to deal with a variety of realities and challenges that projects face on an ongoing basis.

- **Goal setting:** Many stakeholders do not express their objectives clearly and as a result, project goals and success criteria are not always defined properly, where adjectives and descriptions seem to replace the need for specific and measurable objectives. With unclear objectives and requirements, the project team will have a hard time doing the right thing and in turn, the decision makers will lack criteria to determine what success should look like.
- **Team building:** Efforts related to team building need to be tailored to the team's needs; since the stakeholder analysis involves team members, it will provide valuable insight on team members' needs and on how to effectively engage them and improve team performance.
- **Culture:** Stakeholder analysis can help the PM and the BA better understand the organizational culture and existing best practices for engaging stakeholders, sharing information, escalation, and general conduct. No two organizations are the same, and even within one organization there could be multiple different cultures. It is therefore important for the PM-BA duo to understand the environment in which they operate and build an appropriate approach to effectively handle it. The intent here is not to change cultures or organizations—as this is next to impossible, especially for the short term—but rather to learn about the people who make up these organizations and how to approach them. A short-term

prospect for the PM and the BA would be to establish a culture of collaboration among team members and potentially among additional stakeholders. Specifically with team members, such collaboration needs to start with getting people to work together and make a genuine effort to help one another. The PM and the BA need to lead this effort and guide team members toward focusing on helping each other; including facilitating sessions where the main question to be asked is—"how can I help you?" and "what can I do to improve our ability to work together?" Without such effort, existing challenges in the working relations among team members will not be addressed and will typically escalate with time.

The BA's Ability to Contribute to the Stakeholder Analysis

Managing stakeholder expectations is one of the most important tasks in a project and as such, requires meaningful contribution from both the PM and the BA. With the PM typically leading this effort, the BA role is important, both at providing support for the PM, as well as in leading aspects of the expectations management task.

As the BA leads the efforts in several areas within the project, it is only appropriate to have the BA lead the associated aspects of addressing stakeholder needs and managing their expectations. For example, with the BA leading the product requirements management effort, anything that pertains to product requirements should be facilitated and led by the BA; including addressing stakeholder concerns, keeping them informed, and exchanging information with them. Additional areas where the BA should take the lead are related to ensuring that the *product* requirements transition seamlessly into *project* requirements; helping to define objectives in terms that are not only specific and measurable, but also take into consideration all aspects of the project—from product functionality to business needs.

The area of team building is another example of the BA's ability to make a meaningful contribution. The BA typically works closely with many team members and thus, has the opportunity to develop a rapport with them and help generate buy-in among the team members. The BA serves as an agent or an ambassador for the PM, and it is an opportunity for the BA to utilize his or her relationship-building skills for this task. The same skills come into play in building relationships with stakeholders who are not part of the project team. With different personalities, the PM and the BA can double their chances of developing a good rapport with team members and with stakeholders—as communication and interactions can be led by either the PM or the BA, depending on the style and focus areas required.

The areas of planning a specific risk management can also receive significant support from the BA, since the BA introduces requirements related risks into the project risks (as discussed in the Risk section of Chapter 7 of this book). The BA also helps the PM in combating people's tendencies related to instant gratification which may translate into taking shortcuts in planning, undermining the potential impact of risks, and pushing toward moving ahead with producing deliverables with insufficient due-diligence and incomplete planning. The urge for showing immediate results often comes at the price of moving forward too fast and failing to address potential obstacles and challenges along the way.

Having both the PM and the BA *on guard* and in leading positions for the task of managing stakeholder expectations can also serve as a check and balance mechanism that gets the PM and the BA to ensure that their colleague in the duo performs his or her role properly and to the best possible extent.

Sources of Uncertainty

Identifying and proactively managing the sources of risks and uncertainty provides several benefits to the project—it helps the PM and the BA identify early indicators for areas that may lead to risks; it helps address risk areas that are associated with specific stakeholders; and with that, it helps improve the relationship with stakeholders by proactively addressing their areas of concern. Furthermore, it helps communicate risks and areas of risk effectively to the stakeholders and it helps address their concerns, seek alternatives or resolutions, and it brings us closer to being able to satisfy stakeholders' needs. With both the PM and the BA engaged in this process, it improves our ability to cover all areas that may produce risks and plan for most of the events that may threaten our ability to deliver project success, value, and benefits. It also means that the risk events the duo can cover would include project risks, product/requirement risks, business and organizational related risks, as well as events that concern the needs of specific stakeholders.

With the PM and the BA working together, we need to look at common sources of risks that look into deeper areas of PMI's risk breakdown structure, including:

- Requirements
- Complexity and readiness assessments
- Assumptions and constraints
- Environment and political considerations
- Organizational priorities—other projects and initiatives in the organization
- Estimates and plans
- Tools and processes
- Changes to the project

STAKEHOLDER ANALYSIS

The process of identifying, analyzing, and managing stakeholders is not a one-time thing at the start of the project. It is an ongoing process that needs to take place at various points throughout the project. Defining the process and its goals and objectives can help set up a target of how to measure when a necessary and satisfying set of information has been obtained:

1. *Identify the project stakeholders*: The PM and the BA should think together, while also engaging the sponsor, customer, and other stakeholders who are already known to be involved. By definition, a stakeholder is anyone who has an interest in the project, which broadens the scope of stakeholder analysis to beyond those who are involved or impacted. Anyone who has an *interest* in the project has the potential to influence the project and will need to be identified and managed accordingly. Unfortunately, the troublemakers are often the ones who have high interest in the project, but are not impacted or involved because they flew under the radar during stakeholder analysis.
2. *Stakeholder analysis*: Learn about what the stakeholders want, need, expect, what stake they have in the project, and how much influence they have on the project and its results. Also consider their disposition toward the project and toward other stakeholders, along with their expected responses to situations and challenges.
3. *Stakeholder engagement plan*: Develop a plan to engage them and manage their expectations.

Make Assumptions When You Have to

It is likely that, despite their efforts, the PM and the BA still do not have a clear picture of everyone who has an interest in the project, let alone a clear understanding of the stakeholders' characteristics and tendencies. At this point, many PMs often proceed with their planning without completing the analysis, virtually giving up on obtaining this information. While it is not imperative to get a complete set of information about all stakeholders, a certain level of understanding is required in order to proceed effectively and efficiently with the planning of the project.

An effective solution to the challenge of gathering the full amount of information needed is to resort to making assumptions. When information is missing about potential stakeholders, the PM-BA duo can make assumptions about the nature of stakeholder involvement, including their likely positions and reactions to situations. Assumptions should not just come out of thin air or be seasoned by hope—it is important to keep in mind that any assumption needs to be documented and in turn, revisited periodically until validated or refuted.

Stakeholders and the Requirements

There are countless benefits to obtaining vital information about project stakeholders that subsequently leads to engaging them and managing their expectations and impact over the project effectively. One benefit is that it can also help with the project requirements and scoping since it is likely that at some point, the project manager will need to go through the process of prioritizing requirements. The result is either the need to remove some requirements altogether or to change the order in which they are delivered. Removing features, functionalities, and their associated requirements is never an easy decision to make, especially since stakeholders get quite attached (sometimes emotionally) to their requirements. Moreover, cross-requirement dependencies and other considerations make the process much more complex than it was initially thought to be. The PM does not have the capacity, or sufficient knowledge, to ensure requirements prioritization is aligned with the stakeholders; the BA possesses such information and can provide the PM with additional context that can save a lot of hassle and unnecessary changes downstream, if done correctly in the beginning.

Most projects have some sort of prioritization scheme for the requirements: from the Must, Should, Could, Would (MoSCoW) method to functional and technical considerations (and sometimes there are even proprietary methods to rank and prioritize requirements). Despite the strong need and the available tools to assist with this task, it is surprising that in many projects, there is no method or approach for requirements prioritization altogether—leaving it to chance and causing fierce arguments as part of the descoping exercises.

One of the challenges concerning requirements prioritization is that there is often no systematic way of checking which stakeholder is associated with which requirements. This can be managed by gaining knowledge about the association of stakeholders to requirements (i.e., which stakeholder requested, paid for, or needed each requirement). A visual scheme, as demonstrated in Figure 5.1, can then be applied to help map each requirement's importance to the project and the level of complexity associated with it. By placing the requirements grid next to the stakeholder grid (the output from conducting the stakeholder analysis), it gives the PM and the BA an opportunity to map each requirement to the stakeholders associated with it. Complexity is mostly related to technical considerations, and importance is rated by whether a requirement is part of a minimum feature set and which stakeholder is associated with it. The location of each requirement on the grid should be based on these two criteria:

1. *Requirements' complexity*: The level of complexity (complexity refers to technical aspects and dependencies) associated with the requirement is called the requirement complexity. The BA should pursue clear

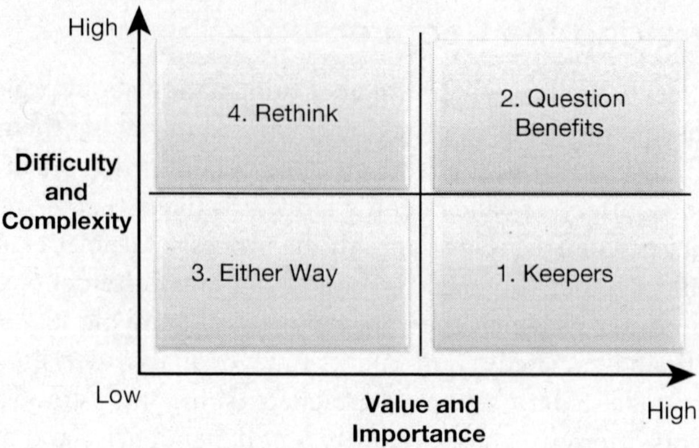

Figure 5.1 The requirements grid

measurements as to what makes a requirement complex. For the most part, the technical team will be able to provide the majority of the answers for these items, allowing the PM to come up with a complexity ranking for the requirements at stake. One method to measure technical complexity can be to count the number of technology components needed to implement a requirement; for example, modifications to interface, database, and the connection between interface and database equals three technology components. The complexity scale will also need to be defined; for example low complexity could mean one to two technology components, medium complexity could mean three to four, and high complexity could mean five or more. The complexity level can be documented as a requirement attribute, and in this example; the complexity level would be documented as medium complexity. The definition of complexity and the complexity scale can, and should, be modified to suit the organization and the project.

2. *Requirements' importance*: Importance is, first and foremost, based on whether a requirement is part of a minimum set of functionality and how critical it is to the success of the project. This information can be provided by the BA. Subsequently, the PM and the BA need to consider the value and importance of the requirement to each stakeholder by determining which stakeholder(s) is/are associated with the requirement and what the implications would be of changing or removing the requirement. This analysis requires multiple areas of consideration, including the stakeholder analysis.

Manage the Stakeholders

The key to the success of stakeholder management is utilizing the information that is gained by setting expectations upfront, engaging the stakeholders appropriately, and maintaining those relationships by dealing in the currencies and values the stakeholders understand and care about, so that their needs are met in a timely manner. Following these guidelines also allows a PM to focus on what matters in the project, which is delivering its value and benefits and reducing the level of distractions.

Being Proactive

The results of the stakeholder analysis should serve as a foundation for the project communication plan and stakeholders' engagement plan; but even after completing the analysis, significant pieces of information may still be missing. The stakeholder analysis results should not stop the project planning process from moving forward, nor should it stop the PM from trying to obtain any valuable, missing information about the stakeholders. Failure to address the needs of important stakeholders or to understand their expectations will end up being costly as the project moves forward.

STAKEHOLDER ENGAGEMENT AND EXPECTATIONS MANAGEMENT

With the knowledge gained during the stakeholder analysis process, it is time to plan for the stakeholder management and engagement process. While related to communication planning, it is not quite a communications plan yet—a communications plan is more tactical, dealing with the day-to-day aspects of the project.

This is more about the strategy and concepts that will shape the communications plan to make it effective, relevant, and appropriate. Effective stakeholder engagement management supports the project by helping us understand both internal and external environments and by enabling us to respond, influence, and initiate actions accordingly. It improves our ability to maintain a consistent approach and maintain sensitivities to specific stakeholders' needs and to policies, procedures, and issues—taking into account the stakeholders' interests and project needs.

How to Engage

The process of conducting stakeholder engagement can be broken down into three elements:

1. *Inform*: There is a need to keep stakeholders informed by providing them with objective, consistent, accurate, and appropriate information. *Appropriate* refers to making sure that each stakeholder gets the information they need to know—no less and no more (especially not more). Giving stakeholders more information than what they need to know will lead to distractions and misunderstandings.
2. *Work with them*: Work together to exchange feedback and ensure that needs and concerns are understood and taken into consideration on both sides.
3. *Collaborate and energize*: Create working partnerships with stakeholders for decision making and process improvements. This includes providing advice to each other, considering each other's points of view, and seeking win-win solutions.

To make the relationship with the stakeholder successful, the PM must utilize the BA to not only leverage the depth that the BA brings to the table, but also the BA's style and personality, as an alternative point of contact with some of the stakeholders.

A commonly used tool that is helpful in managing stakeholder engagement is a table that can help guide us regarding the stakeholders' disposition toward our project and where we need them to be (see Table 5.1). This simple table lists the stakeholders by names or by groups, against their attitude, disposition, or level of commitment as we know it. We then mark where the stakeholders are, where we need them to be for project success, and potentially, where we can still have them at a minimum. Based on this grid the PM-BA duo can now put together a plan on how to approach, engage, and deal with each stakeholder (or group), determine what it takes to move them from their current level of commitment to where the duo needs them to be, and determine what type of alternative approach is necessary (or alternative stakeholder to engage).

DEFINING SUCCESS

The process of baselining parts of the project plan (specifically, scope, time, and cost) is an important step in defining project success because it helps us focus on what needs to be done and to evaluate the results against these plans. Although important, the project baseline is not the only thing we need to do in order to define success—as success needs to be defined and articulated early in the project, possibly during the writing of the project charter, and it has to be directly related to the project objectives.

An important component of defining project success criteria is defining, articulating, and illustrating the impact of trade-offs among the components

Table 5.1 Stakeholder engagement management plan

The stakeholder engagement plan shows stakeholder's current stance toward the project versus the desired state we are trying to achieve. There is also an option to further elaborate and state realistic expectations of where we want each stakeholder to be, as well as a position called "I can live with it".

		STAKEHOLDER ANALYSIS							
1									
2–3	**Level of Commitment**	Stakeholder 1	Stakeholder 2	Stakeholder 3	Stakeholder 4	Stakeholder 5	Stakeholder 6	Stakeholder 7	Stakeholder 8
4	Enthusiastic			D		X D	D	X D	
5	Helpful	D	D		D		X	X	D
6	Compliant			X				X	
7	Hesitant	X			X			X	
8	Indifferent		X						X
9	Uncooperative								X
10	Opposed								X
11	Actively Hostile								
12									
13	**Key:**								
14	**D** - Desired - Level Necessary for Success								
15	**R** - Realistic Level Expected								
16	**C** - Can live with (Minimal level for success)								
17	**X - Current Level**								
18									
19									
20	The Plan:								
21	1. What it takes to move a stakeholder from where they are to where we need them to be								
22	2. What would be an alternative approach when we cannot move the stakeholders								
23	3. What alternative stakeholder we can engage and how, instead of moving an existing stakeholder								
24									

that define success. These components are the elements that are going to be measured as success indicators—some of them are tied to the project constraints and they are referred to as the *competing demands*:

- **Scope:** What we are going to deliver (all the features, functionalities, and functions) is known as the scope. This is a project success measure, since it checks what the project ends up delivering against what the project was supposed to deliver. Most of the project planning revolves around the scope (timelines, resources, and costs are estimated around what we need to do) and the extent to which the product (or service, or result) that we produce ties to quality, benefits, and the perceived value we produce.
- **Time:** This is the schedule and timelines for what we need to deliver, with milestones indicating when we are doing it to provide the promised value (or the scope items that are in the plan). The schedule is a project success indicator, along with being a constraint, that unfortunately, often prevents us from delivering the full value of what we do, due to the need to deliver it on time. Even though it is a project success criterion, it has heavy impact on the product and the business success, it is a visible indicator of success, and it is one of the most common causes of project failure. Failing to deliver according to the milestones is also related to poor quality, thus on certain occasions, the time serves as the most important success criteria.
- **Cost:** Cost management is similar to time management, with two significant differences—(1) the impact of a delay is hard to assess because it varies, depending on when it takes place, while it is easier to evaluate a cost overrun; (2) most delays on projects do not only affect timelines, but also the cost—even if work stops it is likely that overhead costs continue to be expended. Add to that the constant pressure for cost savings even after budgets have been determined and it makes cost management, like time, a major indicator of project success and a constraint that often prevents the project from delivering its full value, or even being completed at all. It is important to keep in mind that money alone is not going to directly help deliver success, as the money has to be spent on acquiring or utilizing resources that help perform the work. To illustrate this point: a pile of cash delivered to a project a day before a deadline will not help the project avoid missing the deadline, unless we have the ability to use this money toward something that can help us meet the deadline—such as acquiring resources, machines, tools, or materials.
- **Resources:** This component of the competing demands is tied to costs (as it costs money to utilize resources of any kind) and although it is an

important means to deliver success, it is not a direct measure of success. At the end of a failed project it is important to check whether resource management contributed to the failure (for lessons learned purposes), but even if resource management has not been part of the problem, it will not change the fact that there was a failure to deliver success. Scope, time, cost, and quality are the main determinants of success.

- **Risks:** Similar to resources, risks are not a factor in defining success, but rather a means to deliver success. Risks (in the context of threats) are events that impede our ability to deliver success; they are not constraints.
- **Quality:** Beyond the *official* definitions of quality, people and organizations have a hard time defining what quality really stands for and how to measure it. For a project to be able to deliver success, we must define what quality is in the eyes of the important stakeholders. Quality is tied to the value, benefits, the characteristics of the product, the extent to which it performs, and whether or not the product does what it was intended to do. But quality can also be tied to the timelines, costs, and functionality (scope) of what we do. Articulating quality is an important step toward defining what is important to stakeholders and toward defining success. By understanding what we view as quality, we can then define what else is important for us and the tolerance levels we will have toward spending more time and assuming risks. It will also help in determining how much money we are willing to spend in order to achieve quality and on which areas and items the money should be spent. There is another challenge regarding quality—delivering the quality standards may be in conflict with other measures of project success, such as time and money.

The PM, the BA, and the Definition of Success

Many of the success criteria have inherent conflict with each other and even within them; delivering project success may not be aligned with delivering the product success that the project tries to produce. Lack of understanding by the project team or by key stakeholders of what constitutes success will lead to multiple versions of what success is—causing confusion and ultimately, project failure.

Narrowing down the competing demands to four key aspects of success—scope, time, cost, and quality—is the first step in defining project success. Then it is necessary to articulate the trade-offs among these areas and to identify a success definition that makes sense to all key stakeholders—especially the project sponsor, the customer, and the project team. Due to the strong integration of the four components of project success (with each other and with other external factors), nothing less than the joint effort of the PM and the BA will be able to articulate success accurately, with the following considerations:

- **Scope:** This is what the project needs to do to produce the product. It is driven by the requirements and there is a critical need to ensure the requirements are streamlined into the project scope properly, with no losses or distortions. This also includes the boundaries of the scope, to ensure that the project does all it needs to—but only what it needs to do. Although the PM is in charge of developing the work breakdown structure (WBS), it cannot be done without input from the BA regarding the requirements and further analysis by the BA, to ensure items are placed on the WBS in a logical way that is intuitive for the team and from a product perspective. The BA can also provide input toward the logical grouping of items on the WBS, to facilitate resource estimates for deliverables, and to ensure all (and only the relevant) activities are identified for each deliverable.
- **Time and cost:** The help that the BA provides will directly and indirectly help the PM come up with time and cost estimates that are in line with what needs to be done, the availability of resources, and the right mix of the competing demands to meet success. Prioritization of the requirements and identification of dependencies among requirements and against any external factors are also coming from the BA and are valuable in ensuring that realistic time and cost estimates are produced, and that the project actually has the ability to deliver on them.
- **Quality:** The integration and the appropriate trade-off among all the considerations that impact success make up quality—in addition to the BA's information regarding not only the functional requirements, but also nonfunctional requirements, stakeholder requirements, and transitional requirements. All of these ensure that standards are defined and that there are plans to meet them, that specifications and documentation are defined, that continuous improvement activities are built into the processes, and that assurance (i.e., audits and process reviews) and controls (i.e., inspection and testing) are planned and accounted for. Safety, security, scalability, maintainability, and other product attributes need to be defined, so they can be planned and accounted for.

The Balloon Theory

An effective way to articulate the trade-offs and the relationships and interactions among the competing demands can be done through the Balloon Theory, as illustrated in Figure 5.2; explaining to stakeholders how the trade-offs work

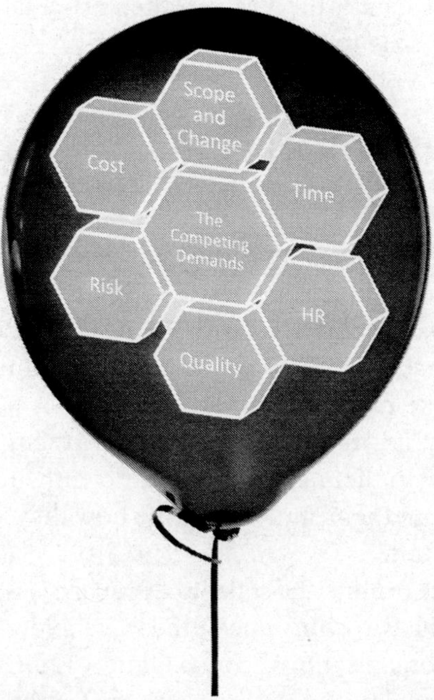

The balloon illustration of competing demands helps articulate to stakeholders the impact of project trade-offs; just like with a balloon—when pressing on one side, something needs to give elsewhere or quality suffers.

Source: Schibi, Ori. *Managing Stakeholder Expectations for Project Success* (2013), J. Ross Publishing

Figure 5.2 The competing demands trade-off balloon theory

and illustrating that, like the laws of physics, one of the competing demands cannot *give* without an equal *compensation* from at least one other. For example, if the customer asks for more functionality, something of an equal value needs to be adjusted—either with the timelines, within the budget (to acquire resources), or by removing an equal amount of work from other functionalities (scope). If the balance is not maintained, it will lead to more risks and ultimately, to the unacceptable result of quality deficiencies.

Many PMs have been in situations where stakeholders promise future considerations, promotions, bonuses, or lunches in return for adding scope items. These do not work, as we must be fully accountable for any pressure we apply against the balloon. The BA can help provide context and assistance in conducting an impact assessment, along with recommendations for reprioritization, whenever the balance of the competing demands is threatened as a result of a request or performance; the PM can then articulate this information and communicate it effectively to the stakeholders.

THE COMMUNICATION GAP

The PM and the BA have a multilayered role when it comes to communications; they need to ensure effective communication takes place with the team, with other stakeholders, and with each other. The value of performing a meaningful stakeholder analysis is already clear, and despite the realization and recognition of the value of doing so, in too many projects this foundational and important task still does not take place. Stakeholder analysis is not only about knowing the people around us; it is mainly about knowing them in context and crafting a strategy to engage with them, keep them sufficiently informed, figure out how to get information from them, and determine how they are expected to respond to challenging situations.

The BA's role in performing the stakeholder analysis is not only important due to the familiarity of the BA with some of the stakeholders, with the product, and often, even with the organizational context; but it is also important that the BA take part in the stakeholder analysis to ensure the BA's buy-in and involvement in strategizing the approach to handle the stakeholders. Furthermore, the BA is also likely to directly handle some of the communication channels with key stakeholders and therefore, needs to have a say about the process, the approach, and the means of communication. The value that the BA adds to this process also involves the application of knowledge and considerations that are part of the enterprise analysis and any insights the BA might have about the success criteria, areas of complexity, organizational readiness, and resource allocation.

Despite the best efforts in conducting the stakeholder analysis process, there may still be gaps in the understanding of stakeholders' needs and styles and even in realization of whether or not stakeholders are involved in the project. Since we are not pursuing perfection in these areas, our goal is to improve our understanding of stakeholders and our ability to communicate with them effectively. We should also note that since we do not live in a perfect world, there is a chance that we may not anticipate certain things and potential reactions even for stakeholders that we thought we understood well.

Similarly, our communication with stakeholders may not be perfect due to styles, *noise* in the system, varying levels of expectations, and other project-related circumstances; we may find ourselves in situations where, despite our efforts to communicate effectively, our message may not go through. Due to various interruptions, a gap may be created between what we say and what certain stakeholders hear and understand. Figure 5.3 illustrates such potential

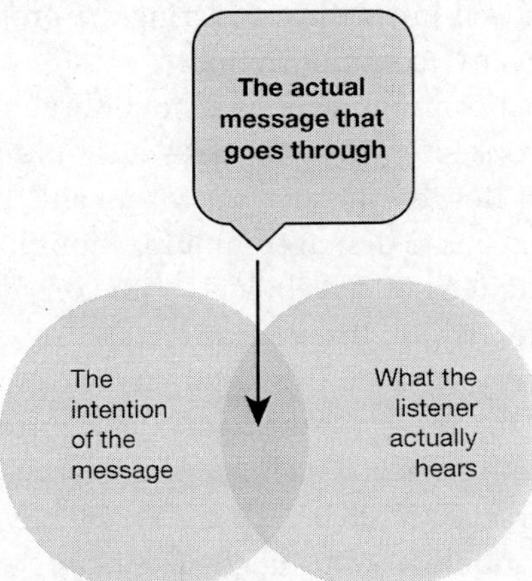

One of the core causes of miscommunications: a gap between what stakeholders intend to say and what their counterparts actually hear. It often results in only a portion of the message actually going through.

Source: www.pmKonnectors.com

Figure 5.3 The communication gap

gaps. One of the important steps to avoid situations like this is to recognize that it could take place, then take measures so that it doesn't. Overcoming this gap is what we mean when we say *effective communication*—which is when the message is sent and received as intended.

Communication Planning and Related Contracts

The goal of project communication management is to design and control project communications in such a way that it will accommodate the needs of stakeholders and, at the same time, promote collaboration and enable project success. One of the most important aspects of the communication management plan is to establish a clear, open, and streamlined route of ongoing communication between the PM and the BA and in turn, to build an approach for delivering a consistent message between the PM-BA duo and the rest of the team and stakeholders. The communication between the duo and all other stakeholders involved requires the maximization of the capacities, abilities, connections, and channels that the PM and the BA have. This is the time to leverage personalities, styles, and relationships so the PM and the BA can effectively *get* to anyone and everyone affected by the project. It is important to note that developing such effective communication capabilities requires significant effort, coordination, careful planning, and ongoing improvement to the process and the approach;

an investment that is well-justified considering the project stakes involved and the importance of effective communication.

The setup of project communications is not only about a generic enabling of communication in a *one-size-fits-all* format—it should proactively establish an effective and efficient flow of information within and around the project. Proactive, in this sense, means to design communications in such a way that it takes the needs and expectations of stakeholders into consideration and maximizes the flow of information within these constraints.

PMs and BAs need to discuss the components of the communication plan and its options with the project stakeholders and introduce the meaning and intentions behind them. When stakeholders understand the reasoning behind certain actions, it increases the chance that they will buy in and support the process. The discussion should also include engaging report recipients and setting expectations about reporting formats to avoid misunderstandings and issues related to the structure and content of the reports.

The Communication Plan

The communication plan consists of elements that ensure the effective flow of information, as well as establish ground rules and expectations about the daily interactions among team members and project stakeholders. Traditionally, a communication plan has two components:

1. *A breakdown of ongoing team and stakeholder communication events*: This will assist with focusing on the deliverable description, method of delivery, frequency, owner, and audience.
2. *A list of specific, one-time (e.g., milestone-related) communication events*: The difference between this and the first component of the communication plan is that this one is aligned with the project milestone list and details the communication events associated with it.

The communication plan document also contains more standard information (some of which may be available from the organization or from previous projects) that needs to be customized to the specific project requirements—including organizational structure, reporting lines, communication processes, and guidelines regarding communication for specific project matters.

Project management standards indicate that PMs should produce a communication plan outlining their communication with stakeholders, and the business analysis standards indicate that BA's should do the same. To avoid confusion and the potential for overlap, the communication plan should be consolidated for both the PM and the BA to provide a single view of the communications between the PM-BA duo and the stakeholders.

TEAM CONTRACT AND GROUND RULES

After the PM and the BA establish their own PM-BA contract for their internal rules of engagements, it is time to build a set of *ground rules* for the team and the other stakeholders to be articulated in a team contract. The ground rules consist of behavioral guidelines that help facilitate communication between the PM-BA duo and the team, among team members, and between the project team and external stakeholders. These ground rules can also be established under certain circumstances for external stakeholders, which will help narrow the gap between stakeholder expectations and the way communication and events take place in the project, thereby reducing the chance for misunderstandings or unnecessary or possibly uncontrolled conflicts. The nature of the guidelines and the level of detail they involve have to be based on organizational culture, on previous projects' events, and on the make-up of the team.

The content of the team contract should be grouped into the following categories:

- Guidelines for general communication
- E-mail code of conduct
- Meeting expectations (including teleconferences)

General Communication

This area deals with establishing general guidelines for communication and for how team members should interact with each other and with other stakeholders. There are two parts to general communication guidelines:

1. *Aspiring behaviors*: These are behaviors that the team should strive to espouse; they are not measurable and therefore team members cannot be held in violation of any of these behaviors, but all team members should commit to following these principles.
2. *Code of conduct and ground rules*: These are like fences that are put in place to help build relationships, set expectations, and protect each other's territory. They *can* be measured, and team members should adhere to these ground rules.

There are similarities between the two lists in places where the aspiring behavior should become more specific. This section focuses on the communication code of conduct and ground rules as displayed in Figure 5.4.

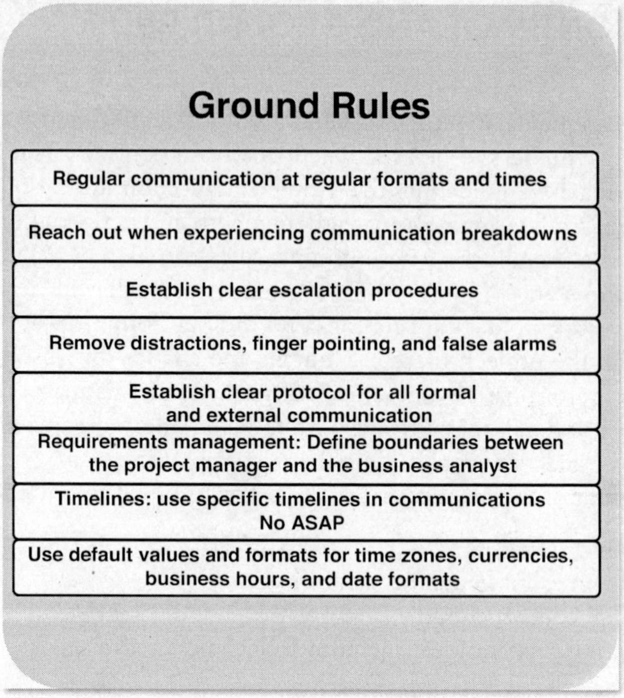

Ground Rules

Regular communication at regular formats and times

Reach out when experiencing communication breakdowns

Establish clear escalation procedures

Remove distractions, finger pointing, and false alarms

Establish clear protocol for all formal and external communication

Requirements management: Define boundaries between the project manager and the business analyst

Timelines: use specific timelines in communications No ASAP

Use default values and formats for time zones, currencies, business hours, and date formats

Figure 5.4 Communication code of conduct and ground rules

E-mails

E-mail was introduced many years ago with the great promise of streamlining communication and enabling almost real-time communication across the world. Since then, many e-mails have been sent and received—and it appears that the promise has turned into one big load of work that consumes a significant amount of time for each and every person in the organization. Although e-mail is a basic function that can be performed and handled (on the technical side) by essentially everyone in the organization, there is a strong need for establishing some ground rules that will govern the use of e-mail, reduce the volume of e-mails, and ensure that e-mail actually adds value to the project, rather than just consuming time and energy. Figure 5.5 illustrates the guidelines for effective use of e-mail.

Meetings

In most projects and organizations, meetings are a drag that, for the most part, can be summed up by describing them as dysfunctional. A PM can get a realistic

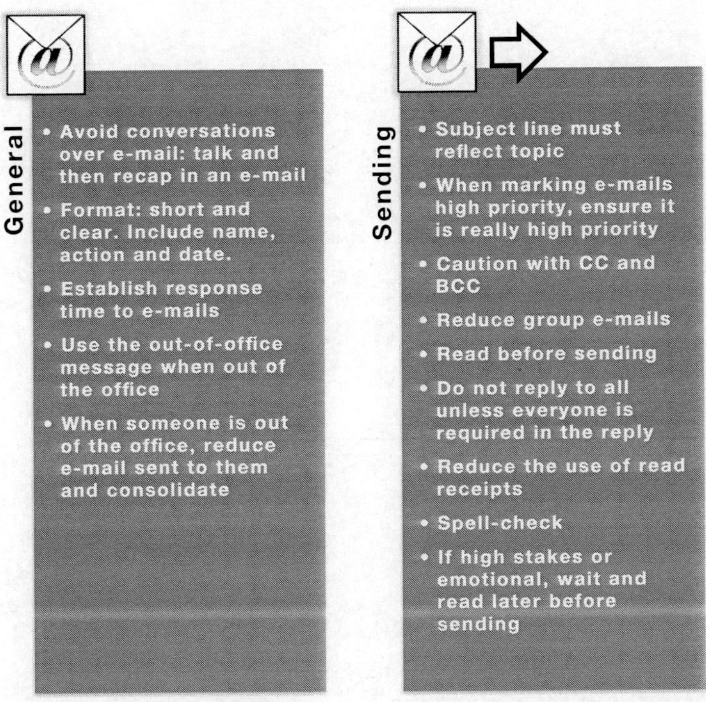

Figure 5.5 E-mail guidelines

picture of the state of a project simply by walking into a project meeting with their ears plugged and *looking* at how the meeting is managed. Project meetings may not only serve as a reflection of the state of the project, but they can often serve as an indication that even if the performance does not lag, there may be signs of trouble.

Well-run meetings are an asset to the project and the organization, and since they are such a rare commodity, they may serve as a morale booster for the team and be seen as a key to the success of projects. To help project managers and team members run effective meetings that add value to the project and the organization, Figures 5.6 and 5.7 recommend guidelines to consider.

CONFLICT MANAGEMENT

We already know that conflict is not a bad thing—or rather, constructive conflict is not a bad thing, as opposed to unconstructive (which is a bad thing).

Meeting Organizer

- Prepare and submit an agenda
- Reduce number of participants
- Specify items to prepare
- Open with a purpose
- Roles required: time keeper, scribe
- Start time: 5 minutes past the hour
- Start on time
- Address disruptions (politely); then one on one
- Consider short stand-up meetings
- Stagger time for participants
- Meeting notes: short; include action item, owner, and date then obtain agreement and distribute
- Assign offline, parking lot items

Figure 5.6 Meeting guidelines for organizers

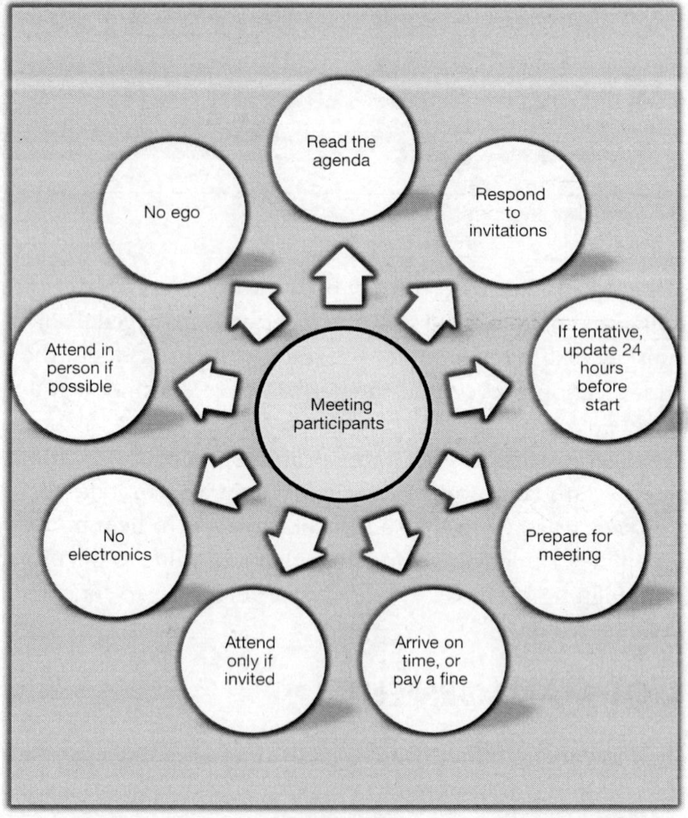

Figure 5.7 Meeting guidelines for participants

Constructive Conflict

Constructive conflict is conflict that is about the merits and the substance of what we do in the project. It is a mechanism to address disagreements about what we do, the way we do things, priorities, capacities, and resource allocation. This type of conflict helps us confront the issue at hand, go through a process to solve the problem, look for ways to collaborate, and seek consensus. Throughout the conflict management and resolution process we focus on the problem; we maintain a civilized, impersonal style; we care about what is at stake; and we keep the emotions contained. At the end of the process, we should be better off working together and moving forward, as we have cleared the issue at hand, with the goal of becoming a stronger team. If this process is handled properly, the team should get stronger and more cohesive as we move ahead in the project. The conflict resolution process may sometimes seek resolutions that are *less than ideal*, with the main goal of making the problem go away in order to clear the way for other project-related priorities.

The approaches that may be looked at can range from ignoring the problem, accommodating one of the parties' needs, making a decision that favors one side, or compromising by meeting in the middle, between two positions. A compromise, however, is not a sustainable, long-lasting solution, as it addresses the parties' positions and not their needs. The intent is to cut the losses and ensure that the most cost-effective approach to the conflict is selected. While the most effective approach is to confront the issues and solve the problem, it comes with a price—it involves a significant time and capacity investment, as the facilitator of the process needs to hear both sides, ensure collaboration, understand the needs of those involved, and pursue a win-win resolution. The time and capacity required are not always available and are not always worth the effort; with the cost exceeding the potential benefits.

Unconstructive Conflict

On the contrary, unconstructive conflict is about personalities, emotions, and arguments that are not about the work that we do, but rather about personal differences, petty issues, and personal styles. The conflict typically appears as an argument and it rolls over and over in different forms and for different issues. Unconstructive conflict distracts the team from the work that needs to be done, focuses on things that surround the work or are about positions (as opposed to interests), and with time it *consumes* the team—meaning that it hurts morale, reduces collaboration, leads to negative attitudes, distracts from work, makes people indifferent, and causes people to be more emotional and to *check out* from the process. At the end of the conflict resolution process, if people do not feel as though the problem has gone away—or has even been addressed properly and fairly—there is no win-win atmosphere, negative emotions run high, and people become reluctant to work together.

Furthermore, team members lose the sense of a team, they do not feel they work together toward a greater cause, and they start attending to their own affairs; trust evaporates, accountability turns into finger-pointing, and performance lags—creating a snowball effect that not only hurts morale but also creates conformity and retention issues. Unconstructive conflict is one of the symptoms of weak leadership where there is no role-model behavior and no leader to hold the team together and facilitate the team building and teamwork processes. A good leader addresses issues with the team, helps members handle conflict, leads the decision-making process, and serves as the owner of team ground rules, trust building, and escalation procedures. The leader must be there for team members to confide in and for professional and interpersonal advice.

Leadership for Effective Conflict Management

A leader does not necessarily need to be the most senior person or the formal authority, but rather someone with a legitimate source of power who steps up to the role. In the project, the PM must assume the majority of leadership responsibility, but due to the various roles, relationships, and areas of expertise in the project (for both the team and the external stakeholders), the BA must step up and become a full partner in leading the project. For the BA to become a partner, there has to be a clear set of rules of engagement between the PM and the BA, a clear division of areas of responsibility, and above all, the need for the PM to be willing to share the leadership responsibilities and to view the BA as an equal partner. The notion of *one entity* must be the guiding principle in this process of collaboration between the PM and the BA.

Conflict—What's in a Word?

As illustrated in this chapter and in alignment with PMI's views, conflict is a positive thing. It helps the team deal with issues, grow, become more cohesive, improve its capabilities, clear the air, and move away from issues that plague performance. Although it is well-recognized that conflict is a positive process that teams need to go through, some stakeholders may not view the word conflict in the same way—misunderstanding its meaning. While PMs and BAs know that conflict, in its constructive form, is a positive thing for the team, the stakeholders may fall into one of these three categories:

1. *People who view conflict as a negative thing*: They try to avoid conflict almost at any cost. The impact is that issues are not properly discussed,

there is no process of collaboration, and the problems linger. Teams that view conflicts as a negative thing tend to remain withdrawn and hold back on issues and challenges—achieving *artificial* harmony and typically not performing so well.

2. *People who get stuck on conflict*: The excitement associated with conflict is addictive to some people. Friction and conflict become prevalent until they consume the team and people turn edgy, reserved, and agitated. Typically, these teams do not perform well, as they are not cohesive and the team members do not conform to the rules.
3. *People who misunderstand the meaning of the word conflict and believe that engaging in conflict is the same as fighting*: Engaging in a conflict does not mean that team members or stakeholders are fighting with each other or exchanging personal insults. A conflict does not need to turn personal, it should not involve emotions, and it must not lead to people getting offended or fearing to express themselves. Stakeholders who misinterpret the meaning of the word *conflict* may try to avoid it when it is necessary to deal with an issue—or think that winning is about prevailing, rather than about achieving a win-win resolution that is sustainable and long-lasting.

The PM and the BA are not only the owners of the conflict management and resolution process, but they also must address the process of handling conflict between the two of them. Beyond the inefficiency, a visible conflict between the PM and the BA will hurt their credibility and their ability to provide leadership to the team. This does not mean that the PM and the BA should not have conflicts, but rather that they must engage in an agreed-upon process that is constructive and out of the team's sight. Once the PM-BA relations are set, it is time for them to establish the ground rules and expectations for their engagement of the team and the stakeholders, as well as guidelines for all team members and stakeholders regarding how to engage each other, what escalation procedures are in place, and how to handle issues and disagreements in a constructive and civilized manner. The set of ground rules proposed in this chapter are crucial for successful stakeholder and team engagement, expectations management, and conflict resolution management.

Conflict Management and Difficult Conversations

PMs and especially BAs have the need to work closely with stakeholders and team members who are often more senior than themselves to provide input and information for the project. This poses a challenge when combined with unclear circumstances, changing priorities, and stakeholders who are less than enthusiastic about their role in the project. This leads to the need to engage in conversations that may be difficult to handle and at times, to engage in conflict that may pose challenging outcomes. The onset of difficult conversations may be due to a variety of issues that range from challenges related to requirements and scoping, to estimating and risks, all the way to divergent views of the process—what we do, and the reasoning behind why we do it.

In addition, the PM and the BA need to address issues related to performance, gaps in expectations, and disagreements and friction among stakeholders. These conversations, along with the occasional need to deliver news that is not in line with expectations, require careful handling, as well as the generation of the highest possible capacity, knowledge, context, and relationship-building skills that can only be put together through a seamless collaboration between the PM and the BA. Such collaboration can only be achieved through open communication, ongoing sharing of information, constant adjustment to the way we deal with each other, and daily informal meetings that will allow us to focus on what matters, leverage the positives, and deal with the challenges.

When the PM and the BA are confronted with the need to engage in a difficult conversation, they may feel that they face only two options: (1) either initiate a conversation—bearing the risk of being ostracized or damaging the relationship or (2) say nothing and simply let things happen. In fact, the PM and the BA have a third option, which involves learning how to engage in difficult conversations while applying an appropriate approach with the confidence that the conversation will yield positive results. Engaging effectively in a difficult conversation involves steering it in the right direction by staying focused on the issue at hand, pursuing an attempt to find a common point of view, and trying to come up with a creative solution that addresses the needs of those involved. Remaining focused involves figuring out what we want from the conversation, from ourselves, and from the relationship, along with what we need to avoid—plus trying to answer the same questions about the other side.

PMs and BAs often find themselves in situations where conversations have turned difficult. *For the PM*, the conversations turn difficult typically in the following situations:

- Managing team members who do not deliver their work on time or to the extent required
- Dealing with functional managers regarding resource allocation
- Facing senior management, the sponsor, or the client to update status; report challenges; ask for more time/money; discuss priorities; break bad news; or review the charter, risks, assumptions, and other documentation
- Discussing changes with the client or with any other stakeholders
- Dealing with difficulties, priorities, and conflicts with team members

- Engaging in a difficult conversation with a vendor about timelines or deliverables
- Managing the timeline when priorities are not aligned and he or she needs to get things done faster than things can get done—procurement, finance, legal, sign-offs, steering committees
- When communicating with the PMO regarding reporting and process
- Attending any meeting that takes a turn toward becoming difficult
- When dealing with any correspondence that is not replied to according to expectations or protocol when there are performance issues—including meeting attendance, replies to e-mails, and style/tone of communication
- When collaborating with the BA—discussing requirements and scope prioritization, change requests, resource allocation, estimates, and processes

For the BA, the conversation may turn difficult during these circumstances:

- With the PM, when not treated like an equal in the partnership
- With the team, about requirements and scoping, estimates, and prioritization
- With stakeholders, about requirements and priorities
- With team members and stakeholders, about resource allocation
- With virtual team members and stakeholders, about change requests and prioritization
- With stakeholders and team members, about processes, improvement, and adherence
- With the team, about performance
- Before, during, and after any type of meeting (typically related to requirements), including dealing with stakeholders who do not attend or do not provide feedback about requirements

The types of challenges in relation to managing difficult conversations show partial overlap between those of the PM and the BA and the most effective approach to deal with and tackle these situations goes back to the PM-BA collaboration. With both roles putting their heads together, utilizing both personalities, relationships, leadership skills, experience, and clout in the organization, there is a higher chance for effective handling of these situations. It can be through the establishment of escalation procedures, engaging stakeholders in different styles, providing another set of eyes and ears in conversations, and dealing with people with an approach that is aligned with their needs, interests, expectations, and values. The combined power and range of available options the BA and the PM can jointly achieve is far greater than their individual powers.

The Dialogue

Engaging in a challenging dialogue is a daily occurrence for the PM and the BA, and their ability to turn these conversations into an effective and efficient discussion will not only allow them to manage the project successfully, but will also increase their credibility in the eyes of the stakeholders and team members. To engage in effective conversations the PM-BA duo (as well as all other stakeholders) needs to follow the following steps:

1. Be open-minded, not judgmental—other people's points of view may also be correct.
2. Separate the conversation from the decision. A two-way conversation is a must; we cannot expect to only express our point of view; it has to be a real dialogue. First, exchange points of view and allow all sides to express themselves, then move on toward reaching a resolution.
3. Treat all others as equals in the process.
4. Keep the emotions away, do not do *accounting* (i.e., bringing up previous arguments and disagreements). Really listen to what others have to say—empathy, acknowledgment, care, and putting yourself in the other side's shoes are all critical factors.
5. Look for common ground and areas of potential agreement.
6. Make assumptions, then document and validate them. Hidden and undisclosed assumptions that are not addressed may turn into risks and may prevent the discussion from reaching an effective resolution.

Win-Win

It is only possible to achieve a win-win resolution by separating the emotion from the situation and judging things by their merits—not by who said what or by attempting to make a point. It is not even about who is right or wrong, but more about the style and the way people feel about each other and about the situation. To help the point come across as effectively and distraction-free as possible, try to apply the following:

- Remain professional
- Focus on the problem
- Stay objective
- Maintain an image of trying to achieve a win-win resolution

The pursuit of a win-win resolution will bring the other side to a state of mind of potential agreement, and will help you build a reputation as a composed individual, who remains focused on the big picture—solving problems and ensuring everyone gets what they need. Taking the discussion of emotions a step further can show that it is not mandatory for people to genuinely like each other or be best friends in order to build productive and collaborative relations. In fact, many alliances were formed among people who had conflicting priorities, did not see things eye-to-eye, and who were not necessarily on friendly terms. Working together toward solving each other's problems was achieved through the ability to take emotions out of the equation—seeing past personal differences, identifying areas of mutual gain, and complementing each other's needs.

A focus on the win-win approach is fundamental for PMs and BAs, not only in building strong relationships and managing projects effectively, but also in negotiations. It is an approach that can be applied to any conflict situation by shifting the focus of the discussion away from a collision course of the opposing positions that are facing off. These positions represent what each side wants and sometimes they have little to do with what the real needs are. Focusing on uncovering each side's interests addresses their underlying needs and is likely to produce a win-win resolution when these needs are met.

In addition, try to further shift the conversation away from viewing each other as the problem—toward focusing on how to solve the problem together by approaching it as *us against the problem*. When people view each other as the problem, there is little progress made toward a resolution, and it usually leads to both sides entrenching themselves deeper in their original positions. Once again, less emotion and more focus on the merits of the situation are the keys to success.

COMMUNICATION IS NOT A 50/50 EFFORT

One of the biggest problems with communications management is that people believe that the responsibility for effective communication is shared 50/50 by both sides—that is, the sender and the receiver of a message. However, when examining the flow of communication, it is clear that this responsibility needs to be shared in a different way—100/100—in order to ensure that the message is properly generated, transmitted, received, and understood; with an opportunity to verify the information with each other, and with both parties owning the information from start to finish. A basic communication model (see Figure 5.8) shows that each message goes through a series of potential interruptions from the time it is generated to the time it reaches the receiver, and each of these potential interruptions may become a potential failure point. The message can be distorted by any bias that the issuer has—by noises in the communication channel it goes through or by the state of mind and the perception of the receiver. The communication model contains a loop that the receiver of a message generates to acknowledge and provide feedback, which goes through a

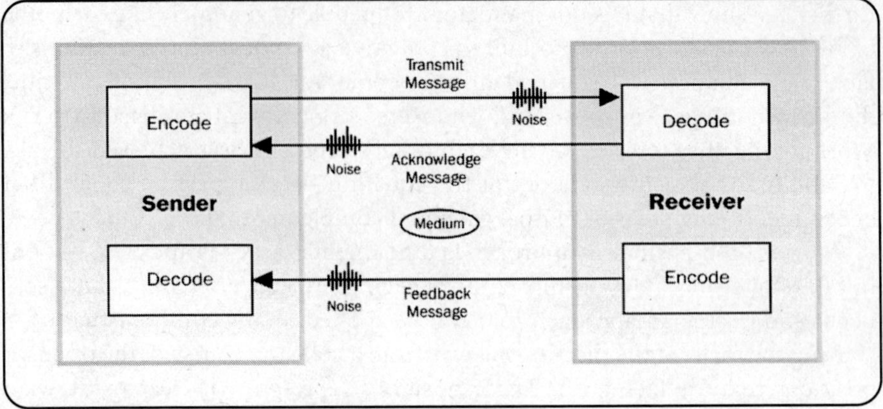

The PM and the BA need to be aware of the potential interruptions to the message when it travels from the sender to the receiver and back. Beside the "noise," perceptions and biases may also interfere with the message.

Source: Project Management Institute, *A Guide to the Project Management Body of Knowledge (PMBOK® Guide)—Fifth Edition*, Project Management Institute, Inc., 2013. Copyright and all rights reserved. Material from this publication has been reproduced with the permission of PMI.

Figure 5.8 Communication model

similar path back to the issuer of the original message through the three potential interruption points in the process.

The responsibility of ensuring that the message is received and understood lies with both sides of the communication loop. In particular, the sender needs to ensure the following:

1. The message is generated and sent out *as* and *when* intended.
2. The message is *received* by the intended recipient.
3. The message was received and that it was *understood* as intended, by establishing a feedback mechanism that encourages the receiver to reach out with acknowledgment and feedback.

The receiver also has a responsibility to ensure the following:

1. When expecting a message, reach out to ensure that it *was* generated and *sent*. It is not enough to passively sit and wait for an expected message.
2. When a message is received, make sure it is clear and *understandable*.
3. Reach out to *confirm receipt* and convey understanding of the message, by paraphrasing, if needed. This will allow both sides to validate that the message was received as intended.

Many projects are plagued by incomplete communications where senders do not ensure messages are received as intended or ever delivered at all, and receivers do not reach out to confirm their understanding of the message. The completion of the communication loop on its own can serve as a major contributor to reducing misunderstandings.

Emotional Resilience

It is hard to take the emotions out of what we do. Emotions are usually the result of caring—and most people care about what they do. Moreover, emotions get involved and dictate the course of action in conflict situations, especially if the stakes are high. People want to be successful; they invest time, money, and energy into doing something, and they become emotionally involved. Yet, without removing the care, concern, and attention that come along with emotions, it is important not to let emotions interfere with decision making, relationship building, or work. When a team member says something that provokes a witty comment, it is the power of not saying anything that should prevail. Even if there is a strong urge to react with a comeback, it can be done one-on-one, after the meeting. Making unconstructive comments will derail the discussion, may deter others from associating themselves with you, and will possibly hurt the person your comments were directed at. While many people tend to forget their commitments, they often hold a grudge and will get even at the worst possible time.

Verbal Judo,[1] which uses martial arts concepts for managing communications, and in this context means *if you are going to say something just for the purpose of making yourself feel better, do not say it*. While easier said than done, there are some techniques that can be applied in an effort to overcome that urge: one of them is the good, *old-fashioned count to ten* technique. When someone tells you something that infuriates you, or when they *open the door* for an inflaming statement from you, take the time to count to ten; and if it is still relevant and applicable after ten long seconds, you can say it then. At the very least, it may stop you from saying something that you will regret later. Keep in mind that almost anything can be undone, except for reversing time and *unsaying* what has just been said.

Another tactic to apply is related to the concept of martial arts:[2] when in a conflict situation and the other side goes on the attack (especially if personal), it is important to resist the urge to retaliate and counter-attack—instead, there should be an attempt to cool down and consider not responding altogether, or to try to take their motion and use it to your benefit by turning the same argument around on the other person so that it serves your point, in an attempt to solve the problem. For that, one needs to have emotional resilience, know the subject matter, understand the situation, realize the stakes involved, and make the point in an assertive, professional, and effective manner without getting personal or antagonizing others.

Virtual Teams

An increasing need that the PM and the BA need to address is the growing number of work environments that are *virtual*. Whether it is easier to handle a virtual type of team that is *hoteling* and working remotely, or the more challenging type, where team members are sometimes dispersed all over the world, the PM-BA duo needs to cope with both the *traditional* communication challenges that exist in any environment, as well as with the *unique* challenges posed by the virtual team.

One of the most effective ways to deal with challenges associated with virtual teams is to establish a set of ground rules. Similar to the ground rules discussed in this chapter dealing with meetings, e-mails, and general communication, it is even more crucial to set up a series of ground rules for the virtual team, to ensure that team members engage with each other based on a specific protocol and that they are somewhat on the same page. The following common challenges for virtual environment can be handled effectively by their respective proposed approach:

- **Different cultures:** Start with ground rules that address even the most basic types of communication, then incorporate culture training.
- **Different time zones:** This can be partially overcome by flexible hours on both sides to locally accommodate off-business-hours needs.
- **Different languages:** Although this is becoming more rare, establishing team signals and symbols, including a set of ground rules can help reduce the negative impact it might have on communication.
- **Different values and norms, including different practices regarding meetings, replies, styles, and timeliness:** Besides addressing these through the ground rules, there is a need for culture-related training, as well as a constant watch by the team leaders (typically the PM and the BA) to maintain alignment and prevent slippage toward chaos.
- **No face time and no personal relationships:** While there is no meaningful replacement for face time, there is a need to incorporate the appropriate technology (e.g., video conferencing), as well as ensuring one-on-one activities take part remotely. If possible, there has to be an arrangement for at least one personal meeting, but with teams that are located on two different corners of the world it may not be an option. With that said, there has to be an investment in addressing the challenge of no face time, including facilitating one-on-one activities remotely.

Ground Rules for Virtual Meetings

Clear procedures around how team members and stakeholders should handle themselves in virtual environments are a significant step in the right direction—they include the following:

- **General guidelines:** Always state your name; make sure that there is no background noise; use concise and clear statements; and refrain from using speaker phones. For the facilitator or the team lead—work with team members one-on-one to deal with issues.
- **Before the call:** Make sure you are prepared, arrive 3 minutes early, then—(1) establish a clear agenda and communicate using clear and measurable objectives, (2) invite only those who need to be there, and (3) remove all distractions.
- **Starting the call:** Always start with energy and momentum—(1) start the call on time, (2) start with a focused question and welcome people when appropriate, (3) establish or reiterate and clarify etiquette/ground rules, and (4) establish one clear purpose for the call.
- **During the call:** (1) Address background noise immediately, (2) ask simple, clear questions—starting with the name of the person to whom the question is being addressed, (3) allow silence after asking a question, (4) acknowledge people's contributions frequently, and (5) do not multitask.
- **After the call:** (1) Establish a timeframe to accomplish all action items, (2) close the call in five minutes or less, (3) go over an end-of-call process that involves asking for a one-sentence take-away or lesson-learned statement, go over the meeting notes and address any parking lot or offline items, then (4) end the call clearly.

For teleconferences, Figure 5.9 lists guidelines in reference to conference calls, which seem to be a growing pain in many organizations.

Mitigated Speech

The PM and the BA can utilize to their benefit (and for the benefit of the project) a technique called *mitigated speech*. It is a linguistic term, describing deferential

- Provide an agenda
- Provide access and alternate contact info
- Host to dial in 5 minutes before start
- Participants to dial in 1-2 minutes before start
- State your name when you speak
- Do not leave in the middle
- Speak one at a time
- No background noise
- Listen: mute does not mean disengage

Figure 5.9 Meeting guidelines for teleconferences

or indirect speech inherent in communication between individuals of perceived high power distance. It was popularized by Malcolm Gladwell in his book *Outliers* and is defined as "any attempt to downplay the meaning of what is being said."[3] There are six degrees of mitigation with which we make suggestions to authority. They are listed here with examples:

1. *Command*: "Strategy X is going to be implemented"
2. *Team member obligation statement*: "We need to try strategy X"
3. *Team member suggestion*: "Why don't we try strategy X?"
4. *Query*: "Do you think strategy X would help us in this situation?"
5. *Preference*: "Perhaps we should take a look at one of these Y alternatives"
6. *Hint*: "I wonder if we could run into any roadblocks on our current course"

The perfect mix of which technique(s) to utilize has the age-old consulting answer of *it depends*—on the people around us, the culture of the organization, and the aggressiveness of the mission at stake. Most effective people employ a well-rounded mix to make communication more effective. PMs and BAs should use these techniques to increase their ability to control conversations and ensure flow of communication at all levels throughout and around the project.

CHANGING PROJECTS THROUGH EFFECTIVE COMMUNICATION

If PMs and BAs apply the easy-to-understand concepts presented in this chapter, it can lead to a change in the way projects are managed and possibly in how project management and its partner profession—business analysis—are practiced altogether. The need to change project management as we know it is not because it is not done right—the methodologies are robust, the PMs do their jobs well (albeit, on their own, without true collaboration with BAs), and ample tools are available to help in the process. However, there are three factors that combine to make project management less effective than it could be and also make projects more difficult to manage—hence, the need to change how project management is performed.

- **A disconnect:** There is usually a wide gap between various stakeholders' views and expectations and the project team's capabilities—there may also be gaps within the project team or between the team and the customer. Project managers have a hard time articulating these gaps, and they often fail to reach out and address them.

- **Lack of meaningful communication:** There is a general statement that is applicable to almost all organizations and situations: people do not listen. Most people operate within preconceived notions and paradigms, and they do not make sufficient effort to pay attention to what colleagues, peers, managers, subordinates, or customers have to say. Moreover, there is little effective communication occurring within the project team or with external stakeholders. No tool can replace the human mind in engaging other people and listening to them, and its far-reaching impact exacerbates the disconnect between stakeholders.
- **As a result of the previous points, project results fall short of expectations:** Poor expectation management, a limited ability to understand customer needs and those of other stakeholders involved in the project, along with numerous other distractions due to poor communication contribute to project failure more so than technical difficulties and project constraints.

Changing the reality of projects does not need to involve applying new tools or enhancing technical capabilities, but rather allowing the project management profession to realize its potential and deliver higher success rates than it currently does. Change can be achieved by recognizing that the current way of managing project communications is not sufficient and that more focus needs to be given to this critical, yet overlooked area. Most organizations and project managers see communication as something that is foundational and basic and as such, it is lower in priority than technical knowledge.

To make project communications successful, PMs and BAs should take a few simple steps:

1. Make communication a top priority.
2. Establish a culture where all stakeholders and team members feel that they share responsibility for communication and fully understand their role in every interaction.
3. Match the communication channels to the needs of the project stakeholders.
4. Keep reviewing the communication processes and methods to ensure that they meet the current project needs.
5. Remain open to opportunities for improvement.

FINAL THOUGHTS ON COMMUNICATION AND STAKEHOLDER EXPECTATIONS MANAGEMENT—*AUT NON TENTARIS, AUT PERFICE*

If there is an area that all PMs should excel at, it is communication—and the way to do it effectively is through establishing a full partnership with the BA. Owning project communications is the key to success for everything else in the project. Communication management, stakeholder engagement, and expectations management are the most important factors in managing people's attitudes and impressions, and it affects every single aspect of the project—from scope and change management, to schedule and budget, risk, quality, resources, expectations, and procurement.

And one thing PMs and BAs must keep in mind—as Ovid[4] said in Latin, "*Aut non tentaris, aut perfice*"—"Either carry it through, or don't make the attempt at all." PMs and BAs who do not possess excellent communication skills are in for an uphill battle that may not yield the desired results. Perhaps the biggest misconception is that PMs and BAs can get by with technical skills, to make up for deficiencies in their communication capabilities.

REFERENCES

1. Based on the book *Verbal Judo: The Gentle Art of Persuasion* (2004), George J. Thompson and Jerry B. Jenkins, Harper Collins, New York.
2. Adapted from http://flamesonfifthavenue.com/archives/310
3. Gladwell, Malcolm (2008). *Outliers*. Little, Brown and Company, New York.
4. Publius Ovidius Naso (20 March 43 BC - 17 AD), Ovid, *Ars Amatoria, Book I*. 389.

6

REQUIREMENTS DEFINITION

"Insanity is doing something over and over again and expecting a different result."—Albert Einstein

Inaccurate requirements gathering has consistently been cited as the primary reason for project failure according to a Project Management Institute (PMI) study. In fact, the percentage of failed projects due to inaccurate requirements gathering increased from 32% in 2013 to 37% in 2014.[1] Reflecting on this information, many project managers (PMs), business analysts (BAs) and other project practitioners can relate to participating in post-implementation review sessions, and when asked why the project did not go so well, everyone points the finger at poor requirements and, indirectly, at the BA. Yet many organizations still lack mature requirements management processes, and some still do not see the value in taking the time to define requirements. We continue to skimp out on the requirements definition phase of the project, then gather around the table to once again discuss why the project did not go so well.

Instead of pointing fingers, we should be working together to solve this problem. How many organizations have projects with fixed deadlines and take shortcuts in the requirements definition and design solutions in parallel? How often is the time to define requirements dictated to the BA? How many times have stakeholders signed off on requirements without having read a single word in the document? How many organizations dive right into scheduling requirements workshops that last days on end, without a clear agenda—leaving stakeholders wondering whether there is value in requirements definition instead of planning for requirements definition first? It is unfortunate that many organizations are guilty of these offenses. Product requirements are an important factor on any project, and project requirements, design, build, and testing are all dependent on clear, complete, and accurate product requirements. Many organizations do realize this importance, but do not understand how to implement strategies to improve the requirements definition process. Most project teams also realize that the definition of product requirements is the responsibility of the BA, and attempt to wipe their hands clean of any involvement in this extremely tedious activity and request to be engaged only when requirements have been finalized. Because of the many dependencies on the product requirements, team members should instead be actively trying to get more involved in the product requirements definition phase of the project, starting with the planning of product requirements.

PLANNING FOR REQUIREMENTS DEFINITION AND MANAGEMENT

PMs have the opportunity to plan out project deliverables prior to executing the project; developers plan their design prior to build activities; and testers have to complete a formal deliverable of a test plan prior to beginning any of their testing activities. This begs the question, why is it that a BA is rarely provided with the opportunity to plan out their requirements definition and management activities prior to scheduling the elicitation sessions? Lack of time is the number one excuse for excluding planning activities; contrary to popular belief, if more time is spent planning for requirements definition and management, the overall time spent defining and managing requirements ends up being less, as time will be saved by executing a well-laid-out plan. The probability of missing dependencies, missing stakeholder groups, and missing requirements will be much lower and the overall project will be less risky. Evidence of a plan also provides stakeholders with the confidence that the project team is organized and can deliver a successful project. A small number of high performing organizations are starting to introduce the new business analysis and requirements management plans, which is definitely a step in the right direction.

The Business Analysis Plan

A common challenge that many PMs face is project scheduling—and schedule overruns in the analysis phase of the project are unfortunately, common occurrences. A conversation between the PM and the BA while estimating the requirements definition work effort, can sometimes look like this: the PM asks "How much time do you need in order to deliver a signed-off requirements document?"—the BA licks his or her finger, waves it in the air, and gives an arbitrary number, "six weeks." The PM then replies with, "I can give you five weeks." There is not much to negotiate at this point as there is nothing tangible to base the estimates on. Creating a business analysis plan provides tangible activity lists that are created from the bottom up, on which to base these estimates that can be used as a negotiation tool with the project manager and steering committee when dealing with a fixed deadline initiative or generally requesting the needed time for requirements definition.

A business analysis plan carefully lists all the activities that the BA needs to perform in order to complete their deliverables, the dependencies between the activities, and time estimates to complete each activity. The business analysis plan can be compared to the project schedule. The PM will manage project activities at a higher level and track project milestones—one of the many milestones being a *signed-off business requirements document*. The BA would document all the individual activities they would need to perform in order to produce a signed-off business requirements document, including all of the elicitation activities, review sessions, and signoff (which usually takes a week in itself) within a business analysis plan. The BA needs to remember to include the time to prepare and synthesize the information from any meetings that are planned for, and keep in mind that a half-day requirements workshop is not just four hours, as there may be prework, such as creating detailed meeting agendas, pre-alignment meetings, engagement requests and/or introductory slides that need to be prepared before the start of the meeting. After the workshop the BA needs to analyze the information that was learned from the meeting to schedule follow up interviews, observation sessions, or additional workshops. The BA may also need time to convert the information learned into another medium, for instance, producing models. The pre- and post-workshop activities will likely take much longer than the actual workshop itself. This time is typically not accounted for when BAs provide estimates to PMs, hence the schedule overruns in the analysis phase.

The BA can then roll up the estimates to provide the PM with the estimated completion dates. With a business analysis plan, the BA also has a better sense of how much work has been completed and how much more is left to complete, at any point in time. With this information, the BA can keep the lines of communication open with the PM to request more time, if needed, earlier rather than a week before the deliverable is due. The additional time can also be justified by pointing to the remaining activities that are left to be completed in the business analysis plan and which activities within the plan took longer than expected. Returning to the conversation with the PM where the BA requested 6 weeks (which is no longer arbitrary, as the activities are documented in the business analysis plan) and the PM responded with "there is currently only 5 weeks allocated to requirements,"—both the PM and BA can now review the business analysis plan together to determine if there are ways to compress the schedule or put together a case to justify an extension to the timeline. If the schedule cannot be increased and some of the business analysis activities need to be sacrificed or not completed, a project risk can be opened and tracked accordingly.

Without a neatly laid-out business analysis plan, many resort to scheduling meeting after meeting with stakeholders to block time with them, without yet knowing what needs to be discussed at these meetings. This results in poor attendance or not having the right stakeholders at the meeting; requiring a meeting reschedule; which is almost impossible with everyone's full calendars; which then results in a delay in the overall project schedule. Creating a business analysis plan is time consuming, but not completing one has proven to be even more time consuming—as described in the previous scenario. Creating a business analysis plan forces the BA to think about:

- What information do they need?
- Who has this information?
- What is the best way to get this information from this stakeholder?
- Are there any predecessor tasks that need to be completed before making contact with this stakeholder? (For example, speaking with a manager before approaching employees to job shadow/observe them.)
- How to confirm that the information received is correct and complete? Usually it means not relying on a single source, which means more elicitation and more time to complete the elicitation. (For example, reading old procedures to help understand the current state of a process; combined with scheduling sessions to observe an employee performing the task; in addition to setting up sessions to determine how to improve the process and finally; review sessions to receive confirmation that everything has been synthesized correctly by the BA.)

With a business analysis plan, meetings with clear agendas can be set-up well in advance, increasing the chances of stakeholder attendance and preparedness. Table 6.1 shows the main components to be included in such a plan. Without a business analysis plan, all of these questions are jumbled in the BA's head. It is no wonder the ball gets dropped, requirements are missed, and projects are delayed. The PM can further support the BA with the business analysis plan by providing the BA the time to complete one. Even if the business analysis plan is not a formal deliverable within the organization, that does not mean one should not be completed for every project. Once a project team takes the time to complete a business analysis plan and the positive results are observed, more project teams will adopt the same due diligence and eventually, creating a business analysis plan will be the norm. The information in the business analysis plan should be feeding into the project schedule for a higher probability of

Table 6.1 An example of a business analysis plan

This table lists the main components of the business analysis plan, including the activities and their attributes.

#	Activity	Participants	Dependencies	Time Estimate (includes prep and time to analyze information)	Challenges/Comments
1	**Conduct Current State Analysis**				
a	Review call center apply-for-credit-card procedure	No other participants required	None	2 hours	Unsure if procedures are up-to-date
b	Meet with call center agent to understand challenges with current apply-for-credit-card procedure and request observation session	Call center manager	None	3 hours	Difficult to get time with the manager
c	Observe call center agent applying for a credit card	Call center agent	1b - Needs to be cleared with manager first	5 hours	Agent cannot be disrupted for questions during observation session
d	...				

sticking to the planned schedule. The same way design documents are expected from developers and test plans are expected from testers, business analysis plans should be expected from BAs.

The Requirements Management Plan

The requirements management plan serves a different purpose than the business analysis plan. The business analysis plan assists with the scheduling of activities, where the requirements management plan is planning the process to manage requirements for the life cycle of the project and product. The business analysis plan can therefore be compared to the project schedule and the requirements management plan can be compared to the project management plan. In fact, the *Project Management Body of Knowledge* (*PMBOK® Guide*) has the requirements management plan listed as a component of the project management plan. The project management plan *describes how the project will be executed, monitored, and controlled,*[2] with the *PMBOK® Guide* implying that the PM is responsible for completing the requirements management plan,[3] whereas the *Business Analysis Body of Knowledge* (*BABOK®*) has the BA as responsible for completing the requirements management plan.[4] As with any of the project activities, it is less important *who* does it, but more important that *it is being completed*, and completed effectively. Most PMs view the BA as responsible for anything related to requirements, including the requirements management plan, despite what might be implied in the *PMBOK® Guide*. The PM-BA duo will, however, need to work together to complete the requirements management plan in order to ensure effectiveness. The requirements management plan consists of the following items:

- **How requirements activities will be planned, tracked, and reported on:** The PM can dictate to the BA how they would like requirements activities to be planned, tracked, and reported on, but a more collaborative approach would be to allow the BA the flexibility to use a method that works for him or her—but, the BA is expected to provide requirements updates per the format specified by the PM. This is likely the same format that is expected from each of the core team members—development, testing, etc.
- **Where the requirements will be stored:** Project documentation and file-naming standards need to be consistent across the project and the organization.
- **How and whether or not the requirements will be traced:** Tracing requirements helps to ensure requirements coverage from the business requirements through the different layers of product requirements, down to design and test activities. The backwards tractability helps guard against scope creep. The PM and BA specifically need to work

together to ensure the product requirements map to project activities in the work breakdown structure (WBS) and vice versa. Listing relationships or dependencies between requirements also assists with the requirements allocation process.

- **Which requirements attributes will be captured:** Requirements attributes can also be used to trace requirements to WBS activities among other items. For less mature organizations, requirements attributes may be a new concept. Requirements attributes are used to describe a requirement in greater detail. Most still document requirements as one liners: *2.1 The system shall have the ability to track the number of times an application was canceled prior to completion.* The result of this is additional questions from the requirements reviewers:

    a. Why is this required?
    b. Who came up with this idea in the first place?
    c. Is there another requirement to report on this?

  Requirements attributes can be used to answer the questions we anticipate from our stakeholders before they ask them. If a requirements management tool is used to capture requirements, requirements attributes are probably already being documented. Think of each requirement as filling out a form and the attributes are additional fields of the form. However, even if a requirements management tool is not used within the organization, it does not mean requirements attributes cannot be used. If a word processing application like MS Word is used, a grid can be inserted for every requirement to capture the attributes (see Table 6.2).
- **How changes to the requirements will be managed:** The PM is responsible for the project change management process, but the BA is responsible for any changes to product scope. The PM and BA therefore again, need to work together to ensure seamless management of project and requirements changes. Most organizations already have a change management process documented within their organizational process assets, but any gray areas need to be defined. This is expanded on in Chapter 9, discussing project and organizational change management.
- **How requirements will be prioritized:** The PM and BA need to collectively decide who has the authority to prioritize requirements and which approach to take to prioritize requirements, to ensure the project team does not end up in a situation where everything is prioritized as *high*. The PM should have a seat at the table to help facilitate the requirements prioritization by enforcing project constraints. The requirements approval process and who has the authority to approve requirements

Table 6.2 Requirements attributes

Requirements should be documented with their associated attributes to answer the questions we anticipate from our stakeholders before they ask them.

Requirement ID	2.1	Unique identifier
Description	The system shall have the ability to track the number of times an application was canceled prior to completion.	Requirement description
Rationale	Canceled applications will be used as an indicator to measure the user friendliness of the application.	To ensure requirement provides value
Author	Cheryl Lee	Useful when more than 1 BA on project
Source	<insert link to meeting notes where this requirement was discussed>	Useful to know who to follow up with if there are additional questions
Complexity	Low	Can be measured by the # of teams required to make changes in order to implement requirement. For example: Low: 1-2 Medium: 3-4 High: 5+
Assumptions	Canceled applications are a result of the application process being too tedious and/or slow.	Requirement level assumptions, constraints, dependencies, risks
Constraints	System constraint: accounts linked to more than 1 canceled application will only be counted once.	
Dependencies	Related to requirement 7.5 providing the ability to report on canceled applications	
Risks	Requirements Risk ID 5	
Traced From	Stakeholder requirement 3.2	Backwards and forward traceability can be managed using requirements attributes
Traced to Design	To be completed in design	
Traced to Test	To be completed in test	

should also be discussed. The PM should be an approver of the product requirements as well, to indicate agreement that the product requirements can be converted into project requirements that fall within the constraints of the project.

The Project Management Plan

Whether formally or informally, the PM and the BA need to set aside time together to discuss the contents of the requirements management plan. In fact, due to the multiple integration points between the requirements management plan and the other subsidiary project management plans, it is imperative for the PM and BA to work together on all aspects of the project management plan, including but not limited to, the following items:

- **Scope, schedule, cost, and quality management plans:** The PM and the BA should decide together how scope, schedule, cost, and quality will be defined, refined, and managed. The PM plans for project scope, schedule, cost, and quality and the BA plans for product scope and quality, as well as scheduling and cost of business analysis and requirements management activities. The scope management and requirements management plans have many integration points, including the change management process to control changes to the project. Analysis being one of the biggest culprits for schedule and consequently cost overruns, the PM and BA should jointly determine how to build the project schedule and ensure it remains within the planned thresholds to monitor costs. To ensure a successful project and product, there needs to be a collaborative effort. Furthermore, scope, schedule, cost, and quality all have integration points. If one is affected, something else has to give. Additional scope could mean additional time and/or costs and/or decreased quality of the overall product. Reduced timelines usually require a decrease in scope and/or quality and/or an increase in costs in order to restore balance. The PM and the BA need to understand these relationships and plan to keep the lines of communication open to identify and manage how changes in one factor causes downstream impacts in others.
- **Risk management plan:** Risk management is a joint activity between the PM and the BA. The PM being primarily accountable for project risk management and the BA is primarily accountable for requirements risk management, with both project team members assisting each other to manage project and requirements risk. An elaborate discussion of risks management takes place in Chapter 7.
- **Process improvement plan:** The PM-BA duo should determine how to evaluate any process improvements to project management and product development together—specifically if there are any additional things they can do to support each other. Each resource has peaks and valleys during the project. The bulk of the business analysis work is during the analysis phase of the project and tapers off for the duration of the project, with a slight increase in testing and implementation. The PM on the

other hand peaks during the beginning of the project in the initiation/planning phase of the project and remains steady through the duration of the project, unless there are issues. Figure 6.1 shows the relative levels of effort and rigor for the PM and the BA throughout the project, with the understanding that the levels of effort and rigor can be different, depending on the size and complexity of the project. If the PM and BA can team up in the beginning of the project, during planning and analysis, and deal with any issues together (with the assumption that a better plan means less issues), there is a much higher chance for project success, in addition to the feel-good aspect that the sense of triumphant teamwork brings.

- **Human resource management plan:** The BA, being the closest to the product requirements, should have a good understanding of what resources are first required for the elicitation of the requirements as well as the skills required to deliver the end product. This is a great opportunity for the PM to leverage the BA, when planning for project human resources.
- **Procurement management plan:** The BA will be the one to document the product requirements to be packaged into the statement of work, so it would be logical to engage the BA in the procurement management planning. Again, because the BA is closest to the requirements, they should also be engaged to help determine the selection process for vendors.
- **Communication and stakeholder management plan:** Both PMs and BAs need to communicate with and manage stakeholders. The BA

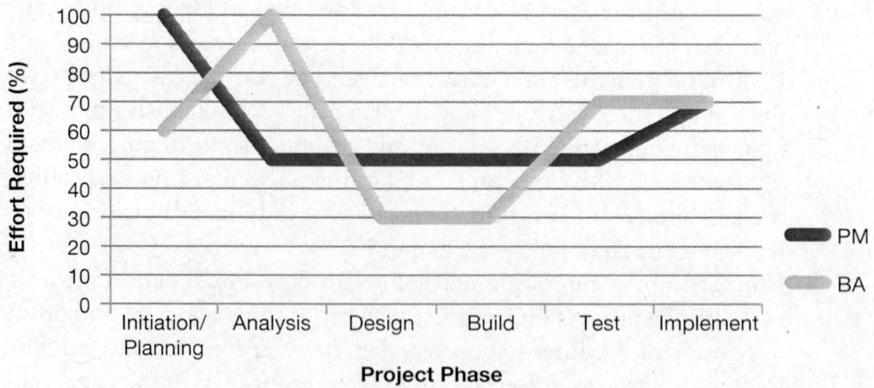

This figure provides a simplified view of the level of rigor and involvement of the PM and the BA throughout the various stages of the project.

Figure 6.1 The PM-BA peaks and valleys

communicates information regarding requirements and requirements status, where the PM would have a broader communication of overall project activities and status. Ideally, a joint communication plan where the BA communication plan feeds into the overall communication plan should be developed, and the integration points should be discussed. The BA is also a prime contender to assist in stakeholder identification and in determining the impacts to each of the stakeholder groups. Sometimes *you do not know* what *you do not know*, and it is through analysis led by the BA, that missing stakeholder groups are identified. Planning to jointly manage stakeholders will help bridge the gap. This was expanded on further back in Chapter 5.

- **Project life cycle decisions:** No single resource on the project team should determine the life cycle that will be used for the project. Inputs are likely required by all team members. Some organizations have developed life cycle suitability surveys to help the project team decide which methodology would work best for that project. Table 6.3 shows the headings as well as a couple of attributes that organizations can use to evaluate agile suitability. As organizations are shifting to using more agile or change-driven methodologies, it creates choices and opportunities to select new and different methods to deliver on the project, based on the business needs and organizational culture. Sometimes a project may not be a clear fit into any one category, and tailoring will be required to better suit the project needs. This may change the set of

Table 6.3 Agile suitability scorecard

	Attributes	1. High Agile Suitability	2. Moderate Agile Suitability	3. Low Agile Suitability	My Project
No.	I. Project Characteristics				
1	Requirements	Frequently changing	Subject to moderate recoverable change	Stable	2
2	Total effort	1,000 to 5,000 hours	More than 5,000 hours	Less than 1,000 hours	1
3					

Headings of an agile suitability scorecard as well as a couple of attributes organizations can use to evaluate agile suitability. Teams would enter 1, 2, or 3 under *My Project* based on agile suitability and an overall score would be calculated and translated into *recommended* or *not recommended* for agile.

deliverables the project will produce and require approval from a higher power, such as a project management office (PMO). A one-size-fits-all methodology or life cycle for projects is yet to be seen. Regardless of the life cycle, even though the set of deliverables may change, the set of activities and integration points between the PM and BA do not. The level of formality and rigor that is applied to each of these activities will, however, vary.

- **Success criteria:** The PM and the BA will need to define a successful project and product, as well as methods and timelines for measurement. The PM or BA on the project may not necessarily be the one who will measure the project success, but they do need to document it somewhere, so it can eventually be measured by someone—possibly within the PMO.

PRODUCT vs. PROJECT REQUIREMENTS

The product requirements are defined based on the business requirements and solution scope defined in enterprise analysis (EA). In Chapter 4, the importance of having a solid foundation was explained. Building product requirements on top of a weak foundation leads to delivering a product or service that does not meet the needs of the stakeholders. Product requirements describe the goods or services that the project will deliver, where the project requirements describe the work or activities that are required in order to deliver the product. The product requirements for a kitchen renovation include the type of appliances that will be included, lighting, the materials—such as the type of countertops (laminate, granite, quartz) dimensions of the counter space, and the color and materials of the cabinets. The project requirements include the resources required to install the kitchen—plumber, electrician, carpenter, the time to complete the kitchen renovation and the budget set aside for the job. The BA is accountable for product requirements and the PM is accountable for project requirements; it is expected that there will be dependencies between product and project requirements. The BA needs to elicit product requirements within the constraints of the project, and the PM cannot determine all project requirements unless the product requirements are known. Sometimes the BA's approach is to *not care about time and cost, because that is the PM's job*—he or she is *only concerned with doing the right thing for the business.* This kind of approach often drives BAs to unilaterally attempt to increase scope without seeing the downstream impacts on project costs and timelines, and it may result in pushing the project toward the full extent of its constraints; causing it to not meet the business needs. As one can imagine, this approach leads to unhappy stakeholders with a lack of trust and confidence in the project team to understand and deliver on their needs.

PRODUCT REQUIREMENTS ELICITATION

Although the product requirements are the accountability of the BA, it does not imply that the BA is solely responsible for the definition of product requirements. Input from multiple stakeholders and support from the core project team is of the utmost importance. Leaving it to the BA to schedule and host the requirements elicitation sessions alone with the business stakeholders is a flaw in the product requirements definition process. The core project team—including the PM, technical leads, and test leads—often do not get engaged until the requirements walk-through just prior to requirements sign-off. The problem with this approach is, from a schedule perspective, the BA thinks that he or she is on track as the product requirements have been elicited and documented from the business stakeholders in order to produce a business requirements document by the date intended. Then during the walk-through, the technical lead speaks up to indicate that the product requirements cannot be delivered with the existing resources (this could mean people resources or even technical resources such as servers and databases) meaning additional project scope—outsourcing and procurement is required, which in turn, means more time and money that the PM does not have for the project. The test lead also points out that there are error conditions that have been missed among other possible gaps in the requirements, which means additional elicitation is required by the BA, now bringing the analysis phase and consequently, the project behind schedule. The business stakeholders who thought the product requirements were ready for sign-off to begin design and build of the solution are also now discouraged that backtracking to elicit additional information is required and the first available opportunity for all stakeholders to get together for another requirements workshop is not until at least a week from now. This downward spiral is frustrating, but all too common.

The core project team does not need to be at every single requirements elicitation session, but there should be key sessions that can be used as checkpoints where they can provide input in intervals instead of at the eleventh hour. Sure, the PM, technical leads, and testing leads will indicate they have time constraints and cannot be made available, but if time is allocated to have these resources available during analysis while the plan is being developed, it should be less of an issue. As a general rule of thumb, whenever there is a need for a requirements workshop with heterogeneous participants (folks with different backgrounds), this is a great opportunity to include the core project team. During the targeted or deep-dive sessions where the BA is setting up an interview or an observation session, the core project team is not required to attend unless there is a specific need; although it could be helpful for them to be present. Requirements workshops are usually more generalized or decision-making sessions where the core project team will likely be required anyway.

Requirements workshops are group elicitation techniques, which typically require more than one resource to run the meeting. Since the BA usually does not have the luxury of a BA peer to assist, this is also a great opportunity for the PM to support the BA by playing the role of the scribe while the BA focuses on facilitating the session. Referring back to the misconceptions of the BA role, despite what many may think, taking notes for every meeting is not the BA's role. Many BAs can recall times in which they worked with a PM who invited them to every meeting the PM chaired, even those where there was no need for the BA to participate or attend, so the BA could take notes. On the other hand, when BAs chair meetings, they are also expected to take their own notes. The authors of this book, through personal experiences, recall responding to one such meeting invitation with, "I can attend and assist with the scribing, but I am chairing a requirements workshop in a couple of days and hope you can assist me in the note taking?" That did not go over well, but it at least opened the door to a discussion on roles and responsibilities that really should have happened a lot earlier in the project.

There are additional benefits to having the PMs attend elicitation meetings, other than supporting the BA with running some of the sessions. During these elicitation sessions within the analysis phase is when many project risks are uncovered. Instead of having the BA pass the message to the PM, or having the BA assist in managing project risks during analysis when the BA workload is already at its peak, the PM can be present to log and manage any project risks. The BA will also be focusing on requirements risks, so it would be helpful if the PM is present to identify any requirements risks that may also be project risks. By allowing the BA to focus on requirements risks as the requirements are being elicited, the PM is indirectly assisting the BA in uncovering gaps or missing requirements. This not only helps the project stay on schedule and within budget, but also decreases the number of unexpected surprises within design, build, or test, that may cause rework.

Throughout the elicitation sessions or the analysis phase, new stakeholder groups may be uncovered and in such cases, the PM should attend the sessions in order to elicit relevant information from the stakeholders for the project. By participating in these sessions, the PM will receive the information directly from the stakeholders and not secondhand from the BA, which will also help reduce the redundancy of having the BA serving as the middle person. It is in the best interest of the PM to support the BA during product requirements elicitation, as the remainder of the project requirements are dependent on the product requirements.

The Many Layers of Product Requirements

1. *Business Requirements*: There are different layers or levels of abstraction in product requirements. In Chapter 5, the business requirements were explained. Business requirements are the highest level of abstraction, and all other product requirements support the business requirements, as seen in Figure 6.2. Business requirements represent the high-level business needs, goals, and objectives of the project and describe why the project has been initiated. An example of a business requirement is: *Decrease customer service representative average handling time by 20%—for instance, 10 minutes to 8 minutes—within 6 months of project implementation*. This example relates to a call center at a financial institution and the average handling time is the average amount of time the customer service representative spends on the phone with the customer.

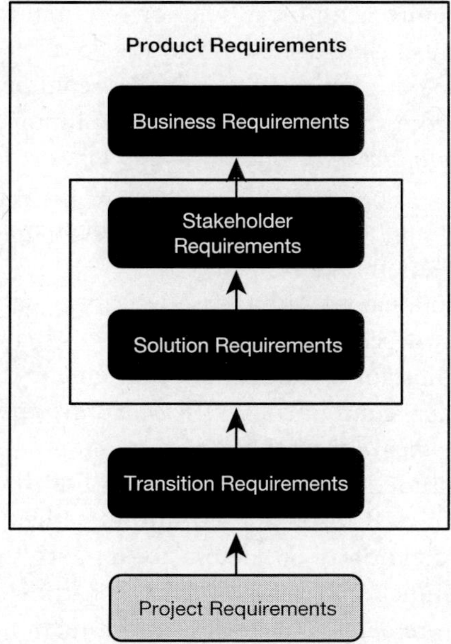

This figure shows the different layers of the requirements hierarchy and how the layers support each other:

- Project requirements support all product requirements
- Transition requirements support both stakeholder and solution requirements
- Solution requirements support stakeholder requirements
- Stakeholder requirements support business requirements

Figure 6.2 The requirements hierarchy

2. *Stakeholder Requirements*: In the next level down, we have stakeholder requirements. Stakeholder requirements support business requirements. They represent the needs of a stakeholder or a group of stakeholders. Stakeholder requirements are typically written from the perspective of the stakeholder. They start with: *The <stakeholder> shall have the ability to...* Stakeholder requirements describe how the stakeholder will interact with the product. Stakeholder requirements are sometimes also known as user requirements. There will most likely be multiple stakeholder requirements mapping back to a single business requirement. An example of a stakeholder requirement that supports the business requirement is: *The call center representative shall have the ability to apply for a credit card directly in the application portal.* After some root cause analysis, it was determined that the average handling times were long for customers opting to apply for a credit card via the phone because the call center representative had to complete the credit card application in another portal and rekey customer information.
3. *Solution Requirements*: Solution requirements are the next layer in the product requirements—and solution requirements support stakeholder requirements. They describe how the solution or product will satisfy the stakeholder requirement. Solution requirements are typically documented from the perspective of the solution, or product. They start with: *The product shall have the ability to...* or: *The system shall have the ability to....* There will almost certainly be multiple solution requirements that support a single stakeholder requirement. There are two types of solution requirements:
    a. Functional requirements describe what the product shall do. They describe the capabilities and behaviors of the product. An example of a functional requirement that supports the stakeholder requirement is: *The call center application shall pre-fill the customer demographics portion of the credit card application.*
    b. Nonfunctional requirements do not directly describe what the product shall be able to do but rather, the ideal environmental conditions or factors to support the product. Sometimes nonfunctional requirements are known as quality of service requirements. Categories of nonfunctional requirements include reliability, maintainability, capacity, availability, and security. A major flaw in nonfunctional requirements is not listing them as testable requirements. For example: *The system shall be fast* is arbitrary, and not testable—how fast? A better way to articulate this example as a testable nonfunctional requirement is: *The call center application shall have a response time of under*

three seconds upon page request. Another common example of a non-testable, non-functional requirement that is seen quite often is: *The system shall be user-friendly*. A better way to articulate this example is: *The call center agent shall be able to complete the credit card application on the call center portal with no training*.

4. *Transition Requirements*: The final layer of product requirements is transition requirements, which support both the stakeholder and solution requirements. Transition requirements are temporary requirements that take you from the current state to the future state. They are temporary in nature—as once the project has been implemented, they are no longer needed. Transition requirements include training or data migration. An example of a transition requirement is: *The credit card application shall be piloted site by site*. It was not ideal to implement the changes across all the call centers at the same time; if there was a major problem with the implementation, there would be a risk of bringing down all the call centers nationwide. This is a temporary requirement—once the credit card application is rolled out to all the call centers, this requirement is no longer required.

Use Cases

Use cases are used often in waterfall projects as supplementary documentation to textual requirements. In projects using the agile approach, use cases alone can be used as the requirements, as use case modeling is a fantastic way to depict both stakeholder and solution requirements. Use case modeling consists of two parts—the use case diagram and the use case scenarios.

1. *Use case diagram*: The use case diagram can be used to represent the stakeholder requirements. The use case diagram can be read as follows: The <actor> shall have the ability to <perform the feature>.
2. *Use case scenario*: Each scenario or oval in the use case diagram can be expanded textually into a use case scenario. The use case scenario consists of the steps that are executed in order to complete the scenario. The use case scenario can be used to represent the functional requirements. Use cases do not have a means to document nonfunctional requirements. Nonfunctional requirements typically relate to the overall product and not specifically to a use case and therefore, should be documented separately. The following list contains the main components of a use case scenario:
   - **Trigger:** What initiates the use case to begin?
   - **Precondition:** What must be true in order to start the scenario?
   - **Post condition:** What must be true when the scenario ends?

- **Normal flow:** The normal flow is also known as the happy path scenario. This is the flow that is most likely taken to execute the scenario.
- **Alternate flow:** Other paths or branches off the happy path that can be taken to execute the scenario.
- **Exception flow:** Errors or disruptions that could possibly occur as the scenario is executed.

The use case scenario can also be represented as a swim lane diagram as the use case scenario demonstrates order, flow, and logic.

Requirements Documents

Now that the various types of product requirements are understood, it is important for both the BA and the PM to understand the timing concerning when they are defined and where they are documented. The business requirements are documented in the business case and transferred into the project scope document. During the analysis phase of the project the business requirements are elaborated into stakeholder requirements. If the organization has a structure where there are *business* BAs and *technical* BAs assigned to a project, there are likely two different requirement documents that need to be completed.

1. *A Business Requirements Document (BRD)—which is completed by the business BA*: Even though the title suggests that the BRD is where the business requirements are documented, this is not actually the case. The business BA would use the business requirements that were defined during enterprise analysis as a starting point, and expand them into stakeholder requirements through elicitation from stakeholders. The stakeholder requirements are what get documented in the BRD.
2. *A Solution Requirements Specification (SRS)—which is completed by the technical BA*: The technical BA would use the signed-off BRD with the stakeholder requirements and elaborate them into solution requirements, both functional and nonfunctional, through elicitation from stakeholders, then include these in the SRS. The SRS is often mistaken as design documentation, partly because the name of the document suggests this. While BAs do design to a certain extent (elicitation drives design and design often drives additional elicitation), the intent of the SRS is not to represent the technical design of the product.

The terminologies BRD and SRS may be different from organization to organization. It is common to see high-level requirements documents and low-level requirements documents used among other varieties. Having two requirements documents completed by two different BAs implies that a business BA would need to go through planning activities and multiple iterations of elicitation and analysis in order to produce a signed-off BRD, complete with supporting models. Then the technical BA would also need to undergo planning activities and multiple iterations of elicitation and analysis in order to produce a signed-off SRS, complete with supporting models. These requirements documents are commonly misused in many organizations—mostly because the different types of requirements are misunderstood. In addition, BRDs are often structured as a bulleted wish list of everything the business wants included in the product sent for signoff (sometimes including solutions like: *A new database to manage client lists is required*). Then the technical BA would take the approved BRD and copy/paste the requirements/bulleted wish list into the SRS template, add any new requirements, and distribute for sign-off again. Using the suggested verbiage for stakeholder and solution requirements introduced earlier in this chapter will help to distinguish the difference between the stakeholder requirements versus solution requirements. In organizations where there is a single BA assigned to the project, there is usually a single document that encompasses both the stakeholder and solution requirements.

Transition requirements are too often forgotten and not documented anywhere, and because they describe the delta between the current state and future state, the future state needs to be well defined before transition requirements can be identified. Transition requirements can be evaluated in multiple phases, including during EA when discussing solution scope. For example, if it is known that the future state consists of a web based application and the current state is using a mainframe application, a couple of transition requirements could be:

- Users shall be trained on using a web-based application.
- Customer demographics data shall be migrated from the old system to the new system.

In the case where there is no intent to move to a web-based application until the design phase, where the product requirements dictated certain functionality that would only be met by moving to a web-based application, then the design decision would have created the two additional transition requirements. With this being said, transition requirements should be evaluated in EA when determining product scope, then reevaluated during analysis when stakeholder and solution requirements are defined, and once more post-design, as design decisions could introduce additional transition requirements.

Product Requirements Sign-off

Obtaining approval on product requirements can be a challenging task. Stakeholders are sometimes unwilling to commit to the requirements and refuse to sign off, or they hide their unwillingness to sign off on the requirements by sending the BA on a wild goose chase of contingent approval, based on multiple minor updates to the requirements documentation. In order to deal with this effectively, the PM and the BA need to uncover the reasons behind the stakeholders' hesitation to sign off. It is likely that the stakeholders are against the change and in such cases, it may become challenging to deal with these stakeholders both during the requirements definition stage and throughout the remainder of the project. People often fear the unknown—a little bit of education and clear communication about the change can go a long way.

There are stakeholders who have the need to put in their two cents worth by nitpicking at the requirements to feel that they provide value to the team. An effective way to deal with these stakeholders is to put something glaringly wrong in the beginning of the document so they feel they can earn their pat on the back, and then we can all move on to more important matters. With the requirements documents being lengthy, another challenge is getting the stakeholders to read the document in the first place. The BA distributes the version of the requirements document that is ready for sign-off, then, asks the stakeholders to review the document and prepare their questions and comments for the subsequent one-hour walk-through. The first question the BA asks at the walk-through is: "Who has read the document?"; only to realize that no one had read the requirements prior to the requirements walk-through. The BA (with the help of the PM, who can help the BA scribe during the requirements walk-through) needs to ensure that the walk-through does not turn into story time with the BA reading the document out loud to a roomful of stakeholders who are not paying attention, and once the hour is over, there is a need to schedule a longer follow-up session to complete the reading of the requirements document. Perhaps it is the name *requirements walk-through* that is misleading people to think it is a requirements reading session. This is not an effective use of everyone's time and the lengthy review process causes delays in the project schedule.

The way it should be done is to schedule periodic review sessions as part of the analysis to confirm the elicitation was accurate. This turns the requirements sign-off into more of a formality, as the approvers or their delegates would already be intimately aware of the requirements through the working sessions. Unfortunately, it is possible that the chunked out review sessions may also not overcome the problem of the stakeholders not reading the requirements documents—and it may require the BA-PM duo to further engage with the stakeholders in this matter.

If there are conflicting product requirements, they need to be resolved prior to requirements sign-off and the PM and the BA should team up to resolve these conflicts. The BA leads the effort to consider what makes the most sense for the product or organization as a whole and how well each requirement maps back to the business needs. The PM needs to consider the situation from the perspective of how each of the conflicting requirements stack up against the project constraints and any trade-offs that may be required. In addition to the need to consider both perspectives, the PM and the BA need to jointly demonstrate effective conflict resolution techniques and stakeholder expectations management skills.

Product Requirements in Agile Environments

In the past people believed that implementing projects using the agile approach meant that documentation of product requirements was not required and that this was what made agile a quicker method to deliver on—as compared to waterfall. But, as more organizations begin to utilize agile methodologies, it is becoming clear that the *no documentation* part was a myth. In fact, agile implementations require the execution of all project activities, just not to the same level of formality. The agile methodology is to break the project into much smaller increments or sprints, where one increment is accomplishing much less than one phase of a waterfall project. By implementing small pieces of the project at a time, dedicated project teams are able to focus and collaborate in order to release functionality into production every two to six weeks. When using an agile methodology, the different layers of requirements are not as apparent, but EA and the development of business requirements still take place—as the methodology is not chosen until there is a project. The stakeholder and solution requirements are still documented, but not necessarily in the same format, and functional requirements are combined into use cases or user stories.

User Stories

While user stories can be used in any methodology, they are more common in change-driven methodologies like agile. User stories document requirements with the user's point of view and focus on the benefits of the functionality requested. Agile is a value-driven methodology and articulating the benefit ensures all requirements provide value. User stories may be confused with use cases, as use case scenarios also focus on the user's point of view. User stories are articulated quite differently from use case scenarios and user stories consist of three parts:

1. *Actor*: The role requiring the functionality
2. *Functionality*: Describes what the actor needs to be able to do
3. *Benefit*: The value the requirement will bring

The components are combined as follows: As an <Actor>, I want to <Functionality> so that <Benefit>. The previous example of the stakeholder and solution requirement for the credit card application can be converted into the following user story: "As a customer service representative <Actor>, I can apply for a credit card directly in the call center application portal <Functionality> rather than logging into another system and rekeying the information; which will reduce the time it takes to complete an application and also reduce errors in the application process <Benefit>." User stories also have acceptance criteria defined for each story and it can be used to confirm that the user story is working as expected. The acceptance criteria can also be leveraged for testing purposes.

The BA needs to have a full understanding of the concept of different layers of requirements in both waterfall and agile, and it is also important for the PM to understand that the different layers of requirements require multiple rounds of elicitation and analysis and there has to be time allocated to complete them. In addition to textual requirements, there is often a need to produce models to enhance the understanding of the requirements and to cater to different audiences. The creation and review of models are time consuming. For these reasons the PM needs to be aware of the work involved in order to create complete product requirements, regardless of the methodology chosen.

DEFINING PROJECT REQUIREMENTS

Eliciting requirements is known to be one of the core functions of the BA. The meaning and intent of the word elicitation is to draw the information out of the stakeholders, because at times, the stakeholders themselves do not know what they need until the BA asks the right questions to extract the underlying needs from them. This back and forth between the BA and the stakeholders is better described as elicitation rather than gathering requirements, as requirements are not lying around for the BAs to pick up off the ground. The *PMBOK® Guide* mentions that the PM collects requirements and it is true in the sense that the PM collects the product requirements from the BA in order to convert them to project requirements, as part of the effort to develop the project WBS. As product requirements are being signed off, there is typically a refinement of the WBS and another round of estimates that are provided by the team. Impacted teams would reevaluate the work they need to perform in order to deliver the product or service specified in the detailed product requirements. The PM combines the information from all impacted stakeholders to create the overall project schedule.

RELEASE PLANNING

There are various reasons why projects may be broken down into multiple releases. In agile projects, this is much more apparent, as more emphasis is put into the prioritization process. Regardless of the rationale for the different releases, it is imperative for the PM and the BA to work together on this task. The PM cannot decide to break up the project based on work that needs to be completed within a specified timeframe without taking into consideration how the product requirements should be grouped. It also does not make sense to split the product requirements while ignoring the project constraints. Each release of product and project requirements needs to provide value and satisfy success criteria that need to be jointly decided by the PM-BA duo.

FINAL THOUGHTS ON REQUIREMENTS DEFINITION

Partnering up during the planning phase of the project and allowing the BA time to complete planning of the requirements definition will set the stage for a much smoother execution of requirements development and management, as well as the overall project activities. Although requirements definition is generally considered to be a BA activity, there are many things that the PM can do to support the BA through this critical phase of the project, including having the PM sometimes step outside of his or her role to help scribe meetings that the BA is chairing. The effort the PM invests in supporting the BA's requirements related activities will pay off with a more streamlined handover of the requirements to the project scope. The chosen project life cycle will also dictate how the requirements are defined and consequently, the project requirements. The relationship between product and project requirements has to be clearly understood and managed between the PM and BA in order to even have a chance at a successful project outcome.

REFERENCES

1. Project Management Institute Pulse of the Profession®. (2014). *Requirements Management: A Core Competency for Project and Program Success.* Newton Square, PA: Project Management Institute.
2. Project Management Institute. (2013). *A Guide to the Project Management Body of Knowledge (PMBOK® Guide)—Fifth Edition.* Newton Square, PA, USA: Project Management Institute, Inc., Section 4.2.3.1.

3. Project Management Institute. (2013). *A Guide to the Project Management Body of Knowledge (PMBOK® Guide)—Fifth Edition.* Newton Square, PA, USA: Project Management Institute, Inc., Section 5.1.3.2.
4. International Institute of Business Analysis. (2009). *A Guide to the Business Analysis Body of Knowledge (BABOK® Guide) Version 2.0.* Toronto, Ontario, Canada: International Institute of Business Analysis, Section 2.5.

7

ASSUMPTIONS, CONSTRAINTS, DEPENDENCIES, AND RISKS

"Risk is like fire: If controlled it will help you; if uncontrolled it will rise up and destroy you."—Theodore Roosevelt[1]

RAID (which stands for risks, assumptions, issues, and dependencies) should be an acronym that comes to the forefront of the mind of a project manager (PM) or a business analyst (BA) when managing a project. With the addition of constraints, we can modify the acronym to C-RAID. Issues are discussed briefly within the context of risks in this chapter but will be revisited when discussing change management (Chapter 9). Assumptions, constraints, dependencies, issues, and risks are commonly identified on projects yet it is astonishing how often they are misused. Most of the time stakeholders and team members log them for no other reason than to protect themselves from possible subsequent criticism or penalties. In many cases, C-RAIDs are logged but never revisited or managed properly. They get copied and pasted from the business case; to charter; to requirements; to design documents; to test plans; and sometimes through to implementation plans for the sole purpose of, if something were to go wrong each person involved can point to the documentation and say, "It's not my fault, because I told you this might happen." Identification is really only half the battle. Ideally, we should be using the logged assumptions, constraints, and risks to proactively validate our assumptions, plan within constraints, monitor dependencies, and reduce or eliminate the probability and/or impact of risks to reduce the number of issues.

Common mistakes also include logging items that are so generic that they fail to provide any value. For example: *If resources are not available when we need them, then our project will be delayed.* If there is a true resource availability concern, such as, if Jane is currently working on a higher priority project that is scheduled to be completed by the time our project begins, then we can assume that Jane will be available by a specific date (the start of our project) and manage it as a risk: *If the higher priority project that Jane is currently working on is delayed, then Jane will not be available by a specific date* (*the start of our project*). Another example of an attempt to identify a risk, but merely coming up with a sweeping statement might be: *We have a constraint that requirements must be signed off before design can begin*; but this is a common dependency for every waterfall project. If there is a more specific concern around the requirements being at risk of being signed off in time for design, then it has to be articulated. For example: *If the compliance concern is not clarified by a specific date, then requirements cannot be completed and signed off before the design start date.*

Before it can be understood how the PM and the BA can work together to identify and manage assumptions, constraints, dependencies, and risks, the difference between project level and product/requirement level needs to be understood. The PM manages at the project level and is therefore accountable for ensuring that project level assumptions, constraints, dependencies, and risks are being identified and managed. The BA manages at the requirement level and is therefore accountable for the identification and management of requirement level assumptions, constraints, dependencies, and risks. However, the PM-BA duo will need to work together to ensure there are no gaps.

ASSUMPTIONS

It is staggering that the large majority of PMs do not like assumptions; and by not liking assumptions, many PMs feel that there is no need to manage assumptions. Unfortunately, issues and problems that are not addressed and tracked tend to stick around and get worse with time—and so do the undocumented and unmanaged assumptions. Like them or not—it is a must to document, track, communicate, and manage assumptions at all stages of the project. Similar to changing babies' diapers or taking out the trash, not liking something does not release us from having to take care of it.

With BAs, the problem with assumptions is even more pronounced, as PMs at least have the perception that they have the luxury to *play* with assumptions—but BAs usually do not take part in any assumption-related exercises. While the PMs' focus on assumptions mainly surrounds early project unknowns, BAs need to not only take part in establishing project assumptions, but also need to lead and facilitate the management of requirements-related assumptions.

Besides not liking to deal with assumptions, PMs and BAs often do not know how to deal with assumptions—what questions to ask or what to do if and when assumptions do not end up materializing the way we were hoping they would. To illustrate how important it is to manage assumptions, we first need to realize that there are several possible outcomes, but three of them are not favorable for the project:

1. *Assumptions may be undefined and, as such—unknown*: If the condition related to the undocumented assumption is not known, we may not take any action about it and find ourselves unprepared when it takes place.
2. *Assumptions are closely related to risks and are often precursors to risks*: An assumption that does not play out the way we hoped it would, may compromise the project's ability to deliver on its commitment or it may derail progress in a variety of ways and areas. Simply put, when an assumption does not materialize the way we thought it would, it becomes a risk and must be managed accordingly.
3. *Dependencies*: Many conditions that are not known (especially early in the project planning stages) are related to various types of dependencies, and if the project's expectations about dependencies are not met, these assumptions once again are potential sources of risk. Most project dependencies are related to resources and to deliverables.

Assumptions can be defined as *something taken for granted*[2] and *accepted cause and effect relationships, or estimates of the existence of a fact from the known existence of other fact(s)*. Furthermore, assumptions must go through a comprehensive examination process before being accepted as reality. Assumptions are conditions, things, and premises that people believe to be true, but they offer no confirmation that they will remain the same as they were upon discovery. They are statements about beliefs related to future events and their outcomes. They are used for planning purposes—as it would be too costly or time consuming to confirm everything at the beginning. We would never exit the planning phase if everything had to be confirmed before moving forward. Assumptions however, should be confirmed as the project progresses. The PM should lead the process of managing project assumptions with the support of the BA, while the BA is the lead regarding the requirements-related and product-related assumptions. The BA also serves as a source of information regarding business and organizational-related assumptions that may not be known to the PM. When considering assumptions, the PM-BA duo needs to keep the project constraints in mind because under certain conditions, and once reaching their limit, constraints will limit the project's planned performance. While having a large number of assumptions may be an early indication for potential risks downstream, having a low number of assumptions documented is not necessarily a good sign, as it may be that the project team failed to properly document the assumptions.

The first step in managing assumptions is to identify and document them in order to be able to track them. Relatively few PMs document project assumptions and even fewer BAs properly document requirements-related ones. In addition, both PMs and BAs usually do little to no follow up to check whether the assumptions turn out the way they planned. After documenting the assumptions, there is a need to manage them on an ongoing basis, which includes a weekly review at the project status meeting and a quick round of updates to assumptions as often as every day, based on the project velocity and the events taking place.

Project Assumptions

The documentation and management of project assumptions can start as early as prior to project initiation, often with the BA's involvement in the feasibility and case study for the project. It then continues through the process of putting together the project charter and in turn, the project plan. The information required to manage assumptions involves the following: what the condition is, any relevant information about the condition, the stakeholders who should provide the information, and the date by which we need to know the information. It is beneficial to log the assumptions, as seen in Table 7.1, as it will be difficult for the PM, the BA, and the team to track and manage assumptions with no central repository to document them. Failing to get any information, receiving information that is not aligned with the assumptions, or receiving the information late will turn the assumption into a risk with all the associated implications.

A valid example of an assumption at the project level would be: *Software package out of the box will meet our needs with no custom coding*. Sure, this is a silly assumption—since when does a software package out of the box meet our needs? Many high paid executives make these assumptions when they attend

Table 7.1 Assumptions log

ID	The Condition	"Expiry Date" Deadline for Decision/Action	Information Required	Stakeholder Involved

The headers for an assumptions log

trade shows and purchase *cool* new tools and then create a need to use them. This assumption is higher-level and relates to the entire project rather than a subset of the requirements.

The management of assumptions includes the following steps:

1. Investigating the validity of the condition identified.
2. Understanding the options associated with the conditions.
3. Defining timelines for resolution.
4. Identifying the stakeholder(s) involved or impacted and those who need to provide information, decisions, or sign-off, regarding the assumptions' conditions.
5. Decide on an action plan. By the time the assumption reaches the date by which information is required, the PM and the BA should be prepared to *move* the assumption to the risk log and treat it like a risk. At that date (sometimes referred to as the *maturity date*), one of three things will happen:
    a. The conditions associated with the assumption *act* according to the plan. At this point we mark the assumption as complete and move on (business as usual), since the conditions materialized in line with our anticipation. For example, we assumed there was going to be an approval for the next phase of the project by Friday at noon, and we got the approval by the deadline.
    b. The assumption did not turn out as expected and the project is now facing a risk that has materialized. With the same condition as in the previous example—this time, by Friday at noon we learn that the plan for the next phase has been rejected. At that point, where one or more risks have been triggered, we need to employ a response strategy for the risk event.
    c. There is no new information or decision regarding the assumption's condition. At this point, we need to treat the lack of new information as a new condition; the assumption should not be viewed as if it did not turn out the way we were hoping it would. If by the deadline no decision has been made, we need to follow up and confirm that there is no decision and with the appropriate stakeholders act accordingly by recognizing that risks have been triggered and communicate the impact assessment of the new conditions we are now facing.

Project assumptions help define and articulate the conditions of the project environment in the absence of certainty or relevant information, and they help test the validity of the plans and estimates, as well as that of the requirements. Managing the assumptions is just as important as the need to communicate them to all stakeholders involved. Failing to communicate is equivalent to mismanaging the assumptions, similar to recognizing that not making a (timely) decision about a condition is equivalent to making a decision to do nothing. All the associated consequences must now be considered and accounted for. Another aspect of assumption-related communication is about ensuring that we not only communicate the conditions, stakes, and dates to the appropriate stakeholders; but that we also illustrate the potential impact of changing the assumption, making a different decision, or failing to make a decision. We also need to follow up with the stakeholders closer to the *maturity date* of the assumption to ensure they are aware of their role and responsibility in the matter.

For large scale, high complexity initiatives, using the assumptions log approach is preferred to make the planning and estimation processes easier by separating the assumptions from the risks. However, for smaller scale initiatives, the assumptions log can be skipped and all project assumptions can be converted into project risks immediately, to be managed in a project risk log. Technically, all assumptions are sources of risks—what happens if the assumption turns out not to be true? All assumptions can easily be converted into corresponding risk events, which is demonstrated as follows:

- **Project level assumption:** The software package out of the box will meet our needs with no custom coding.
- **Corresponding project risk:** If the software package out of the box does not meet our needs, then custom coding will be required, thus resulting in an $x increase in project costs.

The assumption *maturity* date, as described previously, can be used as a risk trigger and documented as the date to be reviewed. Risks that are not worth worrying about yet will not be reviewed as regularly as risks with higher probability and impact scores.

We Managed the Assumptions: Now What?

Another important part of managing assumptions is to ensure that assumptions are clear to move to the next level—we cannot move ahead with the project plan or with requirements without clearing the assumptions and making sure they are out of our way. For example, if the developers are scheduled to start the coding of certain features, we need to make sure that there are no questions, doubts, unclear areas, assumptions, or any misunderstandings in our way. For instance, when at the airport, we cannot start the process of boarding the plane if the aircraft has not made it to the gate yet. We may have an assumption that the plane has to be there by a certain time, but in order to proceed we need to *clear* the assumption and verify that the plane is indeed there.

Based on the options identified previously, our verification process may conclude that the plane is waiting for us at the gate and therefore, we can start boarding; but we may also learn that the plane is not there yet. At this point we treat it as a risk, since it has become more likely that the flight is going to be delayed. The third option considers the possibility that we still have not managed to get an update on whether the aircraft is at the gate or not. We now need to make a decision as to how much longer we are going to procrastinate before we treat it as a risk that has materialized. As a proactive measure, we should communicate the *no later than* point in time for a decision, and possibly start preparing to convert the assumption into a risk.

Assumption Categories

To make it easier to identify and deal with the assumptions, they can be broken down into the following two categories: (1) assuming that something will occur (or not) and planning actions around it; or (2) learning about a condition and making assumptions (for planning purposes) about its consequences.

Breaking down the assumptions into these categories makes it easier to treat them with the appropriate level of rigor. The first category covers events that may or may not happen and helps the team come up with applicable scenarios, while the second one is about events that the team knows will happen, but there is uncertainty about the results or the impact of these events:

1. *Assuming that something will occur and planning around it*: In this case, an assumption is made about something that needs to occur in a certain fashion as a condition for project success. An example would be when a commitment is made by the PM to meet a deadline based on an assumption that the project will have specific resources allocated to it by a certain point in time.
2. *Making assumptions (for planning purposes) about the consequences of a condition:* This type of assumption is made in light of a condition that the project is facing, and it is about the possible scenarios that may take place as a result. For example, if the project is forced to use a vendor that is known for notoriously long turnaround times, to prevent the project from stalling until the vendor provides estimates and plans, the team can come up with an assumption about what the vendor is likely to do. This can give the team a head start in planning around it.

These types of assumptions, which are more like educated or informed guesses, requires the team to also qualify them as risks and plan for the event that things will turn out to be different than the assumption predicts. Known as a risk analysis process, this should establish responses and action plans for the possibility that the risks materialize.

Project assumptions are the accountability of the project manager, but he or she is not responsible for identifying all the assumptions on the project. It is every team member's responsibility, including the BA, to identify and bring these to the attention of the PM. The same will be true when we study project constraints, dependencies, and risks. The identification process can also happen at any time within the project life cycle. New project-level assumptions are usually documented in an assumptions section within the requirements document(s), design document(s), test plan, and implementation plan. The BA can, and usually does, assist with the management of the project assumptions by ensuring all assumptions are consolidated into a project assumptions log and the conversion to corresponding risk events, but is not mandated by their role to do so.

Requirement Assumptions

Most of what was described for project assumptions also rings true for requirement assumptions. A valid example of an assumption at the requirement level would be: *Software package can be configured to display currency fields as two decimal places with no rounding*. By doing some initial tinkering with the software package it was observed that more than one decimal place can be entered for currency fields and the tool would automatically round to two decimal places. If one has worked for a financial institution they would know that a penny up or down is a big deal. An assumption was made that the user input could be configured to only allow entry of two decimal places without any custom coding. This assumption is at the lower level and related to a specific requirement where it was necessary to provide the ability for the user to enter a currency field. The assumption however, can be tied back to the project level assumption that the software package out of the box meets our needs with no custom coding. The BA therefore needs to be intimately aware of the project level assumptions in order to identify requirement level assumptions.

Requirement level assumptions are documented within the requirement using requirements attributes. In order to manage the requirement assumptions, the BA can use their own assumptions log or convert them to risks to be managed accordingly. Similar to how project assumptions can be converted into corresponding project risks, the same can be done for requirements assumptions:

- **Requirement level assumption:** Software package can be configured to display currency fields as two decimal places with no rounding.
- **Corresponding requirement level risk:** If the software package cannot be configured to display currency fields as two decimal places with no rounding, then the accounting may not be accurate.

The requirement level assumptions are usually too low level to bring to the attention of the PM; but sometimes there are requirement assumptions that translate into requirement risks that ultimately do affect time, cost, project scope, or quality. This will be expanded on when risks are discussed later in the chapter.

Assumption Pitfalls

Some common mistakes we make when identifying assumptions include:

- **Listing generic assumptions:** If assumptions can be copied and pasted into any project, they are too generic. For example: *Resources are available when needed.* When converting generic assumptions into risks, it will be difficult to come up with valid response plans since a real threat does not exist.
- **Listing facts as assumptions:** Remember, assumptions are factors that are believed to be true but are yet to be confirmed. When converting these items into corresponding risk events, they will not make sense because it is not possible to put the word *if* in front of it. An example of this could be: *We will be using a software package.* This may be a valid assumption if it has not been confirmed whether a software package is being used or not yet; but if it is a fact, which can be used as a basis for estimating and planning, it should be listed as a decision (in a decision log) rather than as an assumption.
- **Listing scope items as assumptions:** For instance: *Reporting is out of scope.* Again, this may be a valid assumption, if it is not confirmed whether reporting is in/out of scope. Scope items are also used for the purposes of estimating and planning, but they should be listed in the scope section if they are confirmed.
- **Listing process steps as assumptions:** An example of this could be: *Estimates will be revisited post analysis.* This is part of rolling wave estimation and not something we believe to be true but is yet to be confirmed. It is likely already listed in the organizations' project methodology that estimates should be revisited at the end of every phase. These are usually included in the assumptions section with the sole purpose of covering our tracks when providing estimates so that stakeholders know not to hold us to the numbers that were provided.

CONSTRAINTS

Constraints are limiting/restricting factors that affect the execution of a project, program, portfolio, or process.[3] Constraints are important factors to consider in the planning phases. Failing to identify them up front could throw the entire project for a loop. Consider a bathroom renovation—if the homeowner failed to mention that the entire renovation needed to be completed in under $5,000, the designer's grand plans to source a new jetted tub, replace the cabinetry, and install granite countertops would be out of the question and a waste of time. Furthermore, if the home owner failed to mention they were going to live in the home during the renovations, removing the tub in the home's only full bathroom overnight would also be extremely inconvenient.

Project Constraints

Project constraints are limitations or restrictions on the project. Constraints can also be identified at any point of the project life cycle and need to be monitored to ensure that we do not reach the limitations or violate the restrictions.

Some project constraints help articulate project success criteria—typically the triple constraints (scope, time, and cost)—as well as quality. Project objectives have to be communicated by the sponsor, but then further refined and articulated into success criteria by the PM and the BA. The success should be expressed in terms of the four criteria (scope, time, cost, and quality), as well as potentially other performance measures that are important for the customer and the sponsor.

Examples of project-level constraints could be:

- The project must be implemented before the end of the year.
- The project must be implemented in under $500,000.
- A web services resource is not available to start on the project until March 1.
- The software package must be used out of the box with no custom coding.
- All components must be developed in Java.

All constraints can also be converted into:

1. *Corresponding risk events if we are approaching the limitation/restriction*: For example, using the constraint—*The project must be implemented in under $500,000*—when the project is close to having spent all its approved funds, there is now a risk that the project will run out of money. The corresponding project risk can be articulated as: *If the project is not implemented in under $500,000, then funds will have to be allocated from another project*.
2. *Corresponding issues if we are at the limitation/restriction*: If the project has spent all its approved funds, the $500,000; it is now an issue.

Project constraints can therefore be managed going forward in either the project risk or issue log, depending on whether the project is approaching the limitation or at the limitation.

Requirement Constraints

Requirement constraints are limitations or restrictions on a specific requirement or a subset of the requirements rather than the whole project. These are usually identified through requirements elicitation and documented in requirements attributes similar to the requirement assumptions.

Examples of requirement constraints could be:

- This requirement must be implemented by the end of March to satisfy the compliance concern.
- No custom coding will be done to format the currency field to two decimal places with no rounding.
- Input field has a maximum length of 30 characters to avoid truncation in downstream systems.

Requirement constraints are documented to help generate discussion with our stakeholders. Knowing the requirement must be implemented by the end of March assists in the requirements allocation into different releases—which is something the PM needs to be aware of during the scheduling process. If the sponsor had originally agreed to no custom coding of the software application due to additional costs, but is aware that out of the box functionality does not fully meet their needs, additional investment may be made to custom code certain aspects—which means changes in the project funding and reworking the forecasts for the PM. Knowing that the input field has a maximum length of 30 characters will trigger discussions with subject matter experts (SMEs) on whether there would be a scenario where the user would need to input data greater than 30 characters. This may warrant additional system requirements or business process workarounds to manage going forward—both of which may impact project scope, cost, and timelines, which means again, the PM may need to be alerted. These requirement constraints can also be converted into corresponding risk events to work through the impacts, if it is not obvious from looking at the constraint directly. This will be further explored in the risk section.

Constraint Pitfalls

Like assumptions, there are a few things we need to be mindful of when documenting them:

- **Listing generic constraints:** When converting generic constraints into risks or issues, it will be difficult to come up with valid response plans since a real threat or problem does not exist.
- **Not understanding the relationship between assumptions and constraints:** There is the potential for a connection between assumptions and constraints—especially at the early planning stages of the project, when the project team and other stakeholders may not be aware of all the constraints the project may be facing, or their extent. It is therefore important to document this knowledge and ensure that any missing or unclear piece of information is considered and documented as an assumption. Typically, the PM and the BA who facilitate this process will pursue answers for these open questions and in turn, will convert the assumptions into constraints. In some cases, the lack of information may also constrain the ability to move forward with the planning or the project work.

DEPENDENCIES

Dependencies are "relationships between conditions, events, or tasks such that one cannot begin or be completed until one or more other conditions, events, or tasks have occurred, begun, or completed."[4] To demonstrate the importance of dependencies for planning purposes, consider the bathroom renovation example again. If the countertop was installed prior to selecting a sink, it could imply rework or wasted material if the home owner eventually decided on a pedestal sink.

Project Dependencies

Project dependencies establish the links and link types between all the activities and tasks of the project. These also include dependencies on other projects, other parts of the organization, operations, and external links (outside of the performing organization; including vendors, regulators, government, and even competition).

The PM is the owner of the process of defining project dependencies; however this task cannot be performed effectively without the close support of the BA. Similar to the rest of the C-RAID items, the identification of project dependencies should start early on in the project—if possible, while putting together the project charter. Within the requirements document, the BA must also ensure project dependencies are clearly articulated. The work breakdown structure (WBS) is the next place to capture dependencies. As the project team refines the project scope and decomposes the WBS to work packages and activities, dependencies should become increasingly clear. Dependencies are then further evolved during the development of the project schedule, where dependencies will become one of the main drivers in determining activity sequencing. Even if the PM believes it is possible to determine project dependencies without the support of the BA, the need for the BA's involvement in identifying dependencies further increases at this stage, as the BA's knowledge of the requirements and the familiarity with the project's product become major input in identifying project dependencies. Project dependencies are also likely the topic of discussion as the BA is eliciting requirements from the SMEs.

The project management office (PMO) can also be a valuable resource for project dependencies, particularly with identifying and addressing cross-project dependencies. The PMO consolidates all projects' needs in an effort to consistently and effectively avoid any dependency-related interruptions. The PM-BA duo can work with the PMO to ensure all product, business, technical, and resource-related dependencies (including type, availability, timing, and skills) are considered in the appropriate context. In addition to the types of dependencies, the PMO has input from all projects and can provide additional context for urgencies, prioritization, operational needs, and emergencies.

To make it easier for the PM and the BA to identify, articulate, and manage dependencies it is important to discuss the various types of dependencies. As part of establishing their working relations, the PM and the BA need to discuss how they will manage dependencies, who will take the lead for which areas, and how to resolve issues around project dependencies.

Dependencies—Timing and Types

Dependencies can be categorized into one of four generic categories that also indicate the timing in which the dependency introduces itself. There are more effective ways for the PM and the BA to categorize dependencies but as a start, it is helpful to identify when dependencies tend to introduce themselves:

1. *Preconditions within the project*: These are dependencies that indicate that certain things in the project must take place for a successor activity to be performed. For example, testing can start after test cases have been completed and the code is written. Typically, the PM and the BA have the ability to proactively track whether the dependency takes place as required and act, in the event that things do not progress as planned.
2. *Preconditions—external/out of scope*: These dependencies are similar to the previous category in the timing, but here the project depends on predecessor events, actions, or deliverables that need to take place

outside of the project organization. It is much more difficult to track these external dependencies, to identify signs of problems, or to act proactively on the chance for trouble.

3. *Postconditions—what happens next within the project*: These are once again dependencies that are internal to the project; however, they are successor activities that depend on predecessor activities within the project. This type of distinction is essentially the opposite of the dependencies discussed in Category 1; each dependency is viewed as what needs to happen before it (Category 1) and what depends on it in the project downstream.
4. *Postcondition—what happens next externally*: Similar to the relationship between Categories 1 and 3, this type of dependency closely interacts with the type discussed in Category 2. This type is about successor activities that are outside of the project scope and organization and that depend on what predecessor activities need to take place within the project.

Generic Categories

This additional *layer* of dependencies can help PMs and BAs better articulate the type of dependency they are dealing with. It is based on how the Project Management Institute breaks down dependencies:

1. *Mandatory or hard logic*: These dependencies are conditions that are given, for example, the laws of physics. These dependencies refer to situations that the project team has no control over.
2. *Discretionary, or soft logic*: These dependencies are events or conditions that are taken into consideration for the planning and the performance of the project work, but they are based mainly on best practices or other events and conditions that may be subjective. For example, the BA may refuse to complete the requirements elicitation process until certain requirements-related objectives have been met. Although there is nothing that physically blocks the BA from proceeding with the requirements, the decision is based on discretionary considerations. As such, discretionary dependencies may be overridden and the process may move forward even without meeting all its milestones.
3. *External dependencies*: These are dependencies that are a result of predecessor events and conditions from outside of the organization. The PM and the BA have little to no control over influencing these events and therefore should plan around them.

There are also the dependencies that represent logical relationships between any two given activities and they involve the interaction of these two activities with each other, for the purpose of developing a project schedule—Finish to Start (the default type of relationship), Start to Start, Finish to Finish, and Start to Finish. When building a schedule and sequencing activities, the PM and the BA should establish guidelines for themselves and for team members and other stakeholders involved in the estimating process to follow when determining logical relationships between two activities or any type of dependency. The PM and the BA must consider whether to sequence things based on facts that include constraints and actual dependencies, or to do it based on beliefs, perceptions, best practices, availability of resources, and attempts to avoid risks. Sequencing in an attempt to avoid risk can be overcome by assuming the risk and resequencing accordingly. For example, when planning to renovate an office, it would be prudent to schedule the painting prior to the installation of new carpet, to reduce the chance that the carpet will get stained by the paint. This logic is not supported by any physical conditions that force us to do it in this order, and if we need to, we can reverse the order and install the carpet prior to painting. Although it involves risks, it can address the availability of the contractors involved.

The List of Dependencies

The previous discussion provides important context as to what dependencies are and how to understand what they mean. The following list presents the most effective way to list the dependencies under categories that are intuitive, and at the same time, it reduces the chance for confusion, omissions, and duplications. When discussing dependencies, PMs and BAs need to consider the following areas:

- **Deliverable-driven:** This implies a dependency on something that needs to be produced or delivered. It can be further broken into internal and external subcategories. Deliverables could be products, results, processes, reports, completion of activities, or results that we need in order to proceed with our plan.
- **Decisions and sign-offs (stakeholder-driven):** This would include dependency on approvals, go/no-go decisions, passing of a milestone, customer feedback, steering committee decisions, or any other approval that the project requires.
- **Resource availability:** This is one of the most common types of dependencies. It is based on soft logic, but it is also one of the most common types of dependencies that produces the most risk. It involves depending on the availability of the type of resource the project needs, with the right set of skills and experience, at the right time, and for the necessary duration. Many things may not materialize the way the project team had

planned, and in the event that a resource does not report to the project as planned, the PM-BA duo must work together to quickly assess what the impact is, what options are available, and what course of action should be taken.

- **Technical considerations:** This is a dependency that requires input from the BA, because the PM most likely does not have sufficient understanding of the technical aspects of the product. The information is typically reported to the BA by SMEs or by technical members of the team and in turn, the BA puts the report in context and provides the PM with meaningful information to act upon.
- **Risk and assumption-related dependencies:** These are dependencies that rely on conditions that are not finalized or ones that may impact project success. As the PM and the BA work on an ongoing basis to verify and validate assumptions and to manage risks, there should not be too many such dependencies.
- **External dependencies:** This includes cross-project, operational, organizational, and dependencies from outside of the organization—which could even involve events that may take place outside of the project (or even outside of the organization). Dependencies that are *outside of the organization* would include dependencies on vendors, suppliers, and contractors; decisions by regulatory bodies; markets; the environment; and even competition. Within the organization there are also multiple areas that the project may depend on, and the BA has the ability to provide meaningful input. These areas include cross-project dependencies that may contain deliverables from other projects, as well as resource-related dependencies. When a resource works on one project and needs subsequently to report to a different project—there is a chance that events in one project may prevent the resource from reporting to the other project on time, or at all. The value the BA can provide increases when dealing with operational and organizational dependencies, since the BA often has more visibility to the types of considerations that are partially driven by enterprise analysis (EA) and involve considering items that are out of the project scope, but may still have impact on the project. In addition, the BA should keep an eye on the impact that decisions made within the project have on the organization, the business, and the project's product.

When considering external dependencies, the BA, in collaboration with the PM, ensures that there is a two-way interaction when it comes to dependencies: one direction is about dependencies that impact the project and the other refers to dependencies on the project that may impact the product or the organization downstream. In this context, working together with the PM, with active support from the PM, will allow the BA to produce significant value for the organization in the form of early indications on whether or not the project produces the intended value, while ensuring that project objectives remain in line with business objectives.

PMs and BAs also need to consider the nature of the dependency and the severity of its impact if it does not materialize as planned, then put together a plan so the team can act accordingly to ensure that the dependency and its impact are sufficiently and appropriately addressed. Based on all the considerations surrounding the dependency, the PM and the BA need to pick a strategy regarding how to engage stakeholders and manage stakeholder expectations.

Requirement Dependencies

Requirement dependencies are relationships between requirements. There are four different types of relationships between requirements:

1. *Subsets*: A requirement may be a subset of another requirement. For example, the following are subsets of the requirement to provide the ability for the customer to apply for a banking account online:
   - The system shall provide the ability for the customer to select from a listing of valid products based on customer demographics.
   - The system shall provide the ability for the customer to add additional signers to the account.
   - The system shall provide the ability for the customer to transfer a balance from another financial institution.
   - The system shall provide the ability for the customer to review and accept any disclosures.
2. *Implementation Dependency*: Some requirements cannot be implemented until another requirement is implemented first. For example, implementing the ability for the customer to associate multiple mailing addresses to their account cannot be implemented until the requirement to upgrade the software package to Version 10 has been implemented.
3. *Benefit or Value Dependency*: Some requirements in and of themselves provide limited value, but if another requirement is implemented, it may increase or decrease the value of a related requirement. For example, if the requirement to provide the ability for the customer to apply for a banking account online is being implemented, the requirement to provide the ability for call center agents to assist with the online application process increases in value, but the requirement to increase branch staff for account openings decreases in value.

4. *Effort Dependency*: The effort dependency exists when the implementation of one specific requirement makes another requirement easier to implement. For example, implementing the requirement to upgrade the software package to Version 10 will make it easier to implement the requirement to ensure all currency fields in the application allow only two decimal places with no rounding. (This assumes that Version 10 of the software package has an option to configure the rounding settings.)

Requirement dependencies are documented within the requirements attributes. Requirement dependencies play a key role in allocating requirements to different releases, so the BA needs to work with the PM to ensure that all of the requirement-related dependencies are understood, as this information will feed into understanding project dependencies and the creation of the project schedule.

Dependency Pitfalls

Here are some common mistakes to watch out for when documenting dependencies:

- **Listing generic dependencies:** For example, the design start date is dependent on completion of certain requirements. While generic dependencies do feed into the project schedule, there is no value in calling them out in the dependencies section in the charter, then copying them over to the requirements, and so forth.
- **Not understanding the relationship between assumptions and dependencies:** Dependencies are events that need to happen in order for the project to proceed. Although there is a clear understanding that dependencies need to take place, it is possible for a dependency to also be an assumption and therefore, a potential source of risk at the same time. Dependencies should therefore not be taken for granted and should not be viewed by team members or by the PM and the BA as facts. An example of a project dependency which is also an assumption is concerning the approval of the project budget by the steering committee. While it is essential for the project to have funding approvals by a certain date, there is no guarantee that it will happen and hence, the dependency is also labeled as an assumption. It is also possible for an assumption to become a dependency and it should therefore be logged as both an assumption and as a dependency. If assumption logs are not being used, dependencies can be converted into corresponding risk events and can be managed directly in the risk log as well.

RISKS

Risks are uncertainties that can positively or negatively impact a project or product. Risks usually have a negative connotation (known as threats) but positive risks, (known as opportunities) are still considered risks. This chapter focuses on the identification and management of *negative* risks. Risks often get confused with issues and in many projects, items are logged with an identical description in both the risk and issue logs with the same log date. Issues are problems that have happened, concerns, or sometimes a realized risk—things that make us say, "Uh oh, now what?" If a risk event occurs, it is no longer an uncertain event, and it may be treated in various ways, including as an issue. Ideally, a contingency plan is in place so that even though the risk is realized, it is not marked as an issue because contingency kicks in. In order to eliminate the confusion between issues and risks, it is recommended that all risks be documented in an if/then format: *If the condition occurs, then the consequence could happen.* Furthermore, if the risk can be quantified, it can be entered into a risk statement template that is structured as: *If the condition occurs, then the consequence could happen, leading to a quantifiable result.* If something has happened, it would not make sense to put an *If* in front of it and therefore it's not a risk. Risks can also be defined at the project level as well as the requirement level.

Project Risks

Project level risks are those that impact the project. Think about the triple constraints: time, cost, and project scope. If the risk impacts any of those items, it is considered a project risk. The following are all examples of project risks:

- If the software package does not meet our needs, then custom coding may be required.
- If the business SME is tied up on a higher priority project, then he or she will not be available to attend the requirements workshop.
- If an expert on the existing application cannot be identified, then more time will be needed to understand the current state of the application.
- If compliance/risk is not engaged prior to requirements sign-off, then it may lead to rework if changes are identified post sign-off.

The *then* portion of the risk statement in all of these examples is ither time, cost, or project scope—indicating it is a project risk. Project risks are managed within a project risk log. The headings for a project risk log are shown in Table 7.2.

The PM owns the project risk log and is accountable for ensuring that all project risks have action plans, single owners for monitoring, and contingencies

Table 7.2 Project risk log

ID	Risk Description	Impact	Probability	Score	Trigger Event/ Indicator	Risk Response and Description	Secondary and/or Residual Risk	Contingency Plan	Owner	Status	Date Entered	Date to Review

The headers for a project risk log

attached to them. The PM is not responsible for the identification of all risks and certainly does not own all of the risks in the project risk log; in fact, the PM will likely own only a few. The majority would be assigned to the work package owners, including the BA who owns the analysis phase of the project as well as any risks related to requirements management, with the PM on the hook to ensure all project risks are dealt with in a timely manner.

Although the PM owns the project risk management process, the BA should assist, as the majority of project risks are identified within the analysis phase. In the planning phase, we do not know what we do not know—and it is further analysis that converts the unknown unknowns over to the known unknowns. Unknown unknowns being *future circumstances, events, or outcomes that are impossible to predict, plan for, or even to know where or when to look for them*[5] and known unknowns are the risks that can be identified and planned for. The PM is not necessarily part of the elicitation session, and is not required to be, but since the BA is eliciting requirements, he or she should also be making note of any project risks that have cropped up, even if they are not the owner of that risk. The BA can certainly make note of these items and communicate them to the PM to insert into the log so that he or she can follow up accordingly to ensure there are action plans, an owner, etc.—but it would be much more efficient if the BA had elicited all the appropriate information up front and captured it directly into the project risk log. This implies that the BA should also be intimately aware of the project risk management process and managing the project risks log should be a shared responsibility among the dynamic PM-BA duo.

To summarize the project risk management process, risks are identified and documented using the if/then format described. Risk may also be initially captured in multiple documents: the charter, requirements document, design documents, test plans, and meeting notes to name a few. They should be transferred over to the project risk log as a single source of all project risks. After the team decides on an impact and probability rating, an appropriate risk response should be documented along with any secondary and/or residual risk. If residual risk exists, a contingency plan should also be listed. Residual risk is any risk that is leftover after the response plan is put in place; secondary risk is any new risk that was introduced as a result of implementing the response plan. A good test is if there is a new if/then statement upon implementing the response plan, then there is secondary risk. Secondary risks need to be managed as new risks in the project risk log. If the same if/then statement still rings true after a response plan has been implemented, then it is residual risk. There would be residual risk for any risks that have a response of mitigate, transfer, or accept—but if a risk is avoided, there should be no residual risk. In the event that there are many risks that require contingency plans, but the majority of them have a low risk score (the product of the impact and probability), an organization's risk management process may dictate that contingencies are only required for those with a high enough score. What qualifies as a "high enough" score will, of course, have to be defined in the project's risk management plan—and if one of the risks that does not have contingencies is realized, a backup plan will need to be devised as needed.

It is beneficial for the risk management process to identify triggers; these are events or indications that a risk is about to occur or has occurred. Consider risk triggers as things that get our *Spidey senses* tingling (see Image 7.1). Identifying

Image 7.1 Spider-Man's Spidey sense tingles when a risk trigger has been detected

risk triggers is notably absent from many organization's project risk management processes. One of the biggest complaints from PMs is that their risks logs are unmanageable and reviewing risks takes up almost the entire project status calls. If a trigger can be identified, they can be used to set the next review date—keeping in mind that by definition, a trigger can be two different points in time: when the risk is about to occur or at the point where it occurs. Ideally, it would be better to identify when risk is about to occur to give the team enough time to proactively prepare for the imminent threat. Identifying triggers should also decrease the number of realized risks that convert into issues. Referring to the first example of a project risk—*If the software package does not meet our needs, then custom coding may be required*—at what point will the team know that custom coding may be required? They should definitely know by the end of build, but that is probably too late. The team can set the trigger three-quarters of the way through the analysis phase, when requirements are almost firm. A checkpoint can be set to see if there was anything that the technical resources noticed that the software package may not be able to deliver without custom coding. This provides enough lead time to present the information to the sponsor to request more funding and/or time or to modify the requirement so that it will work within the constraints without much rework.

In the case where the technical resources agree that no custom coding is required, the trigger and next review date can be moved to the end of analysis, and keep moving until the project reaches the point where it is clear that there will be no custom coding required by the end of build. A technical resource assigned to the team would be the owner of this risk, with the PM overseeing the process to ensure this risk is monitored appropriately, and the BA on the watch for items that may require custom coding within the analysis phase. If the BA works on the project risk log alongside the PM, they would already be aware of this risk and have it at the back of their minds while eliciting requirements. Hence another benefit to having the PM and BA collaborate on the project risk management process.

The PM should allot time within the status meetings with the project team to follow up with the appropriate owners on risks with an upcoming review date, and to determine if there are any new risks to be added. If, at the review, it is determined that the risk is imminent, this is the time to implement the contingency plans. If there is no appropriate contingency plan, then the realized risk is now an issue that needs to be opened in the issue log and closed in the risk log.

Project Risk Pitfalls

Frequent errors made when managing project risks (aside from not managing them at all) are:

- **Listing generic project risks:** Listing generic project risks is a common mistake that is made across the board, and organizations that include sample generic risks in their templates are usually the ones most likely to make this mistake. The challenge is thinking of ways to manage a generic threat. An appropriate trigger or review date cannot be set on arbitrary risks either. If there is a real threat specific to the project, the risk statement should be modified to indicate that.
- **Not articulating the risk:** Another common mistake is documenting a risk as *resource* or *funding*, without explaining what the resource or funding risk actually is. On the flip side, there are some risks that are documented using an entire paragraph that is riddled with redundancies and in the end, the risk is still undetermined: "We had decided to hire a vendor to assist in the development efforts, since we did not have any of that type of expertise in-house. We are currently awaiting a resource to be assigned. We still aren't sure how much this will cost. We will be meeting with the vendor company next week." This sounds more like an action plan to address an issue that we did not have the expertise to develop in-house. It can also be a risk associated with not having a resource assigned yet—impacting timelines. Articulating all risk events using the risk statement should alleviate this challenge: *If the condition occurs, then the consequence could happen.*
- **Confusing issues and risks:** Using the risk statement will also solve the common confusion between risks and issues: if an *If* cannot be put in front, it is probably not a risk.
- **Arbitrary impact and probability ratings and scoring:** Most organizations do have it as part of their project risk management procedures to assign an impact and probability rating of high, medium, or low without providing any definition as to what high, medium, or low means. It is actually quite amusing that we waste a lot of time and energy arguing with our colleagues over whether the risk impact or probability should be high, medium, or low when the values are arbitrary. A score then gets calculated and there is no guidance as to what to do with a risk of a score of 25 versus a score of five. Tables 7.3 and 7.4 contain guidelines that could be used for defining impact and probability ratings and action plans based on project risk scores.
- **Thinking risk was avoided when it was really mitigated:** In most cases it is no big deal if the response is labeled as mitigated versus as transferred; but avoidance carries special meaning. If an avoidance strategy has been implemented, the probability of the risk event occurring should be decreased to zero, meaning the risk event can be closed and no longer needs to be monitored. If it was mitigated and it was treated

Table 7.3 Project risk impact and probability rating

Rating	Impact	Rating	Probability
5	**High:** Represents failure of the project	5	**High:** (67-99%)
3	**Medium:** Severely reduces project benefits	3	**Medium:** (34-66%)
1	**Low:** May increase project costs and timescales	1	**Low:** (1-33%)

Guidelines for defining project risk impact and probability ratings

Table 7.4 Project risk scores and recommended action plans

Guidelines for addressing project risk based on risk scores

Risk score = Impact x Probability
When determining priority, impact trumps probability

Legend: (priority) score
(1) 25 means a priority of 1 and a risk score of 25

Impact				
	5	(5) 5	(2) 15	(1) 25
	3	(7) 3	(4) 9	(3) 15
	1	(9) 1	(8) 3	(6) 5
		1	3	5
	Probability			

High Risk (score of 15-25):
Critical to address these types of risk.
Recommended responses – Avoid/Mitigate/Transfer

Moderate Risk (score of 5-9):
Cost/Benefit analysis will need to be conducted to determine whether the action plan is appropriate for the threat level.
Recommended responses – Mitigate/Transfer/Accept

Low Risk (score of 1-3):
Monitor to ensure threat levels do not change.
Recommended response – Accept

as avoided, the risk may actually hit the project as a complete surprise because the risk was no longer being monitored and subsequently, did not have a contingency in place.

Requirement Risks

If the risk impacts the product, whether it is an application, process, or service, the risk is considered a requirement risk. The following are examples of requirement risks:

- If the software package currency fields cannot be configured to 2 decimal places with no rounding, then our accounting may not balance.
- If there are more than 500 concurrent users in the system, then the system will crash.
- If the reports are not available by 9 a.m., then teams cannot begin their work.
- If user IDs are not maintained, then unauthorized users may access the system.
- If all data is not migrated within the implementation window, then records may be corrupted if users attempt to access it.

In these examples the impact of the risk or the *then* portion of the risk statement is to the product and not project time, cost, or scope. It is likely that additional requirements may need to be added to address these requirement risks which could ultimately impact project time, cost, or scope, hence the importance of forming a partnership between the PM and BA and ensuring the lines of communication are always open.

The BA will be performing multiple iterations of elicitation and analysis within the analysis phase of the project. As requirements are elicited, the BA should also be eliciting any requirement level risks, which is likely a new concept for many. There are organizations that are well-established in their requirements management processes that already have a requirement risk management process. These are usually the organizations that have formed business analysis centers of excellence dedicated to maturing the organizations' requirements management processes. Requirement risks are not logged in the project risk log: the *Business Analysis Body of Knowledge* (*BABOK*®) lists some of the common requirements attributes that should be captured by the BA as they are eliciting requirements, and requirements risk is one of those attributes implying this is where requirement risks could be captured.[6] To work through some of the requirement level risks, a requirement risk log can be used. The headers in a requirement risk log are shown in Table 7.5.

Table 7.5 Requirement risk log

ID	Req ID	Risk Description	Impact	Probability	Score	Trigger Event/ Indicator	Control	Risk Strategy	Secondary and/or Residual Risk	Workaround	Status	Date Entered

The headers for a requirement risk log

One of the prevalent mistakes that BAs make in the requirement risk management process is leaving it until the end and treating it like a separate process from requirements elicitation—as if it was an afterthought or a chore that had to be done in order to satisfy project audits. Similar to the project risk management process and having the BA enter project risks directly into the project risk log, the BA should also be entering these immediately into the requirement risk log.

The benefits of requirement risk management include:

- **Risk-based testing to allow testing efforts to be focused on specific areas of high risk:** Testers are faced with the challenge of executing the least amount of tests to uncover the most defects in a limited time period. There are an infinite number of tests that can be executed for a given scenario. With a completed requirement risk assessment, they can focus on testing the riskier requirements the most.
- **Assisting with the prioritization of development activities:** Without any specific instruction, the development team may focus on developing the easier and usually less risky requirements first. With a completed requirement risk assessment, they may want to develop the riskier requirements first and have them tested first, as these are the ones that likely produce the most defects.
- **Highlighting residual risk to the business:** Leftover requirement risk is an important factor that usually gets overlooked. After the project wraps up, these items may still continue to haunt the business. By proactively highlighting residual requirement risk and providing business workarounds, the business will be better equipped to deal with them after the project has wrapped up and the project team has moved on. These residual risks should also be included in the transition plan at the end of the project since they will need to be transitioned over to the operational team. The transition plan usually being the responsibility of the PM, he or she should work with the BA to ensure these are included.
- **Identifying any missed requirements:** In the project risk management process the goal is to regularly monitor project risks for changing

conditions so the project team can be more proactive, rather than reactive. In a requirement risk management process, the goal is not to look for changing conditions, but to help poke holes in requirements so the gaps can be filled proactively, rather than reactively—which would open multiple change requests at later stages of the project, resulting in rework. If used appropriately, the requirement risk log can be a fantastic tool in helping flush out missed requirements—one of the top culprits in failed projects.

Requirement risks are also documented using the if/then format in the risk description column with the *then* portion of the risk statement representing the impact to the product. Requirement risks can be tied back to a single requirement or a group of requirements which would be documented in the Requirement ID column. For traceability purposes, the requirement attribute can reference the risk ID in the requirement risk log. There is also an impact and probability rating, and the product of the two will also give a risk score. Note that the impact and probability rating may not necessarily be the same as defined in the project risk management process. Table 7.6 contains guidelines that can be used to define high, medium, and low impact and probability for requirement risks and Table 7.7 can be used to determine the appropriate action plan for requirement risks based on risk score.

In project risk management, the risk response strategies—avoid, mitigate, transfer, and accept—are used in response to project risk score. For requirement risks, a control and/or a risk strategy would be identified based on the requirement risk score. A control is a solution put permanently in place to address the risk. Permanent meaning it survives beyond the duration of the project; and a risk strategy is a solution that is put temporarily in place to address the

Table 7.6 Requirement risk impact and probability rating

Rating	Impact	Rating	Probability
5	**High:** Business processes/activities would stop	5	**High:** (67-99%)
3	**Medium:** A business process or work-around could be implemented for a short period until a fix is implemented	3	**Medium:** (34-66%)
1	**Low:** Business area could live with exposure	1	**Low:** (1-33%)

Guidelines for defining requirement risk impact and probability ratings

Table 7.7 Requirement risk scores and recommended action plans

Guidelines for addressing requirement risk based on risk scores

Risk score = Impact X Probability
When determining priority, impact trumps probability

Legend: (priority) score
(1) 25 means a priority of 1 and a risk score of 25

Impact				
	5	(5) 5	(2) 15	(1) 25
	3	(7) 3	(4) 9	(3) 15
	1	(9) 1	(8) 3	(6) 5
		1	3	5
	Probability			

High Risk (score of 15-25):
Critical to address these types of risk.
Recommended response – define both a control and risk strategy

Moderate Risk (score of 5-9):
Cost/Benefit analysis will need to be conducted to determine whether the action plan is appropriate for the threat level.
Recommended response – define either a control or a risk strategy

Low Risk (score of 1-3):
Monitor to ensure threat levels do not change.
Recommended response – risk strategy

risk—*temporary* meaning that it is something that is done within the duration of the project. Usually *adding controls* means additional requirements and *implementing risk strategies* usually means adding project scope—both of which can increase project time and/or costs. This is why it is in the best interest of the project manager to be well aware of the requirement risks. Many requirement risks can be translated into new project risks by rewording the risk statement.

- **Requirement risk:** If there are more than 500 concurrent users in the system, then the system will crash.
- **Project risk:** If there are more than 500 concurrent users in the system, then additional servers will need to be purchased

It can be assumed that at the time the above risks were brainstormed, it was unknown how many concurrent users were in the system and what the growth rates would be. After some capacity planning, it was determined there were about 350 concurrent users in the system at that time, and that they were not anticipating an increase in that number to anywhere near 500 within the duration of the project. The probability attached to the project risk can then be listed as very low, and that it would not make sense to invest in new servers at this time, but there should be focus on the requirement risk. A control could be implemented for this requirement risk by creating an alert for production support once they reached a count of 400 concurrent users. This alert will require additional requirements to be added, as the alert will need to be developed and tested. Since these discussions would be occurring during the analysis phase when requirements are being defined, it is the perfect time to add additional requirements without risking rework. This requirement may have been missed, without having gone through the requirement risk process—and the alert does not stop us from hitting the limitation, thus residual risk still exists.

A business workaround would therefore need to be identified, which could be as simple as providing a process to request new servers when necessary, and the workaround may or may not be a new process. A workaround to a requirement risk is similar to the concept of contingency in project risk management and the workaround can be thought of as any processes (manual or systematic, existing or new) that will need to be implemented if the requirement risk is realized in the production environment. Any residual requirement risks should also be documented in the transition plan during project handover into the operational environment, given that the requirement risk becomes an operational risk once the project wraps up. The transition plan is typically the accountability of the PM, so the PM and BA once again need to collaborate to ensure the handoff of the residual risks occur.

The following example helps evaluate the controls and risk strategies that could be implemented: *If user IDs are not maintained, then unauthorized users may access the system.* A control could be a process which includes adding a workflow reminder task to management to review user access monthly—and there may also be a need for new screens for management to update user access that was not part of the original requirements. A risk strategy that could be employed in addition to the incremental requirements could be a one-time systematic clean-up of all user IDs currently in the system, where an algorithm is run to remove any IDs that are no longer active. This is something that is done within the duration of the project and therefore temporary in nature.

The requirement risk log, used as a working tool during the analysis phase, should be revisited throughout the remainder of the project life cycle and especially during the design phase. If the BA is not already sitting in on design reviews, it is time that he or she did, as (1) the BA needs to be there for the forward traceability to ensure all requirements can be traced forward to design elements; and (2) design decisions can introduce additional requirement risks. For instance, if the design decision was to use a vendor application to satisfy a certain component of the requirements, not only does this potentially introduce new project risks (which means, the project manager should sit in on review sessions as well), there are also additional requirement risks:

- If the vendor application is hacked, then our customer data may be leaked.
- If the vendor application is down, then the customer will not be able to access our site.
- If the vendor application has a software upgrade, then the customer experience may change or our application may break.

If a change request is opened and the changes affect requirements, this is another opportunity to review and possibly add new requirement risks.

Requirement Risk Pitfalls

Common mistakes made during the requirement risk management process include:

1. **Listing generic requirement risks:** Requirement risks are difficult to leave generic and to be able to copy/paste unless working on a similar project to one that was done in the past. If this is the case, there is a need to learn from the previous project and go right into identifying and documenting the missed requirements to ensure there are no gaps instead of listing the risk first, just for the sake of filling the requirement risk log.
2. **Listing the risk of not implementing the requirement as a requirement risk:** A one-to-one relationship between requirements and requirement risk does not exist. The requirement risk can be linked back to a group of requirements or there may not be any requirement risk associated with a requirement. The requirement risk is also not simply stating what happens if we do not do it. For instance:
   - **Requirement:** The system shall only allow access to users with levels 1 and 2 security.
   - **Invalid requirement risk:** If the system allows access to users with lower levels of security, then the company may be sued. (This is considered invalid because this risk has already been addressed by making it a requirement that access is only allowed to those with the appropriate level of security. This statement does not provide any additional value.)
   - **Valid requirement risks:** (1) If user IDs are not maintained, then unauthorized users may access the system; and (2) If a user transfers departments and their security level changes, there is a

two-week delay in updating the system, therefore we may have a security breach.

These are specific loopholes in the system which are requirement risks that can be discussed further to determine suitable plans of action.

3. **Waiting until requirements are fully elicited and defined before we conduct a requirement risk assessment:** Waiting actually makes the process more cumbersome, as discussions during the elicitation process may have to be rehashed. The gaps uncovered will also require additional elicitation and therefore, more time that was not anticipated or planned for. If communicated to the PM that everything was on track, more time would have to be requested at the eleventh hour. It would be better if gaps were uncovered sooner and it was communicated to the PM that more time was needed earlier on in the process.
4. **Not defining impact and probability levels and scores:** Similar to project risk management, many organizations are guilty of not defining what high, medium, or low impact and probability means which leaves the scoring system arbitrary. It often results in everything being listed as high. In requirement risk management, because we identify and assess business workarounds for items that are not addressed within the scope of the project, stakeholders may be more honest in the rating scale. The fear is that items listed as low probability and low impact may not be addressed at all.

FINAL THOUGHTS ON ASSUMPTIONS, CONSTRAINTS, DEPENDENCIES, AND RISKS

One of the main focus points of the collaboration between the PM and the BA comes down to ensuring that the C-RAID items are under control as much as possible, since any problems that the project or the PM-BA duo faces will translate to a deterioration in the overall state of the C-RAID factors. Further, with the help of the BA function at the PMO, the organization should create measurements around the C-RAID factors and develop threshold values to define acceptable readings for C-RAID. These readings can deliver valuable information regarding project health and provide a set of reliable leading indicators that can help improve planning and forecasting.

The identification and management of C-RAID items occur throughout the project life cycle. It actually begins prior to the project life cycle as project assumptions, constraints, dependencies, issues, and risks are first identified in EA—some will spill over beyond the life cycle of the project and will need to be managed by operational teams going forward. These processes are tedious and time consuming, and we need to make sure we are not doing them for the sake of ticking a box, indicating they have been completed. It is important that the PM and the BA are in sync to manage both the project and requirement assumptions, constraints, dependencies, and especially risks in order to increase the chances for project success.

REFERENCES

1. Riskczar Corporation. (n.d.). *Risk Quotes*. Retrieved February 05, 2015, from http://riskczar.com/risk-quotes/.
2. Based on http://www.businessdictionary.com/definition/assumption .html.
3. Project Management Institute. (2013). *A Guide to the Project Management Body of Knowledge (PMBOK® Guide)—Fifth Edition.* Newton Square, PA, USA: Project Management Institute, Inc.
4. BusinessDictionary.com. (n.d.). Retrieved February 3, 2015, from http:// www.businessdictionary.com/definition/dependency.html.
5. BusinessDictionary.com. (n.d.). Retrieved February 3, 2015, from http:// www.businessdictionary.com/definition/unknown-unknowns-UNK .html.
6. International Institute of Business Analysis. (2009). *A Guide to the Business Analysis Body of Knowledge (BABOK® Guide) Version 2.0.* Toronto, Ontario, Canada: International Institute of Business Analysis.

8

RESOURCE MANAGEMENT

"The key is not to prioritize what's on your schedule, but to schedule your priorities."—Stephen Covey

Resource-related issues (i.e., availability, allocation, and management) are some of the most common sources of conflicts in projects and of project failure. Despite knowing that resources pose a major threat to project success, project managers (PMs) do not provide a sufficient amount of focus on resource management and often neglect to perform basic activities that can reduce the risks and the impact of resource-related challenges. As most organization types are a matrix (weak or balanced), it is inherent that in most projects, resources do not report to the PM and at times, that the resources may be more senior than the PM. Under such conditions PMs have a limited ability to make decisions, mobilize resources, change allocations, or make decisions in favor of the project in a timely fashion—reinforcing the notion of responsibility without authority. With little control as to which of the requested resources end up reporting into the project, PMs need to resort to the full arsenal of knowledge; skills; communication capabilities; access to resources, including business analysts (BAs); and the ability to think outside the box to improve the situation. Resource management is ingrained in virtually every part of the project. Figure 8.1 illustrates the interaction of resource management with virtually all other project components, as well as the importance of PM-BA collaboration to improve the integration.

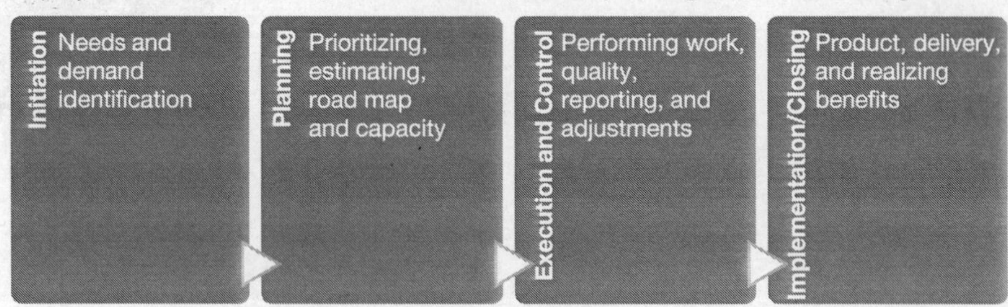

Figure 8.1 Resource management integration

RESOURCE MANAGEMENT INTEGRATION AREAS AND THE PM-BA COLLABORATION REQUIRED

The acquisition, development, allocation, and management of resources integrate with multiple major intersections throughout the project and require attention and focus that can be achieved with PM-BA collaboration. This section discusses the need to integrate and address resource issues and challenges beyond those addressed through human resources, communication, and stakeholder management.

Scope

The first attempt to identify resources required for the project is with the creation of a responsibility assignment matrix (RAM); trying to match resources to scope items (i.e., deliverables and activities). The BA's knowledge of requirements and understanding of the product is valuable in ensuring that scope items are presented with enough clarity so the PM can match the most suitable resource available to the task at hand. Understanding complexities, technical considerations, and any other specific information about the nature of the work will allow the PM to optimize the resource allocation.

Time and Cost

Completing a realistic RAM—that assigns resources to activities, addresses resource gaps, and identifies potential over allocation of resources—is essential in the creation of a realistic schedule that is based on real conditions rather than *auto assigning* generic and theoretical resources to activities with the hopes that a resource will simply appear on time to perform the work. Furthermore, proper assignment of resources (people, machines, materials, tools, and environments) is a major driver in the creation of both schedule and budgets. When considering resources for tasks and activities, the PM needs the BA to ensure timelines and budgets are sufficient to perform activities based on the type of resource assigned for the task. Project resource management and its impact on the scheduling and estimating process is a balancing act, as shown in Figure 8.2. It requires both the PM and the BA to jointly consider their respective specialty areas to ensure they balance organizational available capacity and capabilities with the work that needs to take place to produce the desired product or result.

Resource Allocation

When planning for the resources to perform work in the project, several considerations need to come to mind:

1. Type of resource
2. Skills and experience
3. Availability of the resource (e.g., other commitments, vacation, professional development)
4. Allocation to the activity (%)
5. Number of resources
6. Effort required
7. Duration of activity
8. Timing of involvement (when the resource is needed)
9. Risks associated with the activity and the resources
10. Constraints (related to both the activity and the resources)

The delicate balancing act of what we need to do (the product and project scope), with what we can do (capacity, available resources), requires the PM and the BA to each step up and collaboratively sort out any potential gaps, as required

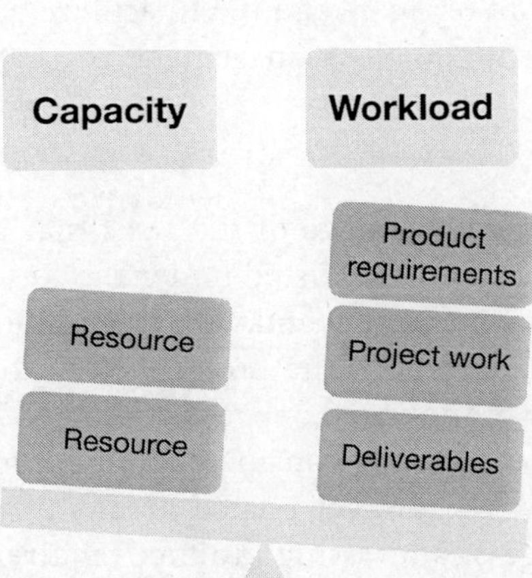

Figure 8.2 A balancing act

11. Consider whether the activity is duration-driven or effort-driven (duration-driven estimates (e.g., a flight) cannot be compressed, while effort-driven ones (e.g., peeling potatoes) can sometimes be shortened by adding resources (to an extent, as the law of diminishing returns needs to be considered).
12. Consider any specific information based on the individual assigned for the task, including productivity rate, specific skills, commitment level, reputation, and attitude toward the project.

The BA is familiar with team members' job descriptions and skills and can provide valuable insights to help the PM in requesting resources that make a good match for the task at hand.

Quality

Quality (i.e., value and benefits) can be achieved when the resource performing the work has the background, appropriate sense of urgency, relevant skills and experience, technical knowledge, and understanding of the task and the stakes involved. The BA, who can unofficially be referred to as the Chief Quality Officer, consolidates quality information related to standards, specifications, and the associated documentation, and champions continuous improvement. The BA supports the PM's resource allocation with guidance and briefing to ensure the resource is up to speed and ready for the work involved. Furthermore, the BA plays an instrumental role in project quality management—from the need to identify standards, specifications, and related documentation, to leading process improvement activities, determining the amount of rigor required to achieve quality, and measuring the costs associated with quality management.

Risk

A large percentage of the risks that projects face are related to resources. Any of the items listed under the Resource Allocation section of this chapter can go wrong, and with it introduce risks (threats) to the success of the activity or even the project. The integrated effort of managing risks gets more pronounced here as we need all hands on board to ensure that all possible threats are considered and appropriately addressed. The PM typically covers the project-related areas that may produce risks, and the BA is in charge of addressing product/requirements-related risks, as well as technical and operational ones.

Communication, Stakeholder Management, and Cross-functional Relations

It is not enough to assign a resource who is technically capable of performing an activity; there has to be alignment of the resource's personality, attitude, experience, and skills to the task at hand, the stakes, the makeup of the team, and other related circumstances such as priority and urgency. In addition to this, the resource needs to be able to communicate, transfer information, escalate, and report as required. The resource must also be able to get along with colleagues and represent the performing organization in front of external stakeholders; including external to the organization, or from cross-functional areas.

Influencing and Motivating

Both the PM and the BA need to realize and develop their ability to influence and to motivate stakeholders. Furthermore, the PM and the BA also need to coach and develop the resources on the team to be able to influence and motivate those around them. Although used in conjunction with each other, there is one way to distinguish between motivating and influencing—motivating is typically a shorter-term task than influencing, as motivating is getting someone to do something for us; while influencing is getting them to change the way they think or do things over a longer period of time.

The word *motivation* can be broken down into three components, that if delivered, we can get almost anyone to do for us what we need them to. The components of motivation include telling the other person (1) what we need from them, (2) why we need them to do it, and (3) what is in it for them.

In order to influence, one should go through a similar process that includes the following steps:

1. *Determine the influencing needs*: identify who is involved and what their drivers are
2. *Check your influencing assets and capabilities*: assess what it is in your arsenal that can help you influence the other party
3. *Plan an approach*: base your plan on the situation and the understanding of the position and needs of the other side
4. *Implement the plan*: execute the process and build the relationship
5. *Make the necessary adjustments*: changes should be made in real time to ensure your approach is aligned with the conditions you are facing
6. *Manage the progress*: monitor the relationship, make adjustments, and move ahead while handling resistance

Conflict Management

The ongoing shift in focus toward people skills and expectations management in both the PM and the BA methodologies reinforces the need of the PM and the BA to recognize that conflict is part of projects and that we cannot avoid it. Therefore, PMs and BAs need to *optimize* their ability to engage in effective conflict management and apply the most applicable conflict resolution techniques. The PM and the BA should also utilize each other in addressing challenging situations and bringing to the table their respective areas of strength to ensure conflicts are addressed and do not linger or reappear. The PM and the BA should also establish ground rules and escalation procedures that can help reduce unnecessary conflict and properly escalate situations constructively and appropriately, while focusing on the merits of the disagreements and on the problem, rather than both sides viewing their colleagues as the problem.

The PM is ultimately accountable for all communication and stakeholder expectations management and the BA is the deputy communication officer. With closer relationships with certain team members and stakeholders, better understanding of the product, and being the owner of parts of the project communication (i.e., requirements) the BA can add significant value in developing rapport, engaging stakeholders, and utilizing the relationship created to achieve goals, motivate, and influence others. Furthermore, the different styles and personalities that the PM and the BA bring to the table widely expand the range of options the PM-BA duo have in reaching out, engaging, and building trust, rapport, and relationships with team members and other stakeholders.

Procurement

The need to procure (buy, rent, or lease) resources, products, services, or results triggers significant changes to the resource requirements for the project. The portion of the scope that is now being procured will no longer require the technical resources to perform the work internally, but it will require a new set of resources to be utilized (along with respective changes to cost, time, and risks). The different resources required include legal, finance, operations, procurement (i.e., contract management and relationship management), risk experts, quality (to ensure standards are being met), as well as technical skills that will perform any integration of the procured work and related product-related activities.

The BA must participate in impact assessment and resource allocation when procurement takes place to ensure the appropriate skills are assigned to the work; specifically in relation to risks, technical work, quality, and anything that may impact the requirements and the scope of the project. Despite what some may think, the BA still needs to define product requirements for solutions that will be delivered via a procured solution. Without the BA's contribution the

PM will have a hard time matching resources to the emerging needs and properly accounting for requirements-related challenges that may arise. The risk and quality portions of the work also need to be performed jointly to ensure changes are properly accounted for and that requirements continue to be properly streamlined into the project scope and subsequent planning.

Change Control

Change control is one of the major causes of problems in projects due to its reach into every area of the project. Project change traces back to product requirements—which is the area that is typically championed and facilitated by the BA. While change is generally a good thing since it brings the scope closer to where the customer needs it to be, when there is too much change in the project, it destabilizes the product, it compromises the performance of the project team and the team's ability to deliver value, it confuses stakeholders, dilutes the ability to focus on producing results, consumes time, adds stress, and leads to conflict.

Although few PMs will admit that, many PMs view change requests as failures in scoping the project. It also indicates failure in the requirements definition process—from elicitation, to analysis, management, and documentation. This sentiment does not lead to pointing fingers at the BA, who typically leads the requirements process, as even the best business analysis work may fail in reducing the risk for subsequent changes in the project—but gaps in the requirements process are a leading root cause of changes in the project. These gaps are predominantly the result of *unruly* stakeholders who fail to contribute sufficiently to the requirements process or fail to pay sufficient attention to it. Even when all the right questions are asked during elicitation, stakeholders sometimes change their minds later on in the project.

The effort related to managing change involves additional resources and stakeholders—beyond the PM and the BA. Team members need to assess the work involved in the change and provide estimates, risks, and trade-offs—external stakeholders may also need to get involved in the process (especially when procurement is involved), the customer needs to provide prioritization and sign-off, and ultimately senior management needs to sign off and authorize funding.

The need to convert the product requirements to project scope and to ensure the quality and completeness of the product requirements and the accurate representation and the reflection of the requirements in the project scope is critical in reducing the need for project change, and is the main change reduction or prevention measure that needs to take place. Making the BA's job easier in fulfilling the prevention part requires, once again, collaboration between the PM and the BA. Stakeholder analysis, requirements prioritization, understanding of the business needs, realization of project objectives, and the definition of success criteria are critical components of a successful requirements definition process. These activities that typically take part, or at least begin, very early in the project must be performed by both the PM and the BA and if done properly, they serve as a healthy and solid foundation for the remainder of the project and its ability to deliver the desired value and benefits.

The remainder of the project change control mechanism can be divided into two components:

1. *Design and establish the change control process*: Due to the impact that changes may have on both the project work and the product requirements, there is a need for a joint effort where both the PM and the BA incorporate into the process the areas they represent; ensuring that the process is clear, formal, and effective, so all changes are captured and all change requests are assessed realistically for their potential impact.
2. *Identify, document, and respond to changes*: Responding to changes and requests is the second part of the reactive part to change requests and here too, there is a need for a seamless effort between the PM and the BA to assess the impact on the project, reprioritize requirements, check the impact on other requirements and on the business, and provide recommendation and impact assessments that are as accurate and realistic as possible. Mishandling change requests or allowing changes into the project with no impact assessment directly leads to scope creep, and may result in defects, the need for corrective action, uncertainty, additional risks, misunderstandings, relationship issues, and ultimately failure.

The change management process is an example of teamwork, as it is intense, fast paced, and condensed—involving multiple interdependencies and high stakes. Proper allocation of the resources to the tasks and seamless hand-offs, combined with trust and accountability are all necessary ingredients for success. A deeper dive into project change management will be conducted in Chapter 9 of this book.

Other Resource Integration Areas

The importance of assigning the right resource for each task goes beyond the project management knowledge areas and includes areas such as assumptions, issue management, dependencies, and lessons learned. The PM and the BA make up the core project management team and together they should lead and manage the project. However, the duo needs the full support of team members in several supporting areas, including the following:

- **Assumption management:** The tasks of identifying and articulating assumptions span over the entire project planning process and extends well into the implementation and control stages. In most projects there is a need to make assumptions about a variety of areas, and it involves multiple functional areas, as well as several stakeholders. As a result, although the process is owned and managed by the PM with the support of the BA, the two need to engage the stakeholders and team members involved, in order to ensure that the assumptions are as realistic as possible and that they are managed and controlled effectively—making certain that they are either *released* when they should be, or treated according to the conditions that ensue (typically turn into risks).
- **Issue and dependency management:** Issues are not necessarily bad things, but they are things that require the immediate attention of the project team. They typically represent situations that are not *big* enough to be part of the schedule—risks that materialized, stakeholders' concerns, or they may also be related to changes. The assignment (escalation or delegation) of an issue for action or follow up must be done carefully, so the most suitable resource is assigned to it; one who also has the capacity to deal with it. This matter circles back to communication as the individual assigned to handle the issue must provide a timely and accurate update about it. Dependencies need to be treated in a similar fashion, as there is typically an oversight when it comes to tracking, following, and handling dependencies. The PM and the BA need the support of team members to handle dependencies effectively.
- **Lessons learned:** The process of collecting and applying lessons learned should not wait for the end of the project, but rather it needs to be performed regularly throughout the project, in conjunction with milestones. This way the project can actually benefit from the lessons learned almost in real time—because if the lessons are collected and realized only at the end of the project, only future projects will benefit from the process. Throughout the project, the PM and the BA need to engage stakeholders and team members in the collection of scenarios and conditions for the lessons learned process. More specifically, the PM and the BA need to perform the collection of feedback at the end of the weekly status meeting. This way the information is collected raw, as it is still fresh in the minds of the team members. Further processing of the information will take place when analyzing it, in an attempt to realize the lessons. When performing the analysis, the PM and BA need to work together and meticulously select the individuals to engage in the effort. There is a balance to strike, so the process should involve those who are deeply engaged in the process, as well as those who can provide the most valuable feedback while being as objective as possible.

RAM—THE RESPONSIBILITY ASSIGNMENT MATRIX

The RAM is the first step in our attempt to match the work breakdown structure (WBS) and the project's scope (i.e., deliverables, activities, and tasks) to the organizational breakdown structure, stakeholders, team members, and other resources. This matching is done through the RAM, where the attempt to connect between resources and tasks has these goals in mind:

1. Ensure that each deliverable, activity, and task is going to have a resource or stakeholder assigned to it
2. Safeguard that there is skill matching and that the most suitable person is assigned to each activity and at the right capacity
3. Get resources and stakeholders to understand the nature and level of their involvement in each activity
4. Find gaps by completing the RAM, which will show us whether or not there is someone who can be assigned to each activity; in the event that there is no one assigned to a certain activity, it means that the activity is not going to get done. It sounds straightforward, but in reality, projects often go ahead without having all tasks and activities mapped out. Many times, project managers mix hope with strategy—and activities with no resources assigned to them on the RAM often get dismissed by saying that they will figure it out later. Unfortunately, any gaps are usually discovered the hard way—later, at which point it is even more pressing than it was previously and the team cannot perform certain activities on the project.

RACI Chart

RACI represents the four capacities for which resources will be assigned to the project's activities and is short for: responsible, accountable, consulted, and informed. For the most part, the RAM serves only as a generic name and, in practice, is often called a RACI chart. The use of the RACI chart is highly common and the letters are a very intuitive way to represent the stakeholders' involvement in each activity. Before proceeding with this discussion, there is another area that requires clarification. Too often, project managers and team members have misconceptions about the RACI roles and if this persists, it may lead to a failure in delivering value in creating a RACI chart—and may even end up backfiring and misleading the team. These are the true definitions of each of the RACI elements:

- **Responsible:** This is the person who is actually assigned to perform the work. Every activity must have a person who is going to perform it because without an *R*, the activity will not get done.

- **Accountable:** Let's start by clarifying that it is not the PM's name that should appear as accountable for any activity. The person accountable symbolizes where the buck stops, and it is often going to be the functional manager or the team lead of the person deemed responsible for performing the work. In essence, the PM cannot be accountable for any task or activity within the project, since the PM is ultimately accountable for the project as a whole and does not have the capacity to be assigned to a specific task. In the event that the PM is only on a part-time basis and also serves as a project resource in the project, it may be possible for the project manager to be assigned as an *A* or an *R* for a task. There should be only one person who is named as accountable for a task.
- **Consulted:** This usually refers to subject matter experts or other contributors who provide input, knowledge, expertise, or other value into the activity, but are not the ones who actually perform the work. There can be more than one stakeholder who is labeled as consulted for each activity.
- **Informed:** These stakeholders are more reactive in relation to the activity, as they are on a need-to-know basis and no action is required by them. For that reason, there can be multiple stakeholders labeled as informed.

It is very possible to have more than one person assigned to perform the work on a certain activity and in this case, many PMs assign multiple persons at the *R* level to an activity. Seemingly, there is no problem with it, but in practice, it is too much of a good thing. When more than one person is assigned to a task, it may lead to an ownership problem or to accountability issues at the *R* level. It is similar to the situation where you send an e-mail with a request to two or more people and each one will see the other name(s) in the e-mail and assume (or hope) that the other(s) will respond to the request. With the letter *R* under more than one name on the RACI chart, people will be busy pointing fingers at others, rather than performing the work. For these kinds of situations, the RACI chart can be enhanced into a RASCI chart by adding an *S* for support:

- **Support:** This is similar to responsible, but it means that there are others who are assigned to the task. The *R* now stands for the lead, who is ultimately responsible for the task or activity, and all the people who are labeled as *S* provide support to the *R*. They perform the work, but report at the task level to the *R*, who serves as a central point for task accountability and reporting. This prevents the need to chase after bits and pieces of information from multiple stakeholders.

Four Steps

Although it is common to have an incomplete RAM, it is actually better than having no RAM at all. Many PMs fail to see the importance of putting together a clear and strong RAM early in the project; others simply confuse the RAM with the project schedule, not realizing it is about the assignment of the resources and not their timing and availability. If it is done properly, it can definitely serve as an important milestone toward building a realistic schedule.

Another benefit it may yield is related to early detection of problems: an incomplete RAM with tasks that have no resources available to be assigned to them is a risk that should be recorded. It is likely that there will be insufficient information to populate the entire matrix, particularly during the early stages of the project; in such a case, once again, the PM can resort to assumptions. The process of developing the RAM can be broken down into four stages that should produce a realistic RASCI Chart:

1. The first step is to take the deliverables and high-level activities (from the WBS or the scoping process) and assign a high-level resource to each of them. *High-level* means defining a *type* of resource that should be assigned to the activity (e.g., a developer, tester, designer, or engineer). This represents a generic resource that will be associated with the task in any of the RASCI capacities. This is done very early on in the project, when the activities are still at a high-level and there is little to no information about the resources and the stakeholders that are going to be involved in the project. At the top of the matrix, resources should only be labeled at a generic level for each of the project activities identified thus far.
2. As progress is made in planning, more information comes to light about resources and stakeholders, and now is the time to get a little more specific about assigning them. This is done by getting more specific about the resources involved by pointing at a particular team, a short list, or a certain skill level that is needed.
3. The third step is a result of detailed planning that should yield a set of specific resources assigned to and associated with each activity in their appropriate capacities. The top of our matrix should now include a name and a role—the name is to make sure that someone does not replace this person with someone else who has the same title; the role is to indicate the skills and experience needed for the activity. This list can be viewed as a set of assumptions; every stakeholder that appears on it is assumed to be able to perform whatever they are assigned to for each of their activities. In the event that stakeholders and resources are removed or changed, the assumptions no longer stand and a

risk should be recorded. This is not done to protect the matrix, but rather, to protect the project. If the RASCI chart indicates a need for a resource, and this person is not available to get involved in the way that was intended, it poses a risk for the project. Recording the risks associated with the RASCI chart and stating their associated impact is part of managing stakeholders' expectations. While maintaining good relationships with the stakeholders, the PM needs to be assertive and stand strong against the removal of resources from the project.

4. This step is about any resource adjustments that will inevitably need to take place. Even if no changes occur in the project, having built the RAM early in the project will probably mean that resources may change at some point. These changes may include availability, skill level updates, cases in which resources were over-allocated, or changes in deliverables, activities, or tasks. These are availability adjustments that may lead to scheduling adjustments if necessary.

If populated properly, the RASCI chart can also serve as an escalation procedure guideline, as it should clearly show each stakeholder's level of involvement—including those who need to be informed about the task. This is a step toward creating a project-wide escalation procedure, where escalation becomes a *turn-key solution*, where it is clearly specified and communicated who needs to know what, when they need to know it, and how it can get done. Communication is another potential benefit of the RAM as it communicates the roles and responsibilities for each activity and ensures stakeholders know what is expected of them and of others.

Who Puts the RAM Together?

Resource allocation cannot be done solely by the PM. If the requirements and scoping processes are complicated in nature (many parts, layers of information, prioritization, and functionality), the task of matching resources to tasks and activities is a complex one. The layers of this task cannot be broken down and there is a heavy level of integration, interdependencies, and risks within it—which make it more like an art. If the PM alone tries to tackle this task, it will be incomplete or insufficient, as the PM does not have enough context about the nature of activities and the impact of assigning certain skills and experience levels, on the overall functionality.

The BA must get involved in the task of assessing resources (for skills, experience, fit) and matching them to the tasks. Since the RAM does not deal with the timing of activities, once again the BA is the most suitable person to provide input, in order to ensure that resources are not overbooked. In addition, when there are no resources available to be assigned to perform certain tasks, it is the BA who can provide the description regarding the skills and experience required. If changes take place, the PM and the BA must work together to figure out the impact of the change—on the resources and on other activities or deliverables.

Beyond skills and experience, the knowledge the BA provides as part of the effort to build a realistic RAM (which will in turn, lead to a realistic schedule) pertains to specific technical skills, understanding of the product, and the capacity of the resource to handle the situation. Any input is helpful and the BA should also engage the resources and even interview them to ensure they make the best fit for the position. With the PM being consumed with trying to populate the RAM, the BA can also help in checking for resource availability against other projects and other operational work. With an eye on business objectives and a strong context regarding the business case and other considerations that go beyond the project, the BA can provide valuable information regarding the availability of resources, other engagements in which they may be involved, and competing organizational commitments that may affect the project's ability to get the resources required.

Cross-project Dependencies

The BA is not the only person who tries to get information regarding other things that go on in the organization—this is also part of the PM's responsibility. Later in this chapter we will discuss a partial application of concepts related to critical chain, where we will try to incorporate the notion of considering cross-project dependencies, define what a dependency is and articulate how to proactively manage such dependencies. It is imperative that the PM and the BA put their heads together and attempt to cover all possible corners when assigning resources to work; if done effectively it will contribute to the effort to mitigate risks and achieve quality.

A lot can go wrong with resource allocation—and when things go wrong, the stakes are high and the pain is significant. On the other hand, despite the task being difficult, there is no appreciation of the importance of the process—and when things go as planned, it is usually taken for granted. Looking at projects in hindsight, PMs and BAs can learn a lot about all the things that went wrong with resource allocation, whereas the most frustrating part is that most of the problems were not only preventable, but also could have been avoided with a modest effort, collaboration, and limited cost.

In simple terms, the PMs and BAs need to sit down together with resource requirements lists and discuss how to share resources; considering what each resource brings to the table, their availability, and what is needed in order to perform the task properly. All of this needs to take place proactively, upfront, and early in the project (for the short-term detailed portions of the plan)—and definitely before there is a crisis.

A Mini RAM?

The RAM is not only a solution for resource assignment and allocation throughout the project, it is also a very effective means to help plan the division of work between the PM and the BA. In fact, the PM-BA duo can utilize another RAM (or mini RAM) to define who needs to do what and at which capacity between the two of them. Since most of the work is done jointly with the PM and the BA alternating the lead on certain tasks and dividing the work between the two of them, there must be a way to identify who does what. The mini RAM can help the duo split the work, define who gets involved when, identify the role each one plays at any stage, and clarify ownership of activities and tasks. Furthermore, it helps set an escalation path, a flow of activities and information, touchpoints, and reporting guidelines within the project between the PM and the BA—and with external stakeholders (and particularly with the sponsor).

Personalities, skills, experience, relationships, styles, and attitudes; as well as role definitions and best practices within the organization all contribute to the dynamic between the PM and the BA and help define where one stops and the other begins. There is no one way to divide the work between the PM and the BA; the important thing is to realize the need for such division, and identify the options and boundaries for the relationship to work—and with this knowledge the dynamic between the members of the duo will help finalize the roles. With time, the PM and the BA will learn from their mistakes, leverage their experiences, and become more cohesive—working as one seamless unit.

ESTIMATING AND SCHEDULING

Beyond the techniques required to build project schedules, there is a series of considerations that PMs must take into account in order for the schedule they put together to be realistic. These considerations include the incorporation of the knowledge and experience the BA brings to the table to ensure the schedule that the PM builds is as realistic as possible, and is built on known conditions, realistic expectations, and assumptions that are as close to *possible* as they can be. The following information captures these considerations as part of the effort to equip PMs with the right information about what to focus on while building the project schedule.

Procrastination

Many people are procrastinators by nature, and it is the PM's job to set up realistic expectations for the team and to build in mechanisms that help the people performing the work deliver on time. When a university professor gives students a deadline for submitting an assignment, often the students will ask, "Is there an extension?" The professor's answer should then be, "Yes, there is an extension, and it is already built into the specified deadline." In lots of ways, many project team members tend to act in a similar fashion—and they have their sense of urgency enhanced only shortly before the deadline approaches.

The solution involves educating the team so that the elevated sense of urgency shows up much earlier. This can be facilitated by the BA, who is also the right person to verify the estimates to ensure they are within an acceptable range. Alternately, under tight deadlines and when the relationship with the customer allows it, the PM-BA duo can orchestrate running two schedules: one for the customer and the other for the team, which depending on the situation, should be several days or even a couple of weeks earlier. This will buy the project some time, however, it will work only in specific situations when the PM (or the BA) have strong relationships with the customer and when the existence of the later deadline that is worked out with the customer can be safely guarded. If the team finds out about the two dates, trust between the team and the PM may be lost.

Language

An aspect of estimating that is closely linked to communications is the terms and measurements that are used in the estimating process. PMs are the ones who ultimately translate resource estimates into a schedule, as they appear on the calendar. However, to ensure that the estimating process is effective and realistic, the questions directed at the resources need to be in terms of *effort*. Since the BA is more familiar with the product and the resources than the PM, it is the BA who should facilitate the procedure of engaging the resources and *process* the estimates before they are given back to the PM. This is not to imply that the PM should sit back and be recused from the process, but the *translation* that the BA can provide, along with the understanding of the product, the resources, and the business context would be very beneficial for the estimating and planning process. With the help of the BA, the PM will then translate these effort estimates into *duration*. Effort is similar to ideal time and is about getting the resources to estimate how long it will take them to perform a task uninterrupted, when they are fully dedicated to doing it.

It is important to set these expectations straight from the start, so resources do not provide delivery dates, but rather effort estimates. These estimates should be as objective as possible, free of bias, and with no regard to any of the loss factors mentioned above.

Delays

One of the most elusive aspects of project estimating is the impact of project delays. It is very difficult to accurately and realistically measure project delays and the schedule impact of various project events, but to make the process easier, it is important to understand that project delays are not linear. When the PM or BA addresses resources work on activities that are not specified in their plan, the resources often dismiss the impact by saying, "It will only take me an hour to finish this before I go back to do whatever is part of the plan." What the resources fail to understand is that the resulting delay may be much longer than one hour, because of the nonlinear nature of project delays. In this matter, the BA can serve as an extra set of eyes, helping ensure that the resources focus on what they were assigned to do and serving as an initial escalation point for issues faced by the team.

Prioritization

In most projects, when activities and tasks are assigned to resources, they are often not clearly prioritized. While there might be an idea of which activities are more important than others, it is often not articulated effectively to those who perform the work. Prioritizing activities is also related to the urgency that is attached to them (in relation to deadlines, dependencies, and stakeholders involved) and the task of prioritization cannot lie exclusively with the PM, since PMs often do not have enough specific knowledge regarding the technical aspects of the project. Since the BA is the champion of the requirements, the BA has detailed knowledge of the requirements and their prioritization so he or she can translate this knowledge into valuable information that can help prioritize tasks and activities that are assigned to resources to perform.

The prioritization process will consider product-related factors, as well as project priorities and cross-project dependencies. Risks, constraints, and any other conditions that may affect the prioritization should also be considered. Combining the BA's product and requirements related knowledge, as well as the BA's familiarity with the resources, with the big picture project considerations that the PM brings to the table makes the prioritization effort realistic, timely, and productive—allowing resources to perform the work that the project needs them to and to make informed decisions as to what to focus on at any given time. Simply giving resources a pile of things to do and expecting them to perform them in an order that makes sense for the project is not likely to happen.

Contingency

One of the most common battles that PMs engage in is asking stakeholders for sufficient time to perform the work. With the most thoughtful of schedules, taking into account all aspects of the project, there are elements completely out of the PM's control such as, sudden illness, organizational changes, professional development, and other events. These losses may add up to 20% or more of the total availability of resources and this does not even take into consideration delays related to sign-offs and customer-driven delays.

Depending upon the nature of the organization, the customer, and historical project information, PMs need to build these time impacts into the project schedule and, as required, stipulate them in assumptions, constraints, and risks. Historical information may also be helpful in providing PMs with an indication of how much additional time it is sufficient to request, depending on similar, previous situations. For example, if senior stakeholders tend to arbitrarily reduce the amount of extra time requested, then PMs should ask for more time than they need, knowing it will be reduced back to a realistic value.

The BA typically has more familiarity with previous projects and of other areas within and outside of the project that may lead to delays and can help set a realistic contingency based on these considerations.

No Backward Estimates

When stakeholders present project teams with deadlines and target dates, PMs must ask for time to come up with a plan and when planning, put the target dates aside and plan realistically how long it should take to complete the work. During the planning, the PM should engage the BA for input regarding the estimates and regarding any additional details or information that the BA can provide, so the PM can go back to the stakeholders with a range of options that are realistic to achieve the target goals.

When completing the estimate, there should be two sets of dates: the target date and the actual date. If they are not the same, the PM needs to present the findings and perform a gap analysis on the date variance, in order to come up with options regarding how to address the gap. The options should illustrate the findings and demonstrate the impact of each action.

Planning backward from the target dates practically guarantees building shortcuts into the schedule, which almost guarantees subsequent schedule, resource, and cost overruns as well as quality issues. PMs should engage BAs to ensure the estimates are done from the bottom up, and illustrate the options available in such a way that portrays them and the stakeholders involved as being on the same side, dealing with the challenges together. Stakeholders should not view the PM as the problem, just because the PM comes up with realistic plans that question the validity of the original target dates.

Estimates for Unknown Conditions

When trying to plan for something that has not been done before, PMs and BAs face significant uncertainty, since they do not have the ability to know what might happen and which risks are even possible. For these situations there are three things to keep in mind:

1. Identify whatever is possible and articulate the conditions that are necessary to do the work. Get buy-in for these conditions.
2. Identify the assumptions that help support the premise and the conditions that are believed to be in place for the purpose of planning.
3. Identify risks associated with the plan. These are known-unknowns that can be identified upfront.

Based on the level of confidence established for the estimates, make sure to price the potential consequences of the impact of what might happen due to risks that have not been considered. This will serve as the basis for contingency planning and potentially for requesting additional time, money, or resources to accommodate these unexpected events.

Non-critical Path Delays

In addition to managing activities on the critical path and ensuring that they are completed on time, the PM needs to engage the BA about activities that are off the critical path. Delays in performing non-critical path activities are less *critical* and by nature, have a smaller direct impact on project delays (in the short term). They may appear harmless, especially early in the project, but if not managed properly by attending to these activities in a timely manner, they may end up being damaging for the project. Most delays in a project, even early ones, are very hard to overcome and therefore, should be accounted for, even if they are not on the critical path. The non-critical path delays will cause these activities to take longer to complete and to finish later than planned. Even if they have no direct impact or dependencies that may affect the critical path, they will cause trouble later in the project since all the non-critical path activities that are currently staggered along the project will start piling up toward the end. At that point, the team is likely to have problems coping with the extra work volumes and these activities will be subject to further delays.

On top of the capacity issues, additional delays may push one or more of these activities far enough to match the critical path, or even surpass it and redefine it by delaying the end date of the entire project. PMs and BAs must make it clear to resources that the fact that an activity is not on the critical path does not actually buy time to delay or extend it, since from the resources point of view, the activity must be completed on its early completion date. The reason is that even though it may appear that activities that are off the critical path can be delayed, the resources performing them are not scheduled for a break after completing the activities, but rather for another activity—that if delayed, will subsequently delay the project. The BA, working closely with the team, should also serve as the *voice of reason*—communicating the message of performing work as early as possible to the team, through coaching and as part of the prioritization process. The PM and the BA need to keep their eye on another type of challenge: when resources see that they are assigned to perform an activity that is not on the critical path, they believe that they have time to spare (float, or slack) and that they can delay the activity. With the help of the BA (with an eye on the resources' other projects' commitments and on the dependencies on the activity in question) the PM needs to ensure that resources perform the activities they are assigned to at the time they are supposed to, in order to avoid additional unforced problems that can be triggered by this type of oversight.

Productivity, Utilization, and Efficiency

Squeezing more work out of people in the form of overtime (and sometimes overworking them) can yield benefits and improve performance, but only to a certain degree—and only in the short term. At some point, people need a break from the constant intensity to recharge—they cannot keep running at full steam over an extended period of time. In many organizations, the culture for project team members is about overtime, over-utilization, and doing more with less.

While PMs and BAs have little or no control over these conditions, it is important for them to recognize when such conditions exist. They should try to warn senior stakeholders about the potential consequences and if needed, identify related assumptions and potential risks. These conditions often lead to reduced productivity, less innovation, team morale issues, and overall inferior performance in the long run. Overdoing overtime, over-squeezing project resources, and ignoring the principle of staying tuned to people's needs will likely lead to a disconnect with team members and other stakeholders.

During peak periods and before deadlines, it is normal and legitimate to squeeze more hours from team members, but after every peak, there has to be a valley with a lull that allows them to regroup and look for ways to improve their performance for the next peak. When team members are expected to constantly produce more with fewer resources, it is no longer about productivity and the PM-BA duo needs to realize the extent of the situation and alert senior management of the challenges that it may lead to.

APPLICATION OF CONCEPTS INSPIRED BY CRITICAL CHAIN

With limited ability to deliver success without the organization providing active support in priorities and resources, PMs need to resort to more cross-project collaboration in the effort to manage resources and dependencies more effectively. The BA can provide valuable input about other projects for dependencies and the impact other projects will have on this project. The concept of critical chain is related to project portfolio management and to enterprise analysis and attempts to identify interdependencies among projects within the organization in an effort to effectively manage resources that are shared across the organization. Critical chain also focuses on bottlenecks within the project in an attempt to allocate the resources to projects based on actual needs, rather than on predetermined schedules that may no longer be valid by the time the resource actually reports to the project. The PM, with the natural focus inward to the project, needs the BA to help with the cross-project dependencies and with the technical needs of the project.

Critical chain[1] provides effective risk-focused approaches that can help minimize cross-project impacts. Operating within multiple project environments, most projects do not have the ability to focus on risks and issues in other projects and even though they may be carefully planned and run effective risk management, they may be subject to cross-project risk, particularly the availability of resources. Critical chain is done by identifying critical resources for multiple projects and ensuring their effective utilization by staggering projects around their availability and protecting each project with schedule buffers. The buffers may be assigned to specific activities, processes, phases, or the entire project. Buffers can also be assigned to off-critical path activities, to ensure that under any circumstances, even if the task is delayed, it will not delay the critical-path task that depends on it. Effective cross-project communication and collaboration among PMs, with support from BAs, through regularly occurring interactions may provide opportunities for establishing early alert systems for cross-project impact areas. With limited ability to plan for resource needs without the help of BAs, PMs should utilize the BAs in planning for resource needs for the short term and present the findings of this exercise to other PMs. The PMs and BAs will then form a mini-committee to discuss the allocation of resources moving forward. BAs should also be present in the meeting to provide impact assessment and alternative analysis should a resource conflict emerge.

Critical chain is difficult to apply in full in most project environments for various reasons, but despite the challenges, it can serve as a platform for the following improvement areas.

Collaboration and Early Detection

Cross-project resource dependencies can be discussed and determined among the PMs who share these resources. Coordination meetings should take place in intervals that depend on the projects' velocities and their focus should be on reaching agreements on how to allocate resources that are shared among multiple projects. It helps PMs shift away from the current inefficient method of fighting and arguing over resources—typically after the fact, when problems have already caused resource scheduling conflicts.

Instead, PMs need to proactively engage BAs to create an early detection system and figure out which project is in greater need to get the right-of-way in resource allocation. This mechanism can help the representatives from each project (either the PM, the BA, or both) improve the quality of the discussion with resource managers and with other projects, and work toward agreeing on resource allocation mechanisms to avoid scrambling as crises happen and events unfold. This approach also helps improve working relations, as now PMs are less focused on fighting with each other and more on doing their jobs, with a more informed set of needs and considerations for resources and allocations—provided by their BAs. It also helps create a momentum of productivity and an environment that other PMs strive to become part of.

Resource Management and Organizational Considerations

This joint effort between PM-BA duos and resource managers (and across projects) to manage resource contentions establishes best practices related to building a problem alert system. Typically when there are problems that cause resources to extend their stay in a project instead of moving on to report to the next project on their schedule, there is no early detection system to give the next PM in line a heads-up. The subsequent decision as to which project gets the priority (and hence the resources) will be much more informed than otherwise, thanks to the input from the BAs, who provide context regarding the availability of the resources, the priority of the activities, the dependencies on the activities, the stakeholders involved and the alternatives available.

Cross-Project Urgency

Most PMs lack the visibility and/or the capacity to look for and worry about problems and challenges in other projects, but the PMs need to become informed of any events in other projects that can impact their own endeavors. The *committee* of PMs and BAs (that is set up in order to discuss cross-project dependencies) will specifically deal with events that if they take place in one project, they may have an impact on other ones. These dependencies are typically related to deliverables that one project produces and another project subsequently requires. The dependencies can also be related to resource-related contention: resource dependencies can take place within projects' components, across projects, and between projects and operational areas.

To make it more challenging, these dependencies tend to appear as a surprise and they often throw a wrench into project plans. The *committee* will discuss resource needs of all projects and operational areas that are scheduled to share resources within a given period of time, and will seek resolution for potential resource conflicts. The *ideal* time frame to plan for should be a two-week period, and the *committee* should include all PMs and BAs representing the projects that compete for the same resources within that time frame along with the respective operational representatives. The reason for two weeks is that one week is too short for holding meetings of this caliber and a month is too long of a planning horizon to have specific resources planned for. The reasons that both PMs and BAs need to attend these meetings is to ensure that decisions are made at the appropriate level and that all decisions are supported by the depth of information provided by the BA, with the impact of the decisions illustrated—representing all projects and all needs. The main objective of this process is to ensure that PMs do not make decisions to give priority to one project over another that are disconnected from organizational considerations and that do not add value to the organization. Functional managers or resource *owners* should also attend the meeting to address any additional issues that may arise as a result of potential conflict between allocation of resources to projects and operational work (or emergencies). Here too, an informed decision is required to ensure all considerations are taken into account. In this case the BA will function on behalf of the organization; ensuring that both the project and the organizational considerations are addressed.

Priority and Urgency Considerations

There is a difference between the terms *priority* and *urgency* and it is important for PMs, BAs, and team members to differentiate between the two words. Referring to each of these words in the right context will not only help the team perform its work more effectively, but it will also streamline the conversation between the team's representatives (typically the PM and the BA) and external stakeholders (including the sponsor).

Project priority refers to the overall priority the project has at the organizational level and it is measured against other organizational priorities, initiatives, and operational work. Within the project, task priority refers to the importance of a task in relation to other things that a resource has to perform. Importance is typically related to whether an item is critical to functionality, to business needs, or to high-profile stakeholders. Projects and activities that are viewed as high priority tend to get more organizational attention and their associated processes are performed with more rigor. Priority level does not tend to change significantly throughout the life cycle of a project.

Urgency, however is different, and can also be measured or articulated beyond just labeling something as urgent—when there are problems, delays, and other pressing situations in projects, the sense of urgency gets elevated. Urgency does not change the priority of things but it will lead to a change in the sequence in which we perform work. Due to defining a situation as urgent, under certain conditions it is possible that high-priority projects or items may temporarily take a back seat compared to other projects or activities, until we clear the urgency from the impacted area.

The priority of projects is not determined by the project team; it should be provided and articulated by the sponsor. However, within the project, the priority of certain items, activities, or deliverables will be determined based on technical and product-related considerations; hence facilitated by the BA. While other items will be deemed as high priority by the PM based on the project objectives, other items' priority will be determined by the BA as a result of the requirements process, or through consultation with the team.

Project urgency levels are likely to change on occasion based on the project's performance and on the nature of its deliverables. Similarly, deliverables and activities within the project may need to change due to delays and other unexpected events. These two situations require input from both the PM and the BA to ensure that items (or projects) get the appropriate sense of urgency for the situation and that no false alarms are sounded. When there are no criteria to identify urgency or when the process is flawed, many stakeholders and team members are too quick to define something as urgent. Building a mechanism with clear criteria that is owned by the PM and the BA can help reduce the number of false alarms and ensure that whatever needs to be defined as urgent is defined as such.

To help with the process, Figure 8.3 provides a set of criteria to determine the urgency of a project (or a deliverable, a work package, an activity, or any organizational matter)—in relation to other organizational considerations. PMs and BAs can track these items over time, and measure them in relation to other projects and organizational initiatives—adjusting the relative weight of each item based on the specific conditions and environment. The level of project urgency can help the organization determine which project or matter requires more attention or resources. Therefore, it is not enough to measure each projects level of urgency in isolation, but they must be put in context and compared to all the projects that compete for the same resources. Since it is common to have a few

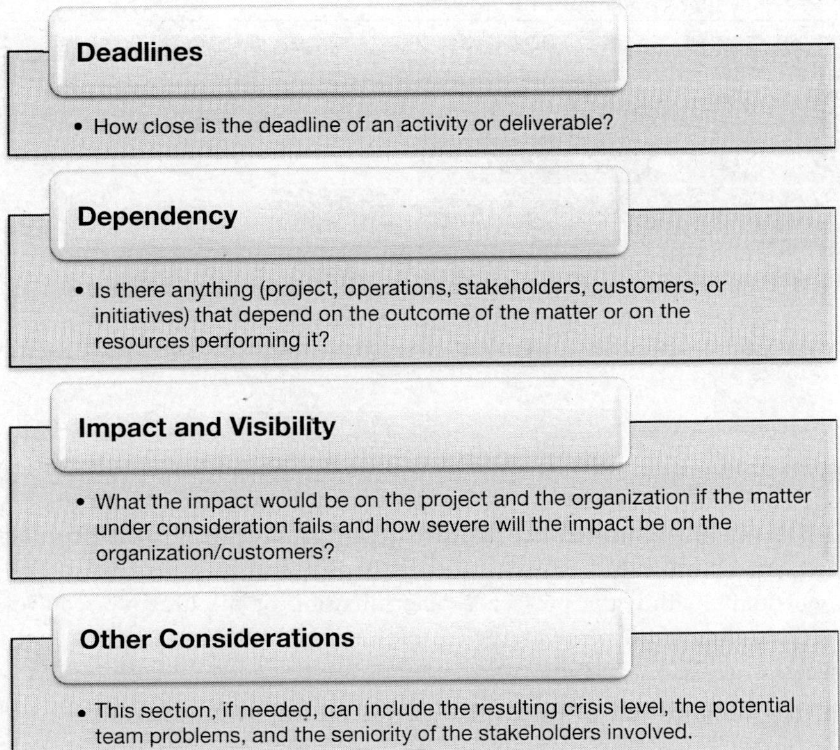

The considerations listed here can help identify the urgency of projects and organizational needs based on a clear, consistent, and transparent set of criteria—to ensure that the discussion is about comparing apples to apples—in an effort to determine the actual urgency of one matter against another.

Figure 8.3 Criteria to determine urgency

projects and other organizational matters competing over the same organizational resources (e.g., people, environments, tools, machines, or money) at any given point, a measurement of their relative urgency will help determine which one(s) gets the right of way.

After taking into account urgency and importance (or priority) considerations, the representatives from each project and from the operational departments that share specific resources should be able to come up with a cross-project urgency ranking mechanism, as illustrated in Table 8.1. The discussions should take place at intervals that are not too long (less than once a month) but not too frequent (once a week may be too often). The discussions are a proactive

Table 8.1 Cross-project urgency scheme

	Project A	Project B	Project C	Project D	Project E
Project A		A	A	D	A
Project B			B	D	B
Project C				D	C
Project D					D

This table helps determine cross-project urgency. It represents the results of the cross-project/operations discussions to establish which project will get the "right-of-way" in terms of resource allocation, in the event of a direct conflict between projects.

approach to consider the needs of each project. The mechanism shown in the table represents the summary of the discussion in terms of which project will get *the right of way* in resource allocation, should a problem cause a conflict of needs among projects.

For items within the project, a determination of the urgency requires an understanding of the product, the requirements, and the project objectives and success criteria. Since these considerations are provided by both the PM and the BA, they need to work together and ensure that the appropriate criteria is applied for each situation that has to be defined as urgent. Projects are still likely to suffer from a shortage of resources, but the urgency assessment mechanism is much more efficient than a series of ad hoc conversations, arguments, and trade-offs that are reactive, riddled with emotions and panic, and that inherently do not take into account the multitude of relevant considerations—before the crisis actually takes place.

TIME MANAGEMENT: MANAGE YOUR DAY

Time management is in many ways an oxymoron, as we do not have the ability to truly manage time, stop it, or reverse it. Time management refers to our ability to prioritize what we need to do, and then do those things in such a way that allows us to complete all the things that we have to do. Managing our time as PMs and BAs is not only critical for the success of our roles and of the project, but it is also part of being role models and coaches for team members to manage their time. The techniques to manage resources effectively that are listed in this chapter are about setting a foundation and an example to the team on how to manage their time. The ability to prioritize activities should, in turn, be transferred to team members, so they can further prioritize their days in line with the mandate given by the PM and the BA—representing the organizational needs and priorities. Any challenges team members have will then be communicated or escalated through the BA, to the PM, in an attempt to minimize the damage or re-prioritize according to the project and the business objectives.

Instead of managing by emergencies and reacting to resource challenges, we should aim toward setting up an environment of prioritized activities—one that enables the understanding of what urgency means. This message will be received positively by team members who, by knowing what they need to do next and which activities are more important than others, will translate it to performance that is both efficient and effective. It will result in a reduced number of emergencies, less false alarms, less last-minute, hasty decisions, and more consistency and focus on the project objectives.

As part of professional development and continuous improvement plans, the PM and the BA should provide team members with guidelines on how to manage their days effectively and how to gain more control over their time. The following list of activities has to be performed in addition to the needs specified in this section (specifically, providing priorities at all levels of the organization and measuring urgencies).

1. Create a Daily Plan

At the beginning of each day, create a plan of the things you intend to do during the day and assign times to each activity—including meetings and other events as they appear on your schedule. It is normal to have unexpected things to attend to, but having a daily plan can help reduce the risk of surprises. Leave time for emergencies and other unexpected events, once again, according to the nature of your work, so it allows you to create a realistic schedule for the day. The prioritization process of what you need to do can also help reduce the number of *emergencies* that will hit you—leaving room for real emergencies, as opposed to those that take place solely because you forgot about them. The prioritization of activities is also beneficial by allowing you to *bump* some of the less important things to do to a later time, until you can get a chance to perform them, or they simply move up on your list.

2. Utilize Your Productive Times

You should set your daily schedule and meetings in such a way that allows you and the team to utilize your productive times of the day. For most people, the morning hours are more productive—so it would be advisable to not schedule meetings in the morning; enabling the team to work in the morning and having more meetings in the afternoon. With the exception of urgent meetings and quick status updates (such as the Scrum meeting in agile environments), most of the day's meetings should move to the afternoon. In any large metropolitan area it is also likely that traffic-related problems may cause people to be late to early morning meetings—by scheduling meetings to early or mid-afternoon, it will increase the chance that more team members will be able to attend. The same line of thinking should also apply for the days of the week: with the help of the BA, the PM should try to stagger team-related activities, events, and even deadlines, so they do not all fall on the same day. Allowing for peaks and valleys to be staggered throughout the week can help reduce the workload, the stress, and the creation of unforced emergencies that all typically occur on Friday. In addition, Monday is also prone to interruptions due to emergencies that were formed or realized during the weekend, or spilled over from the previous week.

3. Track Surprises and Emergencies

When there is a daily plan, it is easier to track what is accomplished and what could not be attended to—it is also an opportunity to determine the actual number of emergencies and surprises that hit you throughout the day. The most basic form of lessons learned should be performed by each individual on a daily basis, to ensure that team members realize what they spend time on. In turn, team members should forward any highlights of their findings to the PM and the BA so that lessons, ideas, and good practices can be proactively leveraged across the team. Further, tracking the nature and the number of emergencies will help the PM and the BA improve processes and adjust practices in an attempt to reduce future surprises and emergencies. It also ties back to requirements management and scoping, as most surprises are associated with change requests, risks that we did not see coming, resource allocation issues, unclear requirements, and items that were left out (or forgotten) in the requirements and scoping process.

Time Wasted

Wasting time does not necessarily come in the form of browsing the web, updating statuses on social networks, or doing personal errands; it can also be the result of performing work-related activities that do not add value, or performing value-added activities in an inefficient manner. The amount of time that can be categorized as waste adds up and can be broken down into three types:

1. *Non-work-related activities*: These are personal matters that people attend to while at work—conversations with colleagues, personal errands, calls, e-mails, online shopping, web browsing, and social media. Not all of it is a complete waste, since it is important to interact

and socialize with colleagues and to attend to personal matters (in good measure), but the bottom line is that it is time spent in the office that cannot be utilized toward adding meaningful progress concerning one's work. Non-work-related activities will always take place and cannot be reduced to zero, and the planning processes must account for the resulting amount of lost time.

2. *Work-related distractions*: Emergencies, changes in priorities and work assignments, work-related discussions, (some) meetings, help and advice to/from colleagues, and unexpected escalations and calls from the client.
3. *Doing non-value-added tasks*: Even when working on things that are important, urgent, and that are related to the project, there is still a chance that they may not be done correctly or that they do not add value to the project. In addition, there are activities that are almost a matter of daily routine for most people, yet they add no value to the project. Non-value-added activities include preventable errors, arguments that are a result of misunderstandings, failing to follow processes, false-emergencies and unnecessary escalations, reactively handling risks and change, and broken communications. One additional (yet damaging) distraction takes place as a result of poor reporting processes that often trigger unnecessary inquiries by senior management (or the customer) and even change requests that would not have been made if the information had been conveyed effectively.

The concepts and ideas presented in this chapter on how to schedule resources, assign them, and introduce ideas that can improve productivity can help the PM and the BA reduce the number of surprises, the amount of time wasted, and the distractions—which help the team achieve the project's goals with less effort and less pain. Getting only one of the members of the PM-BA duo to orchestrate such efforts may not be enough, as the PM and the BA each possess a different point of view and each is associated with different areas of knowledge, interests, and focus. A combined effort will provide a two-tier mechanism that focuses on daily activities (led by the BA) and translates them into project focus priorities (facilitated by the PM).

IN A MATRIX ORGANIZATION

Resource management in a matrix organization can prove to be challenging for the PM to handle, and the role of the BA is once again enhanced and crucial for the success of the project. Conflict around resource allocation is common in matrix organizations; since reporting lines are not clear, resources have essentially two bosses, and the allocation of resources is based on personalities and *deals* more so than on the merits of the situation. As the PM and the functional managers tend to clash often over resource availability, and the PM is also likely to have friction with other PMs regarding the competition over resources, PMs need the help of BAs in defining roles and responsibilities and matching resources to tasks and activities. A clear set of resource requirements and an understanding of the stakes and the options for trade-offs are important ingredients for reducing conflict and improving collaboration around resource allocation.

Beyond the unclear authority, other common problems that plague matrix environments include situations where PMs are actually junior to those whom they manage, and where resources that functional managers are willing to give, may not be what is required to do the job. These conditions cause PMs to feel they were set up for failure, and any help they can get from the BA will serve as *ammunition* in the effort to justify the need for resources and provide support for the claim's needs.

The following techniques and practices can further help manage resources effectively and handle the challenges introduced by the matrix environment:

- Resources should be assigned directly to tasks without assuming that the tasks will get done without resources. Resource requirements should be supported with assumption management to avoid over-allocating resources.
- Realize and articulate to others that effort-driven tasks have durations proportional to the number of resources assigned, but only to a certain degree.
- Duration-driven tasks have durations that are independent of the number of resources.
- Utilize the BA to track the allocation of resources (could be using a resource histogram), to analyze resource requirements, and learn where there are peaks and valleys in allocations that can be smoothed over time.
- In addition, do not schedule 100% of any resource's time since they will always have some distractions they will need to attend to—use time buffers to deal with uncertainty and to absorb minor problems leading up to important deliverables by creating inefficiencies in less critical areas. Also, make sure tasks and activities are always prioritized to ensure that whenever there is a problem, there is a quick turnaround for requirements and scope prioritization that in turn, will also provide clarity to those involved.
- Most importantly, deal with other PMs and functional managers and solve resource conflicts.

FINAL THOUGHTS ON RESOURCE MANAGEMENT

Resource management is an area that not only integrates with virtually every other part of the project, but it is also a lead producer of risks; leading to cost and schedule overruns, conflicts, inefficiencies, reactive responses (and at times panic) to situations, and ultimately quality issues and possible failures. There are many ways to deal with the challenges presented by resource-related issues, but the most effective one is to ensure that PMs and BAs talk to each other, collaborate, and ensure that they cover the task of resource management from all possible angles and that there are no gaps in their approach. While the PM views resources through the lens of project success, the BA does that from two angles that complement the work of the PM: from a product and requirements perspective and from a business and operations standpoint.

The techniques mentioned in this chapter involved improving communication around resource management, as well as protecting the schedules and the allocation of the resources assigned to perform the work. In relation to critical chain, we touched on the subject of buffer management, which involves adding buffers to activities, work packages, phases, or the entire project—based on the specific knowledge and the amount of risks associated with any of these areas. The more risk, the larger the buffer (and with it the contingency reserve for the budget). Risks are commonly associated with product technical and requirements considerations, as well as with resource and dependencies issues. The BA provides a valuable source of information for both risk areas, to assist the PM in making the right decision or recommendation.

One important thing to reiterate—while budget overruns at different points in the project will have a similar impact on the bottom line (or, a dollar spent is always green), delays in the project may have significantly different impacts, depending on when they occur. Running into a friend before entering the train station on the way to a meeting and spending a couple of minutes to greet each other may be significantly more costly, if I end up missing the commuter train; resulting in arriving late to my meeting. However, spending the same time greeting someone after I arrive at the destination's train station will translate merely to an equal amount of delay as the time spent with the friend. This is where many PMs fail to properly account for delays: while they assess the direct amount of time a delay will take, they fail to realistically assess the full impact of the delay on the schedule. In projects, it may be due to availability windows of resources, availability of expertise, environment, tolls, machines, or approvals. The BA can provide additional context in assessing the true impact a delay may lead to, considering resource availability, product dependencies, skills required, and business impact.

The buffers requested by the PM need to be managed and once again, the BA serves as the backbone of rationalizing why a buffer is required and what the impact will be of project events on the existing buffer. Effective buffer management also reduces the need for resources to pad their estimates and inflate them artificially. With the help of the BA, team members can now provide realistic estimates, knowing that they will be protected in the event that there is a problem that leads to a schedule overrun.

With the PM-BA duo, the project team, and the sponsor on the same side—building trust, a sense of accountability, and working together in an attempt to build realistic estimates and deliver success—team members will feel comfortable providing realistic estimates to activities, rather than scheduling backward (or reverse engineering by trying to fit activities into unrealistically short timelines) and not padding their estimates. In return, buffers will be built-in based on a risk assessment (led by the PM-BA duo) and guaranteed by the sponsor. As a result, the resources will not need to make unrealistic estimates, and even if they do, it will be intercepted by the duo. Another element in this system involves not informing the team about the true deadlines, but rather establishing a culture where team members perform the work and complete it by the assigned timelines with no visibility of, or concern for the actual customer-driven deadlines. This allows the PM-BA duo to build additional buffers, if required, to ensure extra protection for the customer deadlines.

The previous approach also helps reduce the team members' distractions, as they now focus on the work to be performed and not on deadlines and procrastination. Furthermore, for activities that are not on the critical path, the float (potential amount of time to spare without delaying the project) will not be viewed by the team as a license to waste time. The task will be treated like any other task on the critical path because the resources are provided with the perception that there is no time to spare, since immediately after the task is completed, they will be assigned to the next task. The extra due diligence suggested here is proven to remove schedule-related distractions and help ensure focus on the task at hand, realistic estimating, and better resource utilization.

Ultimately, everyone around the project benefits from the improved resource management practices, since resources do not provide backward estimates that make schedules look good in theory only, and when estimates need to be squeezed, the BA helps ensure that the discussion is about the merits and that the team can account for the time savings, as opposed to simply or artificially reducing activity durations so they fit in to the schedule. If an activity (e.g., a flight) should take three hours, the only way to reach the destination faster is to increase the air speed of the aircraft. The fact that my manager asks me to arrive earlier does not warrant a (false) promise that I can do it, unless something gives and the impact is fully assessed. The impact assessment is typically facilitated by the BA, and is more comprehensive than just stating the impact on the schedule; it also provides an estimate of the potential impact on cost, resources, risks, scope, and quality.

Unrealistic deadlines, mismanaged expectations, resources' and PMs' fear of saying no, and overly ambitious stakeholders are some of the leading reasons for resource issues, conflicts, and project failures. Early in projects, when things *seem* to be starting well, these factors often introduce themselves. Before long, the project team and the PM are sucked into a vortex of events, that from that point, defines what happens in the project and sets the tone—dragging the team into becoming reactive, putting out fires, and scrambling to keep up with the project events. With the PM and the BA providing leadership and setting direction, the team has better chances of overcoming the problems that plague so many projects.

REFERENCE

1. Based on Goldratt, Eliyahu M., (1997). *Critical Chain*, North River Press, Great Barrington, MA.

9

TWO TYPES OF CHANGE: PROJECT AND ORGANIZATIONAL CHANGE MANAGEMENT

"Slowness to change usually means fear of the new."—Philip Crosby

Change is an inherent element of projects. It is in fact, the reason why we execute projects. Yet, there is always hesitancy to change and often negativity associated with it. A project change request is received and the project team panics and grumbles at the fear of having to start over. A new project is about to roll out citing changes to existing processes, and end users protest—fearing that they do not have the time to learn the new process while executing their everyday jobs, or even worse, that their jobs will no longer be required with the new process. There are two different aspects of change that the project manager (PM)-business analyst (BA) duo needs to be able to manage throughout the project: The first being project changes and the second being organizational change, or the people side of change, which is often overlooked or treated as an afterthought. Regardless of the type of change, in order to effectively manage and execute change, the fear of the new is a roadblock that needs to be removed.

PROJECT CHANGE MANAGEMENT

Most mature organizations have formal change management procedures as part of their methodologies. The challenge is that people tend to find ways to get around the formal change management processes. There have been cases where stakeholders have bypassed the PM and BA and have gone directly to developers to implement what they perceive to be minor changes. The impacts downstream include additional project work that was not planned for, which causes delays and additional cost that was not provided to the project team in the original plan. Since the changes were not analyzed prior to being developed, there is a possibility that the changes conflict with some of the other requirements or that they may not meet actual needs but rather, mask symptoms. Since there were no requirements defined for these changes, the testing team will be unaware of the changes and they likely will not get tested, which may result in a defective product or service being released. Releasing a defective product or service can make the situation exponentially worse, resulting in lawsuits or harm to potential users. Adhering to a change management process is a necessity, not only to pass project audits or for project success, but to ensure the organization is thoroughly researching the changes and their downstream impacts prior to implementing.

Most people understand the consequences of bypassing the change management process, but why do they still continue to do it? It could be because the change processes themselves are too complicated—for example, when multiple layers of approvals are required from change advisory boards, where it takes a couple of weeks just to get on the calendar to present the change. A one-size-fits-all change management procedure does not exist. The change management procedure as documented within the organization may need to be tailored to the project while taking into consideration the size, complexity, and stakeholders on the project. The PM is accountable for the project change management process—meaning that he or she is the enforcer who ensures the process is being adhered to. However, both the PM and the BA equally own the project change management process and any customization of the process that is required—the details of which are documented in the requirements management plan and/or scope management plan jointly by the PM and the BA. The PM and BA should have the authority to suggest modification to the change management process to better suit the project. Guidelines are needed to outline how this is done without the PM and BA overstepping their boundaries or overriding any project governance structure.

On the contrary, the change management process may be too lax, where there are too many changes submitted and the project team is distracted from working on the actual project and spends too much time evaluating potential changes. For example, on one project there were 36 change requests opened during a six-month-long project. Out of the 36 change requests opened, the business stakeholders decided to proceed with one. The project itself ended up about six months over time and 100% over budget. Much of the additional time and costs were attributed to evaluating change requests that stakeholders decided not to pursue. Every time a stakeholder had a new idea, a change request was opened and all changes were evaluated, as long as the form was submitted and the change management process was adhered to. Each one of the change requests was treated like a mini project in itself. The change request forms were submitted as one-line changes that the requestors thought included all of the necessary information to proceed to estimation—for example: *Provide the ability to add additional signer to account*. To a BA, the following questions would come to mind:

- Are there additional disclosures that need to be provided to the client?
- Do additional signers need to undergo an adjudication process?
- Do we need to obtain signatures from each of the additional signors in order to open the account?
- How many additional signers can be added per account?
- Which products can additional signers be added to?

Needless to say, additional elicitation is required in order to have enough information to proceed to estimating project requirements. Elicitation meetings need to be scheduled and conducted. The results must be analyzed and documented as product requirements and reviewed before the change request can proceed to determining project requirements. As project requirements are being determined, the project team must also conduct analysis to determine how the additional work fits in with the work that is already in flight, in order to provide accurate estimates before moving forward with obtaining sign-off to proceed with the requested changes. All of this additional work occurs while the project team is attempting to keep the original project requirements on track. Typically, only when the change request is approved does the project get re-baselined, which can be viewed as a loophole in the process.

In the previous example, time and money spent on the additional project activities involved in evaluating the 36 change requests were not recouped and in the end, came out of the original project time line and budget. The good news is, lessons were learned by the project team and applied to the next project.

In the next phase of the project, the PM and BA worked together to implement a new change management procedure tailored to the project. The business stakeholders remained the same and they continued to ask questions such as: "How much would it cost if we were to add...?" A new approach was implemented where funding and time was secured *up front* for every change request submitted—a process modification that proved to be effective in other organizations as well. It was determined that the project team would charge $2,000 and two days for every change request that was submitted, based on historical data of how much time/money was spent evaluating changes on the previous project. This way, regardless of the decision to move forward with the change or not, the time and costs are recouped for the extra project scope required to evaluate the change.

Another flaw in some change management processes is not setting guidelines as to when changes can be submitted and evaluated. Another factor that adds to extended timelines and incremental costs are change requests that are submitted during the later stages of the project. As a project approaches the implementation date, it becomes much more difficult to implement changes without causing significant rework. Some changes will be required even during the later stages of a project, for instance, changes to meet regulatory, legal, or compliance requirements. However, not all changes fall into this category. Introducing a two-step approval process may help to better control these scenarios. When a change is submitted close to the implementation date, a preliminary analysis should be conducted to determine whether it is worth the time to even evaluate the change and conduct an impact analysis at that stage of the project. The approvers at this stage should include the sponsor—who is funding the project and therefore should have the ultimate say on whether he or she wants to invest time and money to evaluate the change now or save it for a post implementation fast follower (a new release to be implemented shortly after implementation)—and the PM—who is responsible for guarding the timelines, budget, and project scope. The PM would need to consult with the BA and possibly the rest of the core project team, such as the technical lead and test manager, to get a high-level indication of whether it makes sense to evaluate the change at this point. If it is determined that it makes sense to evaluate the change, this is when the seed funding can be collected to conduct the mini project activities to provide the project requirements—time, cost, project activities—in order to execute the change. The findings would be presented to the change control board, which typically includes, at a minimum, the sponsor, the PM, and requestors, to determine if they would like to proceed. If so, this is when the project is re-baselined to include the additional product scope. These details should be discussed between the PM and the BA and documented in the requirements management and/or scope management plans.

Perhaps the most fascinating matter around project change management is the distinction between project change requests and issue management. Since most project environments have no clear distinction, the difference between change and issues becomes a common cause of conflict and friction between the

PM and the BA—negatively impacting project success. There are several definitions and approaches to dealing with issues, but in order to simplify things, let's define them here in a consistent and generic manner:

- **Issue:** An issue deals with addressing problems that arise throughout the project. These are not necessarily bad things, or even conditions that may require additional time or money—but if an issue resolution requires rework in order to achieve original product scope, the project baseline does not need to be reset. However, if an issue resolution leads to an approved product scope change, the approved product scope change becomes part of the baseline and the project needs to be re-baselined. Typically, issues remain confined to project scope, where a change to the product warrants a change request to be opened. The rationale behind it is to ensure that even if timelines, budgets, and resource usages change, this does not change the baseline—so we can see the difference between the plan and actual, upon reaching milestones or at project completion. Unfortunately, it is common for change requests to be incorrectly opened to increase timelines or funding due to estimation errors, and the project is inaccurately re-baselined after these change requests are approved, which skews the results measurement between planned and actual.
- **Change request:** A change request is required for changes to product scope and approved product scope changes become part of the project baseline, against which project success criteria is measured. When the project baseline changes, it signals an acceptance that revised project objectives and success criteria have been approved and additional project work is approved to implement the additional features. With the new baseline, the extra cost and time is now *Kosher* and will not be viewed as schedule or budget overruns.

To recap, when an issue is raised or discovered, its impact is assessed, time/budgets/risks are adjusted, and results are communicated. These issues will not lead to a new project baseline. When a change is requested, the same steps are performed, but if the change is approved and accepted, the approved change is reflected in an adjusted baseline. What qualifies as a project change and guidelines around re-baselining need to be defined in the appropriate plan(s), if it is not already documented within the organization's methodology. With the differences between change and issue management clearly defined, the PM and the BA can work more collaboratively and communicate the impact of events within the project more effectively.

Agile Considerations for Project Changes

On agile projects, the project change management process is quite different. In fact, formal project change management processes do not exist for agile projects. The agile methodology is a change-driven methodology, meaning that product changes are welcomed at any stage in development. Change is an inherent part of agile processes in order to maintain the customer's competitive advantage.[1] Any product changes are simply added to the product backlog. At the beginning of every sprint or increment, the product backlog is reprioritized to determine what is included in the next release.

FINAL THOUGHTS ON PROJECT CHANGE MANAGEMENT

Having an effective, well-defined, customized project change management process to cater to project needs takes the fear out of project changes and they will no longer be perceived as something negative. There is less pressure on the core project team to evaluate new product changes while keeping up with existing project work as new change requests will no longer equate to compressed project timelines. Stakeholders are also more willing to follow processes that have proven to provide value rather than executing them for the sake of executing them to meet project audit requirements. Less time will be spent arguing over grey areas in the process if the PM and BA are able to spell everything out in black and white.

ORGANIZATIONAL AND STRATEGIC CHANGE

When discussing change and change management, depending on who we speak with, there will be a different meaning to the word *change*. When speaking with technical resources, BAs, and team members, the word *change* refers to scope-related changes in the context of project change control. However, when speaking with senior management, the sponsor, and the customer, the word *change* is often used in the context of organizational change.

While the two changes are different (project/scope vs. organizational) they are related to each other and will impact one another. With the word *change* common to both types of change, it is important that the PM and the BA, who are typically consumed by project/scope change are also aware of the organizational change. Further, both the PM and the BA have the ability to impact organizational change with project change decisions. Both roles need to ensure that they understand the relationship between the two types of change and both roles need to connect between the organizational change and their actions in the project. Although one could argue that organizational change is for the project sponsor and for senior management to address in relation to strategy, connecting between the project and the organizational change is key for project success and for ensuring that the organizational objectives are being met.

Project/program management and change management are still considered distinct studies with different approaches and deliverables, yet there is a conceptual overlap between the two that allows for project/program management practices to leverage and benefit from change management as a study. This is an area that also receives focus by the Project Management Institute,[2] along with identification of opportunity areas within the project life cycle where change management concepts and tools may be integrated.[3]

The PM (and the project team) typically do not have a say in the organizational strategy and hence, they do not make the call on selecting the project or whether they choose to perform the project work or not. With that being said, however, the PM needs to ensure (to the best of his or her knowledge) that the mandate for the project is aligned with the organizational objectives. In the event of misalignment, the PM should alert the sponsor, and the BA's role is to help the PM make such a call. How would the PM and the BA know if the project's objectives are aligned with the organizational objectives? The answer lies in activities that take place prior to the project or at the project initiation stage and tie back to portfolio management and enterprise analysis (EA) activities: activities that involve needs identification, reviewing options, completing a business case, justification and feasibility analyses, financial considerations, scoring models, and the project selection process. These activities can be performed by a variety of functions within the organization (e.g., operations, finance) but the BA may also be involved.

The considerations around the selection of projects are related to the strategic objectives of the organization, and are in place to check whether and to what degree the selected project (or the project under consideration) is in line with the organization's strategic goals and how much value it adds toward achieving those goals. Projects and programs are the tactical means by which organizations execute their strategic goals and deliver on their change initiatives; hence the importance of the alignment between the projects and the strategic goals—as any misalignment means that the organization is investing time, resources, and money in initiatives that do not deliver value toward its goals.

Since BAs are often involved in pre-project activities, they have knowledge and context of the projects selected and therefore it is recommended that the BA produce a "welcome package" for the PM with the context and the information gathered in those early steps. The information from the pre-project due diligence and selection process is then incorporated in a concise form into the project charter. The charter captures the essence of the reasoning as to why the project is in place and how the project is going to deliver value for the organization. The charter provides the mandate for the project to apply resources and perform the work required to achieve the organizational goals and in turn, it articulates the project objectives and success criteria that need to be aligned with those of the organization.

CHANGE INITIATIVES

The project, as the tactical means of executing the organizational strategy, represents a small chunk of value to be delivered as part of the big picture. The project authorization and selection process needs to be consistent and performed by the most applicable level of senior management, based on the stakes and the visibility of the project. The authorization process that leads to project initiation also needs to take into consideration the fact that changes may take place between the time the project is approved up until the time the project actually begins. This gap may represent a change in circumstances and personnel or a knowledge and context gap. By the time the project starts, we need to ensure that it is still relevant to the program's and portfolio's goals and objectives and that the BA can act as a knowledge transfer of the relevant information from the pre-project work into the hands of the PM. Failing to provide the PM with context and information about why the project is taking place may lead the PM to make poor decisions and recommendations that will, in turn, reduce the value the project delivers and may even put the success of the project in jeopardy.

The information thread that begins with the business case provides important considerations that tie back to the organizational objectives through portfolio management, with a focus on the following areas:

- Specific information about the project sponsorship
- The seniority and level of knowledge required by the PM
- Key resource needs for the project
- Information regarding budgetary needs, availability, and approvals
- The overall project priority (in relation to other projects)
- The level of urgency of the project
- Any information about the organizational readiness to perform the work

Failures of Change Initiatives

Despite the extensive approval and due diligence processes organizations go through to bring projects to life, it is staggering to learn that close to 80% of change initiatives fail.[4] A 2008 McKinsey & Company survey of business executives indicates that the percentage of change programs that are a success is still around 30% today. With a lack of sufficient hands-on involvement by senior management (i.e., leading by example, providing clear prioritization or timely decision making and sign-off process), it is up to the PM and the BA to assume this responsibility to gather and articulate information with such clarity and relevance that motivate senior stakeholders to fulfill their roles. For example, although it is the role of the sponsor to write the project charter (since it is the sponsor's project), most sponsors delegate this task to the PM, who in turn, can use the help of the BA to put together the charter and present it to the sponsor. It is easier for the sponsor to critique the document and ensure all the required information is there rather than writing the charter from scratch.

The reason the majority of change initiatives fail is not because over 70% of change initiatives are bad ideas, but rather it is due to poor execution of those initiatives. The poor execution is driven mainly by the gap between the pre-project intentions and the actual hand-off of the mandate to the appropriate PM and team. Numerous books, courses, articles, and theories have been written and developed around why change initiatives fail, but only a few realized that it is not the existence of flaws in the ideas that take initiatives down, but rather flaws in execution. Further, the disciplines of project management and business analysis are also somewhat siloed and have only recently started opening up to integrating themselves with organizational change management. Similar to the fact that great initiatives fail due to poor implementation, brilliant PMs and effectively executed projects may fail to deliver value to the organization if they are misaligned with the objectives for which they were taken.

Why Change Initiatives Fail

The disconnect between the strategic goals and the projects undertaken can happen at any point along the way and is commonly related to the following reasons:

- Failing to understand the nature and complexity of the change
- Failing to appoint a PM that is suitable for the task and the rigor required
- Failing to ensure organizational readiness for the initiative
- Incorrectly estimating what is needed to move a change from idea inception to an ongoing program
- Neglecting to properly frame the scope and boundaries of the change
- Underestimating the resistance to the change
- Confusing enthusiasm and determination with planning and preparation

- Quickly running out of steam from the excitement of a big announcement to the hard work of implementing the change ideas
- Failing to consider what can go wrong and how to deal with it
- Remaining locked in a paradigm of *this is a great idea; it cannot go wrong*
- The BA failing to consolidate all relevant information and creating a knowledge thread to ensure continuity and context for success

In addition, stakeholders must realize that the strategic change will have an impact that is likely to be felt everywhere in the organization, and this includes planning for the day after the change and ensuring that people, processes, and tools are in place to accommodate the change. These items require effective communication that can be led by the PM, along with process mapping and improvement activities to be facilitated by the BA.

DRIVING FORCE(S) BEHIND SUCCESS

It is safe to say that throughout the 20th century there were five driving forces behind successful companies:

- **Efficiency of processes:** This includes streamlining processes, process improvement, process integration, and more formal approaches to process management—from ISO to Six Sigma.
- **Effective mass marketing:** People did not buy the best products but rather, those products that were most effectively marketed considering the following key aspects: (1) brand alignment between the brand perception and the customer; (2) authenticity of the brand, as people engaged with campaigns and not necessarily with companies; (3) proactive and reactive thinking, so the brand could deal with any type of backlash before it was too late.
- **Rapid adoption of technology:** This involves the ability to use technology as a competitive advantage.
- **Financial acumen:** This includes cost savings, identification of trends, effective planning and efficiencies (e.g., Lean), proper investments, leveraging, and focusing on value-added activities that put organizations in a position of financial advantage.
- **Human resource skills:** Effective communication, people acumen, understanding and acting upon people's needs, learning people's drivers and motivators, relationship building, stakeholder expectations management, keeping your team happy, and managing perceptions all fall under the umbrella of human resource and people skills—and they have been getting an increasing amount of focus in recent years.

While historically these five areas all yielded a competitive advantage, it is only the last one—human resource skills—that provides a sustainable advantage into the future, and it is the *people component* that is the most essential ingredient in change.

Change and Project Management

Change (i.e., organizational or strategic change) and project management differ in several respects:

- Change is more strategic, whereas project management is more tactical.
- Change is complex (a package that cannot be broken down to simple pieces) and is an umbrella for project management that is in place to execute and implement the change. Project management has complicated aspects (ensuring we follow the processes and best practices) that can be broken down into smaller, more manageable pieces. However, it also has an aspect of complexity (around the management of people and about aligning the project with the change and its complexity).
- Change is about the initiative, the idea, the organizational needs, and the strategic objectives. Project management is about the execution of the strategy, the implementation of the idea, the planning of the details of what needs to be done, and the allocation of the resources to do it. While the change is about the mandate to take action, the project is about hitting the pavement and doing the work, hence the importance of the alignment of the project's authorization, direction, personnel, planning, and objectives with those of the organization.
- Connecting the change to the project and managing the people aspect of the change as well as throughout the project are the two critical success factors of both the change initiative and the project.
- For the project sponsors, the alignment between the project and the change initiative is achieved through portfolio management, which includes allocation of resources, management of capacities, and prioritization.
- For PMs, value is produced by asking the right questions, putting together a charter that captures the essence of the business case, and making recommendations and decisions that are aligned with the stated organizational needs.
- For BAs, it is about the knowledge transfer and maintaining a knowledge thread that goes from the idea generation, through the project selection to the chartering process. While senior management needs to ensure this process takes place; it is the BA who facilitates it, manages

the knowledge, serves as a knowledge repository, and handles the behind the scenes of the alignment.

The PM and the BA already know that their sphere of influence is limited, but they need to draft a plan that acts on this knowledge and that helps manage stakeholder expectations accordingly. The term *managing upward* comes to mind in this case, as the PM-BA duo need to help senior stakeholders realize that their sphere of influence is also limited. Understanding that one cannot impact the entire system will help stakeholders realize what they can and cannot do or expect from the project and the change initiative. Further, it will lead them toward thinking about improving the handling of the people side of things: both at the strategic change level and at the project level. It is important to remind stakeholders that the best team, delivering the most effective implementation will not lead to organizational success if the mandate for the project is unclear, incomplete, unrealistic, or miscommunicated.

As we see so often, the onus for achieving success is on the project team, even if the change idea is not clearly communicated, and even when there are gaps in the handover of the change initiative to the project team. These gaps are typically related to the mandate, its clarity, the capacity and resource authorization, communication, money, timelines, realistic expectations, and considerations regarding organizational impact. Strong sponsorship, a chartering process, and a PM-BA duo will increase the probability of alignment and subsequently, for success.

The link between the change initiative and project management is also about ensuring that the focus shifts toward asking the right questions first, before pursuing the right answers. The right questions can typically be determined with the help of the BA and their due-diligence process and in turn, will lead to a paradigm of looking for the best way, rather than the right way, of doing things. Due to the complexity of change and the ongoing alignment challenges between the change and the project, the search for the *right* answers becomes a moving target because *right* will change—based on the nature of the change, the alignment, and the circumstances. The search for *right* will cause us to become reactive and to erratically search for answers, instead of ensuring we are doing our best as long as we are heading in the right direction at any particular point in time.

Ownership and Resistance

Change initiatives are highly prone to failing due to their challenging nature and due to the need for focus on both the change and the project sides. Success requires the change leaders to effectively delegate not only the work of bringing the change to life, but also the authority and the control over it. In fact, change is best facilitated by developing ownership by senior management in the change process and delegating a large part of this ownership to the PM and in turn, to the BA. The ownership does not only refer to the parts of the initiatives that are confined to the project (and with it the controls required to properly own the relevant aspects of the change). Other pieces of the change can be handed over to the PM and the BA to own, even if it is outside of the project. Utilizing portfolio management and EA processes can allow the PM and the BA to add tremendous value to the change initiative as a whole by helping them achieve effective stakeholder expectations management and ensuring communication, reporting, authorization, information, and context flow to and from stakeholders.

The flow of information within and beyond the project can help provide stakeholders with relevant information, reports, and context that will improve their buy-in and reduce one of the most challenging aspects of change—resistance. Most people do not resist the change itself, but they resist the way things are done; they are upset by feeling misinformed, by the perception that they are out of the loop, and by the pain and the threats posed by the change. As the PM-BA duo is all about expectations management and performing effective stakeholder analysis, it will be a wise decision to apply their subject matter expertise in this area to the entire change initiative. This will also help align the project work with the organizational objectives for which it was taken, in the pursuit of success.

The best way of dealing with resistance is by recognizing it and taking action, rather than suppressing, avoiding, or minimizing it. Change leadership involves helping people make better choices in light of the current reality and then helping them take responsibility for pursuing their choices. One of the challenges that a project faces during its life cycle is planning for and dealing with stakeholder reactions and resistance to the changes they are supposed to achieve. Negative reactions can thwart schedules, compromise the quality, and impact the perceived value and benefits the project produces. Failing to properly deal with the human element of change will lead to roadblocks and resistance all throughout the initiative.

There are six approaches to managing stakeholders' resistance[5] to change, which can be applied and enhanced by the PM and the BA by leveraging their skills, relationships, and areas of expertise:

1. *Education and communication*: investing in informing people about the rationale for the change (when resistance appears as a result of misinformation or a lack of information). Another tactic that has been proven useful is the WIIFM technique—What's In It For Me? This involves putting yourself in the shoes of the resisting stakeholder to

empathize with their situation, and then articulating any benefits specific to that stakeholder or at least how they will be supported through the change. This technique is not easy to implement, especially when emotions, relationships, and residue from past events get involved. In addition, the PM and the BA, being overworked and distracted by day-to-day tasks often do not have the capacity to slow down and put themselves in the stakeholders' position. The PM and the BA already lead a complex set of both formal and informal communications and they can incorporate the change aspect into their ongoing communication and expectation management processes. This, as part of the overall attempt to improve collaboration between the PM and the BA, can help free up capacity and bandwidth for the PM and the BA to attend to important tasks—such as understanding where stakeholders come from. The WIIFM does not require both the PM and the BA to fully dedicate themselves to the task, but rather they should share that responsibility based on the stakeholder, the type of challenge at hand, and their respective areas of expertise.

2. *Participation and involvement*: bringing stakeholders into the change process more as active participants (when resistance appears to be a result of being excluded from the process). Buy-in can be achieved by giving stakeholders a role and making them feel they are part of the solution.
3. *Facilitation and support*: staffing up on emotional and physical/technical support to aid in the execution of the change (when anxiety or uncertainty surfaces as reaction to the change). Facilitation is one of the core roles of the BA and it can be expanded to cover certain aspects of the change.
4. *Negotiation and agreement*: incentivizing the adoption of the change (which is particularly helpful when resistant stakeholders are well positioned to undermine the change and cause serious issues if their needs are not met). This ties back to understanding stakeholder needs and making trade-offs—the PM and the BA already engage in these types of activities.
5. *Manipulation*: intentionally limiting information to some stakeholders and helping to achieve buy-in by giving other stakeholders key roles in the change process (often used when the other methods are deemed too time- or resource-heavy for the change team). Although the word *manipulation* has a negative connotation, PMs and BAs already engage in manipulating stakeholders and even team members, by providing them with only the information that is timely and relevant to them. This is obviously done in a tactful way and this type of manipulation

helps the PM and the BA control the flow of information and improves the ability of team members and stakeholders to focus on the things that are at stake (i.e., Pareto's 80:20 Principle[6]).

6. *Explicit and implicit coercion*: threats of undesirable consequences to the resisters (useful in high stakes situations, such as the organization's survival is in question if a particular change is not adopted). While all five other approaches require the support of the project sponsor and the change leaders, this item in particular cannot be performed by the PM or the BA without the hands-on explicit involvement and support of the senior members of management because they do not have the authority over stakeholders that are external to the project.

As part of stakeholder analysis, the PM and the BA need to include a *situational approach* so they can apply these techniques as part of their effort to manage the change. This does not preclude the sponsor and the change owners from doing their part—which includes understanding and ensuring organizational change readiness, identification of the resisting and driving forces of the change, and engaging stakeholders accordingly.

This list of six approaches to managing stakeholders' resistance to change is another tool that the PM-BA duo can use to draft responses to each anticipated challenge, which will more effectively aid in planning, execution, and overall team morale throughout the process. The PM and the BA need to consider how to combat potential resistance by each stakeholder, discuss it with the team and with the project sponsor, and integrate these tactics and their possible impact on the change initiative into the project plan, schedule, risk, and communication plans and budget accordingly.

Resistance can be broken into two types: positive and negative. Positive resistance is important and helpful to the cause, and it includes inquiries that are intended to test the change, the introduction of open minded questioning, and even disagreeing with the solution. It also involves attempting to promote and lobby alternative solutions while analyzing alternatives, questioning the need for the change, and even challenging the vision. Positive resistance is not only essential to the process, but also needs to be encouraged and in turn, addressed properly.

Negative resistance, however, needs to be overcome before it damages the spirit, morale, attitudes, and dispositions toward the initiative. It involves attempts to sabotage the initiative (or parts of it) and it can surface as being too busy to attend meetings, starting another (competing) initiative, having a phantom initiative, ignoring the efforts that are taking place, or actively influencing others to check out and not pull their weight in the change. These negative efforts may be directed at team members, as well as external stakeholders, thus, the sponsor, the change owners, and the PM-BA duo need to combine forces to combat the damaging effects.

The Need for Integration

The organization needs to establish the formal relationship between the official change leaders and the PM to ensure there is a meaningful integration and collaboration in their respective efforts, so business objectives and organizational value can be achieved. The change management activities need to be seamlessly embedded within the project life cycle, and should not be viewed as a separate or adjunct activity that can be deemphasized. With alignment in place, it will be easier for the PM and the BA to leverage joint opportunities so that stakeholder engagement activities become more streamlined. It also provides the PM-BA duo with better insights into understanding organizational impacts and stakeholder concerns, so the team can modify its approach and proactively minimize potential resistance.

Types of Change

Although the PM and the BA can play a major role in the change initiative, the sponsor and change owners must pull their weight and provide the leadership, set a direction and vision, and perform their role in aligning people with the vision. These activities will serve as the backbone of the change initiative and from here, the change owners need to ensure appropriate and effective division of work and responsibilities with the project management team; addressing such topics as the day-to-day management, efficiencies, problem solving, controlling, and reporting.

There are different types of organizational change[7] that may be pursued, and each will have an impact on a variety of organizational factors, as well as on the project and the project team. There are primarily three types of change that organizations may engage in and each has a different impact on the organization:

1. *Developmental change*: This type of change is driven by a need for improvement in the organization (i.e., improvement of skills, knowledge, practice, and performance). It does not pose a significant threat to stakeholders and its outcome is fairly clear—as it is project-oriented and prescribed against an existing standard. This type of change occurs through training, skill development, communications, and process improvement—areas in which the PM and the BA can, for the most part, lead the change.
2. *Transitional change*: This type of change is driven by the need to fix a problem (i.e., redesign of strategy, structures, systems, processes,

technology, or work practices). It is project-oriented and poses a slightly bigger threat to stakeholders than the developmental change. This change occurs through controlled process, support structures, and timeline, where once again, the PM and the BA are suitable to carry most of the load.

3. *Transformational change*: This change is about survival, and requires a breakthrough to pursue new opportunities—as the alternatives may be either to change or to die. The focus of this change is to overhaul strategy, structure, systems, processes, work, culture, behavior, and mindset—and it poses a significant threat to stakeholders. The desired outcome is not initially known—it emerges or is created through trial and error and continuous course correction. Unlike the other two types, this type of change forces stakeholders to shift old mindsets and business paradigms to new. This type of change occurs through conscious process design and facilitation; high involvement, and emergent process. While the PM-BA duo can lead most of the leg work of this change, it must have significant hands-on involvement of the change owners and the sponsor.

The Change Stakeholders

At the outset of the project, the PM and the BA conduct a stakeholder analysis. It takes into consideration stakeholders from within and outside the project and the organization, but it is oriented toward the stakeholders' involvement, influence, and needs around the project. There are also the change stakeholders, who might partially overlap with those of the project, or not. The change stakeholders are those who are involved with or impacted by the change itself, regardless of the project. Typically, we can identify the change sponsor(s), the change target(s), and the change agent(s), as well as the customers, clients, influencers, and advocates. The change stakeholder analysis should be led out by the change sponsor. Since the PM and the BA already perform project stakeholder analysis, participating in the change stakeholder analysis could benefit the initiative across the board. On one hand, it can help the PM and the BA better understand the context and the story beyond the immediate project organization; and on the other hand, it will leverage the PM-BA duo's experience and work as part of the analysis to help develop, or even lead the change stakeholder analysis.

Attitudes Toward the Change

The PM and the BA need to consider the stakeholders' disposition toward and view of the change, so they can come up with strategies and recommendations on how to handle these stakeholders and how to help them move toward a more favorable position on the change. This is part of the PM-BA duo's involvement in the change stakeholder analysis, and it can serve as a significant stepping stone toward integrating the project's efforts with those of the change leadership. It can also help align the project needs with those of the organization and change leadership; and the knowledge, as a result of this exercise, can provide the PM and the BA with valuable context that will make their decision-making process throughout the project more informed and of higher quality.

Stakeholders may not support the change initiative for various reasons, but in order to engage them effectively, we first need to check whether they are even aware of the change initiative. Once we figure this out, we can move toward checking whether their position is associated with their ability or willingness to be a supporting party of the change initiative. Examples of when stakeholders may not support the change initiative and proposed approaches to gain buy-in may include:

- When stakeholders are not aware of the change, we should communicate with them and provide them with information that will get them involved to better understand the needs, stakes, and context.
- When stakeholders are not able to perform, contribute to, or support the change, we need to provide them with training and coaching so the applicable skills are transferred to them.
- When stakeholders are not willing to support or to buy-in to the change idea, we need to engage in conflict resolution techniques, including: confronting the issue with them, collaborating, demonstrating the value proposition of the change, and getting them involved so they can reframe their view and understand the implications of their position.

Team Building

Any type of project requires a cohesive and effective team to lead it to success. This is especially true when the project tries to implement a change initiative where the need to align the team with the change and organizational needs increases further. Team-building activities are typically part of the roles of both the PM and the BA; it primarily involves turning the group of people who have been selected to do the work into a team that has a mutual goal. Regardless of the leadership that needs to be demonstrated by the change owners, the PM and the BA need to step up, encourage individual accountability, lead by example, define individual work products, and continuously ensure that the team's purpose matches the broader organizational mission. Open communication, expectations management, open discussion, a transparent decision-making process, and situational leadership that clearly delegates and shares the leadership roles are also essential for a successful change initiative.

The results, final products and team's successes need to be collective; problem solving needs to be timely, effective, and transparent; performance needs to be measured directly by assessing collective work products; and decisions need to be consensus-based.

ORGANIZATIONAL READINESS FOR THE CHANGE

In order to improve the chances of achieving the change initiative's goals, there is a need to ensure that the organization is ready for the upcoming change—and for the project that will implement the change and bring it to life. Although it is impossible to guarantee that the organization is fully ready for the upcoming endeavor, there is a need to perform an organizational readiness assessment that will provide the project and change stakeholders with a realistic read regarding the level of readiness of the organization. Organizational readiness assessment presents a series of factors and guidelines to consider measuring whether and how prepared the organization is to undertake the initiative. It also provides an indication of the areas in which the organization is not sufficiently prepared, in order to allow the stakeholders to change their areas of focus to better position the organization for the tasks at hand. The readiness assessment does not measure the intent or the interest in an initiative, but rather whether the organization has what it takes to succeed.

Organizational and project readiness assessment connects back to EA and to portfolio management due to the need to ensure that the organization is ready to undertake the project initiative from an alignment, context, and capacity perspective. While it may be formally out of scope for the PM, it is either the BA or the BA-PM duo who needs to engage stakeholders to ensure organizational readiness. The findings of the assessment are not intended to result in a decision to cancel the project, but they can provide a warning and a call-to-action to help the organization become better prepared for what it needs to do. While the project readiness portion of the readiness assessment takes place early—at the pre-initiation or initiation stage of the project—the change portion of the organizational readiness assessment starts at the same early stages and continues on an ongoing basis throughout the project and the life cycle of the change initiative. The ongoing mechanisms to measure the organizational readiness should be incorporated into the performance gates of the project, ensuring that the progress taking place in the project is aligned with the organizational needs. The input to the performance gates should be provided and defined by the PM and the BA, along with context and information from the project sponsor and the leading change stakeholders. Part of this effort helps the BA define and refine the solution assessment to ensure it answers to the changing needs of the stakeholders throughout the initiative. In addition to the areas mentioned here, and the EA and portfolio management considerations, the ongoing organizational readiness measures also tie back to project and organizational governance and to the integration of all the moving parts in the project.

Readiness Assessment—Making It Less Informal

People plan and conduct informal readiness assessments for most things that they do. Sometimes we use a checklist to make sure we take everything we need when going somewhere (although usually we just have this list in our head). When it comes to our personal lives, it is usually sufficient to have an ad hoc list of items to keep in mind—but in an organization, when larger initiatives take place with more moving parts, multiple stakeholders, along with higher stakes and costs, we need to better organize our thoughts on whether the organization has what it takes to take on an initiative, and throughout the project, we need to check on whether or not we are prepared for the next stage in the change initiative.

At any gate point throughout an effective readiness assessment process, the PM and the BA should have the ability to articulate the organization's readiness for the project and in turn, to manage or change the expectations and the risks associated with the undertaking. There are many ways to measure readiness and the assessment's rigor and thoroughness should depend on multiple factors, such as organizational risk attitude, project and change complexity, and the specific situation at hand. A *proper* readiness assessment may include evaluations of the organizational culture, processes and procedures, leadership styles, resource management, overall complexity and historical performance. Some additional factors to consider throughout the initiative may include progress; alignment with organizational objectives; and solution assessment from a technical, process, and people perspective. The readiness assessment can help identify project and organizational needs and serve as a foundation for planning and subsequently, for scope changes and replanning down the line. Each time the assessment is conducted, the BA would use the results to work with stakeholders to define or refine any transition requirements to assist with bridging the gap between current and future state—e.g., for example training requirements. These transition requirements are then converted into project requirements and therefore, are built into the project scope to help stakeholders adapt to change. The iterative nature between the assessment and definition or refinement of transition requirements to be converted into project requirements continues through the life cycle of the change initiative.

Readiness deals with a variety of matters, where the leading issues are related to resources (i.e., availability, capacity, skills, timing, and fit), project dependencies, domain experience, approvals, budgets, and schedule. The change portion also looks at organizational priorities, allocation of funding, decision-making processes, solution assessment, and product alignment. The readiness assessment can be viewed as a type of gap analysis between where the organization currently is and the capability required for the initiative. Failing to effectively address gaps that are realized throughout the assessment will result in elevated levels of complexity and risk. In some cases, the team may identify areas of the project that indicate a lack of readiness and in others, there is simply a lack of information about some aspects of the initiative. Either way, these are both warning signs to the organization that this initiative requires special attention that can be addressed by identifying and implementing transition requirements.

Why Readiness Assessment?

The simple answer to the question, "Why is there a need for a readiness assessment?" is because it is less costly to do it, than not to do it. If the assessment results show that the organization is ready to take on the initiative, it helps reinforce the need for it and that the direction taken is correct. Indication of readiness also provides validation and helps boost the confidence of and achieve buy-in among stakeholders. However, if the assessment determines that the organization is not sufficiently ready, it will be less costly to look after the gaps and deficiencies early in the initiative, or shortly after they are realized, than it would be later. In fact, the longer the organization waits to deal with areas that are deemed not ready or insufficient, the more expensive and risky it will become to correct its course. Realizing early on that there are gaps in the readiness level also provides stakeholders the knowledge and insight to make a more informed and timely decision about the change, the project, and the initiative, rather than proceeding with the wrong initiative altogether, or with the right initiative but the wrong approach.

In addition to the direct benefits it produces, the organizational readiness assessment also serves as a team building exercise—an opportunity for the PM and the BA to come together and establish guidelines for working together and an opportunity for the PM-BA duo to build rapport with stakeholders. Further, interaction with the stakeholders can help assess their level of involvement with and support of the initiative and contribute to the stakeholder expectations management effort. The downside of performing an organizational readiness assessment, especially the ongoing portion of the readiness analysis throughout the initiative, is that it is difficult to implement—not because of the cost or complexity associated with it, but rather due to the difficulty in *selling* the idea to senior management and in demonstrating its value. The readiness assessment does add to the cost and time at the front end of the project and throughout—with the enhanced gating process—but this is time and money that is essentially guaranteed to be saved later in the life cycle of the change initiative in the form of lower costs, less defects, lower risks, and greater efficiencies.

What the Readiness Assessment Is About

The readiness assessment involves measuring at one or more of the following levels: organizational, program, project, and/or team. It checks whether the organization is prepared to perform the work, how open it is to changing the way things get done (the change) in order to accommodate the new needs, and the overall implementation capability. At a high level, it includes the proposed readiness assessment areas, as demonstrated in Figure 9.1.

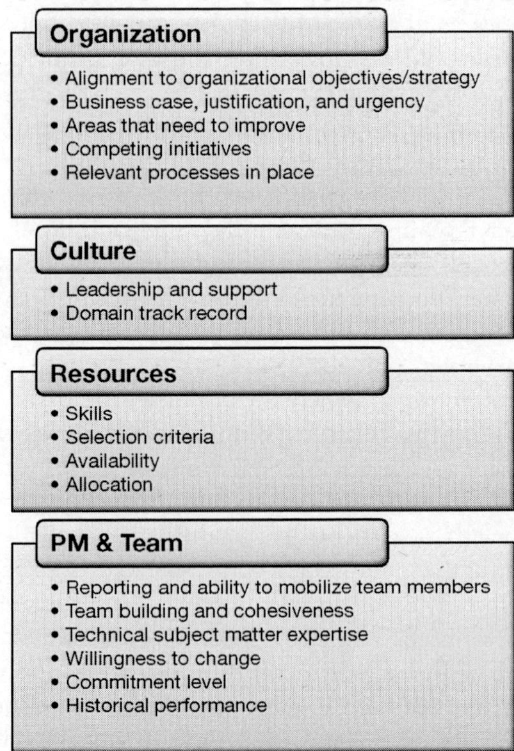

Figure 9.1 Readiness assessment areas

The assessment will help focus on areas the organization might need to prepare for, or to overcome any potential obstacles that may impede the project. Parts of the team readiness assessment may overlap with the stakeholder analysis; this is an example of integration and should not be viewed as a duplication of effort, but rather as an input to the stakeholder analysis and in turn, to expectations management. For the most part, readiness assessments yield results that vary somewhere between fully ready and completely not ready, but very rarely will deem a project as being one of these two extremes. If an assessment produces results that show that the organization is fully ready for the project, this may truly be the case or there is a possibility that the assessment was not performed properly. Generally, it is expected that the assessment will reveal gaps and articulate areas that can help your organization put together stronger teams and focus on the relevant areas of planning that it needs to.

Know If You Are Ready

There are a few questions to ask before starting the assessment, to get a better idea about where the organization stands in relation to being ready:

- Is there an organizational readiness measurement process in the organization?
- Has a lack of readiness been an issue in previous initiatives?
- Did lack of readiness cause project complexity or mire the initiative's performance?
- Is there a formal process in the organization for readiness assessment?

Even if the answers to these questions are less than ideal, it does not necessarily indicate looming trouble; it simply reinforces the need for meaningful readiness planning and serves as a reminder of what might happen if the gaps in readiness are not addressed effectively and in a timely manner.

Assessment Considerations

The readiness assessment aims to determine how aligned the main stakeholders, the organization, and the customers are with each other on the goals, objectives, approach, and capabilities of the initiative. There are several questions to be asked in order to help measure the readiness level. The questions should be treated as discussion points, for which PMs and BAs need to engage in conversations and look for answers, rather than walk around and ask stakeholders direct questions that could be taken out of context. Each question has the potential to turn into a risk, if the answer is not in favor of the initiative's context or when there is not enough information about it. PMs and BAs can build their own proprietary measurement tool by performing a few simple steps, as demonstrated in Figure 9.2.

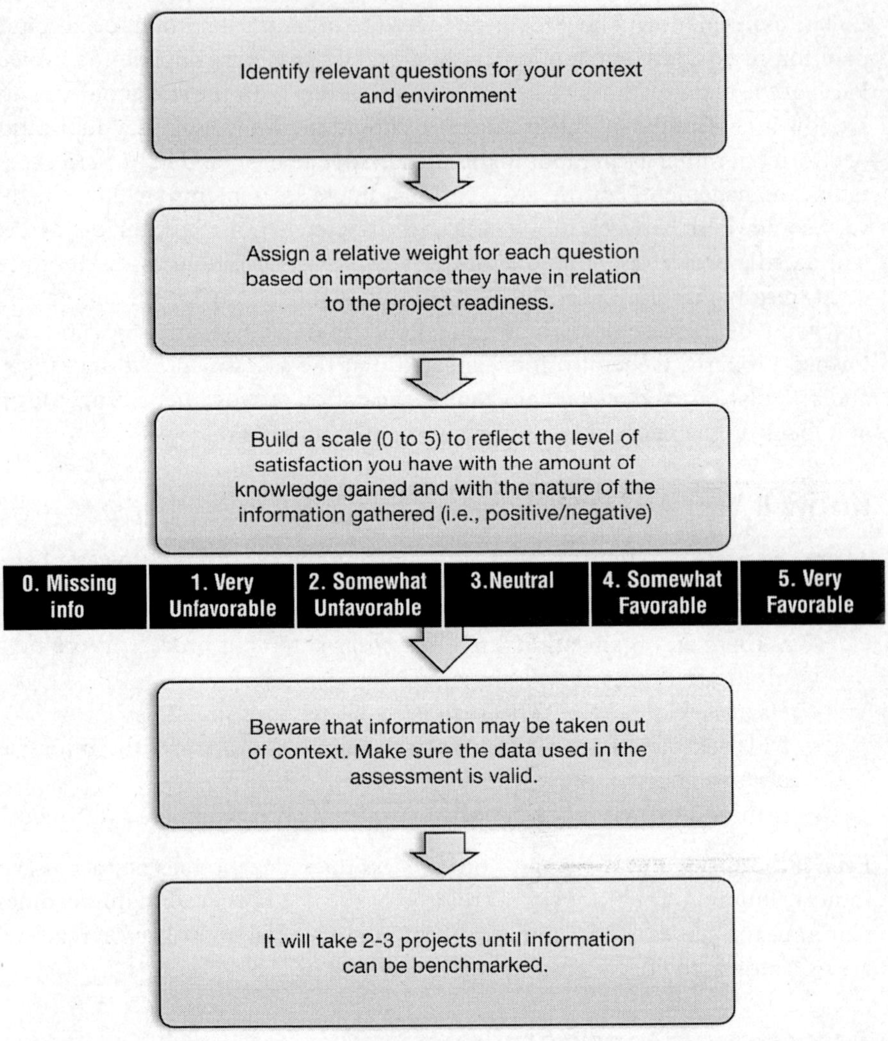

Figure 9.2 Steps to build a proprietary readiness assessment

The Assessment Questions

With the previous considerations in mind, PMs and BAs must remember that some of these questions may not be relevant to every environment and some adjustments may need to take place to ensure relevance to the specific situation at hand. The goal is to have a set of questions to ask that will ultimately provide an indication of whether the organization is prepared to move ahead with a

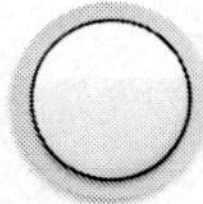

Readiness Assessment Categories

1. Strategic Alignment
2. Enterprise Analysis Factors
3. Organizational Change
4. Organization Priorities and Culture
5. Leadership
6. Track Record
7. Success, Objectives and Quality
8. Resources and the Team
9. Risks
10. Product and Solution Related Capabilities

The readiness assessment categories should be applied for each of the assessment areas that are specified in Figure 9.1.

Figure 9.3 Readiness assessment categories

given change initiative. A simple scale of 0-5 should be sufficient: where 0 indicates missing information and a need to make assumptions; 1 means *strongly disagree*, or unfavorable answer; and 5 means *strongly agree* or that the question has a favorable answer. The list of questions has been organized into logical categories as presented in Figure 9.3. Each category should trigger a series of questions that are relevant for the organization and its environment. In addition, Figure 9.4 provides a list of questions that should be asked for any type of change in any organization.

Assessment Results: How Do You Know When You Are Ready?

The results of the readiness assessment may not be conclusive or specific and they may not give a clear signal as to where things appear to be heading. However, they can give better insight and additional knowledge about the project's environment and possibly, about the overall chances of successfully completing it. More specifically, the assessment may produce value from the following points of view:

- Help the organization identify changes that need to be made to invest in the initiative, including: reassigning responsibilities, shifting staff schedules, and changing the scope, areas of focus, or the cost structure.
- Ensure that the project coincides with the organizational strategy and goals. Beyond the potential waste of effort and resources for pursuing misaligned goals, it may confuse employees and may further impair the

Communication **Who is affected?**

- Is there a clear vision and strategy for the initiative?
- Are priorities set?
- Are all identified and relevant stakeholders informed?

Sponsorship **Is there active and appropriate sponsorship?**

- Is there an executive Sponsor?
- Does the Sponsor have the appropriate seniority?
- How will the Sponsor be involved?
- Are there clear escalation procedures?

Stakeholders **Is there buy-in?**

- Is success criteria clearly defined and articulated?
- Are stakeholders' needs and concerns addressed?
- Is there a plan to handle resistance?

People and Planning **Are people ready for the change?**

- Is there a resource management plan in place?
- Do people know what their roles and responsibilities are?
- Is there a mechanism for tracking progress and reporting?
- Are the project plan and the change plans aligned with each other so the change strategies are scaled to the organizational conditions?

Transition **Is it moving in the right direction?**

- Is there a transition plan in place? Is the organization ready to pick up from where the project leaves things off?
- Is there sufficient training and/or knowledge transfer in place?
- Are all risks identified and analyzed? Both project and business risks.
- Is there anything else we forgot to consider?

In addition to questions that are triggered for each of the readiness assessment categories, this figure lists a series of generic questions to ask.

Figure 9.4 Generic readiness questions

chance for success if the project is not aligned with the organization's overall strategy.

- Indicate whether the organization has allocated adequate budget, staff, and technology infrastructure to the project and that other resources are in place to support it through its implementation.
- Provide input to the organizational priorities and if needed, lead to conversations about resource reallocation.
- Give an indication of where the organization is in relation to the initiative and how prepared the organization is for the project. It may also

provide some insights and answers related to stakeholder analysis and preliminary risk assessment.

- Provide insight into the organization's decision-making process, priorities, handling of emergencies, conflict management, product alignment to business objectives, and solution assessment.

FINAL THOUGHTS ON ORGANIZATIONAL CHANGE MANAGEMENT

The PM and the BA originally signed up for a project and ended up at the forefront of a change initiative. This involves higher stakes, more challenges, and more responsibilities—but the rewards of doing it right will be felt across the organization. This team is the right choice of people for the tasks at hand, since many of the things the PM-BA duo already do can be leveraged from the project to the change and back to the project, and the skills, experience, and context they bring to the table are relevant for the situation. Further, having the PM and BA leading this effort with the guidance and oversight of the change owners increases the chance for a seamless alignment of the project and the change in terms of needs, resource requirements, risks, rigor, communication considerations, and definition of success.

The marriage of project management and change, supported by the BA, is the right way to ensure that a proper handoff from the idea stage on the strategy level, to the implementation stage on the project/tactical level is performed and ultimately, that more change initiatives are successful.

REFERENCES

1. www.agilemanifesto.org. (n.d.). *www.agilemanifesto.org*. Retrieved March 22, 2015, from Principles behind the Agile Manifesto: http://www.agile manifesto.org/principles.html
2. Project Management Institute. (2013). *Managing Change in Organizations: A Practice Guide*. Newtown Square, PA: Project Management Institute.
3. White paper, *One Solution for Project Success: Project and Change Management in the PMBOK® Guide* by T. L. Jarocki (2014).
4. Kotter, John, "*Leading Change: Why Transformation Efforts Fail*," Harvard Business Review, March-April 1995, p 1.
5. Kotter, J., & Schlesinger, L. (March/April 1979). *Choosing Strategies for Change*. Harvard Business Review, 106(14), 45-58.

6. Bookstein, Abraham (1990). "*Informetric distributions, Part I: Unified Overview,*" Journal of the American Society for Information Science 41 (5): 368-375.
7. Adapted from: Anderson and Anderson, *Beyond Change Management*, Pfeiffer Publishing, 2001.

10

PROJECT QUALITY, RECOVERY, AND LESSONS LEARNED

"Every setback is a setup for a great comeback."—T.D. Jakes

What is project recovery? Many people, including project practitioners, do not understand the exact meaning of project recovery. Project recovery takes place when the project's performance reaches a point that can no longer meet its objectives or deliver on key success criteria—recovery means that the project enters a stage of recovering its performance to a level that is acceptable by the key stakeholders. Recovery does not mean fully restoring the performance to its original intended level, but rather restoring to a level that is sufficient to call it a success—albeit to a different extent than originally intended. Recovery also means a change in the project's momentum. Project recovery involves similar activities to the ones that need to take place as part of prevention and planning, with the one difference—that the recovery activities are often done under pressure, after the fact, reactively, and under significantly less favorable conditions. The result is a project that is more expensive than it should have been and typically, longer.

Project recovery takes place as a result of some sort of failure that prevented the project from meeting its original objectives, and is the final step of a series of activities that involve the following steps:

1. *Planning and prevention*: defining standards, identifying specifications, putting together documentation, building plans on how to achieve

them, and setting up the stage to perform quality assurance (QA) and quality control (QC).

2. *Performing QA*: a proactive and preventive approach by ensuring quality in the processes used to develop the product (e.g., conducting audits, process reviews, walk through, and tracking project performance indicators). QA focuses on checking that the processes are correct and that the product we produce conforms to requirements.
3. *Performing QC*: a reactive (yet necessary) process ensuring quality in the product post-product development but prior to launch (e.g., testing and inspections of the project's product). QC focuses on evaluating that the technical performance of the deliverables we produce is according to specifications and that they perform as intended.
4. *Ensuring we did the right thing altogether—part of Validating the Scope*: after ensuring QA and QC, checking that the product we produced is now performing according to project objectives and that it is fit for use and is the product that we actually needed.
5. *Reporting and measuring where we are against the targets*: it includes the planning aspects of establishing reporting parameters, metrics, measurements, performance thresholds, exception handling, and escalation procedures, as well as the actual reporting, including performing earned value management.
6. *Recovery*: the recovery starts with the realization that something is wrong with the project, checking the extent, considering the options, and working toward restoring performance to an acceptable level. Recovery is the result of all the previously listed items. A project with no clear plan or objectives cannot be deemed as failing, and therefore cannot be recovered. In short, the recovery actions are the same as what the prevention activities should have been with the difference that prevention activities are part of being proactive, while recovery activities are reactive in nature, as they try to address existing unfavorable project conditions.

This chapter is centered on project recovery activities and the interaction between the project manager (PM) and the business analyst (BA) during project recovery. For additional context and relevance, and to instill a culture that values prevention over recovery, but that can perform recovery when needed—the chapter also covers quality considerations that shed light on the importance of measuring the cost of quality (CoQ) and QA measures that can be used as project performance indicators. Both the CoQ and the project performance indicators are proactive in the sense that they give the PM and the BA indications of performance based on readings and measures that are tracked before the project's product is produced—that are typically linked to the process of performing the project work. They complete the picture for project recovery and, as part of prevention activities, this chapter also covers the area of lessons learned—from the importance of performing the lessons learned exercises to techniques and effective approaches.

Although project recovery activities are, for the most part, led by the PM, or by the person who is appointed to lead the recovery, the BA has a critical role in leading the technical aspects of the recovery, measuring the project's performance, and providing real time performance data to the PM. For a successful recovery, in a similar fashion to a successful project, there is a strong need for a seamless integration of the PM and the BA work for capturing timely and relevant data and for applying it to an informed decision-making process.

WHAT IS QUALITY?

Quality is anything that matters to the stakeholders who define the success criteria. Quality can be any given functionality that is requested, it could refer to the timelines or the budgetary limits of the project and it relates to the value and the benefits the project produces. In more formal terms, quality is the degree to which a set of inherent characteristics fulfills requirements.[1] It can be defined as a set of activities that is planned to help achieve project quality and to meet or exceed customers' expectations. There are two sub-definitions that complement each other that can further articulate what quality is: conformance to requirements and fitness for use (see explanations in Table 10.1).

Cost of Quality

Cost of quality is a term that is widely used but often misunderstood and as a result, usually overlooked. Phillip Crosby[2] articulated in his book *Quality is Free*, that quality, conceptually, is free because whatever we invest in quality upfront (i.e., in prevention activities) will pay off in savings in the future (i.e., products that work, no defects, and success). With that said, there is a cost to quality[3] and it can be calculated by adding the cost of conformance (CoC) and the costs of non-conformance (CoNC). The CoC includes the need to perform actions and activities upfront (as preventive measures) and then perform additional activities as part of measuring quality (appraisal measures). The CoNC is added on top of the CoC in the form of failures (both internal and external). CoQ consists of four elements,[4] presented in Table 10.2: prevention, appraisal, internal failure, and external failure. The first to articulate the CoQ was Joseph Juran who identified the cost of poor quality (i.e., CoNC, which includes both

Table 10.1 The Sub-definitions of quality

An illustration of the main differences between QA (quality assurance) and QC (quality control) as the two areas are closely intertwined. Many project practitioners tend to confuse them with one another.

Definition	**Conformance to Requirements**	**Fitness for Use**
Articulated by	Phillip Crosby	Joseph Juran
Explanation	Checks how well a product or service meets the required targets and tolerances	Tests how well the product performs for its intended use
Achieved Through	Quality assurance	Quality control
Focus area	Can be viewed as the managerial aspect of quality: process reviews, walkthroughs and audits, and continuous improvement. Aligns with Six Sigma[1] principles. Focuses on eliminating defects in the process.	Can be viewed as the technical aspect of quality: testing and inspection. Aligns with Lean[2] principles and is customer centric. Ensures the product or process meets the needs of the customer.
Answers	Verifies whether the processes are correct	Validates that the results are correct

[1]www.isixsigma.com/new-to-six-sigma/getting-started/what-six-sigma/
[2]http://www.lean.org/WhatsLean/

types of failure costs) as any cost that would not have been expended if quality were perfect.

Multiple observations and much research show that organizations spend more than 20-30% of sales on quality, mainly due to poor quality or failures. Further, it is surprising that most businesses are not aware of their actual spending on quality as they do not keep track of it sufficiently, or at all. Most organizations believe that they spend no more than five percent of their total sales on quality; this number is far from correct and is so understated that it gives a false positive picture to key stakeholders. One of the main causes for high CoQ numbers to be so understated, is the lack of realization that the cost to eliminate a failure once the customer gets the product (i.e., external failures) is significantly higher than it is at the development phase. In addition, the costs organizations incur in order to pay for poor quality (i.e., internal and external failures) are not tracked properly. The reason for the insufficient tracking is mainly because these costs are paid for by different costs centers and departments within the organizations and over an extended period of time that may span long beyond the end of the project. When a project is closed, any additional costs that are added to the organization due to the project's failure to produce a quality product are paid for by other costs centers.

Table 10.2 Quality cost components

Cost Type	Category	Details	Examples
Cost of Conformance			
Money spent during project to avoid failure	**Prevention Costs**	Up-front costs to meet customer requirements. Cost incurred to prevent poor quality and to reduce appraisal and failure costs. This is the cost to "design" quality into the product	Design plans, new product review, quality planning, supplier surveys, quality improvement plans, preventive auditing and process improvement implementation, education, and training
	Appraisal Costs	Costs incurred to determine the degree of conformance to quality requirements through measuring, auditing, or evaluating	Inspection, testing, process reviews, service audits, calibration, compliance audits, and investigations
Cost of Non-conformance			
Money spent during and after project due to failure	**Internal Failure**	Costs associated with defects found within the organization (as a result of testing, inspections, and reviews) before the customer receives the product or service	Scrap, rejects, rework, design flaws, repairs, re-inspection, re-testing, material review, defect evaluation, and downgrades
	External Failure	Cost associated with defects found after the customer receives the product or service	Processing customer complaints, customer returns, evaluation of customer complaints, corrective action, maintenance, warranty claims, product recalls, and possibly legal costs

For example, when a customer discovers *after the fact* that a product has a defect, the costs are now attributed against the departments that handle the call from the customer—starting with the call center, through technical support, and then for the following activities: sending out a technician, assessing the extent of the problem, ordering a new part, sending an engineer to perform the rework, processing warranties, producing a report, and eventually closing the ticket. These costs add up quickly to significant amounts of money that the organization needs to pay, but these costs are typically tracked on a departmental level and are not combined. As a result, stakeholders fail to see the true costs of quality—and especially the full costs of failures. The reason the costs are not tracked properly is because the costs are no longer tracked against a project, but rather each department makes only a small contribution to the effort of fixing the problem. With the lack of a consolidated view, the organization will fail to realize the full extent of the CoQ even though it will need to spend those combined funds.

Effective quality management is about early detection of errors in an effort to reduce costs and subsequently, about tracking the costs associated with quality end to end.

There are many ways to view the desired ratio between the various costs of quality, as illustrated in Figure 10.1. It shows the difference between the actual

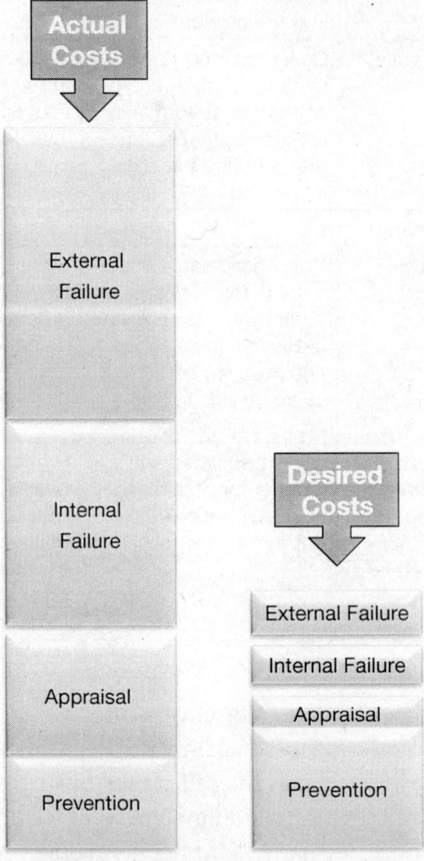

Figure 10.1 Simplified depiction: desired versus actual cost of quality

CoQ and the way it should be (and is mostly perceived to be). However when measuring the true failure costs—including internal, external, and hidden costs—it is safe to say that one dollar that is not spent or that is not spent *properly* during the prevention stage may lead to costs that are 10 or even 50 times greater than that amount in external failure costs that can include compensations, penalties, litigation, and damages.

Measuring CoQ and realizing waste in projects does not need to involve only sophisticated technical considerations. In fact measuring CoQ needs to be performed on an ongoing basis to ensure that day-to-day activities do not consume too many resources and do not produce waste—these measurements should be performed by the PM and the BA. Contributors to the CoNC can be found in the following activities:

1. Working on the wrong project altogether
2. Going through the wrong implementations strategy—leading to rework and delays
3. Not following process
4. Performing an incorrect process
5. Being unprepared because of a lack of planning
6. Not realizing the true complexity of activities
7. False alarms (and all the associated activities up until realizing that it is a false alarm)
8. Weak reporting (not realizing the true status and the triggering of unnecessary change requests)
9. Redundancies (too many layers of reporting, reports that are never reviewed, multiple approval layers, over processing)

A quick glance at the list of contributors to waste and to the cost of failure that were listed previously, triggers the thought that the BA is a natural partner in the effort to measure the costs of quality, and in turn, to interpret them and to try to contain (and ultimately reduce) them. The partnership between the PM and the BA focuses on the fact that most of the areas listed above are related to the role of the BA. This, of course, does not imply that the waste is in any way the fault of the BA, but rather that these areas are typically monitored and controlled by the BA.

How to Measure Cost of Quality

CoQ can be measured by tracking processes and activities, checking how much is invested in them, and discerning where they fail to yield the desired result—leading to the need to undo work that is already performed, then rework to recreate the product. Measuring the CoQ is not a goal or an objective, but rather a means to track performance, check for exceptions, look for areas of nonconformance and proactively identify bottlenecks, problem areas, gaps, and handoffs. By measuring the CoQ the PM and the BA can make informed decisions that are based on actual events in the project, handle situations as they occur—or even before problems are noticed by other stakeholders—and proactively adjust performance and improve processes on an ongoing basis. Measuring the CoQ involves the application of techniques and activities that, for the most part, the BA already engages in, or that the BA should at least be familiar with. The following list (with short explanations) contains activities the PM and BA can perform throughout the project to reduce the CoNC on a project:

1. Prevention and appraisal activities that reduce the CoNC.
    - **Project Charter:** to set the expectations, identify goals and stakeholders, and define performance standards
    - **Stakeholder Analysis (current vs. desired level of commitment):** identifying the stakeholders and understanding their needs is a key step toward defining how to meet performance standards, what activities it will take, what tolerance levels we should expect, and where we should expect challenges and problems
    - **Process Adherence:** defining, mapping, and ensuring the adherence to processes are some of the core activities of the BA and are critical to the success in any organization; and are also the building blocks of *kaizen*[5] (from the Japanese—change for better, or continuous improvement)
    - **Value-Added (VA) and Non-Value-Added (NVA) Activities Analysis:** VA activities change the form or the function of a product, and these are things the customer is willing to pay for. NVA activities are those that do not help create conformance to customer's needs, and they should be reduced, eliminated, or simplified.
    - **Value Stream Mapping (VSM):**[6] VSM is a lean-management method for analyzing the current state and designing a future state for the series of events that it takes to create a product or a service from the start to the point it gets to the customer.
    - **Supplier, Inputs, Product, Outputs, Customer (SIPOC):**[7] SIPOC is a tool that summarizes the inputs and outputs of one or more processes in table form and depicts how the given process is servicing the customer.
    - **Voice of the Customer**[8] **(VOC) Table:** VOC is the first step toward performing quality function deployment (QFD). The

VOC table tries to explore and discover customer needs, in order to help organizations focus their first and best efforts on what matters most to customers and areas where competitors' offerings may be preferred.

2. Activities that represent rework and need to be performed after the fact, once a failure occurs. These activities can also be viewed as part of prevention and appraisal costs, if they are performed proactively on lessons and findings from previous projects. In that case, they are part of an effort to reduce the chance for failure in the current project:
   - **Root Cause Analysis:**[9] is a method of problem solving used for identifying the root causes of problems.
   - **Pareto Chart:**[10] (named after Vilfredo Pareto) is a type of chart that contains both bars and a line graph, where individual values are represented in descending order by bars, and the cumulative total is represented by the line. The Pareto principle is the 80-20 rule that states 80% of defects can be attributed to 20% of the causes. The Pareto chart assists in identifying the 20% of causes that should be targeted to fix 80% of the defects.

In addition, the CoQ calculations should include a list of less tangible impact areas that are harder to measure, but these items are typically missing from the calculation:

1. Indirect costs of delays due to failures, untimely or wrong decision making for the organization as a whole
2. Cost of not performing a different task that was supposed to be performed, instead of fixing the failed one (i.e., opportunity cost)
3. Delays in the organization
4. Morale
5. Retention
6. Reputation
7. Ensuing conflicts and meetings

These additional hard-to-quantify costs increase the CoQ, especially the failure categories, to levels that are excessive, with no justification or accountability for the return that these additional costs may produce. Furthermore, most of the costs associated with quality are not direct costs that are easy to measure (e.g., defects, rework, and inspection); but rather indirect costs that are hard to realize and measure (e.g., rush delivery costs, product failure in the field, complaints, time lost due to rework and failures, and costs of lost sales). Implementing the ideas this book provides for PM and BA collaboration can help improve many of the factors that lead to the above mentioned costs.

Poka-yoke

Poka-yoke, also referred to as *mistake proofing*, is something that is widely used—and while people benefit from it, they are often unaware of its existence. The term was coined in Japan during the 1960s by Shigeo Shingo,[11] who was an industrial engineer at Toyota. The initial term was *baka-yoke* (or *foolproofing*), but this was perceived to be dishonorable and politically incorrect, and was therefore changed to poka-yoke. Poka-yoke is a simple method to prevent defects from occurring in business processes and help people and processes work right the first time.

Poka-yoke can help substantially improve quality and reliability by having products designed in such a way that forces users to use them as intended or, at a minimum, prevents them from making mistakes. The results are less errors, mishaps, damages, and possibly injuries. Examples are easy to find and also documented in Figure 10.2. The PM and the BA both have multiple opportunities

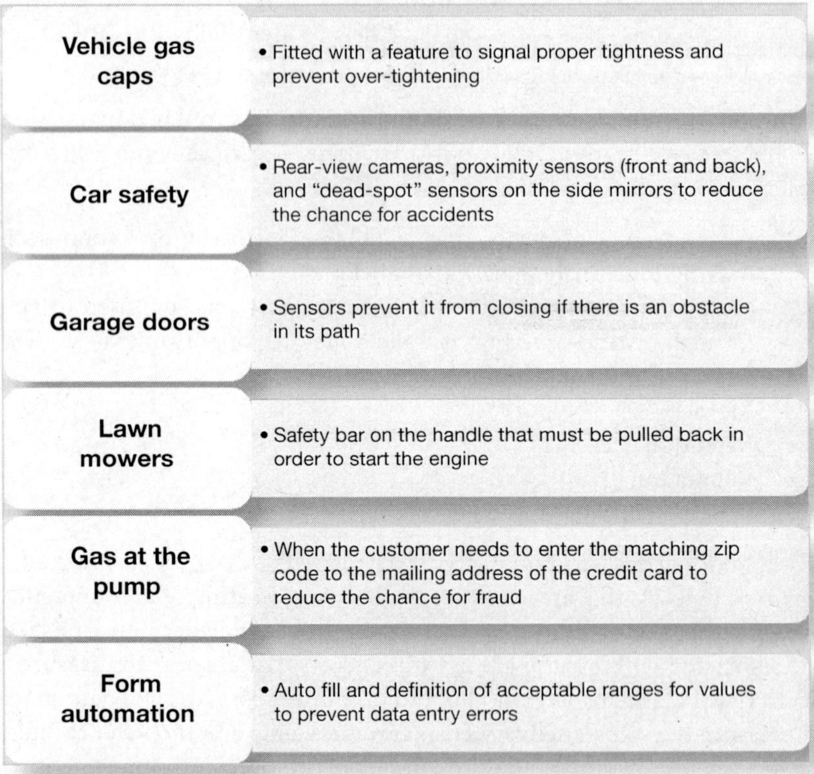

Figure 10.2 Poka-yoke examples

to build in poka-yoke into the project's activities and into processes that are performed by the team as well as in the product itself. Error proofing can be incorporated into processes in the form of automation to reduce human errors and data entry mistakes; into processes through simple checks and balances or threshold definitions; into team members' routines by introducing *cheat sheets*, checklists, or tally sheets; and into any other activity throughout the project by ensuring that success criteria are defined, measured, and enforced.

These measures to reduce the number of errors by forcing the process user to do the right thing are a proactive, lower cost, and effective measure to achieve quality and to reduce errors. It requires planning and design, understanding of the steps to perform the work, and thinking outside of the specific activity's box in order to prevent errors from happening. Poka-yoke measures are not only directly related to quality and to risk management, but also to communication—by introducing ground rules, acceptance criteria, and escalation procedures that help guide the conduct of team members and control the results. To perform their roles more effectively, the PM and the BA must proactively look for areas against which they can apply poka-yokes. In areas to which the poka-yokes are applied properly, the team can operate in *autopilot* mode, which means that as long as these activities or processes are performed within their thresholds, there will not be false alarms or unintercepted failures. When the performance falls outside of the threshold, it will then alert the appropriate team member based on the escalation procedures that are in place. Sufficient application of poka-yokes across multiple activities and processes will free up time and capacity that will allow the PM and the BA to perform VA activities and engage proactively in improvement and in delivering value to the customer.

PROJECT PERFORMANCE INDICATORS

There are many commonly used measures through which PMs and BAs can track quality, as well as *proprietary* measures that serve as early performance and trend indicators. Proprietary measures are those that the team can collect information for and track, but since they are situation-specific and organization-specific, the interpretation of the information they provide must be done internally and over time, so that the data can be benchmarked and compared against other projects within the organization for trends and for context.

These performance and trend indicators relate to quality in two primary ways and many of them can be used both during and after the project:

1. *They provide indications of the project's state and possibly its overall health*: These are interim reads about the state, process, progress, and general health of the project throughout its life cycle to provide

indications about where it is trending. These measures provide a comprehensive analysis of the project and insight into project governance and management oversight.

2. *They act as post project indicators*: Beyond the validated deliverables and the project's product and results, there are a variety of measures that can point at performance levels of the team, processes, and the project as a whole. Even when the project delivers its results and they are accepted by the customer, there may be performance issues that, if addressed, will lead to future benefits and opportunities to avert future problems. Similar to any type of team sports, even after a team wins, the coach will review the game's highlights to learn about plays, mistakes, turnovers, and any other good and bad thing that took place throughout the game. Spotting these plays and analyzing them can allow the team to learn from its actions and avoid making the same mistakes again, help capitalize on positive actions, and above all, recognize what actually took place so successes can be recreated and failures avoided.

These indicators and measures serve, in part, as a proactive mitigation measure and a lessons learned process that needs to take place as part of the continuous improvement process with the intention of capitalizing on benefits and improving weakness areas on an ongoing basis. A discussion about lessons learned takes place later in this chapter.

Benefits of Reviewing Project Performance Indicators

Conducting periodic project indicators checks provides the PM and the BA with real-time findings about areas for potential improvements, along with a chance to review ideas for improvement of processes and deliverables. Although the collection and interpretation of the data consumes time and resources, the investment pays off by engaging the team and providing an opportunity for exchanging information and expertise. The project sponsor, other stakeholders, and the organization as a whole also benefit from the collection of these proactive indicators, with a real-time option to mitigate risk and the ability to quickly address findings about project management practices and processes in the event that organizational-level action is needed.

Project Indicator Measurements

There are multiple ways to measure project health and no two organizations will benefit from the same sets of items. The tables referenced in this section provide potential measures that the PM and BA can use. Values for benchmarking are not provided, as every project and organization needs to develop a set of these values on their own—relative to other projects within the organization. PMs and BAs should also be mindful of the costs and efforts associated with collecting, assessing, and communicating the data; and conduct a cost-benefit analysis to ensure that the measures add value to the project and to the organization. The types of project measurements for the PM to seek and for the BA to collect and analyze are presented in Tables 10.3, 10.4, and 10.5. Table 10.6 lists items for the PM and the BA to consider in regard to the utilization of project resources. Table 10.7 presents a list of considerations to monitor regarding the usage of time and about meeting schedules. Some measurements may not be valuable for certain environments, and in every situation, the BA should ensure the measurements are not taken out of context.

Table 10.3 Project indicator categories for scope and change

This table (1 of 2) covers scope- and requirements-related indicators that can serve as performance indicators of project health to help the PM and the BA identify trends and act proactively to make informed decisions.

	Project Indicators	**Explanation**
1	Requirements Stability	Number of changes submitted per requirement and how much the project's goals changed over the course of each phase. Many changes may signal that the project's goals may not be clear.
2	Defects per Requirement	The number of defects discovered per requirement.
3	Defect Discovery	Trends in defect discovery and who discovers them: project team versus the customer (include timing, costs, and impact).
4	Defect Fix	Time, effort, and cost required to fix defects and how many defects are fixed versus defects that require multiple fixes or not fixed at all.
5	Defects per Change	The number of defects discovered per implemented change request along with the measure above for defect fix.
6	Changes Acceptance Rate	Tally how many of the change requests submitted were actually accepted and to what extent.
7	Change per Stakeholder	Which stakeholders submitted each change request and identify trends in the rate of acceptance versus rejection per stakeholder.

Table 10.4 Project indicator categories for scope and change

This table (2 of 2) covers scope- and requirements-related indicators that can serve as performance indicators of project health to help the PM and the BA identify trends and act proactively to make informed decisions.

	Health Measure	Explanation
8	Cause for Change	The number of change requests submitted as a result of scope addition/change and the number of changes triggered by risks and performance issues that require change to the baselines.
9	Change Implementation	Number of changes implemented as intended.
10	Change Control Process Effectiveness	Quantify how effective the change control process is. Is it clear? Does it produce realistic estimates and impact assessment? How long is the process?
11	Change Control Process Adherence	Check whether the change control process is followed (if not, implement poka-yoke).
12	Risk and Change	The nature and the number of risks associated with change requests.
13	Final Deliverable vs. Original Goal	Compare the final deliverables to the original scope to assess variance against the original targets (even for accepted change requests); this allows a chance to check how effective and realistic the initial scoping process of the project was.

PROJECT RESCUE AND RECOVERY

Performing planning and prevention activities, measuring the CoQ, and identifying areas to measure as project interim health indicators are all important steps toward achieving project success, but unfortunately there are times where projects reach the point where success can no longer be delivered. Projects that face the onset of major risks or performance issues that pose a significant negative impact on their success criteria, may reach the point that the original, intended objectives are no longer within reach. At that point a decision needs to be made to determine whether the project needs to be terminated, or whether it should proceed—and if the project is deemed as worth proceeding, whether to proceed at the existing performance levels, or attempt to fix it.

When the performance falls below a certain level and the project's status turns red, there may be a variety of potential responses to a red status:

- The PM-BA duo needs to determine whether the red color represents a major performance issue, or rather that even though the budget or time status fall in the red color zone, it does not mean that the project is in an immediate or urgent need for repair.

Table 10.5 Risks and issues indicator categories

This table covers risk- and issues-related indicators that can serve as performance indicators of project health to help the PM and the BA identify trends and act proactively to make informed decisions.

	Project Risks and Issues Indicators	Explanation
1	Number of Issues	The number of issues at various milestones against other projects (compare the number of issues generated vs. the number and the speed of issue resolution). Having more issues at a given point than in a previous project is not necessarily a negative trend but it may indicate that the project is facing more challenges than previous, similar projects.
2	Issues Resolution Time	How many of the issues became stale and were not resolved in a timely manner and became a crisis or a risk that materialized.
3	Risk Process Effectiveness and Efficiency	How much time and money does the team spend on risk management and per risk? Are the risks identified at realistic probability and impact rates? How many new, unplanned risks are introduced throughout the project? How prepared is the team for risks that emerge? Are the previously planned responses valid and do they solve the risk?
4	Risk Response Effectiveness	The number of events for which the response plan was inadequate.
5	Escalation	The number of times issues have to be escalated to the sponsor.
6	Risk Stability Rate	Compare at specific points in time whether the team still discovers significant risks and at what rate.
7	Assumptions Remaining	The more assumptions, the more potential for risks to materialize.
8	Project Risk vs. Business Risks	Track the number of project risks that as a result of mitigation efforts may negatively impact the organization (post-project impact).
9	External Dependencies	Track external dependencies and their impact on the project (including the introduction of risks to the project).

- In more extreme cases, there is a need to make a major decision about whether or not the project should proceed—and how:

    1. The sponsor, or customer may realize that the project is no longer feasible and that it is not salvageable. At that point, preparation needs to take place to terminate and close the project. Regardless of the timing—closing activities need to take place.
    2. When *critical to success* areas suffer from significant performance issues and it becomes clear that the project will not be able to meet its intended targets and objectives, yet there is a need to continue the project, a decision needs to be made to shift gears. This involves

Table 10.6 Resource-related indicators

This table covers resource-related indicators that can serve as performance indicators of project health to help the PM and the BA identify trends and act proactively to make informed decisions.

	Resource Indicators	**Explanation**
1	Utilization	Check the actual resource utilization on deliverables vs. planned resources (time of each resource, how many resources).
2	Overtime	Measure the amount of overtime spent on deliverables (even if not charged against the project budget [a.k.a. brown resources or non-billable resources]).
3	Plan vs. Actual	Review the actual progress of each phase and whether it was completed within the expected effort and timelines.
4	Timing of Allocation (Project Issues)	Monitor the time losses as a result of resources reporting to the project when the project is not ready for them.
5	Timing of Allocation (Resource Issues)	Track the total delays as a result of resources not reporting to the project when required.

Table 10.7 Time and schedule management-related indicators

This table covers time and schedule-management indicators that can serve as performance indicators of project health to help the PM and the BA identify trends and act proactively to make informed decisions.

	Resource Indicators	**Explanation**
1	Estimates Accuracy	How accurate are team members' and project estimates? How many estimates need to be adjusted and how many of the adjustments are due to wrong estimates rather than changes to the scope?
2	Delays	If the project is late, by how much is it late and which areas and work packages are the sources of the delays?
3	Non-Critical-Path Delays	If the project is not late (critical path is on target), are there any work packages or activity milestones that are late? If non-critical-path work packages are late, it is an indication that the project's schedule is trending in the wrong direction.
4	Work Package Completion	How many work packages finish on time, early, or late?
5	Effort	How much effort actually had to be expended on activities (even if they finish on time)?

treating the project differently than it has been up to this point, through the re-setting of the expectations for an adjusted set of benefits and kick-starting a project recovery or rescue effort.

What Recovery Is Not About

Project recovery does not mean restoring the original intended performance and recovering the project back to the previously desired level. When projects enter a recovery stage, it is about re-juggling priorities and adjusting performance expectations, so work efforts can be planned for the new targets.

What Is Recovery About?

Once the go-ahead is given for a recovery and rescue operation, the project enters a new phase, which often starts by installing a new recovery manager in place of the PM. While it is common to have the PM leading the recovery efforts, having a different person leading the recovery may help signal a change in momentum.

Once it is acknowledged that the project is failing to meet its targets and that it cannot continue in the same direction, the recovery begins and it should consist of five steps:

1. *Assign a recovery manager*: Whether the recovery manager is the current PM or someone else, the sponsor should make an announcement that the recovery is underway—and formally introduce the recovery manager to the project stakeholders.
2. *Develop a recovery charter and conduct a recovery kick-off meeting*: This will set the tone and the expectations for the recovery and redefine the goals and objectives of the project. The BA can provide valuable information for the recovery charter and take a central role in planning the recovery kick-off meeting.
3. *Conduct a current state assessment*: Any recovery effort starts with understanding the current state of the project—where it is failing and the extent of the problems. The findings from this assessment will determine the nature of the effort moving forward and the end result of the recovery. The BA performs this step and organizes the findings in such a way so the decision makers can make an informed decision. The role of the BA at this stage may be further enhanced, especially if no recovery manager has been appointed, or if a new recovery manager is placed instead of the previous PM. In both instances, the BA becomes the center of the knowledge thread between the existing project team and the new recovery team.

4. *Recovery plan development*: Before the plan is formed, there may be a need to present recovery options to the sponsor and senior management, and wait for them to decide on their preferred option.
5. *Lead the recovery*: Execute the recovery plan; monitor the progress; and control the outputs, outcomes, and results as they are realized. Here, too, the BA facilitates the conversion of data into meaningful information for informed decision making.

The Recovery Team

Whether the recovery team is made up of the project team members or it is a newly formed team, an important activity to be performed early on in the process by the project recovery manager is to build trust and reduce the level of anxiety among team members and other stakeholders. This anxiety is usually driven by the uncertainty about the state of the project, frustration about the events that have led the project to its current state, and concerns about post recovery career implications.

Although it is understandable that team members feel anxious and uncertain under these conditions, it may hinder the recovery effort and hurt the team's effectiveness. To alleviate these concerns, the recovery manager must demonstrate leadership by providing transparency and instilling confidence about the process. Throughout the process, the recovery leader should also encourage members and promote a results-driven attitude rather than a *shoot the messenger* one.

Thoughts on PMs and BAs Throughout the Project Recovery

Although the recovery is a project itself, it is not a regular *business as usual* one. Monitoring the status, controlling the results, and recalibration must take place in shorter intervals than in a regular project to ensure quick response and adjustments if needed. The need for collaboration between the PM and the BA is enhanced here even beyond the need for collaboration throughout the project, since the stakes here are higher and since more eyes in the organization are directed at the recovery effort. Every PM and BA who has had to stand in front of a senior stakeholder asking for a second chance knows that asking for a second chance to deliver project success (and along with it, for more time and money) is never easy. Furthermore, we also know that if this effort fails, asking for a third chance is next to impossible and it is very likely that those who fail to deliver on the second chance will not be there for the third time. The frequent changes and adjustments in project recovery, combined with the higher stakes and the newly defined objectives, translate into higher levels of risk. The recovery manager should manage risk rigorously and thoroughly, while continuously engaging the BA for valuable information about risk, related factors, triggers, and impact areas.

Overcoming previously failed projects (or projects that came close to failure) can be challenging. A negative mindset is directed toward the project, even through the renaming of the recovery initiative; the negative mindset may still present barriers for future success. Having the recovery PM properly utilizing the BA in the recovery effort can play an integral role in overcoming some of the recovery challenges and ensuring the project is successful this time around. Listed below are several important areas where BAs can add meaningful value toward project recovery success.

Understand the Reasons for Failure

In order to avoid making the same mistakes during the recovery that were made during the project—that originally triggered the need for recovery—the recovery PM must understand the reasons why the project previously failed and realize what must change in order to deliver success this time around. The BA can perform root cause analyses on the previous failures and work with the PM and stakeholders to see what lessons can be applied so these mistakes are not repeated. The process of identifying root causes of previous failures involves interviews, assessing solutions, requirements review, and documents analysis. The review should cover the organization, processes, technical aspects, the environment, and the alignment of the project success criteria with the business objectives.

Adjust Performance and Processes

Since most project failures can be traced to poor requirements, a review of the scope and objectives of the previous projects is important, in order to assess which parts of the original scope and objectives are still required for the recovery effort. The BA should then provide a list of recommendations regarding which items may no longer be necessary, in order to increase the chance for success of the recovery effort. The report should also include optional items, or items that can be deferred for a future phase, once the project has managed to achieve a certain level of recovery success. In addition to reviewing scope and requirements-related items, the BA needs to also review the original project charter, plans, and close-out documents. The review should also include a check of which, if any, of the original project's objectives have been met and the conclusion will help adjust the approach and processes for the recovery, which will improve the chance of achieving the recovery objectives.

The review should also produce a set of recommendations on how to manage the recovery. There should also be a new prioritization scheme to ensure that the important things the recovery needs to produce are prioritized higher and other objectives, that were deemed lower in priority as a result of the failed effort, will be pushed down the list or removed altogether. The PM and the BA can now articulate the new value they are set to deliver, help decision makers focus on approvals by providing them with clear new objectives, and ultimately increase the chance for success by reducing timelines and costs, and by achieving a stronger buy-in.

It Is No Longer the Same

The recovery effort signals a second chance for the project, but it also sends a message that it is no longer *business as usual*. Things have changed and with the BA's findings of the root causes of the original project's failure, the PM and the BA can now provide clear approaches on how to avoid the same type of failure, and effectively address the issues that plagued the previous round of effort. The current state assessment can help articulate where we are against where we were supposed to be, and provide clear documentation of processes, factors, and areas that have changed, as opposed to conditions that remain. Combine this with the renewed sense of urgency and the restated objectives will provide stakeholders and the project team with the ability to put together a recovery action plan. In addition, anything that has changed from the original project can now be labeled whether the change is positive or negative toward achieving success. There is no need to even quantify these findings, as all the information gathered should be sufficient to put together an approach for recovery success. Even if the changes in conditions do not favor a recovery success, the PM and the BA can now present these findings and in turn, reprioritize scope items or redefine other success criteria to a lower level of success that can still be achieved.

The Buy-in

The recovery charter, along with the establishment of a recovery team, the building of a recovery plan, and the redefined objectives are all intended to help gain support among stakeholders and achieve buy-in. Many of the stakeholders might be skeptical at this point regarding the chances for success and every bit of support for the recovery may be helpful. The efforts put together toward the recovery are also intended to communicate an elevated level of confidence that this time the results will be better than the ones in the original project. The PM needs the BA in order to provide support for these promises—in the form of numbers, plans, and definition of the new success. The application of previously learned lessons must be demonstrated, so stakeholders do not get a sense of deja-vu.

The effort to generate support and buy-in is similar to the business process, feasibility analysis, and initiation activities of the original project, with one difference—that now there is a need to prove that this time around, the project will indeed deliver on its promise. Beyond the buy-in, the recovery effort needs the organizational commitment in applying resources, priorities, and decisions to the recovery effort—commitment that is on the ground and that goes beyond promises, statements, and expectations. With the help of the BA, the PM can perform an up-to-date and relevant stakeholder analysis and subsequently address stakeholders' needs in a meaningful and timely manner. With the BA's ongoing stakeholder engagement the PM-BA duo maintain their ability to remain up to speed in understanding stakeholders' needs. Furthermore, the traditional analysis tools that the BA utilizes on an ongoing basis helps the PM and the BA better understand the reasons that led to the previous project failure and what needs to take place to change gears and momentum to avoid a second failure. A sober look at the recovery's environment can also help the duo handle the change (organizational change) aspect of the project and the communication and stakeholder engagement needs.

PM-BA Collaboration

While many projects find themselves with the need for recovery due to a combination of mistakes that were made in the implementation, planning errors, unrealistic expectations, and performance issues—other recovery needs are triggered because of less specific and more generic factors that tend to plague many projects. While these are common conditions, effective collaboration between the PM and the BA may prevent the need for recovery altogether, or at least help improve the chances for a recovery success. The following is a list of causes for failure, along with corresponding activities that the PM and BA can perform to prevent the need for recovery or improve the chances for a successful recovery:

- **Unclear success criteria:** Well-written requirements can help articulate and quantify the success criteria, and effective communication will help to set expectations as to what qualifies as success—reducing the chance of failure.
- **Lack of leadership:** Whether there is a leadership deficiency at the sponsorship or at the project level, keeping information regarding stakeholders fresh and up-to-date can help reduce the damage it causes.
- **How can I help you:** Lack of collaboration among team members in general (and specifically between the PM and the BA) is a major cause

of project failure, as team members fail to find time to improve the way they work, and fail to engage their team members in an effort to look for ways to improve the way they work together. This is also related to the previous leadership item, as team members' attitudes toward collaboration and team building initiatives in general all start at the top.

- **Instant gratification:** We live in an era of instant gratification, where management and stakeholders want to see results *right now* with no regard to the effort required. Furthermore, there is a negative attitude toward planning where stakeholders can often be heard saying, "Enough with the planning; show me some progress." Complexity and readiness assessments that are performed by the PM and the BA should provide the duo with the ability to provide a *heads up* to stakeholders about what is expected to take place and to effectively set expectations for the project.
- **Failing to identify uncertainties:** Related to the measure of project complexity, is the handling of risk management. A proactive approach is required by the PM and the BA in their respective areas of responsibilities, to identify areas of uncertainties, common producers of risks and risk triggers, along with addressing *common* producers of risks (i.e., assumptions, change requests, requirements, and estimates).

Prevention Measures

The PM and the BA need to take a series of prevention measures that, if done properly, will reduce the chance for the need of project recovery—but if they are not performed at all, or to an insufficient level, they can serve as a checklist of items to be looked at during the recovery. Furthermore, if the PM and the BA are aware of the following list of prevention activities (in addition to the previous list of PM-BA collaboration items), they can review the extent to which the list was followed and it can serve as a benchmark to what has gone wrong and what triggered the need for the recovery:

- **Effective change control:** Beyond the discussion in Chapter 9 about change control, a simple checklist of items to consider when managing change includes having the PM and the BA ensure that all change requests are traceable, all impact areas are assessed, a cost/benefit analysis of the change is performed, configuration management processes and tools are followed, and the approval levels are appropriate to the magnitude of the change.
- **The communication gap:** The PM and the BA, as the owners of project communication, must ensure that all formal communication is clear and that informal communication is controlled through clear ground

rules. The communication gap simply addresses the difference between what people try to say and what their colleagues hear and understand. The PM and the BA must attempt to reduce the gap between the desired message of the sender and the portion that the receiver understands.

- **Effective risk management, reducing of waste, measuring and acting on the findings related to the cost of quality, application of poka-yoke, and measuring of project performance indicators:** These items, discussed previously in this chapter, are all major contributors to preventing project failure and are all within the responsibilities of the PM-BA duo.

The Recovery Process

If project performance indicators, or actual performance, indicate that a project is failing, it needs to be recovered or terminated. A recovery project is a short-term endeavor that is designed to stabilize a project and bring it back to acceptable performance levels. If there is a decision to proceed with the project through a recovery, the project recovery process is comprised of six steps:

1. *Identify that the project is failing:* This involves the process of monitoring project performance and any indicators, and recognizing when the performance falls below the predefined acceptable threshold.
2. *Initiate the recovery:* This step involves selecting a recovery manager (the original PM, a replacement PM, or a temporary recovery specialist who will try to bring the project back to an acceptable level of performance) and creating a recovery charter. The charter is similar in nature to the project charter, but it has a few notable differences—it comes to signal the change in gears, it identifies the new personnel and objectives, and it instills a renewed sense of urgency to the stakeholders. The recovery charter also defines the scope of the failing project assessment, defines expected recovery goals and deliverables and provides a rough estimate of the recovery cost.
3. *Conduct a recovery assessment*: This involves an assessment of the project to determine the severity of the situation and the prospects of recovery—and creating an assessment report that states whether the project should proceed, and how. The main goal of the assessment is to produce a prioritized list of issues the project is facing, to articulate the urgency of resolving each issue and to highlight show-stopping areas. It also includes the identification of risks associated with the overall recovery process and with each issue. The approach to this stage is done through traditional information-gathering techniques that BAs typically specialize in.

4. *Planning the recovery*: This is when the BA and the PM (or recovery manager) put together a recovery plan, assemble the recovery team, and conduct a recovery kick-off. There are a few options for the recovery and they need to be identified prior to the start of the recovery execution stage. The options involve any combination of the following options: (a) reduce requirements or scope; (b) increase resource productivity; (c) slip the schedule; and (d) increase costs by utilizing more resources or working faster. Adding risks and compromising quality are theoretical options when considering the competing demands, but in reality they will not yield the results we hope to achieve as part of the project recovery. The PM and the BA must carefully consider the options available in light of stakeholder's needs and expectations and come up with the most suitable options that are possible.
5. *Execute the recovery*: This entails taking the project through the recovery activities, including managing the risks, the change, and the stakeholder engagement and expectations.
6. *Closing the recovery*: Once the recovering project's performance is stabilized, it is time to ensure that it is sustained, restore the project's performance by handing over the project to the next level (another PM, or post-completion owners), and transfer the knowledge. It also includes ensuring lessons are captured and applied.

The last two steps of the recovery process should bring the project to its recovered state in order to finalize the stabilization and restoration activities. To conclude these steps, the PM-BA duo need to check to see if the recovery effort achieved its mandated goals, verify that the project is stabilized, perform exit interviews with key stakeholders, ensure all knowledge is transferred appropriately, perform hand-over from the recovery team to the original or newly formed project team or to operations, and in the event that goals have not been met, go back to the drawing board. Figure 10.3 summarizes and illustrates the six steps.

The BA and the Recovery

While the PM is leading the recovery and engaging stakeholders, it is up to the BA to produce valuable information to the PM and to ensure that the information is used properly to facilitate an informed decision-making process. More specifically, there are a few areas that the BA should cover:

- Align and match between business needs and stakeholder expectations
- Envision a clear picture of the recovery solution
- Control and minimize overruns that are caused by rework and scope-related issues

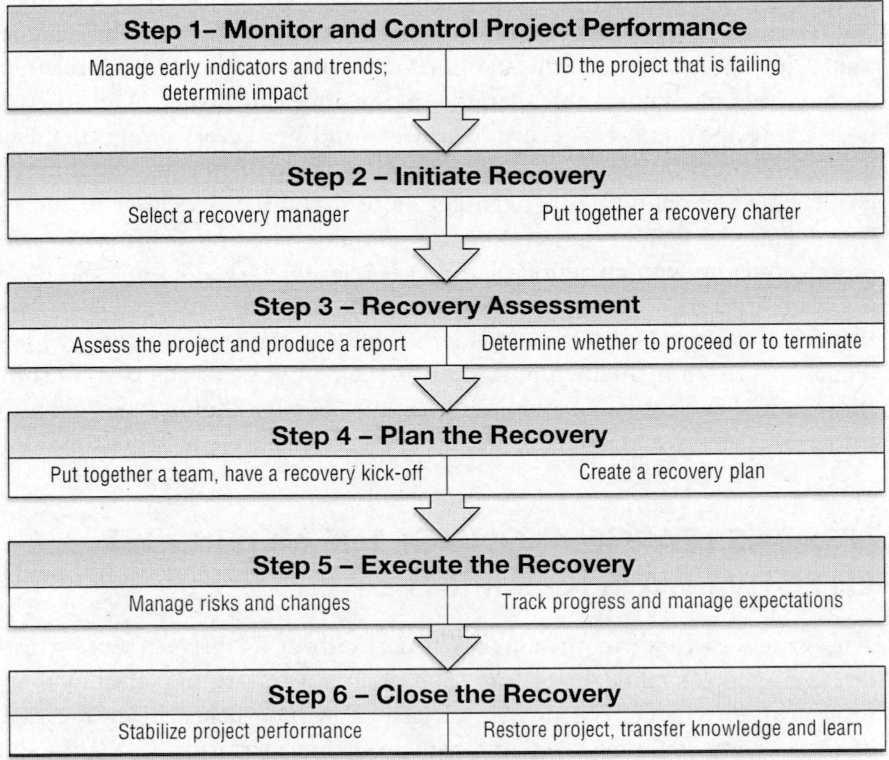

Figure 10.3 The recovery process

- Innovate and maximize room for creativity
- Manage the requirements process end-to-end (a second chance is always more demanding)
- Serve as a liaison and ensure stakeholder needs and expectations are addressed, and that relevant communication is flowing effectively and efficiently
- Ensure that organizational processes and business rules are aligned
- Create a decision support that will provide context for discussions and decisions related to risks, capabilities, assumptions, and dependencies

During the project recovery process, the touch points between the PM and the BA become ever so more integrated, frequent, and significant. As insufficient alignment and collaboration between the roles is a likely contribution to the need for project recovery to begin with, effective PM-BA collaboration is key for any recovery success. With the faster pace, moving parts, and higher stakes during the recovery, the successes and failures of the PM-BA relations become even more noticeable than they are in a *regular* project. While there is no secret recipe on how to recover a project—and since every project that is in need of recovery suffers from different afflictions and is plagued by different challenges—the one thing that can get the PM and the BA closer to success is to follow the recovery process end-to-end and based on the project's condition, come up with an action plan that is relevant and applicable. When all the conditions are taken into consideration—including the success criteria and the stakes involved—the PM and the BA will lead the application of the systematic approach in an attempt to achieve the best possible solution. Rushing through trial and error and attempting for quick wins will most likely not yield the desired results, and in fact, it may further deteriorate the project's condition.

LESSONS LEARNED—ONE OF THE MOST COST-EFFECTIVE WAYS TO IMPROVE

The process of capturing lessons learned is critical for project success, as it leverages people's tendency to learn and applies it toward organizational and project improvement. The process of lessons learned helps us leverage successes, learn to avoid mistakes, and benchmark our performance against similar projects, plus, it also serves as a team building exercise. Capturing lessons should not only take place at the end of the project, but rather, on an ongoing basis throughout the project. The task of collecting, documenting, and learning from events that take place throughout the project is not only highly beneficial for the PM and the BA, but the task also represents the roles of the PM and the BA—from the need for continuous improvement, to the notion of prevention, and the importance of planning. Lessons learned are cheap to obtain—as they already happened—and learning from them means that we are, as a project or an organization, bound to do better the next time (either recapture a success, or avoid a failure). And while it is cheap to capture lessons, it is a resounding waste to miss the capturing and learning, since it is likely that we will stumble on the same problems again, which leads to a growing frustration when the same mistakes repeat themselves.

The process of capturing lessons from the project brings the team together and helps team members reframe the way they view how things took place in the project. It involves a series of activities that, even if they yield no tangible ways to improve processes, gets the team to take a second look and identify areas for personal improvement, and by that, it improves the team's cohesiveness and its members' ability to work together, interact, and deal with challenges.

Most projects conduct their lessons learned exercises at the end of the project. While this is the best time to look at the project in hindsight, the problem is that many resources may no longer be available or even involved in the project—they may have moved on, left the organization, or gotten promoted. Waiting until the end of the project also increases the possibility that the lessons from the earlier phases of the project, such as planning, will be forgotten. A simple way to overcome this problem is to capture inputs for the lessons learned exercise throughout the project at regular intervals. At the end of every status meeting, the team should engage in a quick round-table of capturing lessons for that week:

- The PM asks all participants in the meeting to provide feedback about what took place in the past week. Feedback will be provided by each team member in one sentence that captures the essence, or the highlight of that week, with focus on what went right, what went wrong, any surprises, unplanned successes, or anything that is worth noting.
- No feedback or further discussion is allowed.
- The PM and the BA will create a lessons learned feedback form as shown in Table 10.8, to capture the feedback by recording each participant's comments for the appropriate date.
- The PM and the BA will review the notes once a week and will either come up with actions and recommendations to address them, or identify areas to improve at the end of a project cycle (a period of time, a phase, or at the end of the project). With both the PM and the BA considering the comments and discussing them, they can both apply findings in their respective areas and raise considerations from their respective areas of knowledge. This type of collaboration is about being proactive and, similar to other types of collaboration opportunities between the

Table 10.8 Feedback for lessons learned

The feedback for lessons learned table can be utilized to identify items for consideration that can serve as an input for the lessons learned process. The process needs to take place at the end of the project, but can also be performed periodically throughout the project at certain intervals, upon reaching milestones, in order to capture lessons and opportunities for improvement throughout the project.

Team Member/Role					
Date	**JP (BA)**	**Leah (Developer)**	**Amanda (PM)**	**Robin (PCO)**	**Carlo (Sponsor)**
Week 7: Oct. 22nd	Gaps in requirements traceability	Inconsistent language in some requirements	Unclear role of vendor in the process	No effort estimates	Plan is missing assumptions

PM and the BA, it will translate to overall less combined effort by the PM and the BA since being proactive and well-informed will pay off in the form of a reduction in risks, errors, and miscommunication, along with less rework and waste and a greater level of success.

The information collected will be processed and categorized: (1) items that do not serve as inputs for lessons; (2) items for immediate application for improvement; (3) deferred items for future lessons learned recommendations. This way no information goes to waste by being missed, and the application of the lessons is done in real time. There is no need to wait with recommendations until the end of the project and there is no need to produce a large lessons learned report at the end of the project—a report that will most likely be filed on a SharePoint drive and will never be looked at again. Lessons should be small, nimble, and timely.

What to Ask

There are many general questions that could potentially be asked but not all projects require all areas to be investigated. However, there are five questions that should be included in all lessons learned exercises:

1. What went right in this project—and why?
2. What went wrong in the project—and why?
3. What was a surprise—what ended up being ok despite a lack of planning; was luck a factor in achieving success; and if so, where did luck replace good planning?
4. Did the project differ significantly in any way from others that you have worked on—in what way and what was the impact of this?
5. Did the project events and outcomes differ significantly from the plans—what was expected to be straightforward and ended up being straightforward; and what was expected to be difficult and ended up being difficult?

In addition to the general questions, some lessons learned questions should focus on stages or phases of the project and on events and activities that took place in each of these phases (e.g., initiation, planning, implementation and control, closure, and handover and transition). These questions should be asked about each phase to determine whether processes and activities took place as required and how effective they were—check if the goals of each of the phases were achieved as intended and examine if there were any events that are worth mentioning (i.e., both good and bad).

Post-implementation Review

A post-implementation review (PIR) takes place sometime after the project is completed (often 3-6 months later). The reason it is not conducted immediately after the implementation is to allow time for things to settle and performance to revert back to normal, in order to measure how successful the integration of the project's product was into the business. While the lessons learned process should be a fully shared effort between the PM and the BA, the PIR should be led by the BA, for two reasons: (1) it is focused on the product and the implementation success; (2) it is performed after the project and therefore, the PM may not be around anymore to perform it. Concerning the second reason, it is fair to state that the BA may also not be available to perform the PIR, but when considering the nature of the BA's role in the organization, it is more likely to assign a BA to perform work that is not related to a project, than a PM. With that said, the main reason the BA should be assigned to lead the PIR is the product-driven nature of the evaluation.

Unlike the lessons learned exercise that checks how the project work was performed, the PIR deals with checking how successfully the project's benefits are realized and objectives are met; the PIR is also referred to as the benefits realization check. The project benefits are measured against the quantifiable success criteria and high-level business requirements that were defined for the project. Conducting a PIR requires planning in advance, including allocating time, money, and resources to conduct the work, along with granting permissions for access by the users of the project's product (often the customer). The value the PIR produces is about helping future projects in setting objectives, planning, setting and managing expectations, managing the project overall, and delivering value.

FINAL THOUGHTS ON PROJECT QUALITY, RECOVERY, AND LESSONS LEARNED

Quality, recovery, and lessons learned are all closely related to each other. The effort to define and achieve quality is led by prevention activities; the recovery takes place when quality standards cannot be met as intended in an attempt to redefine the objectives and deliver on them; and the lessons learned complete the cycle back toward the prevention aspect. These three elements are not only tied to each other in a cyclical manner, but they also carry some of the most fundamental activities in the roles of both the PM and the BA. As such, these three activities are important, valuable, and dependent on each other.

- **Quality:** This is identifying the standards and ensuring that the product delivers on them. The product side is championed by the BA, and the ability to deliver meaningful value hinges on the balance that can be achieved via the joint PM-BA effort. To perform their roles effectively, both the PM and the BA need to stand out for their attitude toward quality and to ensure that whatever the customer and sponsor deem important will be delivered and trade-offs will be made around it. The specific aspect of quality discussed in this chapter, CoQ, is the project's ability to track expenses, investments, and costs attributed to quality throughout the project and confirm whether there were sufficient resources allocated to quality. The PM-BA duo's focus should be on performing prevention and planning activities and sufficient appraisal actions, in order to reduce the potentially soaring costs of failure. Failing to track quality related costs may prolong problems and prevent organizations from diverting resources and investments toward higher yielding activities that are preventive by nature.
- **Recovery:** When it is realized that the project cannot deliver on its original goals, a decision has to be made to change gears and redefine the success criteria. This way, the project can take special measures to deliver on the newly defined objectives. But, in order to recognize that there is a problem with the project and to redefine its objectives and targets, there has to be specific success criteria and plans in place. When quality standards are clearly defined in the beginning, it is easier to realize when they are not destined to be met and it is easier to redefine them. In order to effectively identify where there is a problem, what the extent is, and how to take action on it, there has to be strong collaboration between the PM and the BA, in order to make sure that all factors are considered, all conditions are addressed, and all options are explored—with the ultimate goal of restoring project performance to a satisfactory level. Recovery involves everything that a regular project involves, with a few unique elements: (1) failure to deliver, despite previous efforts; (2) the need to change performance quickly and in real time; and (3) alongside with fixing the problem, learn from the mistakes and apply the lessons learned to future projects. This joint integrated effort covers all aspects of the project and cannot be done effectively without both the PM and the BA putting their full set of skills to the task.
- **Lessons learned:** The ability to capture lessons from events that take place in the project and apply them in context for future events or future projects is key in the continuous improvement process that each project and organization needs to go through. Collecting, interpreting, and applying lessons is not difficult and is critical for future success—learning

from mistakes, leveraging good practices, and increasing the chance to achieve future quality. The lessons learned process must also take place as part of a recovery effort, and if done properly, is a key input toward prevention and achieving quality. This process, too, requires the collaboration of the PM and the BA, not only due to the two types of lessons to be captured (i.e., project process lessons and product lessons through the post-implementation review), but also because of the integration of all parts of the project throughout the lessons process: processes, estimates, requirements, risks, team performance, and reporting.

REFERENCES

1. ESS Quality Glossary 2010 Developed by Unit B1 *Quality; Classifications*, European Union, 2010.
2. Crosby, Philip (1979). *Quality is Free*. New York: McGraw-Hill.
3. *Quality Control Handbook* (1999). New York, New York: McGraw-Hill, 5th edition.
4. Based on the ASQ Quality Costs Committee (1999). *Principles of Quality Costs: Principles, Implementation, and Use*, Third Edition, ed. Jack Campanella, ASQ Quality Press, pages 3-5.
5. Europe Japan Centre, *Kaizen Strategies for Improving Team Performance*, Ed. Michael Colenso, London: Pearson Education Limited, 2000.
6. Rother, Mike (2009). *Toyota Kata*. McGraw-Hill. ISBN 0-07-163523-8.
7. Simon, Kerri. *SIPOC Diagram*. Ridgefield, Connecticut: iSixSigma.
8. Adapted from http://asq.org/learn-about-quality/qfd-quality-function-deployment/overview/voice-of-the-customer-table.html
9. Wilson, Paul F.; Dell, Larry D.; Anderson, Gaylord F. (1993). Root Cause Analysis: *A Tool for Total Quality Management*. Milwaukee, Wisconsin: ASQ Quality Press. pp. 8-17. ISBN 0-87389-163-5.
10. Juran, J. M. (1962). *Quality Control Handbook*. New York: McGraw-Hill.
11. Shingo, Shigeo (1986). *Zero Quality Control: Source Inspection and The Poka-yoke System*. Portland, Oregon: Productivity Press.

This book has free material available for download from the Web Added Value™ resource center at *www.jrosspub.com*

BUILDING A PARTNERSHIP: SHARED RESPONSIBILITY THROUGHOUT—PUTTING IT ALL TOGETHER

"It isn't the mountains ahead to climb that wear you out; it's the pebble in your shoe."—Mohammad Ali

The collaboration between the project manager (PM) and the business analyst (BA), as presented in this book, needs to take place from the very start of the project and continue throughout. This chapter completes this book's picture and focuses on where the project hits the ground—to ensure the project plan and sub-plans are realistic and produce the highest possible value. This chapter captures *how* the collaboration needs to take place along with *when* and *where* the collaboration activities by the PM and the BA need to be performed. The PM serves as a subject matter expert (SME) in the project management process and the BA is an SME in business analysis and requirements management processes. Together the PM and the BA must produce a realistic integrated plan that covers all stakeholder needs; addresses potential trade-offs; helps manage expectations; and controls all project communication, changes, dependencies, and impact areas. All this needs to take place while keeping organizational and business needs and objectives under close consideration—ensuring that whatever happens in the project does not negatively affect the business. For example, a decision within the project to remove functionality in order to meet project-specific objectives (such as timelines or budget constraints) and to pass it to warranty, must also be considered against organizational and business considerations—to check the extent of these actions on the organization. There also has to be a clear understanding as to who in the organization is going to pay for dealing with any situations that the project may leave behind. While the decision to promote project objectives is legitimate, it is not the project that will have to carry the subsequent warranty costs. Thus, an informed decision needs to be made as to whether putting project time and costs constraints ahead of organizational priorities is the right thing to do; or if it is more important to deliver the product in full, even if it is late and/or over budget. There is no single answer that would always be correct and this is why both the PM and the BA must work together to ensure that for each situation the right decision is made—taking into account all that there is to consider for the situation. Leaving functionality to be delivered post-project means that someone in the organization will have to pay for it with resources and dollars. While the PM typically wants to pass features to the post-project era, the BA needs to stand strong and ensure the impact is recognized and measured properly. This is not a game of good-cop/bad-cop, but rather having both the project's and the business' points of view considered against the merits, so the most informed decision can be made.

Regardless of the specific skills and experience levels the PM and the BA each bring to the table, this chapter provides a set of timelines and areas of shared responsibility so these two roles can enhance the benefits they produce for the project and the performing organization.

THE PM AND THE BA—INTERTWINED

The PM and the BA are not meant to be SMEs from a product perspective—and in most cases, they are both considered to be generalists. With that said, project management and business analysis are progressively becoming strategic skills in many organizations. When the two roles are integrated with each other and run in proper cycles, it is a competitive advantage for the organizations that can do it right or a major deficiency in the organizations where the PMs and BAs are not properly integrated with each other. The Project Management Institute (PMI), with its Professional in Business Analysis (PBA) Certification, has now put the PM and the BA on the same page, finally using the same terminology, in the same context, and working together under one approach toward adding value to the organization. It is well recognized that the International Institute for Business Analysis (IIBA) put business analysis on the map and redefined the BA's role to what it is today, but the growth in the role of the BA and in the recognition of the BA's contribution to the projects' and organizations' success has been riddled with growing gaps and inconsistencies between the roles of the PM and the BA. The differences in terminology between PMI's *Project Management Body of Knowledge* (*PMBOK® Guide*) and the IIBA's *Business Analysis Body of Knowledge* (*BABOK®*), appear to have been a contributor to the growing gap between project management and business analysis and in turn, to the misalignment, or even hostile attitudes between PMs and BAs. Unfortunately the gaps in terminology have been widened with the introduction of the *BABOK®* version 3. There are more instances of inconsistencies in terminology, not only between PMI and IIBA, but new terminology was introduced in *BABOK®* version 3 to replace some of the terminology that it originally introduced in version 2. A few examples to illustrate the differences in terminology are highlighted in Table 11.1. Conflicting language makes it very challenging to communicate with stakeholders within a project. The newly introduced inconsistencies in vocabulary with *BABOK®* v3 are especially disappointing as the purpose of having a governing body or professional institution is to standardize practices and use a

Table 11.1 Inconsistent terminology

This table illustrates the inconsistencies in terminology for common business terms, including changes between the *BABOK®* versions. These inconsistencies can make the communication between the BA and other stakeholders, including the PM, challenging.

Term	PMI's views	IIBA *BABOK®* v2[1]	IIBA *BABOK®* v3[2]
Examples where IIBA contradicts with PMI terminology			
Risk Responses	Threats (4): Avoid, Mitigate, Transfer, Accept Opportunities (4): Exploit, Enhance, Share, Accept[3]	Consistent with PMI	Threats (4): Avoid, Mitigate, Transfer, Accept Opportunities (1): Increase
Sunk Cost	Could not find a definition but understand it to be a cost that has been already incurred and cannot be recovered.	"Sunk cost describes the money and effort already committed to an initiative."	"Sunk cost describes the money and effort already committed to an initiative." Commitment implies the costs have not necessarily been spent and therefore can be recovered.
Example where IIBA changes terminology between *BABOK®* versions			
Types of Business Rules	Does not specify rule categories in *Business Analysis for Practitioners*	Structural and operative rules	Definitional and behavioral rules

[1] International Institute of Business Analysis. (2009). *A Guide to the Business Analysis Body of Knowledge® v2.0.* Toronto, Ontario, Canada: International Institute of Business Analysis.
[2] International Institute of Business Analysis. (2015). *A Guide to the Business Analysis Body of Knowledge® v3.0.* Toronto, Ontario, Canada: International Institute of Business Analysis.
[3] Project Management Institute. (2009). *Practice Standard for Project Risk Management.* Newton Square, PA, USA: Project Management Institute.

common language—this was unfortunately a step backwards in standardizing the BA role. PMs and BAs must be on the same page and speaking the same language, as project success hinges on this duo working together in harmony, collaboration, and full synchronization—as if they are one entity.

This book promotes extensive sharing of the work between the PM and the BA. The sharing is not intended to increase the volume of work for the PM nor the BA, and it does not attempt to imply that traditional roles of the PM need to be transferred to the BA, or vice versa. The purpose of the sharing is to integrate the two roles together and to strive to foster a partnership, rather than the love/hate relationship that currently exists between the PM and BA. The formation of the partnership requires both roles to sometimes swallow their pride and step outside of their traditional role boundaries to lead the project together. Even though it may initially appear to be more work on both the PM's and BA's behalf, the collaboration efforts translate into tightly coupling project and product objectives resulting in less rework and delivering the intended product the project was set out to produce and hence, a success.

With more projects delivering success, the organization will be able to save on project-related costs (for personnel and for rework), as projects will finish sooner and with less defects and problems. Any additional costs incurred from increasing the allocation of the PM or BA in the pre-project enterprise analysis (EA) planning and analysis phases of the project will be balanced in lower overall project costs. Figure 11.1 illustrates the cycle of benefits that the PM-BA collaboration produces.

The BA is an instrumental part in providing support to the PM and in leading projects to success and as such, the BA becomes a true partner of the PM. While each carries a different set of responsibilities and areas of focus, they both bring to the table their respective areas of expertise that benefit the project most. Overall, it helps the PM focus on delivering project success, and ultimately, it helps the organization by funneling more successful projects, more quickly—leading to efficiencies and cost reductions.

While the integration between the PM and the BA that is proposed in this book suggests virtually every possible area for potential collaboration; this level is not likely to be achieved in reality. What project management and business analysis practitioners can do, however, is to look at the areas that lack collaboration in their environments, or alternately at the areas that, from a benefit-cost perspective, make sense for their situations and apply whatever is applicable, possible, and realistic for their context. There is always room for improvement, and even if not all areas of collaboration are realized, it still allows for an improved relationship and enhanced partnership between the PM and the BA.

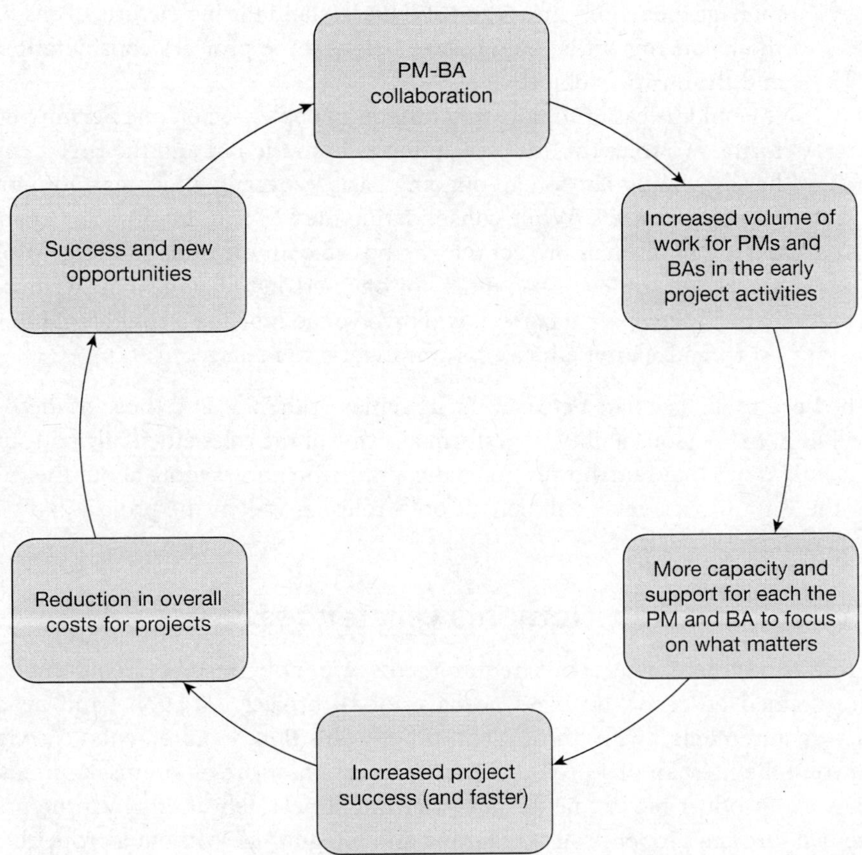

This cycle of benefits illustration shows the benefits that the PM, the BA, and the project realize from the enhanced collaboration between the PM and the BA. The extra effort early in the project pays off later.

Figure 11.1 The cycle of benefits

The PM/BA? Can One Person Perform Both Roles?

Having one person performing both PM and BA roles is possible. It can become easier to apply the notion of *one entity* when it is the same person who performs both roles—however there may be some challenges attached to it:

1. The skills and even personalities that each role requires and utilizes are different and sometimes contradictory. PMs need to be able to see the big picture, especially in regard to the balancing acts of the trade-offs with competing demands. BAs need the attention to detail to effectively

manage the requirements and still understand the big picture, to ensure the balancing act is taking place between the project's considerations and the business objectives.
2. It would be easier to have two different people—when one person performs two roles (in this case acting as both the PM and the BA) it gets hard to *switch hats* on an ongoing basis, especially in larger and more complex projects. While consolidating the PM and the BA roles to one person on a small project may be possible, in medium and large projects it will simply be too much for one person to handle. Furthermore, with all the moving parts, it will involve too much of a conflict of interest (practical, not ethical) for one person to manage.

The need to change hats between the activities of the PM and those of the BA will limit the person's ability to perform any one of the roles efficiently and sufficiently. With that said, however, having a PM who knows more about the role of the BA and vice versa will benefit both roles, as well as the project and the organization as a whole.

Project and Requirements Differences

Projects are temporary, but requirements are not; business requirements are defined based on business needs prior to project initiation—and product requirements (with the exception of transition requirements) survive beyond the lifespan of a project. With that said, there are often misalignments between product requirements and what the project delivers that can be prevented through proper project planning and integration. Without a proper link between the PM and the BA there is a greater likelihood that the project will fail to deliver on its original mandate; even if it produces a working product, it may not be the right product. Although the BA is more associated with the *what* and the PM with the *how*, the forces that shape the project may cause it to drift from the *originally intended what* to an outcome that is too influenced by the *how*. On the other hand, ignoring the needs and constraints imposed by the *how* will prevent the project from achieving the *what*.

The challenges around the project's ability to deliver the desired requirements also relate to the organizational structure (e.g., functional, matrix) and its culture. When there is an initiative with a high priority and with high stakes, there has to be appropriate and sufficient buy-in across the organization—including enabling the PM to make decisions, providing the PM with appropriate authority for the task, assigning the right resources to the project, and providing the project team and the right environment to perform their work. Failing to deliver any of these conditions, friction and misalignment between the PM and the BA, and other ongoing struggles the PM and the BA tend to encounter, especially in functional or weak matrix organizations can severely impede the PM-BA duo's ability to deliver the project's desired outcome.

Project Management 8.4 (It Looks Similar to Project Management BA)

Although every few years someone comes along with a new number for project management that signals a new way of doing things, the results often do not yield a truly better way of managing projects. It may appear that the most notable change in project management may come from the collaboration between the PM and the BA and incorporating it back to the attempts to define what modern project management means. Traditional project management was more reactive in nature—it built mechanisms to handle situations and react to them (e.g., risk and change management). It also viewed the project and the PM as suppliers of results and deliverables with a short planning horizon that separated the project from the business. Modern project management is about changing attitudes toward being proactive, utilizing prevention, and performing more right-brain activities, essentially viewing the PM and the project as business partners that support the customer's needs and that delivers meaningful value, rather than simply deliverables. The benefits that the project produces take into consideration both the short term, as well as the long term—and the project views the customer as a partner. The organization, through the application of portfolio management and EA, helps ensure the partnership between the project, the business, and the customer works in the form of capacity management, long-term thinking, delivery of solutions, and value and engagement for future considerations and benefits—rather than moving the organizational focus toward the next customer. Client retention, relationship management, effective communication, and long-term partnerships become the focus; they can all be achieved by the integration of the PM and the BA and the utilization of each role's skills intermittently and over time, to ensure the right mix between everyone's needs.

Part of the integration of project management and business analysis takes place through utilization of the PM's and the BA's communication skills to promote the values each role brings to the table and to prevent duplication of effort and the concept of working against each other. The PM is the master of communication and expectations management, and the BA is the champion of the organizational landscape, acting as a bridge or a liaison by handling mainly the product side of the change, as well as policies, procedures, and operational considerations. There is also room to integrate the role of the relationship manager and set up an environment where all three roles work in harmony. The key for the success of this integration is to get the PM and the BA to act as equals toward each other and even when the PM assumes a more senior capacity, establish a true partnership between the two. Both roles should be viewed as respective leaders in their areas and in their ability to integrate with each other, and the division of the roles should be clear:

- The BA will lead the definition of the problem and the solution (ensuring the project builds the right solution to solve for the right problem).
- The PM will lead the work toward delivering the solution (within the required deadline, available budget, and resources).
- The BA will ensure the project aligns with business objectives.
- The PM will adjust the project's performance to ensure it delivers on the alignment to the business objectives.
- The PM must demonstrate strong interpersonal skills to manage stakeholder expectations and motivate the team.
- The BA must demonstrate strong interpersonal skills to lead business analysis and requirements management tasks, including but not limited to facilitating requirements elicitation meetings and communication of requirements. The BA can also support the PM's effort in managing expectations.
- The BA must be focused on the solution and on value creation to avoid any type of *overkill* with risks, communication, reporting, or scope. The BA needs to provide a balancing act, including balancing the priorities of the PM to ensure alignment to business objectives, as well as value creation.

TIMING AND CONTEXT

The following section will discuss the roles and responsibilities of the PM and the BA at various points in time throughout the product life cycle. The timing of events will be expressed in the context of a typical project life cycle, but the project management process groups will be referenced throughout. Figure 11.2 illustrates the timing of events between the product life cycle, project life cycle, and project management process groups.

Enterprise Analysis—Before the Project

The PM and the BA should both engage in context-related work (the BA in EA and the PM in portfolio management). Even when the PM's involvement in portfolio management is limited, the BA needs to provide information related to project justification and benefit-cost analysis that typically come as part of the pre-project package the BA needs to give the PM. This package captures the

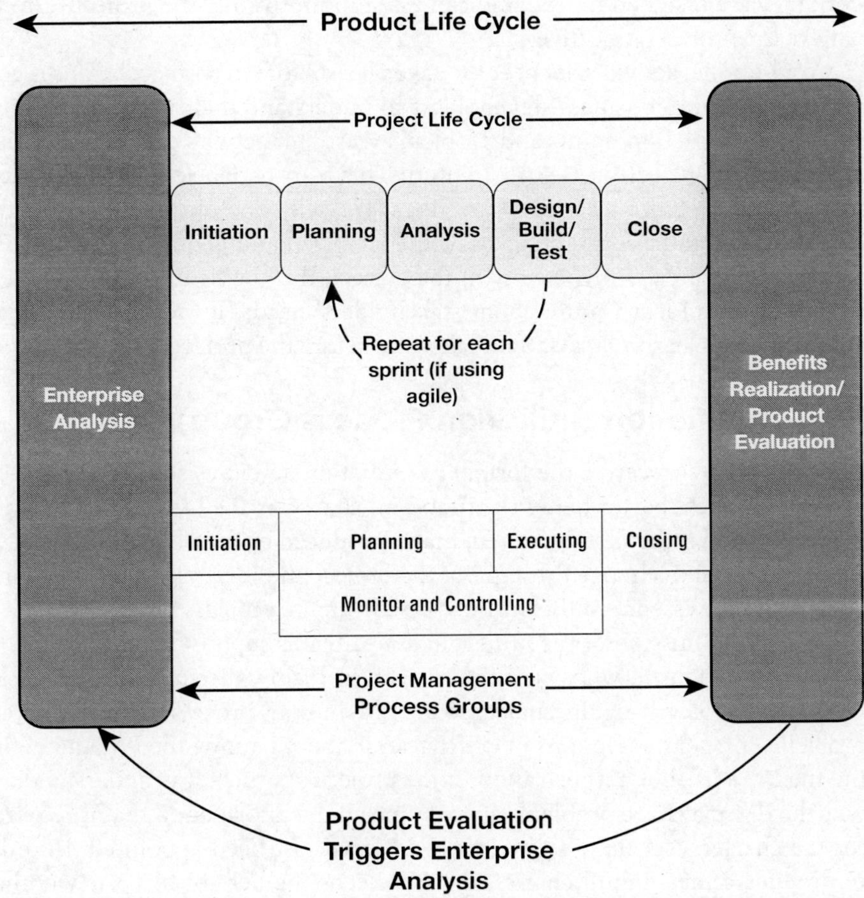

This figure shows the timing of events between the product life cycle, the project life cycle, and the project management process groups.

Figure 11.2 Life cycles

essence of the project, including the business case, justification, feasibility, and readiness, and it allows the PM to get up to speed by receiving an accurate picture of the information available, success criteria, and business objectives. Such a package can be very valuable in enabling the PM to drive the project with the lights on from the get-go. If possible, having the PM act as an SME in the EA activities to assist with high-level estimates, risk identification, and definition of the initial success criteria for each potential project will provide the opportunity for the PM to provide input into the project that she or he could potentially be leading. The PM will therefore have a better understanding of the value of the work they are assigned to lead and can assist in motivating the project team to achieve the project's objectives.

An additional activity that needs to take place before the project begins is getting introduced to business stakeholders to understand their needs and recognize potential friction points and problem areas. This activity can be performed by either the PM or the BA (or jointly). They can be labeled as pre-kick-off activities that require a series of meetings (typically one-on-one) between the PM or the BA and a series of key stakeholders. Depending on whether the PM or the BA are already involved with the project, the goal is to attempt to elicit information and learn more about stakeholders' needs. It precedes the stakeholder analysis and in fact, should take part before the project.

Project Initiation (Initiation Process Group)

Once the project receives the formal *go*, initiation activities start to take place, with the project charter being the first. The charter is the official mandate for the project and is the first document that is produced by the project. The charter is not supposed to change throughout the project and it captures, in short form (1-3 pages) the essence of the business case from the project's point of view. It is the vision and mission of the project and ideally it is supposed to be written by the project's sponsor, who *owns* the project. In reality, the sponsor often delegates the task of writing the charter to the PM, but this process has one inherent problem—one of the sections in the charter is about naming the PM and defining the PM's level of authorization in the project. As such, it is understandable why the PM may have problems articulating all the information that is required for the charter, especially if the PM has indeed just been appointed. In order to produce a meaningful charter, the PM needs the help of the BA (who had worked on the business case) in order to get context and understanding of what the project is about—for this reason, the BA is also sometimes delegated the task of writing the charter. Anything that is not fully clear during the writing of the charter should be qualified as an assumption and in turn, be validated with the project sponsor. Having the sponsor delegating the task of writing the charter to the PM (and in turn the PM getting the BA to contribute to the effort) may make the effort more effective—as it will be easier and more cost effective for the sponsor to review the document and critique it, rather than put it together. Any unclear items or assumptions should be considered and clarified by the sponsor.

The PM and the BA should take advantage of the opportunity to confirm with the sponsor their understanding of the sponsor's stake, level of commitment, and expected involvement; as well as clarify the goals, decision-making style, and capacity and the overall project's visibility within the organization as they are presenting the charter for review. Additional areas to be addressed should include known issues with the required resources, and risks related to organizational and cross-project dependencies and priorities. The intention of this exercise is to raise as many valid questions as possible for the sponsor to address up front and also, to identify key stakeholders for analysis and engage them so they understand what the project is about. Understanding key stakeholders also involves mapping out the decision-making points, who occupies them, and how many decision makers there are at each point. Too many decision makers signal that there is going to be a lot of red tape—and with that come conflicts, duplications of effort, and other inefficiencies that add risks to the project. If the PM-BA duo realizes that there are too many decision makers, it can serve as a heads-up to the sponsor so they can better prepare for the project's realities. The sponsor's handling of the inquiries typically provide the PM-BA duo a strong indication of the sponsor's priorities and style that in turn, will have a strong bearing on the project.

This would also be a good time for the PM and the BA to identify their touchpoint areas and discuss their decision-making process, the authority levels between them, and their interaction style with the stakeholders. Naturally, part of this exercise would be to define scope and requirements boundaries and figure out a change control process and criteria for the project. The understanding of the lay of the land (i.e., objectives, stakeholders, and scope) involves engaging SMEs and other key stakeholders and setting the stage for open communication and trust, so the SMEs can drill down into the subject matter and ask the right questions. With both the PM and the BA engaging the SMEs, it ensures that each question and inquiry will be directed appropriately with the right rigor and toward the right individuals in search of answers.

Finally, the PM and the BA should take all the information that they have elicited and make sure it adds up. Even though the project is a *go*, there may be gaps related to whether the project addresses the right problem, the degree to which the project delivers value for the business, the clarity of the problem definition, the accuracy and relevance of the success and acceptance criteria, and any related readiness and complexity measures to address the gaps.

Project Planning (Planning Process Group)

The planning stages of the project are critical for project success and hence, these stages require the bulk of the PM-BA duo's focus, and reinforce the need for effective collaboration between the two roles. The major outputs out of the planning phase of the project are: completion of the project management plan with all subsidiary plans; refinement of product scope, project scope, and project success criteria; as well as high-level time and cost estimates. The following list contains some guidelines that should be followed while project planning.

- Although the PM leads the effort of putting together a project plan, the BA's contribution to the project plan is imperative to define a consolidated approach for all aspects of the project. Also note that although each of the subsidiary plans may be listed separately in the following sections—implying they are all separate documents—it does not imply they cannot be combined for simplicity, depending on the formality and complexity of the project. As long as the conversations are happening and decisions documented jointly between the PM and the BA, it is sufficient.
- Ensure the voice of the customer is understood and is incorporated into the planning process to reflect customer's needs.
- When referring to efforts that need to be joint between the PM and the BA, it does not mean that all associated activities need to be performed together simultaneously, but rather that there is an option for either the PM or the BA to take the lead in each respective area; depending on the type of challenges, skills required, and experience that each brings to the table. Having only one of the duo's members perform any of these activities without the collaboration with their counterpart may lead to gaps and future issues for the areas that are performed without collaboration.
- The PM and the BA need to balance each other and balance any conflicting priorities they encounter to ensure that progress is made consistently—without neglecting to take the necessary steps to properly assess impacts and consequences of actions or lack of action. With the PM focusing on the project's objectives and the BA on the product's objectives there is a strong need for the two to balance the interests that the other represents, and to do so while considering all aspects of planning—including risks, assumptions, constraints, and dependencies. If there is a need to, the PM and the BA should be able to allow a slowdown to reconsider the plans—to ensure that the progress and the planning remain realistic. It is better to slow down the planning to ensure its effectiveness, than to proceed with unrealistic plans.
- There is a need to maintain balance between planning and progress—while it is sometimes important to slow down in order to plan more effectively, it is important to ensure that it is done in the context of the need for progress, the objectives, and the stakes at hand. The combined expertise of the PM and the BA, along with their accessibility to stakeholders are the main ingredients in maintaining the planning-progress balance and each of the duo's respective knowledge and areas should be

considered and addressed. The balancing act is one of the underlying themes of the joint effort of the PM and the BA, and without it there is a greater chance that the wrong decision would be made—whether it is to remove features in order to make schedule and budget gains, or to include features that may lead to cost and schedule overruns. While any one of these decisions may be appropriate for any specific situation, the balancing act ensures these considerations are consistent across the project, and that they yield the desired results based on the project's and product's objectives. The need to balance the planning and progress, and subsequently the project's and the product's needs, are also major building blocks in managing stakeholder expectations. Effectively managing the expectations is, at times, even more important than actual performance and needs to take place on an ongoing basis throughout the entire project life cycle.

Plan before We Plan

Planning before planning does sound a bit like overkill, but the importance of planning cannot be emphasized enough—plan now or clean up later; fail to plan, plan to fail. Before deciding how the team will tackle this shiny new project, the PM and the BA should take a step back and devise a strategy for planning by considering the following:

- Discuss each other's working styles to determine the best way to collaborate and set any ground rules before any misunderstandings that could lead to a poor start in building a healthy PM/BA relationship.
- Incorporate any lessons learned from previous projects into the planning of the new project; lessons learned are often captured, but rarely used. Build it into the process to review them together and make a list of what is appropriate for the upcoming project. Include what went well in the past that should be continued, along with what did not go so well and ways that it can be avoided or mitigated for this project. The lessons do not necessarily have to be from the PM's or BA's personal repository; also consider reviewing lessons learned from a similar project that was implemented within the organization, and schedule follow-up sessions with colleagues as necessary.

Scope Planning

Determining how scope will be managed is an important part of the planning process, as all other plans are dependent on the scope management plan. Scope needs to be broken down into two aspects: (1) product scope—represented by the requirements (features and functionalities) and defines what needs to be produced in order to meet business needs and (2) project scope—these are the activities to be performed in order to produce the product.

The scope management plan has some overlap with the requirements management plan and therefore can be tackled together and combined into the scope and requirements management plan to avoid duplication of work—but requires the input from both the PM and the BA. The requirements management plan (another subsidiary plan of the project plan) defines the approach to manage requirements through the product and project life cycle and includes how requirements activities will be planned, tracked, and reported on; where project documentation and requirements will be stored; what requirements attributes will be captured; and how requirements will be traced and prioritized.

The scope and requirements management plan needs to contain a carefully planned and articulated project change management/change control process. Although most organizations already have a defined change management procedure, there may be elements of the generic process that need to be tailored to the project needs. The ultimate owner of the change control process is the PM, but the knowledge thread is carried by the BA to ensure that the process qualifies for the following three critical-for-success components: clear, formal, and effective.

- **Clear:** The process for handling change has to be defined and easy to follow, and has to be articulated to all stakeholders and team members involved.
- **Formal:** The process must include a series of steps that are to take place any time a change is under consideration. These steps include reviews of the request, estimates, impact assessments, and recommendations.
- **Effective:** The results of the change control process must include a realistic set of estimates and impact assessments, including risks, resource needs, areas of impact, and impact on business objectives.

Once the scope and requirements management plan has been established, high-level product scope and requirements scope need to be determined. While it is not necessary (and not possible) to have the entire detailed project scope figured out right at the start of planning, there has to be a clear idea of what the high-level product scope is, what the boundaries are, including what is in and out of scope, in order to determine high-level project scope. The information contained in the business case or pre-project package can be used as a starting point, with the subsequent list of activities executed jointly by the PM and BA to follow:

- The high-level product scope/product boundaries should be confirmed with the sponsor and stakeholders who will be representing the sponsor at a lower level. There will likely be some tweaks to the high-level product scope out of these discussions led by the BA.

- Define the high-level project scope/project boundaries for a clear definition of what is included and what is out of project scope led by the PM based on the BA's input.
- Define/refine (if already provided in the business case) the project success criteria and how it will be measured.
- Determine the project methodology that will be used to implement the project (e.g., waterfall, phased waterfall, agile, quasi agile, other). This activity will likely require input from the greater team.
- Define the list of project deliverables to produce, dependent on the chosen project methodology.
- Identify areas that the performing organization is not going to produce and how the project is going to obtain them (via procurement); including all the activities and interactions related to the acquisition of products, services, or results from outside of the organization.
- Produce a preliminary work breakdown structure (WBS), detailing the work to be performed to build the product, including estimates for time (effort, duration). Although the WBS is under the direct responsibility of the PM, developing it must take place with the input of the BA to ensure that product requirements are properly reflected in the WBS. The BA would produce a business analysis plan which breaks down the business analysis deliverables into more manageable pieces of work to be estimated and fed into the WBS.

Estimating, Scheduling, and Resource Planning

The outputs of scope planning feed into the estimating, scheduling, and resource planning. The next few bullets highlight the planning activities related to estimating, scheduling, and resource planning within the planning phase of the project.

- Create cost, schedule, and resource management plans with careful consideration of how scope, cost, time, and quality are all integrated—and how the PM and BA will balance the competing demands.
- Identify resource requirements to perform the work on the WBS; this includes focusing on having the right skills allocated for activities. The resource requirements need to be supported with assumptions and risks to ensure they are realistic and that the impact of risk changes is identified and articulated.
- Determine preliminary cost estimates based on the WBS led by the PM with BA input. The estimates within the WBS will be progressively elaborated as the project progresses.

- Identify required buy-in and approval levels for each milestone, deliverable, and if required, activity within the project schedule.

The PM ultimately owns the process of estimating, scheduling, and resourcing, but once again needs the support of the BA in order to provide context, cross reference, and to engage the team and the stakeholders for realistic estimates. Since in most organizations the problem is not lack of data, but rather too much data available, it is up to the PM to establish guidelines regarding the level of detail required, the level of accuracy for each estimate, and the type of estimate to be applied (e.g., top-down, bottom-up). With the help of the BA, the PM also needs to ensure the estimates incorporate dependencies from within and outside of the project. The PM and the BA need to use a responsibility assignment matrix (RAM) as a transition that allows the planners to map tasks and deliverables (project scope) to resources, before developing the schedule—so the latter is realistic and is based on recognized and existing resources, and their level of experience, skills, and expertise.

The RAM also helps the PM and the BA avoid situations where there are *hanging activities*—these are activities with no resources, which implies they are not going to get done. The process of ensuring specific task ownership should be performed alongside the communication aspect of establishing escalation procedures. Resource allocation should include the input from the BA, for a better skill/role fit, while keeping a close watch so there is no over-allocation of resources—and in turn, a realistic allocation and utilization that is based on best practices and organizational guidelines. Performing the estimating process consistently and effectively requires the PM and the BA to avoid estimating *backward*; that is *reverse engineering* estimates so they fit into an imposed deadline. Utilizing the practice of *reverse estimating* almost guarantees future misunderstandings and unmet estimates, deadlines, and budgets. Instead, when a deadline is provided to the PM and the BA, they need to set it aside and come up with estimates based on the activities to perform and the resources at hand. Once the bottom-up type of estimate (or at least a partial bottom-up) is in place, the PM and the BA can compare the estimates to the deadline and come up with a set of recommendations to present to the decision makers; ensuring that all considerations regarding project success and business objectives success are taken into account.

The breakdown of deliverables to work packages and to activities and tasks is part of the effort to break the project down into smaller, more manageable components, so it is easier to estimate and to assign resources to each of them. Combining this process with the establishment of shorter, more frequent and realistic milestones, manageable deadlines, and gates and checkpoints along the way will help us develop a schedule that is robust, realistic, and at the same time flexible—with its parts compartmentalized so additions and changes can be assessed for impact and sufficiently accounted for. The development of the project schedule and other estimates, similar to the development of the scope, does not have to be done in one sitting for the entire project. In fact, applying the concept of progressive elaboration, which is an iterative and incremental approach to the planning, can allow the PM and the BA to break down the project by its timelines and focus on the short-term parts by developing very detailed plans, while allowing some ambiguity and high-level planning for the longer time horizons. As progress is made and the team learns from its planning processes and from its work experience, the PM and the BA should lead the refinement process of the longer-term planning horizons, as they approach the timelines. Like in agile, this way the team will not *waste* time on detailed long-term planning that is likely to change anyway; it will focus on the detailed short-term planning with the vision in mind for a long-term framework—until the project progresses toward what previously was a longer-term time frame horizon, which now is getting closer.

Building a realistic schedule involves a set of two layers of planning and three aspects of controls. The planning involves (1) establishing guidelines and common understanding (including terminology, such as getting the team to use *effort* and not *task duration* in order to provide estimate), so the team comes up with realistic estimates, and (2) the PM and the BA can put together realistic and manageable schedules that take into account all constraints, dependencies, resource availability, and any other considerations related to the work to be performed. This process involves applying the *mechanics* of building a schedule by adding up the activity efforts and durations properly and presenting it in an understandable way, showing the critical path.

The planning and control process involves the education of the team on how to handle buffers, floats, and dependencies. Although it is the PM and the BA who manage these, it is important to ensure that team members do not pad their estimates (without the PM and the BA knowing that estimates have been padded) and do not take it upon themselves to delay an activity just because it has buffers or time to spare. The PM needs the BA to work closely with the resources to ensure that they perform their tasks on time. When a task is not on the critical path, it may appear as if it simply floats on the schedule, but the PM and the BA need to ensure that resources do not mistakenly allow it to *float* there; as there are usually dependencies on that task, as well as other commitments and activities the resources need to perform once they are done with that task.

Quality Planning

The PM and the BA need to jointly determine how to define quality from both the project and product perspectives so that it addresses organizational needs and meaningful value for the customer. The PM and the BA also need to build checks and balances into the project to ensure quality is maintained throughout.

Quality assurance measures needs to be built into the project scope by building in frequent gates, milestones, and decision points to ensure stakeholders remain informed and that progress is sufficiently measured and sliced to manageable pieces. The need for frequent checkpoints increases further in higher risk environments and in high velocity projects. The checks and balances ensure proper tracking and documentation of problems along the way. Quality control checks, such as sufficient testing coverage should also be included as part of the project scope.

From a product perspective, the BA can build into their product requirements definition process to ensure requirements verification and requirements validation activities are being conducted at regular intervals and not left until the end, right before requesting signoff. This will have to be reflected in the business analysis plan as input into the WBS, to build time to complete these checkpoints.

- **Requirements verification:** ensuring that the product requirements meet quality characteristics: unambiguous, precise, consistent, correct, complete, measurable, feasible, traceable, and testable. It is often referred to as doing the thing right.
- **Requirements validation:** ensuring the product requirements (and ultimately the product) can be traced back to the business needs, goals, and objectives. It is often referred to as doing the right thing.

Activities and costs to achieve project and product quality need to feed into the estimating, scheduling, and resource planning.

Communication and Stakeholder Management Planning

A communication plan covers how we are going to communicate, which includes what we are communicating, the format of the communication (written, meetings—virtual, face-to-face, etc.), frequency of the communication, who we are communicating with, and where are we communicating (meeting room, conference line, repository for documentation, etc.). Both the PM and the BA need to interact extensively with stakeholders—where the PM is accountable to build a communication plan for the project and the BA is accountable to build a communication plan for requirements management. Ideally, the PM-BA duo should put their heads together and create a consolidated communication plan for the project that incorporates the requirements management aspects, including but not limited to, how the requirements will be communicated to the stakeholders. The consolidated communication plan should also outline the escalation procedures that will be used for the project.

As part of communication and stakeholder management planning, the PM and BA should once again join forces to conduct a preliminary round of stakeholder analysis. The roles and responsibilities of all identified stakeholders should be documented (including those of the PM and BA) to feed into the creation of a responsibility assignment matrix (responsible, accountable, consulted, informed [RACI] chart). This is another activity that will need to be progressively elaborated throughout the course of the project to ensure a cost effective, efficient, and clear means to communicate with team members and stakeholders to engage them effectively based on their needs and the organizational context.

Risk Planning

The first step in risk planning is to create a risk management plan which incorporates both aspects of risk—project and requirements risk—with the PM leading the project risk management process definition and the BA leading the requirements risk process definition. Many organizations have risk logs or risk registers, but even some of the more mature organizations lack the structure around the risk management processes. The PM and BA should use what is existing within the organization as a starting point but will likely need to elaborate based on the following for both project and requirements risk management:

- Define the project and/or requirements risk management processes (if not already defined within the organization) or refer to the risk management process if there is an existing process and document any tailoring for the project including any tweaks to the project or requirements risk logs (e.g., added columns).
- Define impact and probability ratings (if not already defined)—it is not enough to have an option to select high, medium, or low from a drop-down list; these ratings need to be defined, since one person's definition of high may be different from another person's definition of high.
- Document recommended actions based on risk score (if not already defined)—plugging in an impact and probability rating will produce a risk score, which is a step in the right direction, but it is also necessary to include guidelines on how a risk with a score of 25 should be treated versus a risk with a score of 9.

After the risk management plan has been discussed and documented, an initial project risk assessment should be conducted jointly by the PM and BA with the help of the extended project team. As part of the project risk analysis, the team needs to consider risks associated with each deliverable, activity, interaction, integration, and stakeholder. Any assumptions, constraints, dependencies, and known issues about any of the planning factors should also be considered. In addition, the PM will need the support of the BA to consider business and operational risks; these are risks to the business objectives and impact areas that may be felt as a result of project actions. The BA needs to alert the PM on such risks so the PM can make informed project decisions and recommendations.

Risk management closely integrates with essentially every aspect of the project, but to effectively identify, plan for, and manage risks the PM and the BA must have a clear understanding of the project's success criteria; considering that an event becomes a risk only if it impacts the ability to deliver success.

Analysis (Planning Process Group)

Within the analysis phase of the project, the bulk of the work burden is on the BA. The PM should be looking for any opportunities to support the BA through this section of the project. The following is a summary of activities that would occur during the analysis phase of the project:

- Elaborate product scope and business requirements into stakeholder requirements and, subsequently, into solution requirements through multiple iterations of elicitation, analysis, and communication to develop detailed product requirements, led by the BA.
- Determine and document if there are any transition requirements.
- Requirements verification—the BA should facilitate structured walkthroughs to ensure the requirements are defect free and adhere to quality characteristics.
- Requirements validation—as lower-level product requirements are being defined, the BA should be tracing all lower-level product requirements back to business requirements representing the business value. Requirements should also be traced to the stakeholders who requested or needed the requirement in order to ensure the project benefits will be achieved. This will also certify all project scope items that the team works on will be linked to value.
- Conducting a requirements risk assessment as lower-level product requirements are being defined to document requirement-level risks, assumptions, constraints, issues, and dependencies.
- An ongoing review of findings from the planning process, including project-level risks, assumptions, constraints, issues, and dependencies.
- Define project requirements—the project scope and the product scope are closely tied to each other; the project scope (ultimately represented by the WBS) is about the work to be performed in order to deliver the product scope (articulated and represented by the product requirements). The product scope is broken down into detailed product requirements through elicitation, analysis, communication, and

management of requirements by the BA. The product requirements that are captured need to be handed over to the PM in a seamless and smooth process, to be converted into full project requirements (detailed project scope).

- Ensure alignment between the product's scope and the project's scope and check for alignment on an ongoing basis to the project's mandate (to deliver value according to the business objectives) as reflected in the charter.
- Refine the stakeholder analysis—are there any newly identified stakeholders?
- Gaps—capacity, capability, resource, and knowledge gaps often form throughout the project and sometimes small gaps that are not identified upfront and early on in the project, widen dramatically during the project. Both the PM and BA need to identify when and where gaps are formed that may pose a risk on the project's ability to deliver value for the organization. The most common gaps are related to capacity, resources, and knowledge that indicates that the project's capabilities may become misaligned with its mandate or with the business objectives.
- Scope creep—while PMs tend to guard against scope creep and they want to manage changes to the project so that they remain within their time, budget, and resource constraints, BAs focus on the product—sometimes with limited regard to the project's constraints. This balancing act, where the PM tries to reduce scope and the BA tries to increase scope is a common source of tension between the two roles, but also the center of their collaboration. The BA must also keep an eye on organizational needs and ensure that whatever is included within the project's scope carries value for the organization. In short, while the PM wants to ensure that the project remains within its constraints, the BA has to provide additional context to facilitate the PM's decision-making process so project-related considerations do not override those of the organization. The *traditional* division of the roles between the PM and the BA reinforces that balancing act, as shown in Table 11.2.
- Subsequent estimating and planning—all subsequent estimating and planning will be based on what the project needs to produce and what work has to take place.

Design, Development, Testing, and Implementation Phases of the Project (Execution Process Group)

During project execution or implementation the bulk of the technical and product-related work is taking place. While the PM and the BA do not (in their

Table 11.2 Traditional PM and BA tasks

Traditional PM Tasks	**Traditional BA Tasks**
Articulate project success criteria	Lead business case effort
Create project plan and all subsidiary plans	Requirements management (elicitation, analysis, communication)
Manage the change scope control process	Manage product related impact and organizational impact of the change control process
Manage time, budget, resource allocation	Help match resources to tasks
Manage project risks	Manage requirements/product risk
Manage issues	Consolidate information for solution recommendation
Ensure project objectives and constraints are maintained/met	Enterprise analysis–provide context to ensure business objectives are met
Manage communication and stakeholder management	Support communication management
Listen to the BA's advice and observations	A balancing act for the PM by being a product and stakeholder advocate

capacities as PM and BA) perform the physical technical work on the project's product, both of them are in charge of performing monitoring and controlling activities to ensure progress is made—to the extent required; according to the plan; and with realistic, accurate, and timely reporting. The PM and BA both play a support role during the design, development, testing, and implementation phases of the project.

- The BA would conduct the forward traceability of the product requirements to design, development, and test components to ensure product requirements are not dropped along the way.
- The PM and BA should jointly conduct an organizational readiness assessment to determine if the organization is ready to accept the new product/solution.
- The BA would define and document any additional transition requirements as a result of design decisions or the organizational readiness assessment, which will need to be passed on to the PM to define additional project requirements.
- The BA supports the testing team by reviewing test plans and test cases to ensure that there is sufficient coverage of the product requirements and all ranges of user behaviors. The BA needs to work closely with the technical team, with users, and with the PM to ensure the testing process is meaningful, effective, sufficient, and relevant.

- The PM maintains focus on approved project work and on performing activities as per the WBS.

Throughout the execution process of the project, the PM and the BA continue to share the responsibilities related to communication, along with the facilitation of meetings for prioritization, change and reporting (led by the BA), and conflict resolution (led by the PM, hands-on facilitation by the BA). The final stages of the execution and the associated control processes involve the BA refining the planning of, and preparing for the product's implementation completion and the solution's smooth and seamless transition.

Tasks to be Performed Throughout the Project (Monitoring and Controlling Process Group)

The tasks related to ensure effective monitoring and controlling of the project are shared between the PM and the BA, where the need for collaboration even further increases from its levels earlier in the project. The enhanced need is driven mainly by the reality of multiple moving parts, conflicting priorities, and stakeholders' emotions that surface in accordance to the progress made and to the expectations.

Monitoring and Controlling Scope

Both the PM and the BA need to ensure that the change control process is followed, and that it yields realistic impact assessments and plans to incorporate the accepted changes. They also need to communicate the results of the process and track the performance of the change items. Depending on the areas of work that are outsourced, the PM and the BA need to ensure they share the responsibility of effectively engaging vendors, suppliers, and third-party partners. Both change control- and procurement-related responsibilities will be determined by the result of the BA-led processes to conduct impact assessments for change and subsequently prioritize the changes. The PM ultimately leads the change control process, but for the process to be effective and meaningful, the BA needs to facilitate most of its due-diligence activities. The BA's involvement in the change control process also focuses on ensuring that the changes are assessed for impact beyond the project—including impact to the business, warranties, services, and any other organizational areas. The BA also has to help ensure that any changes to the requirements are performed efficiently by eliciting requirements and identifying any issues or constraints that pose risks to the project's success. As part of the requirements management process, the BA helps the team maintain focus on the business needs and on the approved and accepted requirements, and that the organization's and team's focus do not divert away from it.

Monitoring and Controlling Cost and Schedule

The monitoring and controlling aspect of the estimating and scheduling process includes: (1) the tracking of whether the project is on the critical path and the status of the activities on it. Generally, it would be considered risky for the project if more than a quarter, or a third, of the project's tasks are on the critical path; the PM needs to utilize the BA and engage the resources to move activities off of the critical path. The PM and the BA need also to track whether there are buffers on the critical path and what to do with them. As non-critical path activities are also important, the controlling process also includes: (2) the tracking of non-critical path activities and ensuring that their buffers are managed properly. Further, when there are delays with non-critical path activities the BA needs to check for the impact of that delay and propose options to handle the situation if action is required. Last, but not least, the process includes: (3) controlling the overall progress in the project. This is also important to ensure that both critical path and non-critical path activities are performed as scheduled and as required. While the project may be on the critical path, it may fall behind with off-critical-path activities; or the opposite—where off-critical-path activities are performed at a favorable rate, giving the impression that the project is ahead of schedule, but it slips on the critical path. It is important to have a clear view of all components of the schedule, and while it is the PM who focuses mainly on the critical path, the BA provides options to address off-critical-path challenges.

The PM needs to lead the effort of tracking and controlling performance early in the project to identify trends and ensure that all delays—even small and early ones—are recognized, and looked after. This involves consulting with the BA to provide a realistic impact assessment and course of action, along with keeping the sponsor and other key stakeholders properly informed. The schedule planning and control processes also require the PM and the BA to clearly prioritize tasks, activities, deliverables, and dependencies (within projects, across projects, and across organizational boundaries).

Monitoring and Controlling Quality

While the PM leads the reporting process and consolidates all the reporting information to present to stakeholders, it is the BA who makes sense of the reporting information, collects it, and turns it from data into meaningful information that is in context with the objectives and the project success criteria. This does not release the PM from setting guidelines and thresholds for the reporting, and it requires coordination and synchronization between the PM and the BA to ensure the information collected is relevant and that waste within the process is minimized. The purpose of the reports is to ensure existing processes are effective and followed, performed properly, and if required—reviewed for improvement or for automation.

The reporting guidelines and the report templates are set during the planning process, and the PM-BA duo need to set the reporting expectations with stakeholders upfront. With that said, the reporting needs and the changing circumstances in the project will trigger a change in reporting needs and the duo will then need to adjust the reports and sometimes even the thresholds. The PM ultimately serves as the face of the project when dealing with most stakeholders, and the BA is the engine behind the reporting process, data collection, and processing. The reporting process and the setup of thresholds also involve the establishment of exception handling—where the PM and the BA define the acceptable performance measurement and build guidelines around them of what to do when the thresholds are reached or exceeded. The exception handling (like the reporting process itself) connects back to communication management, stakeholder expectations management, and risk management to ensure that each situation triggers the appropriate response by the most suitable resource; notifying the stakeholders who need to know. Exception handling helps establish escalation procedures and a sense of urgency when dealing with specific types of situations.

Throughout the controlling process, the communication with technical stakeholders is predominantly led by the BA to ensure that communication is streamlined and to the point. The information is then synthesized and integrated into the project reporting and is transferred to the PM for further handling. As project performance information keeps flowing throughout the execution stage, the BA continuously ensures that the product's acceptance criteria and performance align with the project success criteria and then reports this information to the PM for escalation, stakeholder expectations management, and decision making. Figure 11.3 helps simplify the essence of the controlling process and the importance of reporting in any of its stages to ensure that the project produces the right product, the right way, and for the right purpose.

Monitoring and Controlling Communications and Stakeholder Engagement

Throughout the project, the PM and BA need to certify alignment between performance and expectations, with a focus on the product, functionality, and features aspect of the project. The *noise* produced by stakeholders who feel misinformed often turns out to be damaging for the project's success due to unnecessary reports that are produced, change requests that are made with no merits, and other misunderstandings that cause distraction and inefficiencies. It is, therefore, worth the effort to have the BA engaging the stakeholders and

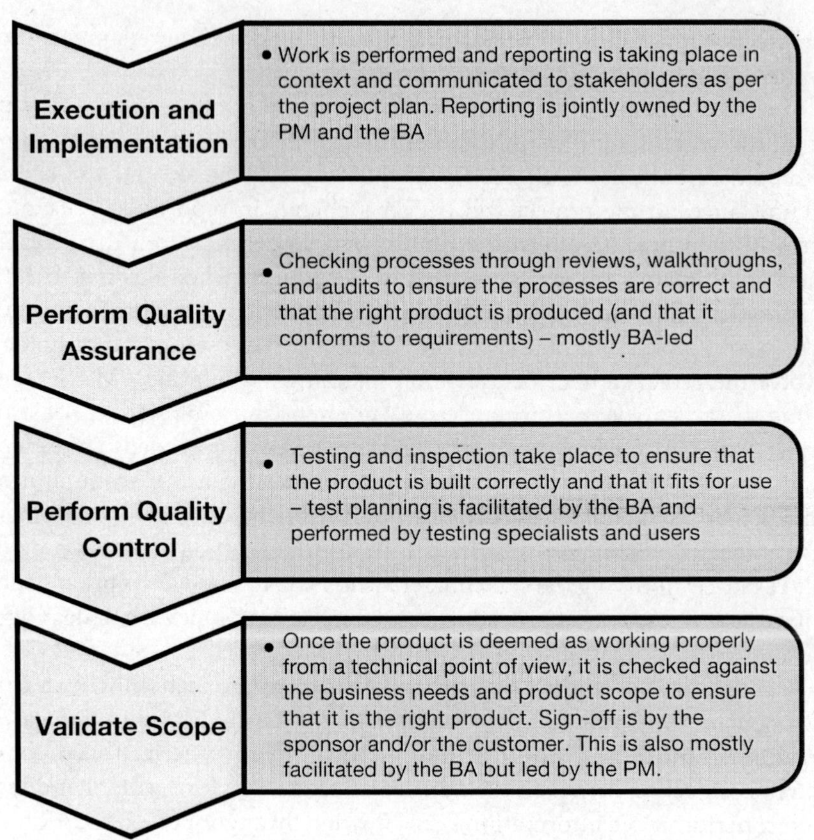

Figure 11.3 The scope and quality control process

ensuring they have a first-hand look at the product being produced at regular checkpoints within the project. The PM does not have sufficient knowledge of the product to effectively keep the stakeholders informed and in most cases; it is the BA who briefs the PM who, in turn, becomes the middleman.

Any challenges, issues, or risks that arise throughout the project should be articulated and introduced or escalated to the most appropriate decision makers in a timely manner, in order to retain the confidence level of the stakeholders. While it is not up to the PM and the BA to decide who makes decisions for the project, they need to articulate the need for a streamlined and efficient decision-making process with a minimal number of stakeholders involved, if possible.

Monitoring and Controlling Risk

Project and requirements risk management is a process that should be happening regularly throughout the project. This includes the regular review and identification of new assumptions, constraints, dependencies, and risks.

Closing the Project (Closing Process Group)

Once the project is deemed a success, or when a decision is made to shut down the project, the PM starts performing the processes and activities associated with closing the project—including closing all contracts and procurement processes, as well as performing administrative closure. The bulk of the activities through the administrative closure require the input and collaboration of the BA, including leading the lessons learned efforts (for the project's processes). The lessons learned should be collected and analyzed by the PM and the BA on an ongoing basis throughout the project and subsequently articulated and refined to meaningful lessons to be applied in the next project phases, or in the next project. As part of the product wrap-up, the BA needs to facilitate the process of handing over product-related information as part of the project closure and transition—including product specifications, requirements of all sorts, use cases, test cases, training related documentation, any type of operating procedures, and any requirements risks.

Projects are Temporary

The integration of the PM and BA roles goes beyond the need to make the project and the product work in the same direction. This integration is also about the marriage of the temporary and the ongoing. Even though projects are temporary, they need to be integrated into the ongoing operations of the organization and the PM and the BA each represent their respective side of this integration. The PM represents the project's needs by being in charge of delivering the project's product on budget and on time (among other success criteria). The PM needs the BA in order to connect between the project's temporary project objectives and the *permanent*, ongoing organizational needs related to operations and the business as a whole. Just as a project's success cannot be achieved without the PM, it also cannot be achieved without the context to be provided by the BA, to ensure that the project's priorities, activities, and deliverables are produced in the context of the organizational needs; with the BA's input the PM has sufficient information to manage the project effectively. The benefits the project produces can now be effectively integrated into the ongoing operations of the organization. The contribution the BA makes toward project success starts with the business case, where the ideas and organizational needs are articulated.

The PM and BA need to take into consideration the needs of the stakeholders who will be supporting the product post-implementation in order to facilitate a seamless transition. The process of understanding the business needs starts at the very early stages of the initiative, along with the business case and the feasibility analysis; it continues through the planning stages of the project and it helps execute the plan effectively. Upon project closure, the understanding of the business needs has to be increased to ensure what is delivered from a product perspective includes post-project support. Based on the product produced, the acceptance to date, communication that has taken place, and the way the customer handles it all, the PM and the BA will need to come up with the most effective, efficient, seamless, and streamlined approach to ensure the customer gets what they need, at the right timing, and to the appropriate extent—so the client can maximize the realization of benefits from the product. Furthermore, the hand-off will also determine the amount of associated support, warranties, documentation, and training required—all based on the reality of the condition of the product being handed over, the plan for the transition, and the terms and conditions in the contract. The PM and the BA must be privy to all of this and must engage the appropriate stakeholders with information about assumptions, warnings, misalignments, and risks that may take place as a result of the transition.

Integration 2.0

Connecting between the temporary and the ongoing operations of the organization is not only challenging, but it also adds another dimension to the word *integration*. While for the most part, the word *integration* refers to combining and mixing all the parts of the project with each other, the mixing of the dimensions gives us a new context for the word integration: integrating the project's product into the organization's ongoing operations. This integration refers to ensuring that the product that we just produced—and tested to ensure it works properly (conformance to requirements)—is validated to do what it is intended to (fitness for use). While the project is supposed to address this part of the integration, it is often overlooked and the handover, hand-off, transition, and shift into the organization's operations are, at times, overlooked.

There are plenty of reasons (or excuses) why such a transition may not take place as required, and they are mostly related to time constraints and the need to move on to the next initiative. The hand-off of the product (or service, or result) to the next level (i.e., operations, maintenance, client) is similar to the passing of the ball to a receiver in any type of team sport. No matter what happens, it is the responsibility of the passer of the ball to ensure that the ball is caught and accepted as intended by the receiver. Any time the ball does not end up in the hands of the receiver (bad or intercepted pass), the person who passed the ball is at fault, because they should not have passed it to begin with. The PM is therefore in charge of ensuring that the transition and handover of the product to the next level is done smoothly, seamlessly, and in such a way that it allows the customer, or the operations of the organization to realize the benefits the product has produced, as intended. In order for this transition to take place as intended, there has to be a plan for the transition, as well as an understanding of what it takes to hand over the product, what information needs to be transferred, what records are to be kept, and the stakeholders who will be involved. While it is the PM who is in charge of the transition planning and execution, the BA serves as the information thread.

The execution of the transition takes place (for the most part) as part of the closing processes of the project, to ensure that the hand-off is done according to the plan and that the receivers of the product (and the information) get what they needed to take possession of the product from that point. Since this part of the integration goes outside of the direct scope of the project, the PM needs the BA for context and elicitation of information regarding the needs of those who will deal with the product post-project. This is similar to the need to engage the BA to get context and information at the beginning of the project from the business case, the feasibility analysis, and any additional pre-project decisions and mandates. Here too, the BA's view of the broader organizational context and his or her understanding of the product and the customer become a valuable compilation of information, so that whoever is in charge of taking over the project's product can do it to the best of their ability and their needs. One item that is often overlooked is the transitioning of any requirements risks into the operational environment. Unlike project risks that should have all been addressed within the duration of the project, requirements risks have a potential to continue beyond the project. As part of the requirements risk management process, workarounds should have been defined so the team is equipped to deal with the requirement risk if it is realized post-implementation; but this information needs to be passed on to the operational team in order to be of any value.

Once the transition has been completed and the operational teams have confirmed the transition to be sufficient, the post-project stakeholders should be all set to move ahead with their portion of the work. If, for example, training needs were identified and training was provided, but the post-project stakeholders did not attend the training or did not follow the process, there is not much the PM and the BA can do. Therefore, all activities in the transition plan must take place as intended and as required.

Although we have discussed a different aspect of integration, it is all related, as the product integration cannot be done without the project integration, and the opposite is true as well—the project integration will not yield the right results without knowing the customer's (or the post-project stakeholder's) needs. Both areas of integration can only be achieved through close collaboration between the PM and the BA, to ensure that all decisions are informed and are made in the right context—for the customer, the organization, the project, and the important stakeholders.

Acceptance

After the BA consolidates reporting and performance information, the PM will facilitate the acceptance process by the business stakeholders and the duo will then close the project and ensure that the lessons are captured and ready to be applied.

Benefits Realization/Product Evaluation

The timeframe to conduct a post-implementation review (PIR)—a process to evaluate the benefits and any challenges with the product after it has been integrated into the operational environment—is dependent on what was defined in the project's success criteria. If benefits are expected to be realized within a year of project implementation, it is wise to schedule checkpoints to evaluate product performance. As this activity lives outside of the project life cycle, this task is often forgotten, since the project team has long moved on—all that time and effort spent on the project and no one checks to see if it was actually a success. This task can be scheduled to be completed by a BA who belongs to the operational team or the BA who performed the initial EA activities where the original success criteria were defined. Some organizations have also leveraged the project management office (PMO) to schedule the PIR. The PIR will sometimes uncover additional challenges with the product that could trigger the start of EA all over again and spawn off additional projects.

SKILLS COMPARISON—THE PM AND THE BA

Many of the skills associated with being an effective PM are similar to the ones associated with being an effective BA—they include strong communication, conflict resolution, negotiation and consensus building, and strong interpersonal and stakeholder expectations management skills. While it is valuable for the BA to have industry and product-related knowledge in order to ask the right questions of their stakeholders, the jury is still out on how important it is for the

PM to have such knowledge. While it is beneficial for the PM, especially if the PM is a full-time employee in an organization, to have product and industry experience, it may not be the case in all situations. For project management consultants it can be less important to possess those specific technical skills—especially since, if there is a strong BA, he or she can serve as the SME who supports the PM. In such a case, it is important that the PM brings to the table the transferrable skills that will benefit the project—such as communication and risk management skills. In fact, in some situations it may be counterproductive for the PM to have too much product and industry experience, as it may contribute to bias and possibly even preferential treatment of certain aspects of the project over others.

Different Types of Skills, Areas of Responsibility, and Role Characteristics

Not all skills for PMs and BAs are the same. Table 11.3 captures most of the different types of skills that effective PMs and BAs need to possess, along with the respective areas of responsibility.

As seen throughout this chapter (and in other chapters in this book), the PM and the BA bring to the table a set of competencies, and each role applies them through a different set of characteristics. This section will discuss these competencies and how the PM and the BA demonstrate them.

Leadership

The PM gives direction, leads by example, motivates the team, and assigns responsibilities to the resources. The PM also serves as an escalation point and owns the communication in and around the project as the PM is ultimately accountable for the project's outcome.

The BA needs to coach, facilitate meetings, lead requirements elicitation sessions, and ensure that senior stakeholders participate in the process—and that they *play along* as required by contributing to the effort. The BA is also the right hand of the PM in working constructively with the team; it is imperative to ensure roles and responsibilities are clear and to synthesize the events that take place within the team to effectively escalate or communicate it to the PM.

Accountability and Responsibility

In many ways the role of the PM is to delegate the work to be performed in the project—in part to the technical resources, but also to the BA. By being accountable for the entire project, the PM, performing at the capacity of the PM, cannot also be a technical lead or a BA. Likewise for a BA, the workload to

Table 11.3 Skills differences between the PM and the BA

PM Skills and Functions	BA Skills and Functions
The ability to see the big picture of the project.	Detail oriented, with the ability to understand the organizational big picture and context for the project.
Develop a project plan including all subsidiary plans. Ensure incorporation of the BA components of the plan.	Contribute to the development of the project plan including all subsidiary plans. Lead the effort in developing the requirements management plan (subsidiary of the project plan). Ensure BA-related activities are incorporated into the project plan.
Lead the stakeholder analysis effort. Work with stakeholders to manage expectations and ensure their needs will be met.	Provide inputs into the stakeholder analysis. Work with stakeholders to understand business needs to ensure their needs will be met.
Owns the process of managing project-level assumptions, constraints, dependencies, and risks. Work closely with the BA to consider gaps and relationships between project level and requirement level.	Owns the process of managing requirement-level assumptions, constraints, dependencies, and risks. Work closely with the PM to consider gaps and relationships between project level and requirement level.
Combine management and leadership skills to lead the project team.	Combine investigative and leadership skills to lead the requirements definition and management work packages (leading from within the project).
Motivate, encourage, and help team members perform their work.	Be the glue between SMEs and resources to ensure everyone is on the same page on how to perform their work.
Make trade-offs and activities to ensure the project delivers its results on budget, on time; a significant balancing act.	Lead the effort to align the product and the solution with the project scope. Ensure the product is built the right way, according to requirements. A balancing act between the business needs with the project's constraints as represented by the PM.
Define and manage project scope to be refined into project requirements with input from the BA.	Define and manage product scope and assist in translation into project scope. Refine product scope into product requirements and assist in translation into project requirements.
Own the process of developing the WBS.	Create a business analysis plan to facilitate development of the WBS for business analysis deliverables.
Build a RAM or a RACI chart for the project.	Assist in populating the RAM and RACI for technical roles and business analysis related tasks.
Manage the change control process.	Manage changes to the requirements and assist in assessing impacts of change.

PM Skills and Functions	BA Skills and Functions
Escalate, manage, and ultimately try to remove issues, problems, and hurdles.	Identify and raise issues, problems, and hurdles; provide facts to the PM to help escalate issues, problems, and hurdles to appropriate stakeholders; and partner with the PM to deal with issues, problems, and hurdles.
Must have the ability to accept the dominant role of the BA, the ability to share the leadership of the project and the fact that the BA will take over certain aspects of the project at certain points in time. Accept that the BA is equal and avoid treating the BA as a junior partner to fulfill admin tasks like note taking and meeting bookings.	Must work closely with the PM and ensure that communication flows in both directions effectively. Need to step up and own pieces of the project to ensure business considerations and product requirements feed in to the PM's decision-making process.

With the different PM and BA functions listed here, the PM must treat the BA as an equal partner and avoid a "bossy" attitude. The BA must treat the PM as the managing partner of the project and recognize that the two roles complement each other and that each role brings to the table a different set of skills that are important for the project and business success: the PM brings project and trade-off expertise and the BA brings product and business expertise.

define and manage the requirements throughout the life cycle of the project is often too much to be able to wear another hat. In the event, especially in smaller organizations and in smaller projects, that the PM or BA plays multiple roles, there has to be a clear definition of when this individual wears each hat and how the time is split between the roles.

As the ultimate point of accountability (leading to the sponsor), the PM should be viewed as the Maestro of the orchestra, where although the PM is accountable for everything, he or she cannot be directly responsible for any product-related tasks. For that matter, (figuratively speaking), the PM does not need to know how to play any of the instruments in the orchestra in order to ensure the symphony plays to perfection. However, as the Maestro of the orchestra, the PM needs to ensure that he or she does not take advantage of his or her authority on the project to dictate how each member of the team plays their instrument, but instead, trusts the expertise on the team. PMs should not dictate how BAs should be defining and managing the requirements—the same way the PM would never think to tell a developer how to design the system.

There are situations where the roles will need to be reversed; for instance in EA, the individual who wears the BA hat leads EA activities and is therefore the Maestro, and the PM is a member of the orchestra. Although the PM is accountable for the entire project, the PM and BA will need to take turns leading certain tasks on the project. Regardless of who is taking the lead on a particular task, both the PM and BA are required to get to the final goal. The PM can be the pilot to fly the project to its destination, but needs his or her copilot, the BA, to navigate the plane in the right direction.

Problem Solving

The nature of projects is that they are riddled with problems. It is not a bad thing, but rather a reality; if projects did not have problems, projects could execute successfully without the help of a PM or a BA (consider it as job security). Without problems, we also may not be challenged to provide innovative solutions. Problems are related to unexpected events like unknown risks or risks without adequate response plans, changes, issues, misunderstandings, miscommunication, and unrealistic or mismanaged expectations. When problems introduce themselves, there is a need to first recognize that they are occurring (the problem needs to be accurately defined): determine the root cause of the problem; assess the magnitude and the severity of the situation; check for impacted business areas and impacted stakeholders; and make a recommendation for appropriate action to reduce, avoid, deflect, or resolve the problem, as well as any recommendations to avoid it in the future. The BA, being the expert in the analysis domain, leads these activities from the perspective of the organization and product, and provides the facts to the PM. The PM will then need to determine how the recommended action translates to impact the project by determining the additional project work that needs to be performed along with the additional time and cost to fix. This may mean escalating the problem and obtaining approval to proceed from a more senior stakeholder—like the sponsor. The PM will also need to manage the expectations of the stakeholders and keep them informed on the issues at hand which could not be done without input from the BA.

Strategic Alignment

The PM needs to maintain awareness of business objectives and ensure the alignment of the project with the organizational strategy. While it is partially done through the functions of portfolio management and the PMO, the alignment can be better maintained with the additional support of the BA through the processes related to EA. The BA serves as the knowledge thread from the business case—and the strategic need for the project to the PM, who represents the project's constraints. This is assuming that the BA working on the project has visibility into the business case, or at least its contents, to understand the business needs and business objectives that spawned the creation of the project. If the BA does not have this visibility, that is the first problem that needs to be resolved early on in the project. The BA needs to ensure that the project decisions made by the PM will not compromise post-project business value and at the same time, that the responses to project risks always take into consideration the impact to the organization and business objectives. A disconnect may lead to project success from a time and cost perspective, but business failure due to quality issues and reduced realized benefits from the project. The disconnect could also introduce a post-project need for undoing some of the work, rework, warranties, service calls, defect repairs, and unhappy stakeholders—which are pricey and painful examples of misalignment between the project's actions and objectives with the business needs and organizational strategy. It would benefit the project if the PM had high-level industry knowledge—complemented by the BA's detailed product and industry knowledge.

Reporting, Influencing, and Motivating

Both the PM and the BA need to step up at multiple points within the project to manage stakeholder expectations. The BA usually focuses on building rapport and relationships with the team and with the customer and the end users, while the PM focuses more on vendor relations—dealing with senior management and the decision makers on the customer side. Both the PM and the BA need to ensure that their style and behaviors are suitable for the situations and the stakeholders at hand, and, if needed, they can rotate the roles of dealing with stakeholders to ensure better matching of styles and personalities.

The reporting is consolidated by the BA and then translated into the *language*, values, and terms that are best understood by the stakeholders—based on the stakeholders' needs. The ultimate goal is to achieve buy-in from stakeholders and to assure that they feel sufficiently informed. By knowing what people value, what they care about, and what their needs are (mostly as a result of stakeholder analysis) the PM and the BA, with combined forces, can influence them and motivate them to do (or not to do) what is right for the project and organization—and in the process, demonstrate to the stakeholders what's in it for them.

Managing Time and Priorities

The PM and the BA need to not only lead by example, but also to help others manage their time and prioritize what has to be done. While the PM articulates the mandate and priorities given by the sponsor, the PM and the BA work jointly to establish criteria for urgency of tasks. The BA plays a major role in prioritizing the work packages (what needs to be done in order to build the product)—as they are closest to the product requirements—and subsequently helps team members prioritize their tasks. This circles back to the PM as input to manage the schedule and make the appropriate informed decisions and recommendations on how to meet the project constraints.

Decisions, Decisions, Decisions

The PM needs to make decisions on an ongoing basis. Some of them are within the PM's authority, and others are recommendations to help other stakeholders with their decisions. The PM's ability to make informed decisions depends on the collaboration with the BA who leads the analysis of the impact of the decisions and the due diligence as part of identifying and analyzing the available options. With that, the BA looks at opportunities for process improvement in relation to the decision areas, and it is the PM who facilitates the sign-off process and serves as the final decision maker in relation to priorities, resources, and schedules. These decisions are then forwarded to higher authority stakeholders. The PM and the BA also jointly facilitate the conflict resolution process within the project and with stakeholders.

How to Collaborate

The PM and the BA need to be able to get along on a personal level, since they need to spend a lot of time working together on the project. The matching of the PM and the BA needs to be done by the hiring managers and the project sponsors. While we do not have control of who we work with, we do have control on how we treat people and our attitude toward building a productive relationship. More specifically, the PM and the BA need to establish, together, how to engage each other and how they are going to handle situations. The building of a framework to establish ground rules starts with the PM and the BA, and will then expand to the team and other stakeholders. The ongoing communication involves the definition of the touch points between the PM-BA duo and a definition of the roles and responsibilities—including who is going to lead which tasks. In addition, the two need to meet regularly and dedicate some time periodically to work on adjusting the relationship, refining the ground rules, and streamlining the trend toward acting as if they are one entity.

Due to the unique nature of the interaction between the two, the relationship requires ongoing maintenance, especially ensuring that both sides do not feel as if their colleague oversteps his or her boundaries. The boundaries, however, change constantly and unexpectedly between the PM and the BA—adding an extra layer of complexity in maintaining a healthy relationship. Like a pendulum, there is a constant shift, within the two roles, in focus, and areas of responsibility as well as areas in which one is more dominant. For example, the BA leads the product requirements development, then the PM takes the lead with developing a WBS, then the BA steps back in to ensure alignment with requirements. Another example is the PM owns the project change control process, but the BA owns the impact assessment; the PM then communicates the recommended action(s) to stakeholders and the BA provides support, depth, and rationale. The shift back and forth must be seamless and appear to be fully streamlined and natural from those outside of this relationship. Any sign that things are not fully coordinated will compromise the ability of the duo to add value, and will reduce the trust and credibility that others have in the duo and the quality of the work they produce.

The factor that is most critical to success when building and maintaining the PM-BA relationship is the building of trust. Trust is the foundation of success in any type of relationship, and the onus is both on the PM and the BA to reach out and build trust. In order to build trust, one must take a risk by introducing a trust-building measure that reaches out to the other side and helps him or her feel more comfortable. As a result, it is the receiver of the trust-building measure who needs to make a concession in return. Making a concession is not about meeting the other side in the middle of the difference area (this is compromise), and it is not about making a concession of an equal size—it is about giving the other side something that is meaningful for them and, hopefully, not very pricy for the giving side. The exchange of concessions will then continue as part of the effort to build trust. Another step in the process of building trust is open communication and the ability to discuss anything that is relevant to the project with each other. Being able to have ongoing, open, candid, and honest communications will allow the duo to address any issues and misunderstandings, and to engage in an effective and appropriate process of conflict resolution.

The open communication also leads to ownership of issues, and being proactive in making commitments toward dealing with problems and issues based on the skills, interests, and experience. Through making the commitments, the PM and the BA continue to raise the standards of their collaboration and their work by being accountable and managing the areas of accountability—removing ego and selfishness from the conversation. This leads to achieving better results and adding an increasing amount of value for the team, the project, the stakeholders, and the organization. This is not about creating a utopia, but rather about a realistic set of actions to take in order to make the most out of the challenges that the project is bound to introduce.

FINAL THOUGHTS ON BUILDING A PARTNERSHIP: TWO ROLES → ONE ENTITY = VALUE AND SUCCESS

This book has looked into multiple ways to enable the establishment and building of a collaborative relationship between the PM and the BA. Countless articles and discussions, along with genuine efforts, have been taking place in an attempt to connect the PM and the BA, to get them to speak the same language and to put them on the same page—countless efforts, but with limited results thus far. The existence of two methodologies (PMI's *PMBOK® Guide* and IIBA's *BABOK®*) that use similar terminology but mean different things has not contributed to the process of improving collaboration between the PM and the BA. The IIBA has been a significant factor in the definition and value proposition of business analysis and the BA role; however, the misalignment between the methodologies has been partly to blame for the misalignment between the PM and BA roles.

PMI recognizes the need for project teams to have a resource with business analysis and requirements management skills in order to deliver successful projects and programs. The establishment of a new standard and a new certification by PMI (the PBA) is part of the cause for the PM's role to shift more toward people management (and the right side of the brain). The certification signals the need to enhance collaboration between the PM and the BA within the context of projects and programs in order to create an equilibrium between the two roles.

This book has provided a buffet of options to align the roles of the PM and the BA, and illustrated virtually every possible way in today's reality to find opportunities for collaboration, apply techniques for working together, and realize the potential of leveraging both the PM's and the BA's experiences, roles, responsibilities, interests, skills, styles, and personalities. A *buffet of options to collaborate* means that not all the ideas in this book may be applicable to all environments at all times, but the concepts, ideas, and techniques introduced here cover a substantial range of options that can bring the PM and the BA to work together effectively. This book is not suggesting an increase in the workload for the BA, but rather a change in how many people perceive the BA's role—to become a true partner of the PM in order to deliver a significant amount of value for the project. Instead of working in parallel and wasting effort, the PM and the BA can now work together in a synchronized manner with a focus on planning, instead of extensive changes, defects, and handling of overruns. The proposed collaborative ways of working together means more upfront volume of work for both the PM and the BA, but it also means a future reduction in their overall effort throughout the project—all in the name of producing more value for the organization in the form of lower costs, faster completion times, and greater rates of success. The real benefits are going to be realized with customer satisfaction, repeat business, process efficiencies, and learning from previous lessons.

The integration of the PM and BA roles, as illustrated by Figure 11.4, combines the product scope, product requirements, product functionality, and business needs (the BA's focus) with the project's competing demands (the PM's focus) in order to achieve business value that is aligned with organizational needs.

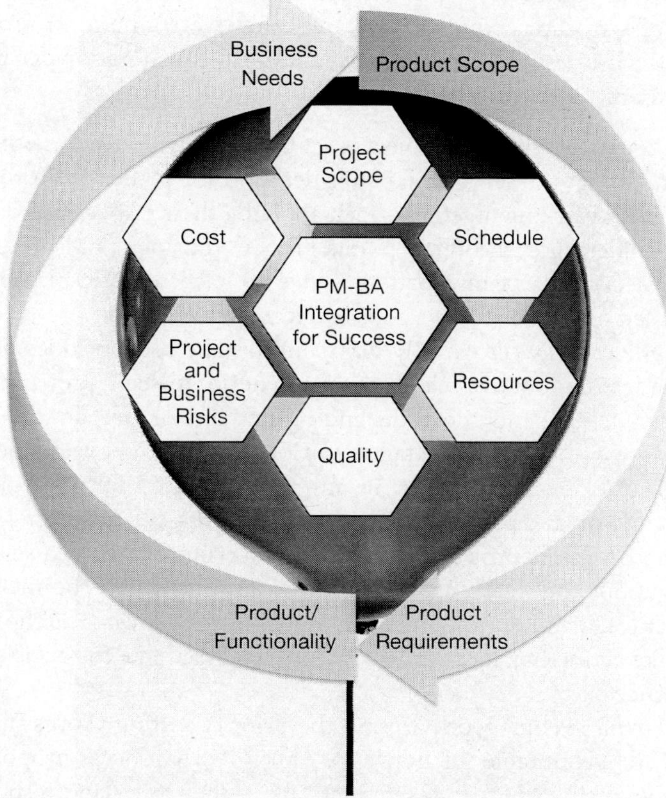

The balloon and PM-BA integration concept taken from Schibi, *Managing Stakeholder Expectations for Project Success (2013), Chapter 7, J. Ross Publishing.*

Figure 11.4 The balloon and the PM-BA integration

More Success and Less Failure

Many research organizations also try to identify why projects fail, and in return, what has to be done to reduce the chance and magnitude of failure and increase success. The findings often shed new or additional points of view on why projects fail and what can be done about it. One research that looks at barriers to success[1] discusses five areas that are common contributors to project failures. While improved collaboration between the PM and the BA may not provide answers to all the challenges surrounding projects, there are several root causes of failures that can get a positive boost from such collaboration. The barriers-to-success research points at five areas that are common in projects, and the following list describes how enhanced PM-BA collaboration can potentially help with them.

1. *Fact-free planning*: A project is set up to fail with deadlines or resource limits that are set with no consideration for reality. With the PM and the BA working together—each applying their respective expertise and considering each other's points of view (business and product versus project)—they run a better chance to have realistic planning that is based on informed decisions and known constraints.
2. *Absent without leave (AWOL) sponsors*: The sponsor does not provide leadership, political clout, time, or energy to see a project through to completion, and those depending on him or her do not effectively address the sponsor's failures. Collaboration between the PM and the BA does not replace, in any way, the need for a sponsor who is hands-on and proactively involved in the project; however, the PM and the BA can approach the sponsor with a more informed set of considerations and clearly articulated set of impacts with recommendation for action. It still may not help, but hopefully it will *wake up* the sponsor to take action in a more timely manner and facilitate the decision-making process.
3. *Skirting*: People work around the priority-setting process and are not held accountable for doing so. The PM-BA process proposed in this book helps educate stakeholders about their roles and responsibilities, and about the impact of their actions (or lack thereof, similar to Item 2 in this list). The PM and BA can also provide tools to better prioritize items and establish the appropriate sense of urgency. These areas, along with the effective management of assumptions, help the PM and the BA to communicate effectively with these stakeholders and possibly introduce options for them to choose that are based on tangible analysis. Not a perfect replacement, but definitely a helping factor.
4. *Project chicken*: Team leaders and members do not admit when there are problems with a project, but instead, wait for someone else to speak up first. The PM and the BA build a set of reporting mechanisms, success criteria, and a gating process that, along with a more robust planning process, serve as early detection tools of project trends, issues, and problems. A proper quality management plan, project health and early indicator measurements, and reporting and control mechanisms—supported by the joint management of project communication—will reduce the chance of project chicken materializing. If someone on the

project makes an effort to hide information it will be hard to discover it, but the previously mentioned mechanisms reduce the chance that things will go wrong for too long without being noticed. This is all about being proactive—and this book proposes multiple ways for the PM and the BA to be proactive. In essence, the delivery of project success goes through the ability of the PM and the BA to be proactive and to build a culture that encourages others to be proactive.

5. *Team failures*: Team members perpetuate dysfunction when they are unwilling or unable to support the project, and team leaders are reluctant to discuss their failures with them candidly. While there are many organizational and cultural factors that may impact team performance and cohesiveness, the PM and the BA, by owning project communication, have a strong ability to make a positive difference in team building, setting a direction, prioritization, effective communication, and escalation. While the PM and the BA do not have the ability to undo all of the organizational issues that may impair the team's performance, they can add a lot of value. Without the PM and the BA effectively owning communication and leading the team, it will be very hard to get the team to perform effectively.

It is likely that the majority of projects have faced any one or more of these five conditions and although a strong PM-BA duo may alleviate some of these challenges to an extent, poor leadership in the organization and certain cultures may put a burden on projects that is too heavy to overcome. The attempts to address these five issues lie within effective communication and stakeholder expectations management, as they combine the skills and areas of coverage of both the PM and the BA. Furthermore, communication and expectations management integrate with all aspects of the project and in turn, enable action and resolution. For example, the most effective approaches to risk management or to estimating will fail if they are not communicated effectively, in a timely manner, and efficiently—as information that is not communicated and acted upon is the same as if it does not exist.

Wrap-up

With the need for communication management in mind, it is time for the PM and the BA to embark on the ultimate career journey—to turn projects around, to deliver success, to positively impact cultures, to help realize benefits, and to ultimately deliver value. It is a known fact that the PM and the BA cannot, each on their own, deliver sufficient value; and furthermore, it is clear that the sum of the PM-BA duo is significantly greater than its individual parts. The large majority of conflicts between the PM and the BA are due to misconceptions, lack of collaboration, broken communication, misunderstandings, and mismanaged expectations. These two roles were born to work with each other like Yin and Yang,[2] as illustrated in Figure 11.5. Yin and Yang is one of the most known and documented concepts used within Taoism and it refers to two halves that together complete wholeness. The PM and the BA are equal partners in this wholeness when they each step up for their part based on the needs of the partnership and the project. Yin and Yang can also be viewed as two opposites or contrary forces that can be complementary and interdependent and in our context—the PM and the BA represent the opposite areas of focus (e.g., project vs. business, project vs. product) but not necessarily opposites of one another. Furthermore, the opposite aspect is about the interdependence and the completeness—as it is likely that deficient areas for one of the duo members will be covered sufficiently by the other.

Whether we call it Yin and Yang, A Love Story, Pilot and Navigator, A Partnership in a Marriage, PMs are not from Mars and BAs are not from Venus, 50 Shades of PM and BA Relations, or simply Collaboration between the PM and the BA Duo—it is about the partnership, collaboration, and proactive approach for delivering project and organizational success together. Reviewing the concepts that this book proposes and explores, then applying whatever is applicable to your specific project conditions will bring your project one giant step closer to success.

The PM and the BA are meant to work with each other.

Figure 11.5 Yin and Yang

This book provides the promise. Now it is time to enjoy the journey!

REFERENCES

1. Research Study: *Silence Fails, The Five Crucial Conversations for Flawless Execution, The Concours Group* and *VitalSmarts* released in October 2006.
2. Taylor Latener, Rodney Leon (2005). *The Illustrated Encyclopedia of Confucianism, Vol. 2.* New York: Rosen Publishing Group. p. 869. ISBN 978-0-8239-4079-0.

INDEX